THE INVENTION OF MEMORY

Also by SIMON LOFTUS

Anatomy of the Wine Trade

A Pike in the Basement

Puligny Montrachet: Journal of a Village in Burgundy

An Illustrated History of Southwold

THE INVENTION
OF MEMORY

An Irish Family Scrapbook, 1560–1934

SIMON LOFTUS

DAUNT BOOKS

First published in Great Britain in 2013
This paperback edition first published in 2014 by
Daunt Books
83 Marylebone High Street
London W1U 4QW

2

ISBN 978 1 907970 52 8

Typeset by Antony Gray
Printed and bound by
T J International Ltd, Padstow, Cornwall

www.dauntbooks.co.uk

FOR

Hana, Iris and Nina
& all their cousins

Contents

MOUNT LOFTUS

INTERLUDE

FAREWELL

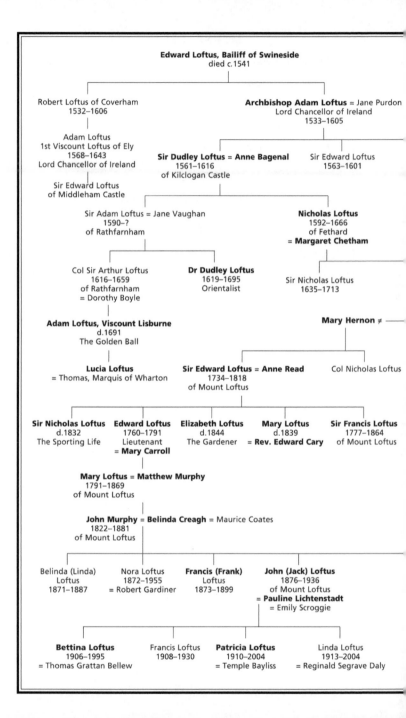

Edward Loftus, Bailiff of Swineside
died c.1541

Robert Loftus of Coverham
1532–1606

Archbishop Adam Loftus = Jane Purdon
Lord Chancellor of Ireland
1533–1605

Adam Loftus
1st Viscount Loftus of Ely
1568–1643
Lord Chancellor of Ireland

Sir Dudley Loftus = Anne Bagenal
1561–1616
of Kilclogan Castle

Sir Edward Loftus
1563–1601

Sir Edward Loftus
of Middleham Castle

Sir Adam Loftus = Jane Vaughan
1590–?
of Rathfarnham

Nicholas Loftus
1592–1666
of Fethard
= **Margaret Chetham**

Col Sir Arthur Loftus
1616–1659
of Rathfarnham
= Dorothy Boyle

Dr Dudley Loftus
1619–1695
Orientalist

Sir Nicholas Loftus
1635–1713

Adam Loftus, Viscount Lisburne
d.1691
The Golden Ball

Mary Hernon ≠ ──────

Lucia Loftus
= Thomas, Marquis of Wharton

Sir Edward Loftus = Anne Read
1734–1818
of Mount Loftus

Col Nicholas Loftus

Sir Nicholas Loftus
d.1832
The Sporting Life

Edward Loftus
1760–1791
Lieutenant
= **Mary Carroll**

Elizabeth Loftus
d.1844
The Gardener

Mary Loftus
d.1839
= **Rev. Edward Cary**

Sir Francis Loftus
1777–1864
of Mount Loftus

Mary Loftus = Matthew Murphy
1791–1869
of Mount Loftus

John Murphy = Belinda Creagh = Maurice Coates
1822–1881
of Mount Loftus

Belinda (Linda)
Loftus
1871–1887

Nora Loftus
1872–1955
= Robert Gardiner

Francis (Frank)
Loftus
1873–1899

John (Jack) Loftus
1876–1936
of Mount Loftus
= **Pauline Lichtenstadt**
= Emily Scroggie

Bettina Loftus
1906–1995
= Thomas Grattan Bellew

Francis Loftus
1908–1930

Patricia Loftus
1910–2004
= Temple Bayliss

Linda Loftus
1913–2004
= Reginald Segrave Daly

Abbreviated Family Tree

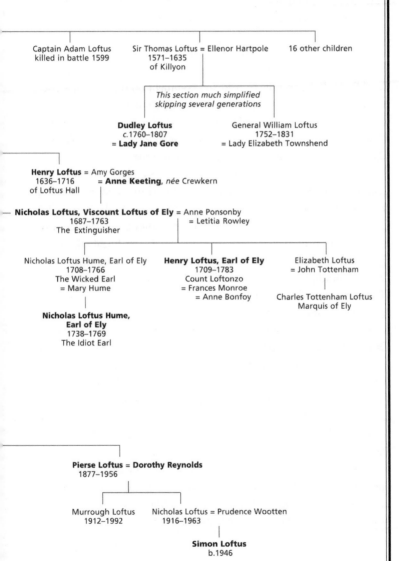

Captain Adam Loftus
killed in battle 1599

Sir Thomas Loftus = Ellenor Hartpole
1571–1635
of Killyon

16 other children

*This section much simplified
skipping several generations*

Dudley Loftus
*c.*1760–1807
= Lady Jane Gore

General William Loftus
1752–1831
= Lady Elizabeth Townshend

Henry Loftus = Amy Gorges
1636–1716   **= Anne Keeting**, *née* Crewkern
of Loftus Hall

Nicholas Loftus, Viscount Loftus of Ely = Anne Ponsonby
1687–1763   = Letitia Rowley
The Extinguisher

Nicholas Loftus Hume, Earl of Ely
1708–1766
The Wicked Earl
= Mary Hume

Henry Loftus, Earl of Ely
1709–1783
Count Loftonzo
= Frances Monroe
= Anne Bonfoy

Elizabeth Loftus
= John Tottenham

Charles Tottenham Loftus
Marquis of Ely

**Nicholas Loftus Hume,
Earl of Ely**
1738–1769
The Idiot Earl

Pierse Loftus = Dorothy Reynolds
1877–1956

Murrough Loftus
1912–1992

Nicholas Loftus = Prudence Wootten
1916–1963

Simon Loftus
b.1946

Acknowledgements

This has been a long project, testing the patience of family and friends. To all of them, and especially to my beloved wife Irène, my heartfelt thanks.

My siblings Belinda and Michael Loftus, my cousins Idrone Brittain and Jack Bayliss, and my friends Hugh Brody, Jeremy Isaacs and Dan Franklin took the trouble to read and comment on the text, in earlier, baggier drafts. Each made vital suggestions, including ruthless pruning, which have improved the end result. My email correspondence with a distant cousin, Guy Loftus, became almost as long as the book itself. Guy read every chapter, supplied a mass of information, references and useful comments, compiled by far the most complete version of the Loftus family tree (www.loftusweb.com/tree.htm) and has been a wonderfully supportive critic, over many years. Thanks also to Liz Calder, Carla Carlisle and Juliette Mitchell. Among the scholars who commented on particular sections I am grateful to Elizabeth Boran, Peter Boyle, Kerry Bristol, Billy Colfer, Ruth Connolly, Robin Darwall-Smith, Jane Dawson, Anthony Malcomson, Helga Robinson-Hammerstein and Clodagh Tait.

Librarians and specialists attached to various institutions helped me with cheerful generosity, notably Melissa Brennan (Rathfarnham Castle), Muriel McCarthy (Marsh's Library, Dublin), Frances Egan (The Dublin Society), Katherine Jones (RIBA Library / Victoria & Albert Museum), Andrew Cormack (RAF Museum, Hendon), Alastair Lindsay (former architect at the Office of Public Works, Dublin) and the wonderful staff at the London Library.

Douglas Matthews made the index – a task that he achieved with wit and clarity.

Thanks, above all, to James Daunt and Laura Macaulay of my publishers, Daunt Books. Their courage and support has amazed me, but should be no surprise to the many admirers of the wonderful business that James founded and continues to run.

SIMON LOFTUS

Picture Acknowledgements

Plate section one

1: Portrait of Archbishop Adam Loftus, possibly 17th century, artist unknown, oil on canvas, 226 x 137cm © The Board of Trinity College Dublin, reproduced by kind permission. 2: (left) Loftus Seal Cup 1593. Silver-gilt. © National Museums Northern Ireland, collection Ulster Museum. (right) Loftus Seal Cup 1604. Silver-gilt, missing its original 'steeple'. © National Museum of Ireland, Dublin. 3: (above) 'The fayre head'. Drawing reproduced by kind permission of National Museum, Dublin. (below) Birds-eye view of Trinity College, Dublin. © The archives of Hatfield House, reproduced by kind permission of the Marquis of Salisbury. 4: Map of 'the Citie of Waterford with the new fortification there', 1591. © The Board of Trinity College Dublin, Trinity College Library, reproduced by kind permission. 5: (above) Engraving from Francis Grose, *Antiquities of Ireland*, 1791. Image © Simon Loftus. (below) Drawing by Thomas Phillips. © The British Library Board KTOP LV (43). 6: (above) Artist unknown, oil on canvas, each 42 x 30 in. Private collection. Images © Simon Loftus. (below) Illustration to P. H. Hore, *History of the Town and County of Wexford*, Vol. 4 (London 1904). 7: (above) Author's archive. Image © Simon Loftus. (below) Image © Simon Loftus, reproduced with kind permission of Marsh's Library, Dublin. 8: Portrait by Garret Morphy, 1680. Oil on canvas, 41 x 35 in., private collection. Image © Simon Loftus.

Plate section two

1: Portrait by unknown artist, 1758. Oil on canvas, private collection. Image © Simon Loftus. 2: Portrait by Thomas Hickey, 1759. Chalk on paper (detail). Private collection. Image © Simon Loftus. 3: Portrait by Thomas Hickey, 1759. Chalk on paper (detail). Private collection. Image © Simon Loftus. 4: (above) Portrait by Angelica Kauffmann, 1771. Oil on canvas, 243 x 287 cm. Photo © National Gallery of Ireland. (below) View of Rathfarnham Castle 1794, by George Holmes. Watercolour with pen and grey ink, 43 x 56 cm. © National Monuments Service, Dept of Arts, Heritage and the Gaeltacht, courtesy of the OPW. 5: Image © Simon Loftus. 6: Private collection, images © Simon Loftus. 7: Image © Simon Loftus. (below) Images © Simon Loftus. 8: (above) Loftus archive. Image © Simon Loftus. (below) Private collection. Image © Simon Loftus.

INTRODUCTION

The Invention of Memory

This is a book about memory. It began with a collection of family stories, told me as a child; became an exploration of how things are remembered or forgotten, the gaps between experience and history; ended in a country graveyard, sitting on a tomb.

To start with, those stories. I inherited a crazy assortment of ancestral legends, featuring the highwayman 'Captain' Freney, the racehorse Hollyhock, the Angelic Miss Phillips and a host of others, vivid as any characters of fiction. When I first visited the old family home in Ireland, at the age of seven, I was able to play with Freney's blunderbuss, marvel at Hollyhock's silver mounted hoof, gaze at a portrait of Miss Phillips. So it seemed they must be true, those wonderful tales.

Later, of course, I began to doubt. But I also became fascinated by the faces of my forebears, the sense of some strong continuing likeness in the family portraits. I wanted to know them. So I pored over documents, criss-crossed the Irish landscape and tried to feel my way into these forgotten lives by exploring their houses and using their possessions – reading their books, grilling my toast on a wood fire with a seventeenth-century toasting fork, cocking a pair of flintlock pistols, shouting through a brass megaphone. All of these things embodied memory; all of them particular to a time, a place, a person.

I found a 'Receipt for a Person in Love', scrawled in a tattered account book. A terrifying scandal emerged from the bottom of a deed box – exploding to life through the testimony of maidservants, tradesmen, wigmakers, doctors, assorted aristocrats and the victim himself. There were bills for 'wonderfully fine soles and a monstrous large turbot', and every necessity of life in a country house in Kilkenny at the beginning of the nineteenth century. And I discovered, to my amazement, that the most improbable stories were rooted in fact.

But I also began to realise how little of what looms large in the political history of the times survives in these ancestral memories. Looking through the eyes of my forebears is like viewing Ireland's past in those distorting mirrors that you find at the end of the pier. Sometimes the proportions seem more or less familiar, but the witnesses are easily distracted. Sometimes we catch the merest glimpse of famous events from the corners of their glance.

That contrast between private and public memory is particularly acute in a country where all history rushes towards myth, where rival mythologies are expressed in brilliantly coloured fables, leaving little room for the maddening inattention of daily experience. This is a function of form. Ireland's history, for many, is still a matter of oral tradition – episodes are shaped for dramatic effect, in response to the speaker's audience, as I know only too well. I was brought up in the belief that you should never let the facts get in the way of a good story. But the facts are stubbornly there – sometimes buried deep or wrapped in layers of retellings, or in plain view but unnoticed. And the big, inescapable fact is the bitter history of England's first colony.

For a hundred and fifty years after the arrival of Adam Loftus in Ireland, in 1560, the experience of colonial conquest dominates the family records. But the eighteenth century brings a change of mood, and the stories seem increasingly detached from the harsh confrontations of religious and national identity. A strange silence, fraught with ambiguities, even surrounds that defining moment, the rising of 1798, when Ireland came closest to shaking off the clasp of its colonial master. For a long time I was troubled by this, as I tried to weave together the private and the public histories of my family and of Ireland, and found the great themes slipping away; sometimes, it seems, deliberately ignored. But gradually it occurred to me that the passions and preoccupations of my ancestors, their daily concerns and childish enthusiasms, their eccentricities and achievements, might constitute an alternative narrative of Irish history – inconsistent, privileged, partisan, riddled with gaps – but no less real, in its way, than the eloquent myths of suffering Hibernia. Hence this family scrapbook.

Now, when I think about those family stories, they seem like memories of a wished-for world, inventing the past to absolve it – but 'invention' originally meant discovery, with the implied sense of something waiting to be found. I love the confusion between this archaeological meaning and its modern sense, of forging something new – the ambiguity that runs through all the narratives of Ireland's history. As I explored the different ways that family legend intersected with public myth, I became more and more interested in how stories were made, why some things were recorded and others forgotten, the merging of fact with fiction, the invention of memory.

11 Feb: 1773

Ellis Sc.

COVERHAM ABBY, IN COVERDALE, NEAR MIDDLEHAM, YORKSHIRE.

PRELUDE

CHAPTER 1

In the Great Wood

'They say also that Agnes wife of Robert de Lofthus entered into the great wood, and there killed a lamb and carried it to the house of Philip Moye. She was insane at the time and is so still. Therefore nothing is done.'

And that is all. The clerk of the baronial court at Wakefield in Yorkshire was more concerned with recording every detail of the fines that were levied that session, in the third year of the reign of Edward Longshanks (1273), than in satisfying the curiosity of future generations. Poor, mad Agnes. Was she driven by undeclared passion, or was her madness truly haphazard – a moment of blind slaughter in the deep shadowed silence of 'the great wood', followed by a perplexed awakening?

I long to know more about those peasants 'de Lofthus' who eked out a livelihood at the margins of the lord's land and were constantly in trouble for stealing wood or allowing animals to stray: about Adam the Grave, who was summoned in 1277 for the escape of a hundred sheep, and Little Hugh, fined 6d. in 1285 'for the escape of 4 beasts, and 2 cows out of the pale of the great wood'; about Malle, in trouble 'for carrying ivy beyond the palisade' and Malina (daughter of Custe de Lofthus) who was fined 3d. in 1297 for stealing brushwood. At the same sessions an exemplary fine of 5s. was levied on another Adam 'for breaking the pale and carrying away brushwood', while his father Thomas got away with 4d. for the escape of a couple of pigs.

I can hear the baaing of those hundred sheep as they stream through a gap in the palisade, smell the bristly pigs (squealing when they are caught), but the clues to personality are more elusive. Adam the Grave and Little Hugh and Malle and Malina are shadows scratched in faded outline by the cramped hand of an anonymous clerk.

They came from the parish of Stanley that included the hamlet of Lofthouse, a few miles south of Leeds. Now this is a suburb of Wakefield with a constant background roar from the intersection of two motorways, but then you could hear the sound of larks above the meadow, until you reached the darkness of the Great Wood and its silence.

Variant spellings of Loftus are scattered across the map of Yorkshire – it is a Norse word (meaning 'house with a loft' or simply 'high house') and dates from the Danish sea raids of the ninth century. I spent a blustery week, camping in an eighteenth-century tower as I explored this vast county, tracing the paths of my forebears as they gradually moved inland, from the coast to the Dales. I discovered a tiny cove where Norse longships landed near the village of Loftus, north of Whitby. I gazed across the cornfields and meadows that surround the ancient farm of Loftus Hill, near Knaresborough. I tried to recapture the scent of the past in the fumes of traffic at Lofthouse, near Leeds – searching in vain for a glimpse of the Great Wood. And I followed the river Nidd upstream, tracking its winding course towards the windswept moors until I found the place that I was looking for, another Lofthouse. This small hamlet, tucked below a steep bluff, still has the air of an old settlement – and up above sits a farm (High Lofthouse) with sweeping views to the south, in a landscape of small, stonewalled fields, rushing streams (gills and becks) and wild, unfenced moors, with the shadows of clouds rippling across the hills. The moors are pitted with abandoned quarries and mineshafts, for the Dales were the source of a great deal of building stone and most of the lead that roofed the churches and monasteries of medieval England, and much of this was monastic grazing land, prior to the Reformation – huge flocks of sheep and herds of swine.

That past is preserved in a name – Swineside – once a monastic grange, now no more than a huddle of stone houses and small barns, crouched below the moors, just north of Lofthouse. The views are fine but even on a sunny day there is a sense of imminent wind, brisk and chill, and in winter it must be harsh. This is where memory begins – for it is here that the great Adam Loftus was born, in 1533.

CHAPTER 2

Dissolution

When I was a boy, my father handed me a treasure – a battered folder containing a manuscript life of Archbishop Loftus, compiled in the eighteenth century. The faded brown ink, handmade paper, archaic spelling, cramped and illegible notes pasted in the margins made it seem immeasurably ancient, almost magical.[1] I deciphered it with rapt fascination, dreaming of a glorious past as I read the opening words:

> Adam Loftus was born at Swineshead in Yorkshire; his Family was accounted both antient and honourable in that Country, and had been formerly possessed of a considerable Estate there, which was a good deal lessened when Loftus first appeared in ye World.

A decade later, in a remote corner of the University library at Cambridge, I discovered that Adam was the second son of a monastic bailiff, whose forebears were yeomen – the noble ancestry and great estates vanished in the autumn mist.

Truth was more troubled. One of Adam's earliest memories, as a boy of three, was of the monks whom his father served as bailiff being evicted from their comfortable abbey, in the spring of 1536. It was the first phase of a social revolution that enriched his family but provoked armed rebellion in the North. Schooled by Catholic priests who treasured the old rituals, he was sent as a young undergraduate to Cambridge at the most radical moment of the English Reformation. Ordained as a priest under Bloody Mary, he was appointed Primate of Ireland by Queen Elizabeth. It would be hard to devise a more extreme rollercoaster of faith and its confusions, at a time when these could be lethal.

Those passions seemed far in the past, remote from common experience, until I drove along a country lane in Ireland, where flags marked the sectarian divide between Catholic and Protestant. Time flickered and jumped.

*

Adam's father, 'Edwardo Lofthouse de Swyneside', was bailiff of the Premonstratensian Abbey of Coverham. The abbey was well endowed but the community had gradually dwindled to fewer than a dozen monks, who left the management of their lands to their bailiff. Occupying a fine complex of stone buildings in the sheltered valley of the Cover, they were forbidden meat – except under special circumstances – but were well provided with fish, from their own fishponds, and with vegetables and fruit from their gardens and orchards. The stream that fed the ponds also powered the monastic watermill, which ground the monastic flour from grain grown on the sheltered slopes of Coverdale. All in all, there is evidence of peaceful prosperity. Their predecessors may have cared for the lepers whose remains were recently discovered in a small field next to the graveyard of the parish church, but the sixteenth-century monks lived comfortably in their calm cloisters, among their gardens and fishponds, in the meadows above the river. And they gave thanks to God – 'There was good singing at Coverham.'[2]

That singing ceased in April 1536. A few months earlier the government inspectors had arrived, searching for scandal and taking detailed note of the monastic rents. Their report was a foregone conclusion, designed to justify a classic piece of Tudor propaganda – that 'the idle and dissolute monks and nuns who live in these little dens of vice' were guilty of 'manifest sin, vicious, carnal and abominable living'.[3] The monasteries must be closed and their wealth forfeit to the Crown, using the pretext of reformation to pay for the King's extravagance. Coverham was one of the first victims; the Abbot was given a pension, the monks encouraged to relinquish their vows and William Blytheman, the King's Receiver, began the task of stripping the abbey of all that could be moved. Valuables were sent to the royal treasury – everything else was intended to be sold.

But the work was interrupted almost before it had begun by the outbreak of rebellion.

The Pilgrimage of Grace started as a riot in Lincolnshire and rapidly spread to Yorkshire, with a series of mass risings. On 12 October Lord Scrope wrote urgently to his father-in-law, the Earl of Cumberland, warning him that the commons of Mashamshire and Nidderdale had risen the day before, occupied Coverham Abbey and Middleham, and were advancing towards Bolton. Their grievances were many, and united all classes of society – resentment at the encroachment of the King's government on the semi-autonomous fiefdoms of the North, rancour at the King's taxes at a time of economic hardship, anger at Henry's execution of Anne Boleyn and his hasty remarriage to Jane Seymour. But above all, there was deep offence at the changes to the Church liturgy and the suppression of the monasteries. The rebels wanted to reverse the course of the Reformation, and one of their first acts was to restore the White Canons to their abbeys at Easby and Coverham.

Inevitably, it seems, the rising failed, and Henry VIII ordered the Duke of Norfolk to make a 'terrible example' of the monks of Easby, for daring to return to their cloisters. I can find no record of similar vengeance being wrought on their neighbours at Coverham but the canons were certainly expelled from their monastery, this time for good, and the task of dismantling the abbey continued. Oxen and cows, sheep and lambs, wool, corn and hay – almost everything moveable was sold, including some of the minor church ornaments and furniture; but the King retained the best – reliquaries, vestments and the like, plus '781 oz of silver plate and 3 oz gold' – according to the careful account kept by William Blytheman. Lead was stripped from the roofs and smelted into pigs, using rafters to fire the furnaces. Six bells weighing 2000lbs were lowered from the tower, and readied for dispatch to the royal armouries, to be cast into cannon. But lead and bells remained in the ruined cloister for more than twenty years, until the abbey itself was sold.

On the eve of the Dissolution of the Monasteries there were more than 800 religious houses in England, containing about 10,000 monks, nuns, canons and friars – owning a sixth of the nation's land. Four years later there were none. It was one of the greatest social upheavals ever undertaken in this country, and change so radical shook the ancient certainties. It was a moment of opportunity, and the 'new men' of Tudor England seized the new day. One such was Edward Loftus, former monastic bailiff.

In some ways it seemed that little had altered, that he simply swapped landlords, from Abbot to King. But the King was far distant and the opportunities endless. There were no monks to feed and keep in comfort, no one but himself to account to. Within less than five years – before his death in 1541 – Edward was able to ensure that his young sons were well provided for, and in the decades that followed his relatives accumulated more and more of the old monastic lands. They moved from the windswept ridge of Swineside to the gentle valley of Coverham.[4]

That tiny journey had huge significance. Swineside is only a few miles up the dale from the abbey but feels utterly different, and much more isolated. When the descendants of Edward Loftus bought lands in Coverham they acquired a sense of leisure as well as space, of order and of prospects, and suddenly they were closer to the world. For the first time in centuries it must have seemed possible to make decisions about the future that were not limited by the parish boundaries. Other members of the family who remained at Swineside – or Swineshead as it was often called – are referred to in the records as they had always been, as yeomen, but the move to Coverham signalled a social transformation. Henceforth they were gentlemen.

Robert Loftus, the bailiff's elder son, lived for most of his life in Yorkshire and grew rich – while his younger brother Adam made a brilliant career in Ireland. For Adam, in particular, the Dissolution changed his life. It gave his family the wherewithal to send him to Cambridge University – to the great new college of Trinity, which had been founded by King Henry with endowments of monastic land. And it gave Adam himself the knowledge that society and his place in it were not immutable. Fired by intelligence and ambition he left the Yorkshire moors, never to return.[5]

CHAPTER 3

A Radical Education

The manuscript of Adam's life that so much absorbed me as a boy seemed to echo with the man himself – a resonant, somewhat daunting brogue – as he told his story in ways that brooked no contradiction. Even now, this is true. When I read that he was sent to Cambridge with an unusually generous allowance from his father, which he used to procure 'the love and esteem of his contemporaries in the University' and the 'friendship with those who were most distinguished there for their virtue, learning and family interests,'[6] it sounds like the old Archbishop, re-inventing his youth as a tale of earnest endeavour. The facts were otherwise. Adam's father had died when he was a child, and the friends that he made at Cambridge included dangerous fundamentalists, intent on religious revolution.

It was a drastic break with his past, for the Yorkshire of Adam's childhood was a stronghold of recusancy, and the tradition in which he was raised was Catholic in all but name. When his father died I think it likely that he was sent to Richmond, to lodge with his relatives Gabriel and William Lofthouse and be taught by their friend John Moore, who was master of the school that had long been associated with the Chantry of Our Lady. All three of them were priests – Gabriel had also been a monk – and they clung to traditional Catholic ways, despite the introduction of new forms of worship. They believed in the saints, prayed for the dead, sang God's praise.[7]

So the youth who set off for Cambridge, a year or two after the founding of Trinity College, was moving from the heartland of the old faith to a place in ferment, seething with radical ideas. King Henry was dead – succeeded by his clever but sickly son, Edward VI – and the Council of Regency was packed with men committed to reform on the continental model. This meant that Court and university were briefly in accord as to the future of the English Church, for Cambridge had long been a centre of Protestant debate and a magnet for reformers from Germany and Geneva. 'Germany' had even become a nickname for the White Horse Inn, where they gathered to discuss the teachings of Luther and Melancthon, Zwingli, Calvin and Martin Bucer. Those debates shaped the views of a brilliant generation – including a future archbishop, Adam Loftus, and his future friend Thomas Cartwright.

For men such as these, educated in the bracing air of Cambridge radicalism, reading the Bible in English and discovering the primitive force of scripture, Puritanism was the breath of belief. 'And there appeared unto them cloven tongues as of fire, and it sat upon each of them. And they were all filled with the Holy Ghost and began to speak with other tongues as the Spirit gave them utterance.' That sense of the Word, of the purifying flame, is hard to capture in the subsequent tangle of Adam's life but it was, I feel sure, the spark that fired him, when he was young.

Those exciting days ended quite suddenly, in 1553, with the death of King Edward at the age of fifteen. Edward's half-sister Mary (whose mother and husband were Spanish) reversed his radical changes with Catholic vengeance, and burned those who refused to recant their heresy. Adam left Cambridge without taking his degree, was ordained as a priest and hid himself in the country. He was appointed to the parish of Outwell in Norfolk – thirty miles north of Cambridge – and then moved again to Gedney, in the fens of Lincolnshire. He stayed there, in quiet obscurity, while more notable dissenters were torched at the stake.[9] It took five years of apparent conformity before the accession of Protestant Elizabeth ended this reign of terror.

Yet somehow in these years of dangerous upheaval the young Adam Loftus came to the notice of a great and cunning politician, his lifelong protector. For lurking in the shadows of this story, unmentioned in any account of Adam's early life, is the man 'to whom I was best known, even from my youth,' William Cecil.[10]

None of the flamboyant favourites of the Elizabethan Court exercised greater or more enduring power than this ruthless chameleon. A convinced reformer with close connections to Cambridge, Cecil had risen from relatively humble origins to hold high office under King Edward. He survived the perilous transition to the following reign, conformed to Catholicism and served the new Queen, but even before Mary died he was in secret communication with her sister Elizabeth. One of her first decisions as Queen was to appoint him Secretary of State.

I have no idea how preacher and politician came to meet, or what so impressed William Cecil about the unknown Yorkshireman. But the evidence is clear, as Adam always acknowledged, that this was the man 'whom in all my good causes I have found a special patron and defender.' I think it was Cecil who found a quiet parish in his native Lincolnshire where the young Loftus could hide from persecution when Mary was on the throne, and then, when the climate changed, set him on the path to preferment – by recommending him as chaplain to his friend the Earl of Sussex, the Queen's Lord Lieutenant in Ireland.

Adam Loftus embarked for Dublin in June 1560, and it seems that he seldom looked back. He certainly never returned to the small stone house on the ridge at Swineshead where he was born. But many years later, when he was grand, he was granted a coat of arms: trefoils for the shamrock of Ireland, a chevron of ermine for his robes of state. The crest was a boar's head, snarling against the sky – punning reminder of the place he had left behind.

ADAM

CHAPTER 4

Faith in the Word

On a fine summer day in 1560 Adam Loftus followed the Earl of Sussex to Christ Church Cathedral, where his master took the oath of office as Lord Lieutenant of Ireland. Fringed mantles, tunics of saffron and red, long 'trouses', strange hair plaits, the clamour of Gaelic – even in this most anglicised of Irish cities, the presence of another, very different culture was palpable and constant, for this was a foreign land, under English occupation. A lavish dinner, hosted by the Lord Mayor, was followed by a play – 'in which the Nine Worthies were acted' – and at night, after more 'sumptuous entertainment', they processed by torchlight through the streets of Dublin, to the sound of music. For a brief moment, it must have seemed like a dream.

Awakening was harsher. First impressions of the colourful strangeness of Ireland were swiftly overwhelmed, for Protestant Englishmen, by the classic colonial prejudices – fear and contempt of the 'barbarous' natives – and this was particularly true for the clergy. Preaching the Gospel in Ireland was a very different matter than it had ever seemed in England, and few wished even to attempt it. There was, for a start, the barrier of language. The 'mere' Irish were famously fluent in Latin but ignorant of English – the vernacular, for them, was the Latin mass, not the 'Gospel for ploughboys' of Tyndale's translation. No Irish Bible was printed until the seventeenth century, and none of the English reformers spoke the language of their flock. For the Protestant Bishop of Kildare (to whom Adam was appointed chaplain soon after his arrival) the fact that he could 'neither preach unto the people, nor the people understand me' was his 'continual and daily torment.' And he complained that 'there is not a preacher to assist me in setting forth God's Word, or the Queen's Majesty her proceedings, saving one Mr Loftus.'[11]

That conjunction of 'God's Word' and the Queen's 'proceedings' is even more telling than the sense of mutual incomprehension, for the Anglican Reformation was seen by both sides as an instrument of conquest. The spur was a constant nightmare that haunted the Queen's Council: the threat of Catholic Ireland allied with England's enemies. Every possible effort must be made to prevent this – so religious as much as civil conquest was a priority of state, however limited the chance of success.

Able and determined preachers were hard to recruit to such an unpromising task, which helps to explain the astonishing speed of Adam's promotion. Soon after arriving in Ireland he felt confident enough to marry and chose as his bride Jane Purdon, the twenty-one-year-old daughter of a prosperous English settler.[12] The following year he was given his first Irish benefice and a few months later the Queen instructed the Dean and Chapter to elect 'Adam Loftehouse, Professor of Divinity' as Archbishop of Armagh and Primate of all Ireland.[13] His appointment to the primacy, at the age of twenty-eight, was unprecedented.

Reality intervened, just as it had done the previous year when Elizabeth issued new silver shillings to replace the debased Irish coinage then in circulation. 'Bad money drove out good' as people continued to use the older coins and hoarded or melted down the new shillings. Likewise with Adam's appointment as primate, the Irish were having none of it – for Armagh was in O'Neill territory where the English writ meant little, and the Cathedral Chapter was stuffed with 'temporal men and Shane O'Neill's horsemen'.[14] Ulster was so lawless that the value of the primacy amounted to little more than £20 per annum, and it was not until March 1563 that Adam was formally consecrated archbishop.[15]

A year later, the Queen set eyes on her new primate for the first time – and a romantic story was born, which I learnt as a child. This told how the redhead Elizabeth 'happened to be present' at Cambridge when Loftus delivered the formal Latin oration for his 'degree of Batchelor in Divinity'. They were exactly the same age – and Elizabeth was dazzled. Adam's 'fluency and purity of expression' and his 'fine

manner and very handsom Person' so impressed the Queen that she
'gave him her royal promise that she would soon promote him,
immediately admitted him as one of her Chaplains: & soon after sent
him into Ireland.'[16]

There is a core of truth in this garbled memory. Elizabeth's only
visit to Cambridge was in August 1564 – when Adam's career in
Ireland was already well established – but her ceremonial inspection
of the university seems to have coincided with the return of the
young Archbishop to take his long-delayed degree, and we have her
own testimony, a few months later, that she was delighted with the
handsome preacher. On 6 January 1565 (Twelfth Night, a traditional
time for royal gifts) the Queen sent a letter to her Lord Justices in
Ireland, declaring that she intended to promote Loftus to a richer
diocese, when one came free, and in the meantime requested that he
be given the Deanery of St Patrick's for his support:

> We had heretofore by good report of ye Archbishop of Armagh, for
> his learning & other good Qualitys meet for that Vocation, so have
> we now by good Experience perceived him to be very well endued
> with singular good gifts meet for ye Place & Dignity, wch he holdeth
> in ye Church.[18]

Her favour, often fickle, survived for the rest of her reign, despite
occasional outbursts of fury. Loftus served longer in high office than
any other servant of the Queen.

At the beginning, Adam seemed full of hope. He returned to Ireland
with a commission 'for removing all reliques & superstitious Images
from Churches' and determined on radical reform.[19] When he learnt
that dissenting ministers were being sacked in London for refusing to
dress in 'popish rags' (the traditional vestments beloved by Archbishop
Parker), Loftus sent a long and astonishingly outspoken letter to
William Cecil, his ally on the Queen's council, demanding that he
protect them. Passionate conviction is implicit in every word – this the
closest we get to hearing him preach.

> O crafty devil and subtle Satan, when he cannot overthrow (no nor
> once shake) the chiefest points of our religion, what ado he makes

about trifles and light matters. . . O what inconvenience were it to thrust out of their livings and ministry so many godly and learned preachers, only for this, that they will not be like papists, the professed ministers of Satan and Antichrist, in superstitious and wicked order of apparel and outward show?

Adam even threatened his great patron with hellfire and urged him to follow his conscience, and to clear away 'all the monuments, tokens and leavings of papistry; for as long as any of them remain, there remains also the occasion of lapses into the abolished superstition of Antichrist.'[20]

But his position was so exposed that Loftus needed allies; he invited his Cambridge friend, Thomas Cartwright, to join him as his personal chaplain and began a dangerous correspondence with John Knox. Knox was in Scotland and to be involved in any way with this dour prophet was to be snarled in intrigue, tainted by the murderous treacheries of Scottish politics.[21] Cartwright, by contrast, was a trusted friend, who arrived in Dublin in the autumn of 1565. The Archbishop and his chaplain lured dissenting ministers from Cambridge to assist in the task of reformation, and eventually set off together to the rich recruiting grounds of their old university. Loftus had been given permission to spend a year in England, to 'cure his gout', and used his time there to take his doctorate in Divinity, while searching out fellow Puritans to serve in Ireland.[22]

While at Cambridge Adam became convinced that his task was hopeless, unless the ageing Archbishop of Dublin, Hugh Curwen, were replaced by a true reformer. In October 1566 he wrote to Cecil 'from 'Trintye Colledge', pleading for Curwen's removal, and a month later wrote again, 'from my lodgin in Sowthworke', asking to resign his diocese – 'neither is it worth anything to me, nor [am] I able to do any good in it, for that altogether it lieth among the Irish.'[23] The following January, back in Ireland, Adam combined with the Lord Deputy, Sir Henry Sidney, to urge the promotion of Christopher Goodman, Sidney's private chaplain, as Curwen's successor.[24] Faced with the prospect of appointing this ardent Puritan (who had shared Knox's exile in Geneva), the Queen decided to proceed with her earlier proposal – that Loftus himself be 'translated' from Armagh to the much richer diocese of Dublin. The news of this appointment was given him by Sidney on 11 March 1567; 'the church's reformation is now at hand'.[25]

When it was clear that Loftus would get Dublin, Sidney had suggested to Cecil that Goodman should succeed him as Primate.[26] Cecil was far too canny to advocate a scheme that had no chance of royal assent, but Loftus, undaunted, proposed that Goodman should become Dean of St Patrick's and that Cartwright – the champion of Presbyterian democracy – be appointed Archbishop of Armagh.[27] The prospect of such a radical reformation, on continental lines, was more than the Queen could stomach.

Cartwright found another platform, as Professor of Divinity at Cambridge, where his increasing fame was accompanied by mounting official concern. In 1570 he gave a series of lectures so critical of the established Church that he was hauled before the authorities to explain himself. Suddenly the professor was a subversive, dangerous to know, but the Archbishop of Dublin came boldly to his defence – asking Cecil to show his 'honourable lovinge favor to my deare frend, Mr Cartwright, of Cambridge. If peradventure he should be deceyved, he were with learninge and mekenes to be perswaded, and not with violence to be molestd or greved.'[28] Such protests were to no avail. Cartwright was dismissed from his post and fled to Geneva.

Loftus had not yet given up hope of fundamental reform, but those he counted on as allies recognised that the cause was lost. Christopher Goodman refused to embark on another campaign in Ireland, claiming that his previous attempts (with the Archbishop's help) had been frustrated by the civil authorities. Adam promised to 'sustain all the blame that shall therefore arise' and invited him to stay at his castle at Tallaght. But Goodman was clear that such a mission would be doomed to failure. He might long for an Irish reformation similar to that of 'Germany, Savoy and Scotland', but unless the Queen's Council in London could be persuaded to allow 'one year's trayel of a Reformed Church at Dublin – it will be none other in my opinion but a striving against the stream.' Adam did his best to enlist support at the highest levels, even persuading the Earl of Essex to write to Secretary Walsingham on his behalf, but Goodman was right, and nothing came of it.[29]

God's anger was prompt, or so it seemed, for 'there was a pestilence at Dublin so great that City was in a manner depopulated, so that grass grew in the Streets and the doors of the Churches.' The Archbishop, in the manner of an Old Testament prophet, 'proclaymed a fast to be observed over all his diocese, that the Lord might withdraw the heavy affliction from this land' – but the Queen had lost patience with prophets.[30] In 1577 she ordered the Archbishop of Canterbury, Edmund Grindall, to put a stop to Puritan proselytising. When he refused, she suspended him. The crackdown had begun.

It was at this point that one of Walsingham's army of informers remembered that the Archbishop of Dublin was a Puritan sympathiser and had employed Cartwright as his chaplain. 'Being advertised of Her Majesty's heavy displeasure conceived against him', Adam embarked urgently for England but was driven back by contrary winds. As the royal fury subsided, Loftus wrote to Walsingham to clear his name. It was a brave and skilful letter, in which he claimed to be 'utterly ignorant what the terme and accusation of puritane meaneth' but declared his 'love and favour' for Cartwright. He ended with a plea for tolerance. 'I will not trouble you with any longe discourse of this matter, but will leave the judgement thereof to god almightye, who knowethe that the purest of us are all impure and fowle, bothe in bodye and mynde.'

But the 'pure' spirit of Geneva radicalism was only too easily corrupted by the 'fowle' realities of the world, as the Archbishop knew very well, for his hopes of converting Ireland by piety and preaching were constantly undermined by some of his strongest supporters – fierce Protestant adventurers who despised the Irish and all their ways, and believed in the summary 'justice' of martial law.[31] 'Civility', for them, had nothing to do with traditional Brehon law, extended kinship, 'papist' religion or other marks of difference – nor much to do with law in any form. It meant 'Englishness' in all its pride, enforced by military conquest. And their contempt was extended to the traditional basis of English power in Ireland, the Lords of the Pale – Catholic 'Old English' grandees whose loyalty was increasingly tested by the financial burden of the 'cess' (taxation to support the government's military campaigns) and pressure to conform to the Protestant religion. All of which pro-voked mounting discontent, open resistance, defiant recusancy.

The result was depressingly plain: after twenty years of continuous effort the Irish reformation was an utter failure – not enough committed preachers, too much church property used to remunerate government officials, a hostile population and lack of support from the civil authority.[32] Outside Dublin and the most anglicised parts of the Pale, the Protestant faith was something remote, and even within the capital attendance at Protestant services was sporadic, or purely nominal.[33]

Confronted by the strength of this opposition, the Archbishop's faith in the Word, the gift of tongues, seemed like a futile dream.

CHAPTER 5

Death of an Archbishop

Exhausted by his lack of success, Loftus sailed for England in 1577, intending to resign. He was only persuaded to stay when the Privy Council ordered Sir William Drury, Lord Justice of Ireland, to make greater efforts to support the Irish reformation, by building schools, repairing churches and reviving the Commission for Ecclesiastical Causes – 'especially in compellinge Noblemen, Gentlemen & People of all sorts to come to ye Church in tymes of Services & commen praiers.' If preaching had failed, it was time for coercion.[34]

Within a few years Adam Loftus was one of the most powerful men in Ireland but the young Archbishop, passionate for reform, gradually vanished from view.

One of his first victims was a hotheaded Catholic malcontent, James Eustace – member of an Old English family, traditionally associated with the FitzGeralds, the Earls of Kildare. Eustace had lived in Rome in the 1570s and returned to Ireland fired by the militant ideals of the Counter-Reformation. His contempt for Protestant compliance eventually provoked Loftus to summon him before the Commission. He spent a night in jail, was fined 100 marks for attending a mass, and had to listen to a sermon from the Archbishop on the folly of his ways.[35]

This and other prosecutions enraged the Catholic magnates of the Pale and provoked a fierce enmity between Loftus and Eustace, who inherited the title of Viscount Baltinglass soon afterwards. Matters came to a head when Gerald FitzGerald, Earl of Desmond, launched a dangerous rebellion in the west of Ireland. Baltinglass conspired with him, and eventually linked up with Feagh M'Hugh O'Byrne to launch their own rising in Leinster. It was a powerful combination, because Baltinglass brought with him numerous of his 'Old English' friends, while O'Byrne commanded widespread Gaelic allegiance. Lord Chancellor Gerrard wrote to Burghley on 3 August 1580 in gloomy terms – 'the Archbishop of Dublin is affraid all our throats will be cut' – and his fears seemed confirmed three weeks later, when the forces of the newly appointed Deputy, Lord Grey, were defeated at the Pass of Glenmalure, close to O'Byrne's stronghold in the Wicklow hills.

The rebellion dragged on for over a year – inflicting a great deal of damage – but never again seriously challenged government troops. More worrying, in some ways, was that several Old English grandees, headed by the Earl of Kildare, were suspected of giving covert support to the rebels. Kildare was denounced by Chancellor Gerrard and Archbishop Loftus, arrested and charged with sedition. He survived, but Loftus became a marked man. The rebels burned his towns and killed the inhabitants, and his own life was 'daily and hourly sought for'. In July 1581 Lord Grey wrote to Walsingham and warned that 'if on their pardon, the Lords of the Pale [Kildare and others] are released, the Archbishop of Dublin will be murdered. He now lives in my house [Dublin Castle], or he would have been a dead man before this.' He recommended that Loftus be relieved of his post and made Bishop of Ely.[36]

Adam stayed in Ireland and was made Lord Chancellor – the second most senior post in the civil administration – but the rebellion brought about a marked shift in his attitude to the use of force.[37] Frightened by the consequences of his own uncompromising actions – which had to some extent sparked the revolt – he was shocked by the brutality of the Deputy. For Grey was a monster, who boasted that in less than two years in Ireland (Sept 1580 to July 1582) he had executed nearly 1,500 'chief men and gentlemen' by martial law, 'not accounting those of meaner sort and killing of churls, which were innumerable.'[38] In his new role as Chancellor, Adam recognised that greater respect for legal norms needed to be restored if the administration was to have any hope of regaining the loyalty of the Old English, and he joined with the Earl of Ormond to plead with Elizabeth and her Privy Council to embrace more 'temperate and peaceable government'.[39] Their pleas were heard, for Lord Grey was sacked and Loftus and Sir Henry Wallop were appointed to act in his stead, as Lords Justices. They disagreed about much, as Wallop later testified, but the two years of their administration were relatively peaceful and unusually economical (which pleased the parsimonious Queen) – and Loftus made plain, right from the start, that he intended to replace brutality with mercy. He wrote to Burghley a few months after his appointment, urging him 'to comfort Her Majesty's people, who now in great numbers perish miserably from famine,' by binding up the broken state of Ireland, giving pardon to the Earl of Desmond and withdrawing the soldiers from Munster.[40]

Adam was even prepared, when asked to make a judgement that might embroil him in the private quarrels of dangerous men, to let justice take its course in unconventional ways. When Conor M'Cormack O'Conor and Teige McGilpatrick O'Conor accused each other of treason in September 1583, the Lords Justice stepped out of the ring and let the combatants fight it out, trial by combat, in the inner court of Dublin Castle. Both were said to have shown great courage and the issue was decided when Conor was slain. Heaven knows what the Privy Council thought of it when the matter was reported to them, but it was certainly less dangerous, and much cheaper, than military intervention to keep the peace.[41]

As Conor's corpse was cleared away, an arrest took place that led within a few months to another contest, involving Adam himself – a trial of conscience, trapped within a political arena from which there was no escape.

In September 1583, after spending two years travelling in disguise around Ireland as he ministered to his diocese, Dermot O'Hurley, Catholic Archbishop of Cashel, was seized at the castle of his protector, the Protestant Earl of Ormond. He was taken to Dublin and 'kept in chains in a dark, dismal, and fetid prison' until the following year, just before Easter, when he was brought before Loftus and Wallop. It was said that they tried to bribe him – promising large rewards if he converted – and then to persuade him by religious arguments. 'Dermot, not relishing this – bade them, stupid and ignorant men (such was his high spirit), not to offer ridiculous and false doctrines to him, an Archbishop, and doctor of celebrated academies.'[42]

Loftus and Wallop were faced with the challenge of what to do next. Like most politicians, their instinct was to unload the problem onto someone else, and the obvious route was to ship their captive to England. So Loftus wrote to Walsingham for further instructions, and then sought every excuse to avoid what the Queen's spymaster demanded, which was torture. 'We want here either racke or other engine of torture to terrify him, and thought that in a matter of so great importance, the Tower of London should be a better school than the Castle of Dublin – and therefore do we wish we had direction to send him thither.'

Walsingham was implacable, and sent back detailed instructions on how to proceed. Loftus and Wallop nonetheless did all that they could to put off the evil day. They interrogated O'Hurley over several months before finally admitting defeat and handing him over to Walsingham's trusted agents, 'Mr Waterhouse and Mr Secretary Fenton, to put him to the torture, such as your Honour advised us, which was to toast his feet against the fire with hot boots.' It is only too clear that the Chancellor-Archbishop was determined to place on record Walsingham's responsibility for this savagery, rather than face his own compliance in such a terrible act.

The torturers extracted some sort of confession from their agonised victim but even the Crown lawyers were doubtful of proving a case of treason in open trial – so Loftus and Wallop sought the Queen's authority 'to have him executed by Martial Law'. Walsingham wrote back with her decision, 'That the man being so notorious and ill a subject', if an 'ordinary trial' was not possible 'then her pleasure is that you take a shorter way with him by Martial Law.' That letter was written at the end of April, but it took another six weeks, until 19 June, before the execution finally took place.

The killing of one archbishop marked the death of another – the moment when preacher turned politician. For the rest of his life the Lord Chancellor busied himself with the accumulation of wealth and power, affairs of state, material things, intrigues and distractions. It was only at the end, faced with a reckoning, that he finally acknowledged 'the greate & heynouse Offences which I have committed' and proclaimed his hope that 'ye merrits & passion of Christe Jesus hath blotted out all my Synnes.' As he tried to fix the record 'for posterities hereafter', I think that he was whistling in the dark.[44]

CHAPTER 6

A College for Learning

When Queen Elizabeth sent a letter to her council in Ireland, authorising the foundation of a university in Dublin, she called it 'a Colleage for Learninge, whereby knowledge and civility might be increased.' That small word 'might' sounds a note of caution, and the story of this foundation is one of greed, corruption and intrigue, played out in the claustrophobic microcosm of the English Pale. Knowledge was clouded by self-interest and civility a distant dream.

At the heart of things was the Chancellor-Archbishop, Adam Loftus – the man who did most to frustrate and then to accomplish the Queen's will. Trinity College Dublin, for better or worse, was his creation.

His portrait still looms above a noisy throng of students, with an air of disapproval. Tall dark hat, vanishing into the dark background; long dark cloak, lined with fur; pale, grey-bearded face; black boots. The boots have bright red heels and soles, and sharp square-cut toes, astonishingly dandy, and the Chancellor holds a large red purse, richly embroidered with the royal arms and trimmed with golden tassels – symbol of his office as Keeper of the Great Seal. It is a powerful, sombre image, combining preacher and politician – but those red-soled boots keep dancing in my memory. They tap out the telltale codes of wealth, privilege and the vanity of power. Those elegant boots may have peeped from beneath Adam's cloak in the Council Chamber of Dublin Castle or paced the Long Gallery of his own castle at Rathfarnham but could never have trod outdoors: far too fancy.

Fancy footwork was needed for a man who survived one of the most turbulent periods of Irish history, in the highest offices of Church and State. He outlived the Virgin Queen and the coming and going of numerous Deputies, acquired a fortune, married his swarm of children into the greatest families of the day and outmanoeuvred all his enemies. It was a remarkable achievement for a bailiff's son from Yorkshire – particularly so because Elizabethan governance was a matter of frightening insecurity. Its practitioners fought for favour in a world of intrigues, spies, habitual and institutionalised corruption, flamboyant patronage, sudden falls from grace, imprisonment, torture and execution. Alert for rumour, constantly watched, Elizabeth's officers of state kept every order, copied every letter, as evidence for their defence. Building alliances of kinship and obligation, sending tokens of love and allegiance with dispatches of state, they sought protection in multiple ways.

For the English administrators in Ireland there was the added problem of distance – communication with the Court was less certain, rumours more difficult to counter – and the constant military danger stretched resources and tempers to the limit. There was also the puzzle of geography – of geographic ignorance – for maps of Ireland were sketchy and inaccurate. It was difficult for the English to have much sense of where they were going, or how to get there. And even when they knew, the roads were few and mostly dreadful.[45]

They arrived with fierce notions of conversion or conquest, as Adam himself had done, and always they failed. Overcome by the bogs and the damp of Ireland, the incomprehensible kinship and feuds of the Gaelic lords, their customs and claims and shifting intentions. Defeated by the lack of resources – money, men, provisions and leadership – grudgingly supplied by a distant Privy Council. Infected by men like themselves who succumbed to greed and compromise, as they fought a war they could never win, while pretending to the Queen and her councillors that things were getting better.

The archives are full of orders and accounts and reports to the Privy Council, signed by the Chancellor-Archbishop, as that war dragged on. There were even times when he went on campaign himself, complaining bitterly of age and illness – and his sons were sent to fight, as I describe in a subsequent chapter.[46] But a glittering thread weaves its way through the records: the trail of Adam's corruption.

Exchanging gifts for favours and dipping a glove in the public purse – such things were taken for granted – but Ireland was exceptional. The example was set by the Queen's viceroys, whose rapid rotation in office was a goad to their greed, as Fynes Moryson made plain. 'For Magistrates often changed like hungry flyes sucke more blood, and as the Devill rageth more because his tyme is shorte, so these Magistrates feareing soone to be recalled, are not so much bent to reforme the

Commonwealth, the fruite whereof should be reaped by the successor, as they are vigilant to inrich themselves and their Followers.'[47]

What made Adam unusual in this context was not avarice but longevity – over forty years in public office. He survived the plots and rivalries that did for so many others, outlived his most powerful patron and his Queen, and continued to accumulate wealth. He was thrice made Keeper of the Great Seal before being appointed Chancellor in 1581 – an office he retained for the rest of his life – and he served several times as Lord Justice. Each promotion provided the means to enrich himself on a grander scale.

My sympathies are confused. When faced with Adam's baleful gaze I catch a glimpse of my own reflection, and his willingness to compromise (for a quiet life and personal gain) seems less repugnant than the bleak ferocity of his opponents. Most were Protestant adventurers, out for profit, whose remedy for this lovely land was massacre and plantation, 'civility' at the point of a sword. On the whole I prefer corruption.

For two years, from 1582, the Chancellor-Archbishop and Sir Henry Wallop governed Ireland in the absence of a Lord Deputy, with no one to countermand their decisions except the distant Privy Council in London. The opportunities were endless and Adam took full advantage, as Wallop later made plain, when he refused to serve in harness with him for a further term.

> I found when we were last joined my colleague chiefly sought his own profit, and the pleasuring of his friends, which are many in respect of matches made, and to be made, with his children. Besides by nature he is and always has been, inconstant and oftentimes passionate. He is a very good preacher and pity he is not employed only therein.[48]

It was during his time as Lord Justice that Adam acquired Rathfarnham. Burghley refused his initial request for a grant from the confiscated estates of Viscount Baltinglass – yet somehow, within a year, the Chancellor-Archbishop took possession of several thousand acres of Baltinglass land in the Wicklow hills to the south of Dublin, at the nominal rent of thirty shillings per annum. And there he built his castle.[49] Loftus might claim that he needed a stronghold for shelter and that his massive new fortress provided a bulwark for Dublin against the raids of the O'Byrnes, but the scale and magnificence of Rathfarnham were far beyond any military need. Gossips questioned how it was paid for, and everyone knew that the castle was a monument to Adam's pride.[50]

Pride took a fall before the place was finished, when a new Lord Deputy was appointed, in June 1584. Sir John Perrot was sworn in at St Patrick's – in a ceremony presided over by Adam Loftus, whose reign as Lord Justice was thereby brought to an end. I suspect it was hatred at first sight.

One of Perrot's first actions was to order his subordinate, Robert Legge, to devise a law for the suppression of wolves. It seems like a satire on his time in Ireland, for the new Deputy treated most of his colleagues with scornful contempt, as predators on the state, and used Legge to find the evidence for their prosecution. But many suspected this was only the means to replace one pack of wolves by another, as Perrot and his cronies took charge.[51]

In the curious way of such things, the chosen battleground seemed far removed from the real quarrel, for it took the guise of an argument over education. Perrot arrived with instructions from the Privy Council to revive a long-mooted scheme to divert the revenues of St Patrick's Cathedral to establish a university, and announced his intention of converting the church itself into a new home for the Law Courts, and turning the houses of its Dean and Chapter into Inns of Court. All were agreed on the need for a Protestant university but the means proposed were violent trespass on the Archbishop's turf. Perrot's scornful justification – that Dublin had two cathedrals, Christ Church and St Patrick's, and the latter had 'a superstitious reputation' – was typically tactless, but the real motivation, for both antagonists, was more mercenary. Loftus suspected that Perrot and his friends were keen for a share of the spoils, and the Deputy knew for certain that the Archbishop had diverted to his family's use many of the rich livings that Perrot now wished to appropriate: 'He and his children received by ye said Cathedral Church 800 Marks a year.'[52]

Their subsequent battle was a fight without quarter, with both men acting like angry children. Loftus dispatched his archdeacon to London, 'to solicit the Queen's mandate against this mischievous scheme.' He claimed that the revenues of the cathedral were used to maintain fifteen university graduates (besides himself) to preach in the Pale – there being only three other preachers in the whole of Ireland – and the survival of St Patrick's was essential to the Irish reformation. In a subsequent letter he threatened to resign unless the Queen expressly forbade the dissolution. Perrot clamoured equally hard to be heard, as he claimed that the Archbishop was enriching himself from church revenues, and questioned the means by which he built his castle at Rathfarnham.[53]

The matter dragged on for months, with charge and countercharge. Loftus obtained a letter from the Queen, instructing her Deputy to leave St Patrick's untouched, but Perrot swore 'that he would not be crossed'. He threatened Adam that 'he would be my utter Enemy; he would sift me, disgrace me, & would do I know not what', and accused him of conspiring to defeat his measures in Parliament.[54] Loftus expressed astonishment at 'how without Blushing the Friends of Malice [could] impute any Default, or blame unto me in that matter,' but Perrot was convinced of the Archbishop's double-dealing. Nothing could be proved, which provoked the Deputy to such 'outrageous fury' that Loftus feared for his safety, and pleaded for Burghley's protection.

At this point the story gains a sub-plot worthy of the most convoluted Elizabethan drama. For it seems that Adam's private secretary was hoping to marry the daughter of his counterpart, Philip Williams, Secretary to the Lord Deputy. In pursuit of this courtship he was a frequent visitor to their lodgings and managed to call one day when Williams was absent on his master's business. The door was open and on Williams's desk he noticed a large sheet of paper, setting out a series of accusations against the Chancellor-Archbishop. He quickly wrapped up the paper and rushed to Dublin Castle, where Adam was sitting in Court – to whom he presented the document as if it was a petition. Adam was angry at being interrupted but his secretary bravely persisted, so he took the paper, 'read it seriously over' and returned it, promising a suitable answer. 'So the Lord Chancellor's Secretary left these Articles of pretended Treason in the place where he found them, without any notice that he had either taken or seen them.'

As soon as he had a chance to rise, Adam went home and wrote to the Queen, Burghley and other members of the Privy Council. He accused the Deputy of having no regard for religion or learning but simply wanting to gratify his friends and his pride by founding 'Perrot's

College', and gave a detailed rebuttal of the charges against him. He acted fast and was just in time to catch a favourable wind. The wind then turned – 'So the Lord Deputy's Pacquet, having not been in readiness, was stop'd on this Side so long, that before its departure, Letters of Approbation were returned to the Chancellor from the Queen & the lords of the Council: as Also a sharp letter from the Queen to the Deputy, reproving him for so groundless an attempt against her Chancellor.'

The Queen expressed 'great mislyke' of their quarrels, and ordered Perrot and Loftus to be reconciled. In obedience to her command, Archbishop and Deputy took communion together on Easter Day 1586 – but the 'old bickerings' soon broke out again: 'Such is the State of Ambition, as it never sees any way but by the stairs of its own climbing.'[55]

The language of Perrot's fury was brilliant in its colour but dangerous for being so memorable. He raged at his colleagues: 'What care I for the Council? They are all of them but a sort of beggars and squibs, puppies, dogs, dunghill churls – yea even the proudest of them come hither with their hose patched on their heels.' And he dared to scorn the Queen – 'God's wounds, this is to serve a base bastard piss kitchen woman,' and 'Ha, silly woman, ha, fiddling woman, now she shall not rule me, now she shall not curb me,' and 'This fiddling woman troubles me out of measure, it is not safe for Her Majesty to break such sour bread with her subjects.' It was madness, because every word was noted down, either by his own secretary or by powerful enemies such as Loftus and his brother-in-law, the Bishop of Meath, and used as evidence of treason when Perrot fell from favour.[56]

The Deputy's arbitrary ways made him so many enemies that his government became increasingly ineffective. The Old English gentry – whose support, however equivocal, was essential to peace and good order – repeatedly voted against his measures in Parliament and paraded their Catholicism as a badge of political opposition; while most of the New English officials, 'concealing their secret mislike, wrought privily against him with their Friends.' When Loftus complained that Perrot's government was 'loathed and abhorred of the better sort', he was speaking no less than the truth.[57]

Perrot was recalled to England in January 1588 but the Deputy's downfall was overshadowed by other, more dramatic events, for the long-feared Spanish invasion – possibly via Ireland, with Irish Catholic support – now seemed imminent. A vast fleet was being assembled to carry an invading army, and rumours were rife. The defeat of that Armada – and the subsequent wreck of numerous Spanish warships around the Irish coasts – was cause for great English rejoicing, but celebrations were much more muted among Old English Catholics, let alone the Gaelic Irish. Most found some excuse to be elsewhere when a Service of Thanksgiving was ordered to be held in every county. 'In Dublin itself the lawyers, in term time, took occasion to leave the town for the purpose to absent themselves from that godly exercise – so bewraying in themselves, besides their corruption in religion, great want of duty and loyalty unto her Majesty.'[58]

This crisis renewed the Archbishop's determination to crack down on recusants and to revive the project for a Protestant university in Dublin, in which he now took the lead. Adam had strong personal reasons to bring it about, for if he could somehow obtain sufficient endowment for the new college, his own cathedral – and his family's revenues – might be safe from future threats. He persuaded the Mayor and Aldermen of Dublin to make a grant of the former monastery of All Hallows, which lay just outside the city, south of the river, by reminding them of the prosperity of the great university towns, Oxford and Cambridge, and promising glory. 'You will thereby receive honour from the whole World [and] will in this time of Reformation dazzle the Eyes of the Papists with the lustre of well-doing.'[59] Leading by example, he 'gave £100 out of his private Bounty' for the new foundation.

The Queen granted her Royal Licence and 'The College of the Holy and Undivided Trinity of Queen Elizabeth near Dublin' was finally established in 1592. It took its name and much of its constitution from the Archbishop's old college in Cambridge and Adam was named its first Provost.[60] Ambition and public policy were at last united.

Public opinion was another matter. The Queen had written that one of the main reasons for founding a college in Dublin was to put a stop to the Irish habit of travelling to 'Fraunce, Italy and Spayne to get Learning in such Forraine Unyversities, where they have been infected with Poperie and other ill Qualities, and so become evill Subjects.' Her Catholic opponents were equally clear about its purpose, as a place where 'Irish youth may be taught heresy by English teachers.'[61]

CHAPTER 7

Signior Gloriosus

His colericke complection was testy as a goose that hath yong goslings, yet easy to be pleased againe with a handfull of otes.

That wonderful description by Barnaby Riche tells me more about Adam Loftus than all the records in the National Archives. Here at last is the man, 'inconstant and oftentimes passionate,' in the words of one of his critics, but the proud father of a vast brood of children, whose monstrous appetite for gold was partly for their protection. When fed his 'handfull of otes' the choleric gander was 'pleased againe'. This jaunty wink at the prelate's enjoyment, his clucking pleasure, is all the more surprising given the author. For Riche was a classic Elizabethan adventurer – soldier, scribbler, spy – who wrote those words having fled for his life to England after Adam's servants tried to kill him on the streets of Dublin. His long campaign against the Archbishop combined bitter outrage with half-admiring relish – the recognition of one scoundrel by another.

'Signior Gloriosus' figures in a complex, rambling satire that Riche published in 1592, but has long been recognised as a portrait of the Chancellor-Archbishop – much less dignified than that which glowers down at us in the Dining Hall of Trinity College Dublin, but perhaps more lifelike. Loftus is compared to a hag from hell, or the personification of vice from a morality play, with beard cut into points, straggling hair and tall hat, padded like a clown and fanning himself like a whore. It is a fantastical image, worth quoting in full.

The loftiness of his lookes was much to be marveld at, but the manner of his attire was more to be laughed at. On his head he weares a hatte without a band like a Malcontent, his haire hanging downe to both his shoulders, as they use to figure a hagge of hell; his beard cut peecke a devaunt, turnde uppe a little, like a vice of a play, his countenance strained as far as it would stretch, like a great Monarcho: his coller turned downe around about his necke that his throat might be seene, as one that were going to a hanging should make way for the halter, his dublet bolstered with bombast, as if he had been diseased by the dropsie: upon that he wore a loose Mandilyon [jerkin or surcoat], like a counterfeit souldiour, in his hand a fanne of fethers, like a demye harlot: riding thus, casting his eies to and fro, seming by his demeanure, as if he had a common wealth in his head, without any word speaking.[62]

Barnaby Riche is a frequent footnote in literary history (two of his tales were sources for Shakespeare's plays) but he played a shadier role in Adam's drama, slouching on stage with two confederates while behind, in the shadows, lurked the sinister figure of Francis Walsingham, the Queen's spymaster. Riche's accomplices were Robert Legge, a civil servant in the Irish Treasury – whom we have already met, as author of the statute on wolves – and Robert Pipho, a long-serving official in Ireland and procurer of informers; 'knaves who will be bought for money.' All of them were Walsingham's creatures and Pypho was his cousin.

The spying began a few years before Riche and Legge appeared in Ireland, when Loftus was appointed Chancellor in 1581. Walsingham's first report came from Andrew Trollop, a tight-minded English lawyer who despised the Irish as 'savages and brute bestes', viewed the Old English Catholics as traitors to their Protestant Queen and scorned those who governed them as venal fools. Trollop declared that 'enything almost will be suffered in Ireland for gayne and friendship' and singled out Loftus for particular criticism. He itemised the cost of maintaining his children, purchasing land in Kent and other expenses that had brought the Archbishop into debt – and that 'to pay this and defray all charges and get more money for his sons and daughters, many think makes him have a very cheverelle conscience' – meaning as pliant as kid leather.[64]

Those envious lawyer's details, the accounting of evidence, suggest only too clearly a world of informers, where officials were constantly watched. Trollop's report is also the first record of Adam's lifelong concern for his children, which became a dominant theme in the tales of his corruption. But family ambition – marriages, dowries, alliances of property and interest – was only part of the story, and I long to know more about the intimacies of family life. Brief glimpses, a few bare facts, are all that I can find.

Adam had twenty children, by a single spouse – even by the standards of the day, this was remarkable. It suggests that the Archbishop was strongly attached to his wife and that she was a woman of resolute stamina – able to cope with his gander's 'testiness' while bearing a stream of 'goslings'. I know her name, Jane Purdon, and that she came from an old Cumberland family, which had settled in Ireland. I know that her sister married one of Adam's closest allies, Thomas Jones, Bishop of Meath. And I know that she was highly regarded by even such a gloomy Puritan as Christopher Goodman, who concluded a letter to Adam with his 'hearty commendations to good Mrs Lofthouse'. But that is all.[65]

As for those goslings and other relatives, Adam's pecking on their behalf – for land, employment, favours of every sort – is a constant refrain in the records. Within two years of his arrival in Dublin, he petitioned his patron Cecil for the rectory of Dunboyne for his brother Robert – and sent him a couple of hunting hawks, as a sweetener.[66] And so it continued, for year after year. In 1578 the Dean and Chapter of Christ Church in Dublin became so tired of his pestering for livings and lands, for himself, his friends and his family that they made the Archbishop promise to ask for no more favours. But Loftus, shamelessly, tried to extract one last request, as the record of that promise was being entered in the chapter books.

This is the truth that Riche so clearly recognised, as he and his confederates attacked Adam's corruption. Riche's first onslaught, in 1589, was a long essay on the negligence and abuses of the Anglican clergy in Ireland. He was careful not to name names, but – as he later explained to the Privy Council – this was the 'orygynall whye the Lord Chancellor and his brother the Bishoppe of Meathe conceyeved their first displeasure agaynste me.' Then came a damning report to Burghley from Robert Legge, who was out for revenge, having been dismissed from office some months earlier. In fourteen angry pages he charged Loftus, Jones and other Councillors with corruption on the grand scale. Confronted by Legge's findings, the Chancellor-Archbishop abused him with 'foul terms and reproachful names, as knave, slave, rascal – and he grew into such choler as he wished the ship's bottom out which brought me over [from England].'

Adam's wrath was born of fear, for Legge's evidence was damning. He described how the Chancellor pocketed fines intended for the Crown, falsified documents to conceal the appropriation of 'spiritual livings' for 'his own children and kinsmen' and blackmailed Dublin merchants by threatening to denounce them as papists. The report concluded with an extraordinary image of Adam as Gargantua, devouring all that came near him – written I guess by Riche, since it rings with his flamboyance.

> He is chief Commissioner in the High Commission, and Principal for the Faculties and Archbishop of Dublin, and Lord Chancellor, so he is all in all. Certain hogsheads of salmon sent to the Lord Chancellor's cellar procured the release of Sir John O'Dogherty from the Castle, and that too, without the poor constable getting his fees. If he grant an injunction to restrain any man it is an easy matter to get it released or dissolved to-morrow, whereupon all people cry out upon him. Some think that angels, beasts of the field, and fowls of the air do fly or run to Rathfarnham.[67]

Legge's battery of charges was sufficient for the Privy Council to order his reinstatement in office, but his patron Walsingham was close to death and Burghley continued to protect Loftus from the Queen's wrath. So, too, did Perrot's successor as Deputy, Sir William Fitz-william, who had served in Ireland before and acquired a well-deserved reputation for corruption. He defended the Chancellor – 'so wise, temperate and useful in affairs of state' – and did his best to keep him in office, while concentrating on his own enrichment. He was said to have taken a bribe of gold from Tyrone, together with sufficient other kickbacks to fill a fifty-three-page book of complaint to Lord Burghley, compiled by the indefatigable Legge. But Fitzwilliam, like Loftus, was a protégé of Burghley, and nothing was done – save that he and Legge came to blows, and Legge was expelled from office for the second time.

Then Riche renewed the attack, delivering a seven-page 'Caveat' to the Queen herself and following it with a 'small book' expanding on these charges. But the Chancellor-Archbishop seemed strangely invulnerable – so his adversaries combined forces to reveal in extra-ordinary detail the scale of his defences, the vast web of relationships that Loftus had managed to construct through the marriages of his numerous children – 'he himself being but of mean lineage out of the north of England.' It was not so much the corruption involved in providing dowries for his daughters and sustenance for his sons that now provoked their outrage as the network of mutual interest and protection that these arrangements bought for him.

> There is not any one house or family, that is of any high degree, name, fame, credit, reputation, or most substantial in riches and forces of followers, for the most part of the English Pale, but that one way or another, through the stock and the cross, and the enterchaungle lines and degrees of marriages and kindred of those wherewithal he has matched his children, the Archbishop has allied and strengthened himself, in some kind of degree either of consanguinity or affinity, to purchase himself into a multitude of lines of friendship, to heighten and uphold his loftiness unmeasurable, and his ambition insatiable.[68]

Adam denounced his accusers as men of no account. Riche was described as 'very needy, by nature immodest and subject to many and very gross infirmities,' in league with 'some papists and atheists of this kingdom to disgrace our persons for our profession's sake,' while Legge was 'a late officer of Her Majesty's exchequer, a man noted and detected of great lewdness, dishonesty and corruption' – and both were 'joined in league of friendship with one Pypho, a renowned Atheist, and most filthy liver.'

Such insults were commonplace in the small and jostling world of sixteenth-century Dublin, but this quarrel was dark enough for violence, and on two successive days there was brawling in the streets of the city. According to Loftus it was Riche who provoked the first fight (on Tuesday 13 June, 1592), when he 'assaulted one of my poor serving men, and after some spiteful words used against him because he was my servant, almost even at my heels, with his drawn sword cut off one of his fingers and desperately wounded him.' Riche's version of events was very different, for he claimed that Nicholas Walsh – accompanied by his brother Piers and others of the Archbishop's henchmen – accosted him with 'shameful words, sodaynly struck me with hys fist, and stabbed me three or foure times' with his dagger. 'Being driven to defend my selfe I gave him a small hurt.'

Riche was imprisoned but released the following day when others testified that it was Walsh who struck the first blow – only to find the Archbishop's men lying in wait for him. It happened that evening, as Riche was walking home with a friend along 'the high street of Dublyn'. He described how six men had been 'layde to murther' him, three hiding 'behind a Cundytte [conduit] with their swords ready drawn to do the act' and three in a nearby house. Thanks to a stout cudgel, the intervention of a couple of passing strangers and an open door that allowed him to slip to safety, Riche escaped with his life – but his account is terrifying in its detail and highly revealing. He claimed that more than a hundred Dubliners stood by during the fight, and none pursued the attackers, who 'went their ways openly through the streets, towards the Lord Chancellor's house' – and that the Mayor of Dublin, who rushed to the scene 'by reason of the rumour', dared not arrest the culprits, 'knowing to whom they did appertain'. Loftus himself, 'understanding all what had passed' took no action. 'I was enforced to flee the country for the safeguard of my life.'[69]

Riche took refuge in London and entertained himself by writing convoluted satires in which he pilloried his enemies to his heart's content. In the first of these (*The Adventures of Brusanus*) Loftus appears as Gloriosus, who 'bending his brow answered: thou base borne fellow, what doest thou thinke I would a companion of thee' – which rings as true as the lovely image of the 'testy' goose. But it was the second (*Greenes Newes both from Heaven and Hell*) that contained the most damning litany of accusations.[70] With evident relish, Riche described Loftus as someone who ignored his pastoral duties, preferring to arrange marriages for his children, 'in theyr very infancie, and when they are under age,' and to 'builde houses, and purchase rents by corruption, extortion, and briberie, that dooth eat and drinke the sinnes of the ignorant people dayly at his table; that will not admit of a pardon from the Pope, yet dares not bee without five or six severall pardons from the Prince, for treason, for murther, for theft, for robbery, for conspiracy, for confederacy, for rasyng, for forging, for extortion, for bryberie, and for many other filthy matters, shameful to be spoken off – and what though from a base and beggarly parentage, he could shewe himselfe lofty in minde, lofty in lookes, and lofty in all the rest of his demeanours.' Bitterness and wonder were twined in a sour knot, never to be disentangled.

Though Riche continued to rumble, like ever more distant thunder, Adam was beyond his reach. Allegations that Loftus had pocketed £24,000 from the Irish revenues, had released a 'Romish bishop' from imprisonment in Dublin Castle and turned a blind eye to the disorders of the O'Byrnes – 'in whose countries you have fostered your children' – prompted a suggestion that commissioners be appointed to investigate.[71] But Adam responded with a mixture of vigorous denials and disarming admissions, while claiming that he had always acted in the Queen's interest.[72]

In fact, as was widely suspected, the Chancellor's dealings with O'Byrne were designed to preserve an outward show of power, in which Feagh M'Hugh was a willing conspirator. Neither he nor Loftus wished to provoke unnecessary conflict. Both would exaggerate a few cattle raids or punitive sorties, for their own purposes, but the reality was a tacit understanding, possibly strengthened by gold. In June 1600, for example, Adam tried to provoke sympathy with news of an attack on his castle, claiming that the rebels had seized 'all the cows, horses, sheep, and other cattle that I had, and have not left me so much as one beef or mutton to feed my family. The Lord in His good time be merciful unto us, for we are in great misery.' But Cecil received another message, by the same post, from Sir Geoffrey Fenton, who dryly advised him, 'that your Honour will hear that the Lord Chancellor was distressed by these rebels in his house at Rathfarnham; but I wish your Honour to believe that as historical, but not as canonical.'[73]

No one paid much attention, because the Privy Council had long since abandoned the threatened commission of enquiry, having decided that none of the charges of Riche and Legge could be made to stick. Or perhaps it was simply too late, and the mischief had been done. Loftus struck attitudes of outraged innocence, complaining that 'not being searched into has given boldness to every discontented and malicious detractor to revenge themselves by such monstrous and false accusations' – confident that his bluff would not be called. The storm had passed.[74]

It was then, at his apogee, that Adam commissioned 'the chief and greatest' of his Seal Cups, to celebrate his triumphs. Gilded angels dance on the finial of its cover, but that was a piece of careless iconography – the man himself was sceptical of angels. The real meaning is in the material, for this magnificent cup – like two other later ones, recorded in his will – was made from the silver matrix of the Great Seal of Ireland. The inscription, too, is worth decoding. It makes no mention of Adam's ecclesiastical titles, proclaiming instead that the cup was made in 1593, when Loftus was 'then Lord Chancellor. He was also Lord Justice in 1582 and 1583 in which year he built his house at Rathfarnham.' It was a statement of wealth and power.

Rathfarnham was another such statement, even bolder, but one that Adam censored when writing to the Privy Council in Westminster. He described it as 'my poor house', afraid that this mighty castle – the scale of it, the lavishness, the stupendous cost – would prompt awkward questions. But visitors to the Castle were staggered by the elk's head and antlers, dug from an Irish bog, which hung on the screen in the Hall, and the 'Basins and Ewers of pure Silver' that were proffered to guests to wash their hands, and the 'great standing white Bowles, which were brought by Mr Newcomen out of England,' and all the other treasures that filled this famous place. For even by the standards of the day the Chancellor-Archbishop had feathered his nest like a prince.

But this was the highest tide of Adam's glory, for his network of protection in London had begun to unravel: Burghley had lost his hearing and suffered some sort of stroke; Elizabeth was old and cantankerous. Burghley retained the Queen's ear until his death in 1598, but his devious son, Sir Robert Cecil, came increasingly to dominate the proceedings of the Privy Council. The Chancellor-Archbishop found himself having to plead for the new man's favour, and to purchase his goodwill with a series of gifts. It was a hard and mercenary world.

Sir Robert's great passion (apart from the exercise of power) was the building of ever grander houses as a setting in which his small, misshapen frame could command the respect of his peers – and he was ruthless in exacting tribute from those who needed his patronage. In October 1596, for example, Loftus wrote to confirm that he had arranged to have quarried for Cecil ten tons of 'touchstone' – probably the famed 'black marble' of Kilkenny – 'good for doors, windows, chimneys, stairs or other building.' He asked whether it should be polished in Ireland, and to which port it should be transported. Cecil decided this was not enough, and by the following spring the Chancellor was writing to assure him that twenty-four tons of the stone were on their way to England, including three large blocks that 'are great in the form of tombstones'. It reads like a sardonic joke.

That enforced gift may have caused Adam to wince, but counted for little compared to Cecil's next demand, which was that he should send one of the treasures from his own castle – the antlers and skull of a giant deer, the extinct Irish Elk – so proudly displayed at Rathfarnham. It was a conscious demonstration of Cecil's power, and the Chancellor-Archbishop had no choice but to concede. 'I have now with some difficulty taken it down without breaking, and delivered it safely to Lumley, the bearer of your letter, who hath promised to carry it carefully unto your Honour; which, when you see, I wish might be the rarest monument in Christendom, or such one indeed as my love to your Honour might the more appear in the bestowing thereof upon you.'[75]

Those professions of love, the repeated bows to 'your Honour', remind me of feudal Sicily and the wheedling voice of Irish beggars, long ago. For the Chancellor-Archbishop was suddenly brought low – forced to write as supplicant to the son of the man who had always been his patron – and the death of Burghley in 1598 left Adam bereft. 'I do now want the staff whereunto I leaned, during whose days none durst have presumed either to have undermined my credit or to have wrought my disgrace with Her most excellent Majesty.'[76]

Even the pleasures of power began to lose their savour. Though his favour at Court was in decline, Loftus was twice more appointed Lord Justice (with Sir Robert Gardiner in 1597 and Sir George Carey in 1599) but each term of office weakened his dominance of Irish affairs. The first earned Adam a tirade from the Queen, for what she saw as feeble incompetence in the face of the most serious rising in several decades, while the second coincided with a spiral of deepening misfortune, as the endless wars now took a personal toll. His namesake son was killed in an ambush in May 1599, and his daughters fled to Rathfarnham, in fear of their lives, with 'their husbands, children and families – all come to me for refuge, not having left to them so much as bread to put into their mouths'. The pessimism of a man at bay can be read in the Chancellor's bleak report to the Privy Council, in January 1600: 'Her Majesty may make this sure account (such is the desperate pass things are now brought to), that, without great killing, this State will not be resettled.'[77]

That was a desolate change of mind for someone whose comfortable venality depended on compromise, on turning a blind eye in return for a bag of gold or a barrel of salmon, on temporising with 'traitors' as neighbours to be pacified. Adam may often have bounced from one extreme to the other – 'he is and always has been, inconstant,' in the words of Sir Henry Wallop – but consistently opposed the harsher measures of martial law. His call for 'great killing' reads like an admission of despair.

The new Deputy, Lord Mountjoy, needed no urging to ruthless action, but his arrival in Dublin, in February 1600, added to the Chancellor's woes. Mountjoy seems to have distrusted Loftus from the start. He dismissed one of the Archbishop's sons from his command in the army, much to Adam's dismay, and encouraged the old man's enemies to renew their attacks with increased vigour.

One charge was new – the accusation that Loftus had taken a bribe of £40 from the 'arch-traitor' Tyrone, which he 'laid in a bag under his bedside'. In earlier times this might have been shrugged aside – the evidence was far from clear – but now, as Adam ruefully admitted to Cecil, 'the practices of mine enemies have so far prevailed to work in Her Majesty's royal heart a hard conceit against me.' There was insufficient proof to disgrace him, but enough to refuse his latest request for a grant of land to relieve the 'iniquity of the times'. Adam sent a blizzard of letters, bewailing the injustice of his fate and demanding that formal charges should be brought, so that he could clear himself 'of all dishonesty and corruption'.[78] Eventually, in November, Cecil showed signs of relenting – whereupon, seemingly without shame, the old Archbishop asked for further favours.

Adam was growing old, as I realised one day when looking over the 1603 accounts for 'The Victuellinge of the fforces in Connaught'. Mountjoy's ugly campaign is reduced to columns of neat figures on thirty skins of the finest vellum – thin, supple, creamy white – but the confident, perfectly ordered script is endorsed by a shaky, quivering version of what had once been a proud flourish; the Archbishop's signature, Ad. Dublin. It is the mark of an ill and exhausted man.[79]

This was the low point, when it was rumoured that Adam's confidence suddenly failed him – and that 'he betook himself to read Catholic books, and, as was blundered abroad, meditated how to recant and repent before being called to account.' Upbraided by the Lord Justice, Sir George Carey, 'Adam had to justify himself privatelie, and after that publiclie by a sermon on Catholic doctrine.' Most historians have rejected this story as implausible propaganda, for it depends on the testimony of a single, partisan witness – a Jesuit priest, Fr Henry Fizsimmons, who was arrested at Adam's instigation and imprisoned for several years in Dublin Castle. I can find not a scrap of evidence to support his account – but sometimes I wonder whether such an unlikely tale could have been wholly invented. It has the curious colour of truth.[80]

Loftus survived, outlived his great Queen and was re-appointed Chancellor under the new King James – but suffered from a 'languishing sickness'. In January 1605, knowing he was close to death, he made his will.[81] Facing eternal judgement, this was Adam's plea for his defence.

> In ye name of God Amen. I Adam Loftus, Lord Chauncellor of Ireland & Lord Archbushopp of Dublin, beinge in perfect health & memory do make this my last will & Testament in manner and forme following.
>
> I bequeath my Soule into ye hands of Allmightie God, whoe, as my full truste & absolute hope ys in his free grace, hath called me to be a member of ye misticall boddy of his holly Churche – renouncing all other helpes, invocations, assistaunce, merrytts & prayers of Saynts, Aungels or any other Creatures, & only relyeinge on Christe Jhesus myn only Savyour & Redeemer in whom only God is well pleased, which Fayth synce I was called to be a Bushopp & minister of Gods holly word, I have allwayes both publickly preached & privatly acknowledged, & doe desire yt this my Faith & profession be made known to posterities hereafter so longe as any Memory be hadd of my self in this World.

'Lord Chauncellor of Ireland & Lord Archbushopp of Dublin.' Reading those words aloud, letting the sounds be shaped by the original spelling, I can hear the Irish in his voice – and the preacher. But then, without a break, the Archbishop turned to the disposition of his material goods – his 'Basins and Ewers of pure Silver', the 'great standing Bowles and lesser white Bowles' and the famous silver cups made from the Great

Seals of Ireland. And 'my mannors, Honnors, Castles, Lands, tenements, messuages, Rectories, Tythes and hereditaments'.

The 'memory of myself in this world' that lingers in the mind is the image of an old man, naming and caressing his treasures, one by one – for Adam, like his biblical namesake, had tasted the fruit of the tree of good and evil, and loved the golden apple.

CHAPTER 8

Band of Brothers

'What ish my nation? Ish a villain and a bastard and a knave and a rascal. What ish my nation? Who talks of my nation?'

The confused anger of Captain MacMorris, in Shakespeare's *Henry V*, is the most poignant contemporary expression of Irish despair at the English assault on their sense of national identity. Beneath the comic brogue lurks a feeling of irreparable loss. The play was written in 1599, as the Earl of Essex left London at the head of a huge army, vowing to suppress the Irish 'rebels' once and for all. For the 'groundlings' of the Globe, this was a topic of immediate political interest, and Shakespeare flattered their chauvinism with speeches of heroic splendour, threaded with Irish allusions. But his own most subtle perceptions are expressed in a voice that no one takes seriously.[82]

'What ish my nation?' Such questions became ever more acute during the 1590s, as the entire project of Irish pacification seemed in danger. The determination of militantly Protestant Elizabethan governors to impose English law and custom, and above all the English religion, over the whole island of Ireland, provoked violent resistance from the Irish and great mistrust among the Catholic 'Old English' settlers. Behind it all loomed a wider fear, of the Protestant island of England under attack from Catholic Europe. The defeat of the Armada in 1588 had merely proved that such fears had substance.

Small wonder, then, that a renewed and repeated emphasis on Englishness pervades the documents of Elizabethan officials in Ireland, and shapes the writings of 'New English' colonists like the great traveller, Fynes Moryson (Secretary to Mountjoy, Elizabeth's last and most effective Deputy) and the poet, Edmund Spenser. For Moryson it is clear that 'English' meant uncontaminated Protestant – an identity that excluded the old-established settlers, whom he referred to as 'English Irish' and scorned for having been 'infected with the barbarous Customes of the mere Irish and with the Roman Religion,' and for speaking Irish rather than English. They had lost all traces of English manners and were agents of the Antichrist.[83] Spenser agreed, expressing astonishment that 'an Englishman brought up in such sweet civility as England affords, should find such liking in that barbarous rudenes, that he should forget his owne nature, and forgoe his owne nation.'[84]

That complacent notion of English 'civility' was founded, at least in part, on righteous conviction – the Protestant faith as God's word incarnate – and contempt for the 'Romish' superstitions (and papal politics) of the Catholic Church, and it was this religious divide, more than anything else, which now brought into question the identity and allegiance of the 'Old English' settlers. In earlier times they had seen themselves as English, however much they may have intermarried with the Irish and adopted their customs, just as the Irish had traditionally made a clear distinction between *Gaedhil* (natives) and *Gaill* (foreign settlers). The new and aggressive breed of Protestant English planters challenged that assumption, and the Irish themselves recognised a changed reality. Absorbed over time into a common culture and sharing a common faith, the Old English were now seen as part of the Irish nation.[85]

For Dudley Loftus, the first of his family to be born in Ireland, confusions of loyalty were bred in the bone. The Archbishop's eldest son may have been raised in his father's household as one of a brood of siblings (English, Protestant, righteous) but as a youth, if rumours were true, he was fostered by the O'Byrnes – to build an alliance with Adam's most troublesome neighbours. Such bonds, for the Irish, were almost as strong as kinship of blood and the experience must have taught Dudley much about the people whom the newly arrived English 'Adventurers', greedy for land, sneered at as barbarous savages. He would have been fluent in the Gaelic tongue, conversant with Brehon law, at ease with Irish customs. And then he was sent to Cambridge, to learn to be an Englishman.[86]

In 1589, at the age of twenty-seven, Dudley made his first visit to Court, with a letter of introduction that described him as 'an honest young man, loved and well disposed'.[87] The recipient was the Queen's Principal Secretary, Sir Francis Walsingham – old and ruthless, responsible for many terrible deeds. It was he who had ordered Dudley's father to torture and then to execute Dermot O'Hurley and had, on occasion, instructed his spies to keep close watch on Adam himself. But Dudley seems to have charmed him, and his father thanked Walsingham for the 'many honourable favours' shown to his son.[88]

Soon afterwards the Archbishop sent 'the dearest jewel I have in the world' on a very different mission – to persuade Feagh M'Hugh O'Byrne to come to Dublin and give evidence concerning Sir John Perrot. O'Byrne was 'a man very fearful and full of distrust,' but the assurance of safe conduct from Dudley Loftus – whom he may have regarded as his foster-son – was enough to persuade him. I have a sense of Dudley's dual identity, not entirely English, and his ability to get others to trust him – but also that he was being used, for devious purposes, his life plotted by his father.[89]

It was the great Archbishop who arranged for Dudley to be granted the Manor of Kilclogan, on the Hook peninsula in County Wexford, and to be married in the summer of 1590 to Anne Bagenal, one of several daughters of Sir Nicholas Bagenal, marshal of the army. Both were steps towards his own independence, but each tied him more closely into the ruthless intrigues of the Elizabethan pacification of Ireland.

Kilclogan Tower stands solitary, darkened by age, in the middle of a green meadow – but was once a strategic stronghold, overlooking the broad estuary that led to Waterford harbour. In Dudley's day this was a lawless land, despite a long history of English settlement. One of those settlers, Edward Itchingham, acted as receiver of stolen goods for the local pirates, and the rocky coastline suffered periodic raids from Barbary corsairs, who seized young men and women to sell as slaves.[90] So the grant of Kilclogan was intended to restore order but there was another, perhaps equal motive: the appetite for land – for the castle was held direct from the Crown and most of the larger estates on the Hook paid a 'head' rent to it, an arrangement that dated back to the time of the Knights Templar. The 'Old English' tenants of those estates were closely entwined with their Irish neighbours, and the new Protestant colonists doubted their loyalty. If they were ever evicted, Dudley or his heirs might claim possession.

Equally carefully considered was Dudley's choice of bride – their alliance of interests and fortunes was part of the vast web that his father spun, through the marriages of his numerous children. But this particular knot had unintended consequences, for Dudley's marriage made him brother-in-law to two very different men: Henry Bagenal, who succeeded his father as marshal, and Hugh O'Neill, Earl of Tyrone.

Tyrone married the twenty-year-old Mabel Bagenal in August 1591. The ceremony was private, in a friend's house, but was conducted by the Bishop of Meath, brother-in-law and closest ally of Archbishop Loftus – who must certainly have known that the wedding was planned and may even have been present. At one level it seemed like a natural conclusion to the long-standing friendship between two of the most powerful families in Ulster, which began when Tyrone's grandfather, Conn O'Neill, gave shelter to Mabel's father as he fled the English courts after killing a man in a brawl. Such an alliance, across the divides of religious and tribal allegiance, implied great political promise, a hope for peace. It seemed like a love match, following a famous courtship, but their wedding caused a scandal. Tyrone had eloped with Mabel in the teeth of her brother's fury, and partly to spite him.

Henry Bagenal was described by a contemporary as 'a greedy adventurer, restless, rapacious, unscrupulous.' [91] A fierce Protestant, he was determined to obliterate the memory of all that his family owed to the O'Neills and to consolidate his power in Ulster by diminishing that of the Earl – and the previous year had accused Tyrone of treachery. It took all the latter's charm to persuade the English Privy Council to give him the benefit of the doubt, and to strengthen his defences he married the marshal's sister. Bagenal was so angry that he refused to part with his sister's dowry and never forgave her husband – the 'arch traitor' – for insulting his family's honour.[92]

Tyrone, for his part, had a bigger game to play. Memorably portrayed by Camden as 'so profound and unfathomable a dissembler, that some foretold at that time, He would either prove the greatest good or the greatest hurt to Ireland' – he fought tenaciously to be recognised by the Irish as rightful successor to his formidable uncle, Shane O'Neill, and by the English as heir to the Earldom of Tyrone.[93] Like Dudley Loftus, a dual identity was bred into him – for the Gaelic boy had been fostered by the English, initially in the household of Sir Henry Sidney and then by the family of Giles Hovenden. When O'Neill went to Court to flatter and dazzle the Queen, he played on his almost-Englishness, while never forgetting his claims as an Irish chieftain – and used his uncertain allegiance as a weapon to deceive his enemies.[94]

So Tyrone's choice of Mabel Bagenal as his third wife was an expression of cunning, as much as love. One of the consequences, which he must have foreseen, was that it drew him into the network of kinship centred on the Chancellor-Archbishop – whose connivance at the wedding added another twist to his relationship with Tyrone, from whom he was later accused of having taken a bribe. And the Archbishop's eldest son was now addressed as 'brother' by two men who hated each other.

That strange brotherhood, and the questions of identity and allegiance that it posed, were thrown into ever sharper focus. On 10 October 1593, Bagenal and Tyrone were marching in uneasy alliance along the bank of the river Erne – in what is now County Fermanagh – when they encountered the forces of Tyrone's son-in-law, Hugh Maguire. There was a brief and bloody skirmish – Maguire's men were routed and two or three hundred killed – but accounts of what happened differed from the moment that the rival commanders sat down to write their reports to the council, on the morning after the battle.

Bagenal's dispatch, from his 'Camp on Connaught side, near the ford of Golune', announced a 'splendid victory over Maguire's full strength' but made almost no mention of Tyrone's part in the engagement, other than to vent his anger at the Earl's unwillingness to stay out of the way, while he led the crossing of the ford with 'Sir Patrick Barnewall, my brother Loftus, and Captain Henshaw'.[95] Tyrone himself was nursing a wound in the leg but sent two long letters, one to the Deputy and council and the other to Lord Chancellor Loftus, 'from the ford of Athe Cooloyne near the castle of Beleek.' Even in their spelling of the place, Bagenal and Tyrone were at odds.

Tyrone told how he was wounded in the Queen's service and rescued by his foster brother, Henry Hovenden – and that 'my brother Dudley Loftus behaved himself very valiantly.'[96] Knowing that personal heroism and English kinship would not be enough to dispel the suspicion of covert treachery, he turned for support to Dudley's father – praising his son's courage. 'After his horse was killed under him with a Scottish arrow, he slew no less than a dozen of the enemies with his own hands; which news I thought good to write to your Lordship for your comfort.' Then came the crucial part of his letter – 'having not many friends that will make true report of me or my services to Her Majesty, and the Lords of Her Privy Council, I shall desire you to do me that favour.' [97] The Chancellor-Archbishop 'found to be true' all that Tyrone had told him, and forwarded his letter to the Queen's most powerful councillor, Lord Burghley, praising the Earl's 'honourable carriage and valour'. [98]

Truth was hard to determine. Maguire was angry at the meddling of English officials in his lordship of Fermanagh – having given 300 cows as a bribe to Lord Deputy Fitzwilliam, on the understanding that he would be left in peace – but the story that he had fallen out with Tyrone is hard to credit. [99] The latter did his best to confirm the rumour – writing with extravagant regrets that 'it was not my hap to have ventured my life upon him, who like a perjured man as he is hath broken his word with me and sought to stain my honour' – but it was widely known that Maguire had recently married one of Tyrone's daughters. [100] Many suspected that he was acting as the Earl's proxy, to test the English response, and that Tyrone marched with Bagenal to hinder the marshal's forces in the guise of an ally.

These ambiguities of allegiance were woven through the fabric of the opposing armies. Tyrone emphasised that Dudley Loftus's horse 'was killed under him with a Scottish arrow' – as if to make clear that the forces of Hugh Maguire were mostly professional soldiers, Scottish bowmen and galloglasses – but Tyrone's 'Irish' troops were also stiffened with Scottish mercenaries and may have been trained by English captains. [101] As for the 'English' army, commanded by Bagenal, it was largely composed of 'meere Irish', of dubious loyalty. And the main protagonists were all related. So what did it mean to be English, or Irish or Scottish? And what did it mean to be 'brothers'?

Dudley Loftus was knighted for his part in the battle of Beleek and continued to fight in the English cause – but without much to show for it, as his father complained in a letter to Sir Robert Cecil, in 1596. 'He has been employed in all the journeys, and has taken as much or more toil and travail as those who have had greater entertainment.' 'Entertainment' meant reward, so when the Chancellor requested a warrant to increase his son's troop of horse from twenty to fifty, the close-fisted Cecil knew that this implied further demands on the English Exchequer, and turned him down. Even the promise that the enlarged company would be 'all English, or Englishmens sons (most fit for this service) as tall men and well furnished as any in Ireland,' was not enough to sway things. Dudley resigned his troop to his youngest brother, Adam, and returned to his castle on the Hook.[102]

I suspect he was glad to be done with the wars, and the endless intrigues of his father, and the loud-mouthed bigotry of the new English settlers. The windy Hook was a good place to escape from all of that. In 1598 he was listed at the head of the 'Principall Gentlemen of the Shire' – 'in co. Wexford, being wasted, Sir T. Colclough, Sir R. Masterson and Sir Dudley Loftus, the only English there inhabiting.'[103] That meant English Protestants, but Dudley's neighbours were the long-established 'Old English' Catholics – Redmond of the Hooke, Laffan of Slade and Lewes of Leweston – so despised by the new settlers. Dudley seemed at home there. He served on various commissions, acquired land and seldom left 'his Manor house of Kilcloghan'.[104]

His brothers of blood and wedlock went on fighting. In the summer of 1597 three of the Loftus siblings – Edward, Thomas and Adam – marched north with Lord Deputy Burgh. Edward sent a letter back to his father, describing fording the Blackwater by night, taking the enemy's fortifications and skirmishing with Tyrone's army for most of the following day. Then they were set to work, constructing a rudimentary fort to guard this strategic river crossing, five miles north-west of Armagh.[105]

By the following year this fort was threatened by Irish blockade – so Edward found himself heading north again, to relieve it. His troop was part of a large army, 4,000 strong, but more than a thousand were untrained Irish recruits and they were led by Dudley's ill-fated 'brother', Henry Bagenal – who had insisted on taking command, against the wishes of wiser men. On 14 August 1598 his army was attacked by the combined forces of Tyrone, Maguire and O'Donnell, at the Yellow Ford, in a fight that eerily echoed the battle of Beleek, five years earlier. This time there was no ambiguity about who was friend or foe. Bagenal himself was killed, along with more than 800 of his best troops; 300 of his Irish recruits deserted to Tyrone and less than half the English army made it back to Armagh. It was a huge defeat, from which Edward Loftus was lucky to escape with his life.[106]

Thousands of English settlers from Munster and Connaught fled in terror to the cities, or to England, as their own tenants joined with confederate Irish forces, and Dublin itself seemed under threat. To cap it all, the government of Ireland was now in the hands of two old men with no military credentials, Archbishop Adam Loftus and Sir Robert Gardiner. They panicked and sent an abject letter to Tyrone, referring almost in passing to 'the late accident that happened to part of Her Majesty's forces in Ulster' and begging him to spare his captives, lest he 'incense Her Majesty's indignation'. Since his 'ancient adversary the Marshall' was now dead 'we hope you will cease all further revenge towards the rest.'[107]

Loftus foolishly enclosed a copy of this letter with a long dispatch to 'the Lords of Her Majesty's Privy Council', in which he tried desperately to impress them with the gravity of the crisis – 'We have no means left to help ourselves' – and urged that a new Governor be sent with adequate reinforcements and a competent commander. 'Otherwise we shall not be able to render any other account to Her Highness than that her realm is lost.' Scrawled on the outside of this message, underlined with fierce strokes of the pen, was a repeated instruction to the courier, 'Haste, Haste, Haste, Haste, Haste.'[108]

Almost immediately the old Archbishop realised his mistake. He wrote again to the Privy Council, claiming that his letter to Tyrone had been a pretext to allow its bearer to assess the strength of the rebel army, and that he had in any case countermanded the order for its dispatch – but the Queen was furious. 'We may not pass over this foul error to our dishonour, when you of our Council framed such a letter to the traitor after your defeat, as never was read the like either in form or substance for baseness! Being such as we persuade ourselves, if you peruse it again when you are yourselves, that you will be ashamed of your absurdities.'[109] Nor did the Queen spare her criticisms of what she saw as military incompetence. 'Though the Universality of the rebellion may be used as a reason, yet it is almost a miracle that with an army of 8 or 9 thousand men the provincial rebels of Leinster & Wexford should not be mastered.'

So the Queen's much-indulged favourite, the Earl of Essex, was dispatched to sort things out, with the largest English army ever sent to Ireland. But Essex wasted his resources in a meandering progress around the south and west of the country, while the Irish concentrated their attacks on smaller expeditionary forces, with devastating results.

In May 1599, at a stream in Wicklow not far south of Rathfarnham, a contingent of 600 men led by Sir Henry Harrington was routed by the O'Byrnes – and Adam Loftus (namesake son of the Archbishop) was mortally wounded. The key to this disaster, as so often, was the habit of stuffing the ranks of an occupying army with recruits from the same 'septs' as those they were fighting, a point repeatedly made by commentators like Moryson and Spenser, and repeatedly ignored.[110] Adam Loftus's 'company of foote', supposedly the rearguard, 'were all Irishe, and most of them lately come from the Rebells' – and it was known even before the battle that they could not be relied on. One of Adam's fellow officers complained bitterly of their indiscipline: 'Captain Loftus his answere was, that he could not mend yt, for yf he should find faulte they would run all to the rebels with his armes, and therefore prayed me to rest contented.'[111]

Harrington's report to the Archbishop was that of a man thunderstruck by catastrophe: 'I cannot but with greef write unto your Lordship of this unfortunate day.' He tried to soften the news that the old man's son was wounded, by emphasising his bravery. 'Capten Loftus [was] hurte in the legg, but I hope without daunger; noe men could serve better then his, whilest one man was able to stand; he lies in the castell of Wyckloe, wanting a good surgion, of which I wish your Lordship to have care.'[112] The surgeon failed to arrive before Adam Loftus died of his wounds, and then a very different truth emerged, of cowardice and incompetence. His troops had become separated from the main force because Loftus had allowed his lieutenant, an Irishman named Piers Walsh, to lead them astray, and when Harrington decided to return to Wicklow, 'beaten back with the bitterness of the weather', Loftus's men once again took a different way, and some of them deserted to the enemy. All day long, in the cold and rain, the O'Byrnes had stung Harrington's column with musket shot and arrows, while flitting through the woods or skipping over bogs where their foes dare not follow them, and now they attacked in force, as the English forded a stream.[113] As if at a prearranged signal, Lieutenant Walsh seized his captain's colours and fled towards Wicklow – causing panic among those who remained. Some of the pikemen fled with him, others flung down their weapons, stripped off their clothes and ran, as a desperate shout went up, 'Turn, Turn for the honour of God.' That frantic voice may have been Adam Loftus – a last despairing cry, knowing that he had failed and hoping, at the end, to rally his men. But it was all too late, and what others remembered was his weakness: 'Captin Loftus all that daye never lighted of his horse, nor never drew sword, but his poynarde.'[114]

The following day his body was carried to Dublin, to be buried by his father in the Loftus vault in St Patrick's Cathedral. And then, as he pondered this disaster, and the bitterness of his son's death at the hands of his old adversary and neighbour, O'Byrne, the Chancellor-Archbishop was confronted by the immediacy of danger, even in his own household. On 30 June he woke to the news that eight of his servants had slipped out of the house during the night, to join the enemy.[115]

When the Earl of Essex returned from his progress, with 'his men wearied out, distressed, and their companies incredibly wasted,' he lashed out at the failures of others, ordering savage reprisals for the Wicklow disaster – but the disaster was repeated in August, when a small company of Irish, led by O'Rourke, ambushed a vastly larger force of under Sir Connyers Clifford and killed a third of them.[116] Having achieved nothing, Essex negotiated a truce with Tyrone that left the Irish in control of all their recent conquests and the Queen almost speechless with fury. And then he embarked to England, against her express orders – on a journey that finally led to his arrest, imprisonment and execution. 'At My Lord's parting' on 24 September 1599, five new knights were added to the profligate list of eighty-one created during his brief stay in Ireland, including Edward Loftus and his brother Thomas.[117]

Sir Thomas served under the newly appointed Deputy, Lord Mountjoy, criss-crossing Leix, Munster and Monaghan in pursuit of an elusive enemy, but Sir Edward was suddenly discharged, to his father's 'discomfort and great disgrace, after he had been at great and extraordinary charges to furnish his company.'[118] Just over a year later, in May 1601, he died at Kinsale, followed soon after by his wife – giving birth to a daughter who lived for only a fortnight.[119]

This cluster of small mysteries (why was he discharged from the army, what was he doing at Kinsale, was his death violent or natural?) can be added to a meagre bundle of tantalising facts about this most elusive of the brothers. I know that Edward studied at Jesus College Cambridge, was trained as a lawyer and was appointed the Queen's Prime Serjeant-at-law in Ireland, in 1597 – shortly before marching to war. I know that he married an heiress and that he spoke French – a French law dictionary, inscribed with his signature, survives in Marsh's Library in Dublin. And I know that he was a friend of John Donne, for whom he stood surety on his admission to Lincoln's Inn, in May 1592, when the poet was still a Catholic and had struggled to gain admittance to the Inns of Court on account of his religion.[120] But that, frustratingly, is all – enough to intrigue, too little to satisfy.

Five months after Edward Loftus's death at Kinsale, a Spanish invasion force seized the town, in the classic attack from the rear that the English had always feared. Mountjoy hastily scratched together an army – including Sir Thomas Loftus and his company of foot – and marched south. The Spanish within Kinsale had some protection from the Irish winter but the English were camped outside the walls at the worst time of year – so poorly clothed that they 'dyed for colde in great numbers, to the greife of all beholders'.[121] Counting on this fearsome attrition, the Spanish were determined to prolong the siege as long as they could, while awaiting the arrival of Tyrone, and were adept at deception. On 9 Nov 1601, Sir Geoffrey Fenton wrote to Cecil from Dublin, announcing that 'Sir Thomas Loftus arrived here today from camp and brought news of messages passing between our troops and the enemy. You may think that when parley is offered the place will not long hold out.'[122] In fact it was another two months before Mountjoy won a surprising victory over the combined forces of Tyrone and O'Donnel, who had finally arrived to support the Spanish. It was this decisive battle, on Christmas Eve 1601, that tipped the balance of the war and eventually led to the submission of Tyrone, six days after the death of Queen Elizabeth.

*

'Pacata Hibernia.' Those comforting words form the title of the best contemporary account of these terrible wars, but it was desolation, not peace, that ended the fighting.[123] For a sense of the real horror you must turn to Spenser, whose description of Munster, in the aftermath of 'these late warres', is a vision of hell.

> Out of every corner of the woods and glynnes they came creeping forth upon their hands, for their legges could not beare them, they looked like anatomies of death, they spake like Ghosts crying out of their graves, they did eat the dead Carrions, happy were they could finde them, yea, and one another soone after, insomuch as the very carcasses they spared not to scrape out of their graves, and if they found a plot of water-cresses or Shamrocks; there they flocked as to a feast.[124]

That haunting, hallucinatory prose has led some to think it a fiction – a nightmare of dreadful rumours – but the truth that Spenser depicts is echoed by other, sober witnesses. It seemed to many a barren victory – destroying the land in order to conquer it, at huge cost in men, money and hope. More than two million pounds was expended; thousands of English soldiers died from cold, disease and hunger (far more than were killed by the Irish); none of the great families escaped unscathed; and the bitterness that divided the English from the Irish was sharper than ever, as the deepening rift between Protestant and Catholic became the pretext, more and more often, for the seizure of land. Old arguments about the rights of English lordship, the security of the state from foreign invasion, competing notions of 'civility' and faith were now excuses for a stronger imperative: the greed of speculators.[125]

When the old Archbishop dictated his will only seven of his twenty childen were left alive – two sons and five daughers – and the brothers had quarrelled. Their father's final words were a plea for reconciliation. 'I charge my son Sir Dudley Loftus and his Son and heirs not only to suffer my said son Sir Thomas Loftus quietly to enjoy all the use of the things that I have bequeathed unto him in this my last Will and Testament but also to use him with good respect in all brotherly love and kindness, and this I charge both him and them upon my blessing.'

But Dudley and Thomas went their different ways, and may never have met again.

Dudley died at Kilclogan in May 1616, a few weeks before his 'brother' Tyrone, who perished in exile in Rome. Sir Thomas was the great survivor. He escaped violent death on several occasions to outlive all his siblings and expire at the age of sixty-four, in 1635. It was a year of unusual calm in Ireland, when the only event of note was the passing of an 'Act against Plowing by the Tayle, and pulling the Wooll off living Sheep' – one of the first pieces of legislation against cruelty to animals. Cruelty to humans was another matter. The worst was yet to come.

ACTS OF SETTLEMENT

CHAPTER 9

A Trew Discription

Brave ships of war, sails billowing and pennants fluttering, bob across the placid sea towards a deeply indented coastline, guarded by forts bristling with cannon. A peninsula is dotted with tiny castles and its tip is marked with a beacon tower. Two naked ladies loll amidst the convoluted scrollwork of a cartouche which frames the announcement that this is 'The trew Discription of the Cittie of Waterford & the New Fortification there, Also – the fort of the Rock. The Trew Course of the River. The new worke at the Passage, And of the fortification at Doncannon. Erected in Anno 1591.'

This brightly coloured map is preserved in the formal splendour of the library at Trinity College, Dublin – but has the magic of a make-believe world, of sandcastles on the beach and paper flags and treasure islands and summer smells of the salt sea air. Reality, of course, was more bracing. The map was drawn a few years after the defeat of the Spanish Armada, at the high tide of Elizabethan glory. It was intended to depict the coastal defences of Waterford and the Hook peninsula, as proof to Her Majesty's Council that her realm was properly protected against any renewed invasion. The cartographer, proud of his handiwork, has signed his name with a flourish: ffranciscus Jobsonn descripsit.[126] But there is also a darker side, for the castles which seem to us now like childhood images of adventure and derring-do were originally built by the descendants of earlier invaders, the Normans, as fortresses to subdue a conquered people, the 'native' Irish. By the time of the Armada they had been domesticated as homes for the land-owning Ascendancy – most of whom were of English origin – but they remained well fortified against insurrection.

Kilclogan was granted to Dudley Loftus, eldest son of the Archbishop, in 1590 – a year before this map was drawn. Over the next century his descendants acquired more and more land on the Hook, until they owned the entire peninsula, including all those tiny castles and the great tower on Hook Head, Europe's oldest lighthouse. For three hundred years this was their kingdom.

It is a wild and windswept place, surrounded by sea. Waves pound the carboniferous limestone of this rocky shoreline, rolling fragments of fossil-bearing rock into smooth round pebbles, and grinding them ever finer into gritty black sand. There are small, sheltered coves and a few tiny harbours, where crabs and lobsters are landed on stone quays, built by my ancestors. Most of the trees on the southern end of this promontory were cut down centuries ago, to feed the beacon fire, and those that survive are stunted, leaning sideways in the salt air of the prevailing winds. Huge skies, wonderful sunsets and the cry of gulls; it feels like home.

But the landscape, seemingly so familiar, so invested with family legends, is a palimpsest of history, much of it erased. And I am forced to recognise that memory implies forgetting, for my family seems to have forgotten most of the seventeenth century. Tales of the great Archbishop are still vivid, if sometimes mythical, and remnants of scandalous gossip from the Court of Charles II are sharp as if told yesterday, but there's a long gap in between: silence, possibly shame.

Meditative hours contemplating the physical evidence of portraits and possessions, and trawling through archives of letters, pamphlets, official documents, have left me convinced that the absence of oral anecdotes represents a deliberate turning away from terrible times. It was also, I think, the consequence of confusion, of not being able to make coherent sense of multiple civil wars – so complex and at times so meaningless that the shaping of fact into narrative was beyond the power of all but the most polemical witnesses. The decade of continuous violence between 1640 and 1650 seems to have overwhelmed the memory of the years before and after, until the Act of Settlement imposed an official forgetting, at least for the victors. The victims were left to mourn, without hope of redress.

That sense of confusion, of dislocated episodes, is echoed in the chapters that follow; I cannot smooth into narrative shape the grim realities of those times. Think for a moment of the recent Balkan conflicts, and you will recognise what I mean. So you may prefer to skip, and leap forward to meet one of my great ancestral eccentrics, a man of many tongues, whose power of selective attention allowed him to ignore the rest of the world, whenever it suited him to do so. Then you can return to the Hook, when the sky is clear. But I must brace myself, for the storm.

CHAPTER 10

A Peaceable Kingdom

In 1639 Nicholas Loftus (son of Dudley, grandson of the Chancellor-Archbishop) commissioned his favourite Dublin silversmith, John Thornton, to make a communion cup for his parish church at Templeton, in County Wexford. The following year he had a silver paten made, for the same purpose. These are some of the earliest and loveliest examples of Irish silver to have survived – but they are also remarkable for another reason, since each is engraved with the Loftus crest and coat of arms, on a flamboyant scale. The arms embrace the bowl of the cup, as if claiming ownership of the sacramental wine, and on the paten they spill across the gentle concavity of the dish, where the wafers would have lain. This extraordinary fusion of sacred and profane, religion and property, epitomised the Protestant conquest of Ireland – for the English God was a Lord.[127]

Another version of that conquest, another myth, survived in the libraries of the great Ascendancy houses, the memory of a past that never was.

> Thus was the present Government most sweetly tempered, and carried on with great lenity and moderation; the Lords Justices and Council wholly departing from the rigour of former courses, did gently unbend themselves into a happy and just compliance with the seasonable desires of the people.
>
> Moreover, the Roman Catholicks now privately enjoyed the free exercise of their religion throughout the whole Kingdom, according to the Doctrine of the Church of Rome. And for the ancient animosities and hatred which the Irish had been ever observed to bear unto the English Nation, they seemed now to be quite deposited and buried in a firm conglutination of their affections. The two Nations had now lived together 40 years in peace, with great security and comfort, which had in a manner consolidated them into one body, knit and compacted together with all those bonds and ligatures

of friendship, alliance, and consanguinity as might make up a constant and perpetual Union betwixt them. Their intermarriages were frequent, gossiped, fostering (relations of much dearness among the Irish) together with all others of tenancy, neighbourhood and service interchangeably passed among them. Nay, they had made as it were a kind of mutual transmigration into each others manners, many English being strangely degenerated into Irish affections and customs; and many Irish, especially of the better sort, having taken up the English language, apparel, and decent manner of living in their private houses.[128]

This idyllic picture of an island at peace (as the English 'degenerated' into local habits, while the 'better sort' of natives adopted the 'decent manner of living' of their colonial masters) can be found in the opening pages of one of the most bloodcurdling accounts of the Irish Rebellion ever written – whose author, Sir John Temple, was a prominent member of that 'most sweetly tempered' government. He published his book in 1646, within a few years of the events that he narrates, as an unreliable but influential witness. Temple's version of events – 'Barbarous Cruelties and Bloody Massacres' – is one that his Protestant audience took to heart as a dire warning against native treachery, and his book went through numerous editions, for decades to come. It fuelled the war it describes. [129]

As with most propaganda, truth was mixed with deception. The beginning of the Rebellion was undoubtedly marked by extraordinary savagery, as vast numbers of Protestant settlers were driven from their lands, destitute and half naked, and thousands were killed. Even the dead were not immune from vengeance. 'John McGarret Coghlanes souldiers' dug up the floor of Tessauran church in search of Protestant corpses, and broke open their coffins, 'and among the rest the carkesses of Mr Richard Loftus & his wife which they layd naked upon a hedg where they were left exposed to publique view and to be devowred of doggs, swyne or any thing els that would fasten on them.'[130] But tales of such atrocities grew in the repetition until it seemed that any nightmare might be true, creating myths of sectarian bloodshed that stained the collective memory for centuries to come. And the subsequent civil war provoked multiple betrayals – of friendship, family and honour. It was, and remains, one of the most confused conflicts ever fought within these isles.

Confusion was compounded because Irish Rebellion, Scottish War of the Covenant and English Civil War were inextricably entangled in the War of the Three Kingdoms – and the shifting pattern of alliances made it ever harder to draw a political map. The danger to English settlers from the hordes of Papist Irish was interpreted as a potent warning to all who believed that Charles I was a covert Catholic, in thrall to foreign princes – but what could one make of a 'rebellion' in which Irish 'traitors' proclaimed their loyalty to the Crown and were ruthlessly opposed by the King's bitterest enemies?

A brief encounter, in September 1642, summarises these ambiguities. Lieutenant Edward Loftus (a supporter of Parliament, like most of his family) encountered a Royalist acquaintance, Adam Beaghan, in St Nicholas Street, Dublin. Beaghan denounced the English Parliament as traitors, 'for that the king had called them soe by his proclamation,' which provoked Edward to declare that Beaghan 'would not leave of talkeing untill his short neck were stretched three inches longer.'[131] Loyalty and treachery were no longer the fixed poles of a common political compass – even within the same social circles. The needle had lost its bearings.

In such a murky world, as disparate factions fought for their own advantage, the conflict could often seem like the random encounters of murderous gangs, in thick fog. Occasionally the fog lifted to reveal the corpses of a skirmish, echoes of a battle, or private murder, the settling of scores. Ireland reverted to tribal warfare. But the battles of tribes are always, in a sense, a struggle for power, and power had a simple definition for most of the colonial period – it meant property, ownership of land. The brute force of that imperative, more than any other loyalty, shaped the actions of those who had most to lose, and most to gain, as the Old Irish, Old English, Protestant English settlers and Presbyterian Scots fought for their stake in the ground.

When the King's Deputy, the Earl of Strafford, raised an army in Ireland that he offered to lead against the rebellious Scots, he also raised a bogeyman to frighten the English Parliament. Pym and his friends at Westminster believed, with good reason, that such a force might be used against them by King Charles – so they brought about Strafford's impeachment (in May 1641) and disbanded his unpaid army. But the prospect of disgruntled troops roaming throughout the land was so frightening to both King and Parliament that several of the Anglo-Irish grandees were reluctantly persuaded to settle their overdue wages. Adam Loftus, Vice Treasurer of Ireland, contributed to a large 'loan' which a furious King Charles demanded from the Irish Privy Council (and had to stand surety for others to a total of £4,000) because 'the moneys in the Irish Treasury fell short to pay off their arrears' – while his brother Nicholas and other members of the family 'took up great sums of Monies upon their credits, to help them disband with quietnesse: which great sums His Majesty is to make satisfaction for hereafter.'[132] It was all in vain; for huge numbers of unemployed soldiers, most of them Catholic, promptly joined the rebel cause.

This was the moment of government weakness for which the insurgents were waiting, enabling them to strike. With numbing suddenness they did so, on 23 October 1641, seizing Charlemont, Dungannon, Mountjoy and Newry on the first day of the rising. They seemed poised to attack Lisburn and their fires were visible from the walls of Belfast. It was the most dangerous threat to English rule for more than a hundred years.

Fear bred panic and fury. The Privy Council in Dublin ordered the Earl of Ormond 'to stay and destroy all the Rebels & their adherents and relatives by all ways and means he can; and burn and destroy and waste and consume and demolish all the places towns and houses where the Rebels are, or have been and all the hay & corn there, and kill and destroy all men capable of bearing arms. No quarter to be given to any Irishman, or to any Papist born in Ireland.' Among the signatories to that order were Sir John Temple, author of the myth of 'sweetly tempered' government, and his friend Sir Adam Loftus (grandson of the Archbishop) – the vice treasurer of a bankrupt realm.

A short time earlier Sir Adam's brother Nicholas had moved house, from his cramped tower at Kilclogan to a larger castle at Fethard – on the opposite side of the Hook – which he had acquired together with 600 acres of land in a complicated swap with the Bishop of Ferns.[134] He took with him the communion cup and paten that he had commisioned a few years earlier and placed them in the church at Fethard, where they survived, miraculously, through all the troubles to come – but he himself was barely settled in his new home before the Rising that began in Ulster spread to the rest of the country and forced him to flee the Hook, together with the rest of his family. He escaped just in time, for 'on or about 1 December 1641' – the day that his wife Margaret gave birth to the twelfth of their 'dear children' – Fethard was attacked by 'Dermott McDooley Cavanagh, the head of the Rebells there.'[135]

The castle was garrisoned by a small band of English servants, commanded by Loftus's son-in-law, Nicholas Devereux, whose wife Jane had left with her father for Dublin. Though nominally a Protestant, Devereux came from a long-established Old English family and his sympathies were divided. The day before the attack he 'made some termes with the Irish partie' and returned to his home at Ballymagir, in the salt marshes of southern Wexford. Devereux threw in his lot with the rebels, fortified his house with 'a brestworke, mote & drawe bridge', raised a troop of horse and never saw his wife again.[136]

The English servants left in charge at Fethard were forced to surrender the castle. Henry Palmer, a bricklayer, later described what happened. He remembered the Irish leader's warning – 'begon you English doggs, for wee doe only take your goods now, but worse shall follow' – and told how the rebels 'went into the Church and cutt the pulpit Cloth & the Ministers books in peeces, & strewed them about the Church yard, and caused the Piper to play whilst they daunced & trampled them under their feete, and called the minister a dogg, and stript him of his cloths.' Palmer himself was 'robbed and stripped' but seems to have struck up some sort of camaraderie with his assailants, one of whom confided this fantastic rumour, to justify their rebellion. 'Welsh of Killculen bridg in the County of Kildare, Inkeeper, tould this Deponent that he, the said Welsh, knew that the King was in the north of Ireland & ridd disguised and hadd glassen Eyes [spectacles] becaus he wold not be knowne and that the King was as much against the protestants as he himself.'[137]

The minister and the makeshift garrison of Fethard escaped lightly compared to many northern Protestants, who died in the first furious eruption of the rebellion in Ulster – where tribal antipathy, religious hatred and the lure of plunder made for fearsome retribution. In the softer south, plunder alone was often sufficient to sate the appetite for revenge. James Sutton, one of the rebels who had joined in the attack on Fethard, took advantage of the general mayhem to become 'a pyrate, and went to Sea to Robb and spoyle the English.' Another rebel, Peter Esmond, was sent to attack Duncannon, 'the day before Christmas eve 1641.' He left the garrison unharmed but 'with others brought from the said Forte a prey of cowes and sheepe, which sheepe belonged to Sir Arthur Loftus because they were marked with A:L.'[139]

Arthur was away in the army, serving as Lieutenant Colonel in Sir Charles Coote's Regiment, while his brother Dudley kept lonely guard at the family fortress of Rathfarnham, encircled by rebel bands. Their father Sir Adam was in Dublin – a city cut off from the few remaining outposts of English rule, with its defences constantly tested by the rebel armies.

Many die, and great numbers fall sick, by the hard duties they are forced to take, and the often sallies we make to beat off the enemy. On Saturday last we received intelligence that Sir Morgan Cavanagh, with above a thousand men came to Deansgrange, within five miles of this City; we sent out part of our Garrison and put them to flight, and killed above threescore of them.

That which now most afflicts us, is that extream want in Droheda. If God afford us not fair weather, and winde to relieve it by Sea, we must of necessity march to the relief of it by Land, and so put the whole Kingdom to hazard; but God I hope who hath been miraculously with us, will not now fail us in this great exigent.[140]

Sir Adam's language was typical of the times, for it seemed to the Protestants in Ireland that a threatened tribe was fighting for its survival, engaged in a holy war, but his letter to Sir Robert King in London was also calculated for maximum political effect. For some time past the Justices and Council in Dublin had been conspiring with the English Parliamentarians to devise a new and ruthless policy for Ireland's settlement, treating war as an investment – and Sir Adam knew that the vital prospectus, an Act for Adventurers, was about to be debated by the Commons. He and his friends on the Council were determined to influence that debate by emotive tales of danger, while also endeavouring to reassure potential investors that their dividends would be paid, in confiscated land. So Adam enclosed with his letter a proclamation that had been issued in Dublin a few days earlier, naming a long list of Irish rebels whose estates were declared forfeit to the Crown and placing a price on the head of each of 'the said Traitors' – ranging from £1,000 for 'Sir Phelim O Neal' to £300 for the lesser notables. 'We have indited of Treason all the [Catholic] Noblemen, Gentlemen and Freeholders in the Counties of Dublin, Meath, Kildare and Wickloe; which I hope will be of a great advantage to the Crown, and good to this poor Kingdom, when these Rascals shall be confounded, and honest Protestants planted in their places.'[141]

An Act for Adventurers was passed in London the day after that letter was written, as one of the last pieces of legislation to be enacted by the joint authority of a reluctant King and his upstart Commons. It went even further than Sir Adam had imagined. Ten million acres were to be confiscated from the Irish rebels, of which a quarter – all profitable land – was to be granted to those Adventurers, or 'undertakers', who advanced money towards the £1m which was deemed necessary to crush the rebellion.

The reality of this bargain was summarised by a Royalist pamphleteer.

An inhumane designe to eradicate and extinguish a whole Nation to make booty of their lands, (which hopes the London Adventurers did hugge, and began to divide the Bears skin before he was taken, as His Majesty told them) an attempt the Spaniard, nor any other Christian State ever intended against the worst of Savage. The conceit whereof infused such a desperate courage, eagernesse and valour into the Irish, that it made them turn necessity into a kind of vertue.[142]

Much of the money raised from those Adventurers was spent on financing the Parliamentary armies in the English Civil War, but the investors eventually demanded their collateral, which Cromwell ruthlessly delivered.[143]

CHAPTER 11

Joyful News from Ireland

On a sleepy afternoon at the London Library I was consulting various obscure seventeenth-century pamphlets, as a gentle susurration of snores rose from the leather armchairs at the far end of the Reading Room. The archaic language and complex phrases of what I was studying had a similarly somnolent effect. Even when I turned to *Joyfull Newes from Ireland* (written by my forebear Edward Loftus) my eyelids continued to droop. Then I noticed that a brief and urgent note had been scrawled on the final page: 'Sr. Tho Bedingfield ye Reccorder of London committed to ye Tower, for refusing to Pleade for Mr Attorny gnrall. This news comitted by ye Lord[s].' Suddenly I was wide awake, because I knew that this particular copy had originally belonged to James Stuart, Duke of Richmond – a cousin of Charles I. This was his writing, scribbled in haste, on the first piece of paper that came to hand.[144]

Six months earlier this rich young Scotsman had loaned the enormous sum of £30,000 to his perennially indebted monarch, been rewarded with a dukedom and posed for his portrait – face like a whippet, sitting at his ease in a billowing white shirt, his hand on the neck of a favourite hound. It was one of those extraordinary images of a doomed generation of young cavaliers, immortalised by Anthony Van Dyck. Glamorous, haunting, superfluous, they strutted like fashion models in silk and ribbons and lace that would soon be torn, dragged in the mud, and stained with blood. Richmond himself survived the Civil War, but his younger brothers were less fortunate. George died at the battle of Edgehill, John expired from wounds received at the battle of Cheriton, and Bernard was killed at Rowton Heath – all extinguished before the age of twenty-five.

Death was foreshadowed when the Duke received a crucial message from the House of Lords, on 9 March 1642, and jotted a note on my ancestor's pamphlet. The news was bad, for the political skirmishing between King and Commons had at last found its focus with an extraordinary tactical blunder by King Charles – the affair of the 'Five Members'. England was on the brink of civil war.

Stubborn conceit was at the heart of things, because the Stuarts as a family almost completely lacked that essential attribute for royal survival, a true instinct for politics – and it was Charles I's misfortune that he was opposed by one of the most brilliant political opportunists in English history, John Pym. The short, plump Member for Calne was a prosperous Puritan who hated Spain, feared Papism, was trained as a lawyer and needed little sleep.

Eventually Charles was so goaded by Pym's cleverness that he tried to arrest him, together with four of his closest allies, within the supposedly privileged walls of the House of Commons. On 4 January 1642 he marched to the Commons with his guards, only to find that 'the birds had flown', warned by their friends at Court. Parliament and the City combined in demonstrations of outrage. Within a week the King had fled London and Pym was carried in triumph back to Westminster, in a procession of barges along the Thames.

George Digby, a close ally of the King, was impeached by Parliament for his part in this affair and so too was the Attorney General, Sir Edward Herbert. Digby fled to Holland but Herbert was committed for trial and the House of Lords appointed Sir Thomas Bedingfield as counsel for his defence. The Commons saw no place for legal representation in a case of privilege and Bedingfield himself was reluctant to act. The Lords sent him to the Tower, to reflect on the realities of politics, and someone rushed to the Duke of Richmond to tell him what had happened. The urgency with which he scribbled this news, as soon as he learnt it, underlines its significance. This was an omen of all the disasters to come.

As I contemplate the Duke's note on the back of my forebear's pamphlet it occurs to me that *Joyfull Newes from Ireland* was itself hot off the press, having been published by order of the Commons a day or two earlier. Richmond may not even have had time to read it before using it as a memo pad, for yesterday's news was already stale – a few flimsy pages that had been urgent, for a moment.

This churning onrush of news and argument found vivid expression in the astonishing blizzard of paper that poured from the presses during the 1640s and '50s. Five, ten, even twenty crudely printed pamphlets appeared every day – more than 22,000 of these Civil War tracts were collected by Milton's friend, the bookseller George Thomason, and even his vast accumulation was not exhaustive.[145] This was the invention of propaganda as a sustained instrument of revolution, startling in its suddenness and scale, but conflict also made for chaos and there was little effective censorship once the taste for pamphleteering took hold. Radical arguments for 'root and branch' reform could be found on the booksellers' racks alongside skilfully slanted news, written for emotive effect, and wild propaganda, conjuring ogres.

This pamphlet warfare, in all its confusion, reflected a wider reality – that the two sides in the Civil War were fluctuating, amorphous alliances, combining a mass of prejudices and opinions under the banners of King or Parliament. Differing views about power, privilege, religion, nationalism, individual liberty, and even (to a strange and largely unexplored extent) about male fashion – flamboyance or sobriety, long hair or short – inspired the pamphleteers. More arcane still was the war of the astrologers, in which the Royalist Wharton battled it out with his Parliamentarian rivals, Booker and Lilly, hurling obscure prophecies and vicious insults through the medium of the printed page.[146]

Among the pamphlets printed on a single day in March 1642 were *Grand Plutoes Remonstrance* – a crazy, satyrical squib with a crowned and priapic devil leering from the woodcut on its cover – and *Two Letters of Note*, incorporating a reprint of *Joyfull Newes from Ireland*.[147] The latter demonstrates the astonishing speed with which these leaflets were produced. The original dispatch from Edward Loftus (son of Sir Dudley, grandson of the Archbishop) was dated from Dublin 27 February. Even allowing for favourable winds and fast messengers his letter must have taken several days to reach London, but it was ordered to be published by Henry Elsing, Clerk of the House of Commons, on 7 March.

The 'joyful news' was certainly dramatic. Four months earlier, on 4 November 1641, Sir Henry Tichbourne had occupied Drogheda with a force of a thousand men, to hold it for the Crown as the last strong outpost between Dublin and the north. He was almost immediately surrounded by vastly superior numbers of Irish, commanded by Phelim

O'Neill, who stretched a chain across the River Boyne to bar access to the sea. After two months of siege the garrison was 'driven to eat horse-flesh' and surrender seemed inevitable – but at the last minute help arrived. This was the story that Edward Loftus so urgently wanted to tell, and Parliament to publish.

> Noble Sir, In my last to you, I signified the difficulties which were likely to befall us by the releeving of Droheda, but God by his infinite mercy hath freed us (I may say miraculously) from that hazard: for when our men there were driven to that extremitie to eat horse-flesh, Sir Henry Tichbourne sallied out of the Town with only fortie Musketiers, and fortie Horse, and beat off foure hundred of the Enemies, killed above threescore of them, recovered fourscore Cowes and Oxen, and two hundred sheep; burned foure Towns, and brought home two of their Colours;
>
> Besides, I must relate unto you Gods abundant goodnesse unto us, in that the night before the releefe and succours which we sent by Sea from Dublin to them, should have entred into the Harbour of Droheda, (which was strongly fenced over with a Chain and severall boates) there happened a storme which broke their chaines, and gave our men so free a passage, as with little difficultie they came safely to the Town.
>
> Our Soldiers are in great want of money, which causes a generall want of all other necessaries, yet notwithstanding God hath infused such courage into them (for undoubtedly it is his work) that they think there is no danger so great, but they may attempt it.
>
> The enemy though their numbers be verie great, even beyond beleef, yet their hearts begin to faint, and I believe they repent their furious madnesse.[148]

Joyfull Newes from Ireland was an instant bestseller, running through several different editions in the space of a few weeks, as the confrontation between King and Parliament came to a head. 'I must relate unto you Gods abundant goodnesse unto us,' wrote Edward Loftus and his letter defined a genre – a town besieged, relieved by God's providence and men's fortitude – and became a parable and leitmotif of the Protestant / Parliamentarian cause.

For a brief moment, it seemed a beacon of hope.

CHAPTER 12

A Family at War

Sir Arthur Loftus rode out from Dublin on 2 April 1642, with a force of 3,000 men led by the Earl of Ormond and Sir Charles Coote. Eldest son of Sir Adam, son-in-law of the great Earl of Cork, a soldier by training, Protestant by conviction – this was 'a person of very good note', according to his own account of the pacification of the Pale.[149] Sir Arthur told with great satisfaction how they 'banished, hanged and killed all the Irish and Papist in the Town of Naas' and moved '50 families of poor, stript English Protestants' into the Town, 'besides many Tradesmen, all English Protestants'. After a brief battle at Kilcullen, when the Irish fled in confusion, leaving 'Pikes so thick that they covered the ground,' Loftus was appointed Lieutenant Governor of Naas, 'to fit the Garrison; now raising Forts, filling the Towne with Corne and serching in daily preyes of Cattle.' And he drank a great deal of wine, according to the records.[150]

'This is my true relation, for I writ it my Self, and my Self was all the time there.' But Sir Arthur's account made no mention of the bribes that he took from a rebel leader, Morrice Fitzgarret, to leave his stronghold unmolested, nor that his own castle on the River Barrow was attacked by his brothers-in-law, Robert Hartpole and Walter Bagenal. They were chased away by English troops but the sharpness of betrayal must have penetrated even Sir Arthur's ironclad conceit.[151]

There was, nonetheless, a sense of deliverance, of the tide having turned, which continued for a few weeks longer, as Sir Charles Coote led his troops south and won a series of famous victories. Pamphlets poured from the presses to celebrate these exploits, and new heroes were made. One such was Sir Christopher Loftus, 'a noble Gentleman lately come out of the Low-countries, and now Commander of a Regiment of Volunteers,' who captured Waterford by stealth on 15 April while the main body of the rebel garrison was pillaging and burning the neighbouring villages.[152] Hardly pausing to rest, Sir Christopher marched out the following day with 1,500 men and surprised a much larger force of rebels. 'They tooke them to their Heeles, but our Bullets was nimbler than they, and soon ended their Journeys, for of 5,000 Rebels there escaped not above one thousand, as we might guesse by the dead Bodies which they left behind to intombe the ground, which should have beene their graves.'

'To intomb the ground, which should have been their graves' – that line of blank verse, Shakespearian in its cadence, gives me pause. As so often when reading these short pamphlets I am struck by the energy of language, the quickness of successive images, the sudden shift from bombast to pathos. But the words seem too fluent, too poetic, for the merchants of Cork or Dublin who apparently wrote these letters – they suggest a dramatist's hand, a professional propagandist. Did Sir Christopher Loftus exist? I have no idea – but he appears to have sprung from nowhere, before vanishing without trace.

The partisan vigour of such ephemera is an unreliable guide to a much more confused reality. When I read the formal phrases that stifled communication between the King and his Irish Privy Council or consider the conflict of loyalties within my own family, clarity is lost behind a cloud of ambiguities.[153] Consider, for example, the six sons of Sir Dudley Loftus.

The eldest, Sir Adam, lived in splendour at Rathfarnham Castle, close to Dublin, and was adept in the treacheries of power. He owed his lucrative offices at the Irish Treasury to the King's Deputy, Thomas Wentworth, Earl of Strafford, but turned against the King when Strafford was dead. As one of a small circle of Protestant grandees – related by blood, marriage and property – who dominated the Irish Council, he plotted with Parliament to transform Ireland into a network of Protestant estates, for the benefit of himself and his friends.

Adam was yoked in office with his brother Nicholas, the Deputy Treasurer-at-Wars, whose loyalties were to his neighbours on the Hook – mostly 'Old English' or Irish Catholic – and to the distant but somehow sacred King. When the troubles began, Nicholas worked tirelessly for the survival of an Irish government that was dominated by the King's enemies but he himself was 'zealously attached to the Royal Cause', and 'sent £800 to King Charles I to Oxford, as a Help against the Parliament.'[154] He faced intense family pressure to abandon his allegiance to the Crown, 'which promised no other recompense than

Ruin to himself and Family, whereas by the other side he was sure to be a gainer.' Nicholas replied to their pleas with admirable simplicity: 'No I will never lift my hand against the Lord's anointed, nor shall I ever to the reproach of myself or my dear Children do Unjust Actions to Increase my Property by wrong or robbery.'[155] After the King was dead he joined the winning side, but by then he had lost almost everything – his lands, his goods, his friends, his sovereign and his certainties.

Brother William was a Catholic but the record is tantalisingly brief, that he 'died a religious in Spain' – mighty strange fate for the progeny of the Protestant Ascendancy. His closest sibling, the equally elusive Dudley, had chosen the opposite side in these wasted wars of religion. He was killed on the Isle de Ré, in a futile attempt to relieve the French Huguenots, besieged in La Rochelle.[156]

Edward the lawyer lived for eighty-seven years with the certainty that God was a Protestant, whose triumphs he hymned in 'Joyfull Newes from Ireland'.[157] He married a neighbour, Anne Hartpole, whose family stronghold on the River Barrow lay a few miles upstream from the Loftus castle of Cloghgrenon, on the frontier of the Pale, and together they had nine children. But most of Anne's family were Catholic and her brother Robert sided with the rebels, for complex reasons of affection and honour – as did Edward's cousin (another Edward Loftus, whose mother was a Hartpole) who 'employes his stock and mony in buying and provideing munition & other requisites to further this rebellion.'[158]

Finally there was Samuel, the youngest boy, who married his doubly connected cousin Mary Bagenal, one of a family of Protestant settlers with whom the Loftuses had been entwined for generations – but Walter Bagenal, Governor of Carlow, was related to the Catholic Butlers and he, too, took their cause.[159]

Nothing, it seems, was predictable.

Three weeks after the cocksure Sir Arthur rode out from Dublin, in April 1642, the Council wrote an urgent message to his uncle, 'our very Loving Friend Nicholas Loftus Esq at Mr Perkins house att the signe of the shipp in fleete streete.' No words were wasted on flowery greetings, for sick and wounded soldiers were dying for lack of treatment. The Council sent a shopping list of what was needed and asked Nicholas 'to move to ye Parliament most Earnestly' to pay the relevant suppliers – £120 to 'Francis Clay Druggist & Merchant at ye signe of the Beare & Mortar in Lombard Streete', for surgical supplies, and £250 to 'Anthony Tysher Druggist at ye lower end of Cheapside', for medecines 'for ye Apothecaries.'[160]

Large grants of funds were voted by Parliament in the spring and summer of 1642 but despite the flow of money the government's increasingly successful efforts against the Irish rebels almost ground to a halt by the end of May, when the Catholic Confederacy was formed to bring together the native Irish and 'Old English' in 'loyal opposition' to the government in Dublin. The Council responded by revoking all previous guarantees of safety for those who brought goods to market, as seeming to offer protection to covert rebels – 'the very Plowmen and those that keep Cattle, having continually Arms lying by them in the Fields, to murther those his Majesties good Subjects when they find them weakly guarded; and on the other side when they find them strongly guarded, they seem to go on in their Plowing and Husbandry, shewing those Warrants for their safety, and seeming to be poor, innocent, and harmless Labourers.'[161] That image of a treacherous world could be transposed to any colonial war, in any age.

The first shock of the rising decayed into a long war of attrition. Famine and disease killed far more than died in battle, and each side wasted the land to deny the other sustenance – burning crops, slaughtering cattle, destroying houses. For Nicholas Loftus this meant an endless, frustrating struggle to secure supplies – nothing glorious, little reward. The English Parliament was reluctant to vote for further substantial aid, fearing that an Irish army could be used against it by the King, and its attention was fully absorbed by its own skirmishing for power, while the Justices and Council in Dublin expressed increasing desperation.

In August 1642 they wrote to Loftus in Chester, complaining that the latest shipment of 'treasure' was inadequate for the needs of the troops, and urging him to make arrangements to ship the balance as soon as possible.[162] They were concerned to get their hands on it before events overtook them but already it was too late. A few days after that letter was sent King Charles raised his standard at Nottingham – marking the formal beginning of the English Civil War and the end of hope for English intervention in Ireland. Nicholas managed to escape from Chester with two well-armed pinnaces of the latest design, just in time to prevent their brass ordnance being seized for 'the malignant party', but came away without any of the promised treasure.[163] When he wrote from Dublin on 21 September to his friend Mr Allen in Fleet Street – 'at the signe of the 3 ttuns right againste Dunstan's Church' – his news was bad. 'Our men lessened by sickness and death, our stores of powder, match, ammunition and all sortes of armes soe far wasted and spent as if the Enemy com to Dublin and give us a hard siege we shall hardly be able to hold out in our defence above xiiii days.'[164] And thus it continued, as the Irish Council sought help wherever it might be found, from men whose only shared allegiance was the preservation of English rule in Ireland.[165]

That confusion of loyalties was mirrored by their opponents. The 'Confederate Catholics of Ireland' swore an oath, *Pro Deo, Rege et Patria Hibernia Unanimis*, proclaiming their allegiance to the King while disowning his Protestant government. It was a convenient distinction but had fatal results, for both sides hesitated, uncertain of their allies in the fast-evolving wars. Such conflicted loyalties could divide even the closest families, as Nicholas Loftus discovered when his daughter Jane fled to live with him in Dublin. Her husband, Nicholas Devereux, had renounced his Protestant faith, taken the Oath of Association, fortified their home in County Wexford and sided with the insurgents.[166] And the political compass was set spinning without direction when Lord Deputy Ormond sent Protestant troops to Wales, to fight for the King, while the Confederacy sent Catholic troops to Scotland, for the same purpose.

As far as the Irish Protestants were concerned, hesitancy ended with 'The Cessation' of September 1643, when Ormond concluded a cease-fire with the Confederation, on behalf of the Crown. The King's decision to negotiate with the Irish Catholics – in return for their support against his enemies in England – provoked a furious Protestant backlash, which extended beyond the conflict in Ireland. Scottish Presbyterians raised an army to fight against King Charles, in support of their cousins in Ulster, and most Irish Protestants promptly declared for Parliament but now found themselves excluded from the Irish government. Sir Adam Loftus was expelled from the Privy Council and subsequently imprisoned, being held captive until September 1645 when he and some others were exchanged for three Anglo-Irish Royalists, 'now prisoners in the Tower'.[167] Two of his sons shared their father's allegiance – Sir Arthur was accused of treachery for siding with Parliament, while the scholarly Dr Dudley wrote a pamphlet denouncing any compromise with 'the rebels then in arms' which he signed, defiantly, '*Philo Britannicus*'. But their younger sibling Walter Loftus was a confirmed Royalist who met his death at Youghal, struck by a cannonball as he patrolled the ramparts.

This was the loneliest time. With those around him intent on their own advantage and most of his family committed to Parliament, against the King, Nicholas Loftus continued in office, scratching around for money and supplies to keep the 'rebels' at bay. Parliament ignored his pleas and the Royalists were facing defeat. By the beginning of 1646 things were so bad that Nicholas was struggling to find a few hundred pounds to pay a firm of London apothecaries, for drugs supplied three years previously.[168] It was, in any case, almost impossible to get supplies shipped to Ireland because the port of Chester was under repeated Parliamentary assault and the seas were swarming with Irish privateers, hunting in packs to attack English ships. But in February 1646 Chester surrendered, after a fifteen-month siege, and Parliament was soon victorious on all fronts, except Ireland. King Charles was captured by the Scots Covenanters in May and Oxford fell in June, thus effectively concluding the last Royalist resistance in England.

Secure in its victory, Parliament turned its attention to Ireland. £10,000 was paid to Nicholas Loftus, Deputy Treasurer-at-Wars, as the first of several large instalments, accompanying equally substantial supplies of arms.[169] This sudden profligacy was accompanied by a maddening obsession with detail. In July 1647 the Parliamentary Committee at Derby House briskly agreed the allocation of a further £40,000 (many millions in modern money) to prosecute the Irish war, but added the rider that a small part of this sum was to be 'reserved for purchases and dispatch of knapsacks. These are necessary, as the means for carrying victuals are defective.' A few days later the Committee ordered that £10,000 was to be sent to Dublin, 'except £150 for providing knapsacks,' and shortly afterwards issued a warrant 'to Mr Loftus to pay £150 to Mr Dobbins, to pay for and transport 2,550 knapsacks to Dublin.'[170] Nothing much has changed in the way that committees work.

Equally typical was Parliament's sluggishness in paying its dues, which frequently meant that its own most loyal supporters risked imprisonment for debt. When the Scots agreed to exchange their captive King for £400,000 army back pay, they had so little trust in English promises that the negotiations required a brief exchange of hostages, including Sir Edward Loftus, son of the late Lord Chancellor of Ireland.[171] A few months later Dr Dudley Loftus and Col Bailey petitioned the House of Commons for payment of £1,000, long overdue, which they had guaranteed to Capt. Plunkett for supplies to the troops in Ireland – 'If the money be not paid, Plunkett must arrest them.'[172] In January of the following year (1648) Sir Arthur Loftus wrote urgently to the Speaker of the Commons, from 'Westminster in ye Market Place,' having been arrested for debts incurred on Parliament's behalf. 'Sir, since yesterday in the afternoon I have been under restraint.'[173] It was not until July that the Parliamentary Committee finally appointed a subcommittee, 'to treat with the creditors of Sir Arthur Loftus.'[174] Arthur's father, Sir Adam, was also imprisoned, 'for great debts in the King's Bench in England' – but in his case there was good reason to suspect corruption.

By the spring of 1647, with all hope for the Royalist cause apparently at an end, Ormond prepared to surrender Dublin to Parliament. Determined to secure safe passage abroad for himself and thousands of Irish troops, he sent Dudley Loftus to London to negotiate terms on his behalf, with the Parliamentary Committee at Derby House. The learned Doctor was a surprising intermediary – eccentric, unreliable and a vehement propagandist for Parliament – but seems to have been friends with Ormond, and his family had political and social connections with leading men in the new English government. The negotiations went slowly and Ormond began to suspect that Loftus was dragging his heels, but the latter wrote from his lodgings in St Martin's Lane on 12 May to explain that all decisions were being delayed because of disputes between the army and Parliament and emphasised that he was building a strong coalition of allies, 'those whoe will befriende you.' His father Sir Adam Loftus – reconfirmed in his old position on the Irish Privy Council – had also arrived in town, and 'hath since his comeing to

London engaged severall men of greate power to give their assent' to
Ormond's plan.[175] Eventually, despite the delays, the plan was approved
and Ormond sailed for France – but it was a decision he came to regret,
as the war in Ireland was renewed with increased ferocity, and his allies
urged him to return.

> Sir William Parsons hathe by late letter advised the governor to the
> burninge of corne, and to put man, woman and childe to the sworde,
> and Sir Adam Loftus hathe written in the same straine. They both
> live in a fat contrie, and are out of the danger of gunshott [Parsons
> and Loftus were in London]. I woulde they were put in the front of
> the battle to act what they write. The greatest cowardes are observed
> to be the most merciless men.[176]

After escaping from his captors, in November 1647, the King negotiated
a secret treaty with the Scots, promising support for Prebyterianism if
they agreed to invade England. It was the reckless reverse of his former
plan, to bring an Irish army to fight against Parliament, in return for
Catholic toleration – but the Scottish invasion provoked a renewal of the
English Civil War, which encouraged the Irish Catholics in their long
resistance. Parliament immediately issued an ordinance to raise a further
£50,000 from the Adventurers, 'on the credit of rebels' houses in Ireland',
but both sides were desperate for the cash.[177] By the following spring Sir
Adam was being urged to make haste to get the latest instalment (£5,000,
then lying at Bristol) loaded onto any of Parliament's ships, because the
port itself was in danger of Royalist attack. 'If this money should miscarry
it would be a great blow to the affairs of Ireland.'[178]

The Royalist revival in England was short-lived, ending with
Cromwell's decisive victory over the Scots at the Battle of Preston,
but the War of the Three Kingdoms continued across the Irish Sea.
Ormond landed at Cork at the end of September 1648 with arms for
5,000 men, paid for by the French, and renewed the King's promise of
Catholic toleration. The Confederation was formally dissolved, as
Catholic Royalists in the south seized the chance of ending a war that
O'Neill was determined to pursue. But the English Parliament was
preparing to put King Charles on trial – his cause was clearly lost.

The trial was brief, the King condemned to death. On a bitterly cold
day at the end of January 1649, a large crowd gathered outside the

Banqueting House in Whitehall. Charles I stepped like a wraith through a first-floor window and uttered a few inaudible words on the scaffold. As the axe fell on the King's neck there was a deep, collective groan. The executioner wore a hood to disguise his identity but it is often said that he was an Irishman.

It was about this time, after seven years of civil war, that Nicholas Loftus and his wife Margaret had their portraits painted. Their sad, exhausted faces gaze out at us as they stand, dressed in black, on either side of a small, linen-covered table. Through an open window I can see lurid storm clouds above a brooding landscape, dotted with fortifications. He clasps a letter addressed to 'Nicholas Loftus Esq, Surveyor of his Majties Court of Wards & Liveries' and she holds a valuable hemispherical watch, with a gold case and domed glass. A diamond-mounted ring hangs at his throat and she wears a rope of pearls, with more pearls braided in her hair and dangling from a pendant of flat-cut diamonds at her breast. But none of these signs of wealth and status have much enduring impact – it is the sadness that lasts, and a sense of foreboding.

For a time, when I first discovered these portraits, grief was all I saw but gradually, as I looked closely, it seemed that a more complex iconography of Royalist mourning was encoded in the painting. Nicholas himself has the unmistakeable nose of a Loftus, but his long hair, moustache and Vandyke beard are worn in the style made fashionable by Charles I. The letter clasped in his hand celebrates his role as Surveyor of a Royal Court whose outmoded functions (administering feudal dues owed to the King, for certain lands and inheritance) had been abolished by a rebellious Parliament in 1646 – rather than his much more important role as Deputy Treasurer-at-Wars. The black clothes and austere glimpses of linen at collar and cuffs (no ruffs, no furbelows), the watch (symbol of time and mortality), the table like an altar (complete with clasp-bound prayer book), the mourning ring that he wears – everything conspires to suggest that this was an elegy for King Charles.

But it was also, in some deeply instinctive way, a statement of endurance.

*

Endurance was tested to its limits by the rapid changes of fortune following the King's execution. In February 1649 Parliament declared the end of monarchy, but when Prince Rupert landed with an army at Kinsale and learnt of the death of his uncle, he immediately proclaimed for Charles II – the King is dead, long live the King. For a few months more, against all expectations, the Royalists were successful in Ireland. By June the Parliamentarians had been driven from every stronghold except Dublin, Drogheda and Derry, and would have been completely overwhelmed if O'Neill had joined the fight, instead of sulking on the sidelines. Drogheda fell in July and Ormond prepared to besiege Dublin by taking the nearby fortress of Rathfarnham, which was held for Parliament by Dudley Loftus.

Three different versions survive as to what happened. Ormond's letter to the exiled Charles II announced that he 'gave command to Sir Thomas Armstrong, with his Regiment and Sir William Vaughan's, to fall upon Sir Adam Lofthouse his house at Rathfarnham, which in 24 hours surrendered, with much treasure in it. All that were in it made prisoners; and though 500 soldiers had entered the castle before any officer of note, yet not one creature was killed.' Parliament's version (published in a contemporary pamphlet) tells of a fierce attack, with numerous casualties, until Lord Inchiquene's men got close to the castle walls and found a way into the yard 'through which the brooke ran'.

> So those within were forced to fly into the Towers, to treat for quarter, which was granted them upon Treaty. Dr Loftus and his brother, and all that were there then taken prisoners, and there were only 50 Armes and some small proportion of powder and bullet, which the enemy took. But the house is one of the most stateliest in all Ireland, some 2 miles from Dublin, in which was some hundred pounds worth of goods which the enemy took.

Dudley's own account, that he was 'basely betrayed, by some who pretended to take sanctuary with him,' is essentially the same story. But Ormond and the learned Doctor were friends, and I think the latter may have trimmed his sails to the prevailing wind and surrendered without a fight.[179]

Within a week the wind had changed. On 2 August 1649, the Parliamentary commander, Michael Jones, sallied from the city, launched a daring attack on Ormond's army and won a brilliant victory at the battle of Rathmines, two miles north of Rathfarnham. Thanks to this 'astonishing mercy' Cromwell landed unopposed at Dublin, two weeks later, with the seasoned veterans of his New Model Army and a train of heavy artillery.

CHAPTER 13

The Wrath of God

Tis madness to resist or blame
The force of angry heaven's flame.[180]

Andrew Marvell's ecstatic view of Cromwell as the Wrath of God was shared by his hero and that implacable fury – English, Protestant, righteous – still chills the heart, centuries later. The most telling witness for the prosecution, in the case of Cromwell vs. Ireland, is Cromwell himself. On 12 September 1649 (less than a month after his arrival in Dublin) he wrote to Speaker Lenthal at the English House of Commons, with his account of the sack of Drogheda – an atrocity that damns his memory to this day. 'Our men were ordered by me to put them all to the sword. And indeed, being in the heat of the action, I forbade them to spare any that were in arms in the town, and, I think, that night they put to the sword about 2,000 men.'

Most historians now agree that about 3,500 soldiers (and some civilians) were slaughtered at Drogheda by Cromwell's troops, for the loss of 150 men. He himself led the final assault and gave the order to make a bonfire of pews in the Protestant Church of St Peter, beneath the steeple where some of the Royalists had retreated. Cromwell's account is a vision of hell, describing without any hint of pity how those trapped in the tower cried out as the flames reached them, 'God damn me, God confound me, I burn, I burn.' He claimed his victory as 'a righteous judgement of God upon these barbarous wretches [which] will tend to prevent the effusion of blood for the future.'[181]

'And thou profoundest Hell receive thy new possessor.'[182] Blind John Milton is describing Lucifer – with the strange, mesmerised admiration that lends such force to his vision of *Paradise Lost* – but this is Cromwell, Milton's friend, the destroyer.

Terrible force was combined with methodical efficiency. Artillery proved crucial to batter the walls of Royalist cities like Drogheda, but equally important was the fact that Cromwell's troops were paid at least a month's wages in advance and were extraordinarily well supplied – with tons of food and other provisions shipped from England, and a treasury of £100,000. These were radical innovations in a war that had hitherto brought ruin to the most vulnerable – as poorly provisioned troops plundered the land – and Cromwell backed those preparations with effective discipline. Less than a week after his arrival in Dublin he issued a proclamation forbidding all looting and other crimes against 'the country people', and hanged a couple of soldiers who dared to disobey his edict.[183]

Thanks to his supplies, Cromwell was able to keep an army in the field for months on end; and thanks to his discipline he was able to protect the populace from violence. But for those that crossed him, he was ruthless. The sack of Drogheda was a shock of extraordinary force. Even by the standards of the time it was seen as terrible, and it echoed down the centuries with increasing horror in the telling. Cromwell's name, even now, is spat with scorn in Ireland – Crum'ell, the monster.

It is impossible to know when Nicholas Loftus switched sides. It may have been the imprisonment of King Charles that persuaded him the cause was lost, or the King's execution in January 1649 – or perhaps he was simply tired of the endless war and of losing so much, for nothing.[184] The decisive factor, it seems to me, was the sack of Drogheda. Faced by that horror, Nicholas became 'a very active instrument in engaging all the inhabitants of Wexford to be subservient to Cromwell's purposes.'[185]

On 22 September 1649 (a fortnight after Drogheda) he wrote to his 'verie loveing friend Mr. Pierse Laffan' at Slade Castle, having arranged a safe pass for Laffan to join him in 'Parliament's Army' as soon as they arrived in County Wexford. 'I shall be in the Army and will endeavour all that possible I can to preserve the inhabitants of that County from harm.' Loftus assured Laffan that the 'English Souldiers' had been ordered, on pain of death, to harm none except 'those which they find in armes against them, and noe Souldier shall take from any man whatsoever, to the value of a penny'. He concluded with this enigmatic note (to which I shall return) – 'I have put Nicholas Wogan in the passe, bring him with you.'[186]

That letter was probably written from Rathfarnham, where Loftus seems to have joined the Parliamentarian army as Cromwell paused on the road south to hold a council of war – and to install a garrison of English troops to guard this strategic fortress. Then Cromwell was off again and arrived at the walls of Wexford on 2 October. Nine days later – exactly a month after the sack of Drogheda – he stormed Wexford with similar ferocity, while its surrender was being negotiated with the help of Nicholas Loftus. It was a ruthless lesson, and intended as such.

The news spread terror. On 14 October the Royalist governor of Duncannon, Thomas Roche, wrote to Ormond to say that the fort had insufficient men, provisions or ammunition to sustain more than three days against attack; and announced that he was in negotiations with the enemy. 'I received from Mr Nicholas Loftus two several letters whereby he requested a safe conduct of coming hither, to ye end, as he setts fourth, of imparting matters of consequence that might redound to yor Excie's availe. I have this day sent him a safe conduct, and upon his coming will sound out his Intent, or send him to yor Excie, if that be his pleasure.'[187]

This was certainly not to Ormond's pleasing, because the strategic fortress controlled the entrance to the best harbours on the south coast, Waterford and New Ross, and he knew that even when ill supplied it was capable of withstanding a vastly more powerful enemy, for months on end. Unlike Slade and those other enchanting towers on Jobson's map of the Hook – fortified houses in a wild landscape – Duncannon was a gun emplacement, entirely military in nature. It dominated the broad estuary of the River Barrow and was protected on its landward side by poor roads, thick walls and an awkward angle of fire. Cromwell's assaults on Drogheda and Wexford had depended on his ability to bring artillery by sea, until close to the city walls. That advantage was impossible at Duncannon, so he hoped for the time-honoured tactic of treachery, to open the garrison gates.

Treachery was prevented because Ormond acted fast. Two days after receiving Roche's letter he sent money and munitions to Duncannon, together with 120 officers and men of his own Life Guard, to reinforce the garrison – and he appointed Colonel Edward Wogan as the new commander.[188] Wogan arrived on the same day that another of Ormond's correspondents sent him this urgent note: 'Although captaine Edmond Furlonge, who is entrusted to oversee the provision to be made for the fort of Duncannon, be a man for his past cariage unsuspected, yet he is a Creature of the Loftusses; and I should be sorry it should lye in his way to express his gratitude by any practise under the fort of Duncannon in favor of a victorious enemy with whom his patrons do side.'[189] It was a classic denunciation, seething with suspicion, but the man who saved Duncannon was himself a turncoat – 'the renegade Wogan', as Cromwell called him.[190] Wogan had defected from Parliament's forces to fight for the King and knew that surrender, for him, meant almost certain death. His resolve stiffened by that knowledge, he held Duncannon against the might of Cromwell's army until Waterford itself was captured, ten months later.

As I ponder these tangled loyalties, other notions occur to me – that Edward Wogan, the defender of Duncannon, was related to Nicholas Wogan, the friend of Pierse Laffan (both were natives of Kildare) – and that Nicholas Loftus knew this, and hoped to use this knowledge to influence Edward's allegiance. 'I have put Nicholas Wogan in the passe, bring him with you.' Whatever the truth, this was a time of expediency, not honour.

Cromwell's conquest was completed by his son-in-law, Henry Ireton, and peace was enforced by martial law. Nicholas Loftus's nephew, the Orientalist Dr Dudley Loftus, was an instrument of this brutal settlement, as Deputy Judge Advocate of the Province of Leinster – and he recorded the reign of terror, day after day, in the minutes of a court-martial that sat in Dublin (sometimes at the Castle, sometimes at 'Patrick's Church') for more than two years, from February 1651. The very first case gives a flavour of the rest. A woman, Kathleen Farrell, was arrested as a spy at the village of Killincarrick, by soldiers who were posted there to watch the Dublin mountains for signs of rebel attack. Brought before the court, she was summarily condemned and swiftly hanged. It got worse. Dudley Loftus's notes, preserved in Marsh's Library, record this terrifying judgement.

At a Court Martial held 23rd September, 1652, at Dublin Castle, under the presidency of Colonel Arnop, Dudley Loftus, Advocate General, being informant, and Murtagh Cullen and wife defendants, it was put to the vote whether it appeared on the evidence that one Donogh O'Derg had been harboured by the said Cullen and his wife? It was resolved in the Affirmative, and Decreed that they should suffer death; but both parties after sentence pronounced were permitted to cast lots, when the Lot of Life fell to the said Murtagh, and the Lot of Death to his wife, who, being with child, was reprieved until the time of her delivery.[191]

Then, presumably, she was killed; and so it went on, for two long years. More than a quarter of the accused were sentenced to death.

Eventually the last of the resistance petered out, leaving a sense of impotence and despair, which promised future fighting. On 26 September 1653, after twelve years of civil war, the English Parliament finally declared 'that the [Irish] Rebels were subdued and the Rebellion appeased and ended; and thereupon proceeded to the Distribution of their Lands.'[192]

CHAPTER 14

Taking Possession

Sometimes in the winter I take down a long ebony cane, embellished with silver mounts, that hangs beside the fireplace. I slip a thick slice of bread into the hinged double hook that dangles from the end of this seventeenth-century toasting fork, and hold it to the fire. The warm combination of smells, toast and woodsmoke, immediately suggests that all is well with the world – and I can easily imagine that for Nicholas Loftus, too, this elegant device had talismanic meaning. He acquired it when he took possession of the Hall estate on the Hook, in the aftermath of violent civil war, and scratched his name on the pommel, to mark and claim this moment – the beginning of peace.

Along with the toasting fork, Nicholas found two other treasures abandoned at Redmond's Hall: a sword and a sash. The 'enormous ancient two-handed sword' was said to have belonged to Strongbow (Richard de Clare, Earl of Pembroke) and a visitor to the Hall in 1780 was told that 'it was with this weapon that Strongbow cut his son in two to punish him for cowardice.'[193] Strongbow was a violent man who had joined together with Raymond Le Gros (Norman ancestor of the Redmonds) to seize much of Wexford – but the legend that he slew his own son is a classic Irish myth and the sword itself was probably a sixteenth-century claymore. For Nicholas Loftus, myth was more important than trivial truth. The sword was connected with the Norman victory at Baginbun, in 1170 – when 'Ireland was lost and won' – and thus forged a link with the earliest colonial past.

Likewise with the sash, woven of red silk and silver thread, which was also believed to be ancient and was certainly beautiful. Romance declared that it was Strongbow's, although Nicholas must have guessed that it was much more recent in origin, possibly made for his predecessor at the Hall, Alexander Redmond. Whatever its history, this was an object that evoked the complex knots of Celtic calligraphy and the splendour of twisted torques, buried in ancient raths.

Each of these objects symbolised the appropriation of Ireland's

identity that accompanied the seizure of its land, for this was a colonisa-
tion of Ireland's history, geography and identity as the place was
remade in the minds of its conquerors. The 'meer Irish' were thrust to
the margins – driven into the mists of the west or down to the base of
society – and the old process of assimilation, described by Sir John
Temple, was replaced by a determination to re-invent what it meant to
be Irish.

That 'invention' (or 'discovery') of Ireland was made possible by three
remarkable men, who supplied the new settlers with the crucial markers
of identity that Camden's *Britannia* had so effectively provided for the
gentry of England: a past, a context and maps. The past – comfortably
distant but subtly linked to the present – was the work of the great
antiquarian Sir James Ware, who researched the history and imagined
the prehistory of Ireland, which he published in a series of learned
volumes. The context was described by a Dutchman, Gerard Boate,
whose *Natural History of Ireland* – published in 1652 , but written seven
years earlier – was composed as a prospectus for the Adventurers,
extolling the climate, the topography and the natural resources of this
misty island. The maps were undertaken by a brilliant Surgeon General
from Cromwell's army, William Petty, whose Down Survey (1654–5)
plotted the land and its ownership in extraordinary detail, providing a
'new testament' to property rights based on unambiguous facts.

Forget for a moment the rights and wrongs of it all and imagine the
excitement.

The first of those interpreters, James Ware, came from an old
Yorkshire family. His father had arrived in Ireland as secretary to a
newly appointed Lord Deputy, in 1588 – like that other successful
Yorkshireman, Archbishop Adam Loftus – and in fact there were close
family connections between the Wares and the Loftuses, which may
have originated in England. Ware's sister Cecilia was married to Sir
Dudley Loftus of Killyan, a grandson of the Archbishop.[194]

Ware himself was a protégé of the learned Dr Ussher, and in this
respect his life shadowed that of another Dudley Loftus – a precocious
Orientalist and favourite of Ussher who, like Ware, owed much to the
patronage of Boyle and Ormond. Loftus helped negotiate Ormond's
surrender of Dublin to Parliament, in 1647, and Ware was nominated as

one of the hostages for the performance of its terms. When Parliament stripped Ware of his office of Auditor General, his replacement was Loftus's future son-in-law Dr Robert Gorges. Ware was Archbishop Adam Loftus's first biographer, and much of what we know about Dudley Loftus can be found in the extended edition of Ware's Works, revised by his granddaughter's husband.

From his first published book in 1626, until shortly before his death forty years later, Ware interpreted the history of Ireland in ways that made sense to its new inhabitants. 'He took from fable its extravagance, disembarrassed truth from the drapery of romance, based Irish history on recorded and incontrovertible evidence, and confounded the slanders that were derogatory of a nation's honour.'[195] That bold claim, written two centuries later, has a thread of truth – however odd this may seem when we read Ware's chapter on 'The Origin of the Irish':

> Girald Barry, commonly called Cambrensis, and other writers give an Account of the Arrival of Caesura, Noah's Niece, in Ireland with a colony a little before the Flood. It is said also that in the three hundredth Year after the Flood Bartholanus the Son of Sera, of the posterity of Japhet, having vanquished some Giants in that Island, intirely subdued it.'[196]

Such fables must be read in context. Ware was a disciple of Archbishop Ussher, who invented a biblical chronology that remained unchallenged for centuries after his death – and behind the gobbledygook of an imagined Old Testament ancestry there lurks a crucial insight: that Ireland was conquered and colonised by successive waves of invaders, from her earliest past. This was critical for the latest settlers, providing an historical precedent that in some way diminished the claim of the 'mere Irish' to be aboriginal owners of the land and its myths.

There were other important aspects to Ware's work. One was his love and respect for the old Irish annals, which he explored with the aid of a succession of Irish scholars whom he maintained in his house to transcribe and interpret Gaelic documents.[197] Another was his determination to bring that history up to date, through his lives of the writers and bishops, by which he managed to suggest that there was an unbroken episcopal chain between the earliest Irish Christians and 'our own [Protestant] times' – as if the most profound divide of all was merely a transition, from one historical epoch to the next.

The cumulative effect of Ware's writings was to appropriate Ireland's history in ways that acted as subtle propaganda for the English settlers, old and new. He allowed them to claim Irish antiquity as part of their own heritage – a cultural ancestry – in comparable fashion to numerous English kings who seized the throne by force but 'proved' a continuous bloodline through ingenious mapping of their family trees. They were heirs, not interlopers.

In that sense, at least, Ware was an old-fashioned figure; the classic genealogist, writing in Latin, in love with the past. His counterpart as Ireland's topographer was a more assertive entrepreneur – the Dutchman, Gerard Boate. A newcomer with a scientific bent, Boate viewed Ireland as an investment, and with the wealth gained from being the King's physician in London he subscribed to a fund that enabled the Dutch to participate in the 'Adventure' of Ireland, in return for grants of Irish land. It was from this perspective that he wrote his brief but influential *Natural History*, as a prospectus for his fellow countrymen and for the English 'Adventurers'.

Boate made it eminently plain that he regarded Ireland as a land of rich potential, neglected by the Old English and by 'the Irish themselves, as being one of the most barbarous nations of the whole earth' – and only properly exploited 'by the New-English, that is, such as are come in during, and since the reign of queen Elizabeth.'[198] He even suggested that the wetness of Ireland was the fault of the Irish, who attracted rain-clouds by failing to drain the bogs, and made clear that only the Protestant ethic could dispel superstition and encourage enterprise. Boate cited the example of the Lords Justice (Richard Boyle, Earl of Cork, and Adam Loftus, Viscount Ely) who had managed to disprove the stories of 'St Patrick's Purgatory' as 'meer illusion' and to develop profitable ironworks where there were none before – Boyle 'in divers places in Munster' and Loftus 'at Mountmelick, in King's-county'. The colonists, in other words, deserved the land that they acquired.

That acquisition, the scale and the speed of it, was only made possible by the achievement of William Petty, a man of extraordinary energy and self-confidence who became one of the leading polymaths of his day. After an astonishing career that somehow managed to include education by French Jesuits, a spell in the Navy, a period working for Hobbes in Paris and election as a fellow of Brasenose College, Oxford – all before he was thirty – Petty arrived in Waterford in 1652 as Physician-General to the Parliamentary army. He immediately set about reforming its medical services and establishing his own private practice as a doctor, before contracting to map the whole of Ireland for a fixed price per acre.

His work was partly based on the evidence of landholding collected at about the same time by the commissioners of the Civil Survey, but that was the recording of oral testimony, not the measured data that Petty required, and he constantly complained about its accuracy. So hordes of sturdy surveyors were dispatched to plot a country without roads or any tradition of boundaries to landed property, establishing the shape of the land and the ownership of every acre, barony by barony. The task was completed with unprecedented accuracy in thirteen months. Ireland was mapped in greater detail than any country in Europe and Petty deservedly made his fortune.

Petty's survey provided the necessary data for an enforced change of ownership of about two-thirds of Ireland. Some of the former owners stayed on as tenants of the new landlords – as did those at the bottom of the social scale, who continued to scratch a living, as they had always done – but for a vast number of people this process resulted in a forced migration to the west. Boate's vision of a land remade by the 'New English' was to a large extent realised, as new estates were formed, land drained, fields walled, ports built and industries established. All of which unexpectedly led to what might be called a 'New Irish' cultural renewal – as practical Protestant Englishmen discovered the anarchic energy and wit of the Irish use of language, and the verbal tradition of history that Ware had honoured.

The work of these three men helped redefine the place in ways that shaped the future, creating an Irish identity which may have been remote from the Gaelic past but was equally distinct from the English present. The colonisers came to think of themselves as Irish, rooted in the place and its history, and the image of Ireland that they held in being – increasingly cracked and crazed as the 'mere Irish' asserted their own, more ancient vision – lasted for more than two hundred and fifty years. If it now survives only in the memory of the dispossessed, the Anglo-Irish, it may be said to have fully conformed to the archetype of Ireland's myths: the tales of loss.

The 'invention' of Ireland was of course accompanied by an actual seizure of land – but the process was less straightforward than is often described. Eleven years of civil war, plague and famine had claimed the lives of vast numbers of people and wrecked Irish agriculture. It was said that a man might ride for twenty or thirty miles without meeting a trace of human habitation, and the rich pastures were so denuded of stock that meat had to be imported from abroad. Wolves prowled in enormous packs and travellers were attacked by maddened dogs, grown accustomed to the taste of corpses.[199] Land was accounted of so little value that even the best was reckoned at no more than four shillings an acre. Boate's prospectus, written before the ruin, must have seemed like a hollow promise.

Thus it was that so many of the English soldiers and 'Adventurers' preferred a quick profit on their allocations to the dangerous un-certainties of holding Irish land – and the real beneficiaries of Cromwell's Settlement were established Protestant proprietors, enlarging their estates. Certainly this was true on the Hook.

Prior to the civil wars, Nicholas Loftus already owned most of the tip of the Hook, south of a line curving east from Duncannon to Poulfer – with the exception of the estates of Lewis of Lewiston, Redmond of the Hall, Laffan of Slade Castle and a patchwork of smaller landholdings near Fethard.[200] North of that line he owned a couple of isolated farms. By the time that the Civil Survey was finished, in 1656, the entire peninsula of the Hook was Loftus land.

About a thousand acres of confiscated land around Fethard (previously belonging to several 'Irish papists' and to a family of 'Old English' colonists, the Whittys of Dungulph Castle) were granted to Nicholas Loftus as a reward for services rendered during Cromwell's conquest of Wexford, together with a further 260 acres in Lamberstowne and Great Graiges, formerly the property of James Lewis, descendant of the Norman Knights Templar. He also purchased about 600 acres from 'several Adventurers and Soldiers', including the Hall estate and other parcels of land in the south of the Hook, which had been 'assigned and sett fourth unto ye Souldiers in part of satisfaction of their arrears for their service against the rebels in Ireland.'

The previous owner of the Hall, Alexander Redmond, had courageously resisted the Parliamentary forces but was forced to surrender to Cromwell in 1649 – from whom 'he obtained favourable terms, namely that in recognition of his advanced years, he being then in his 76th year, he was permitted to end his days in peace in his ancestral home.' He died at the Hall a year or two afterwards, but his son was transplanted to Connaught. Feelings ran high at the time and continued to do so for generations to come. An eighteenth-century map of the Loftus Hall estate bears pencil scribbles by G. O. C. Redmond, dated 13 April 1900: 'Redmond Hall it was and Redmond Hall it is. The Loftus family seized it by plunder and disloyalty.'[201] In his outrage at my ancestors this scrawling Redmond had conveniently forgotten that his own forebears were Norman adventurers who seized their lands on the Hook a few centuries earlier, with ruthless indifference to the Gaelic inhabitants of the time. The history of grudges is never simple, particularly in Ireland.

Possession of those forfeited estates was nothing like the 'quiet enjoyment' promised in later deeds, and a series of Acts of Parliament and Orders in Council was necessary to assure the new owners of Ireland that they held their lands 'in real and true seisin and possession'.[202] Certainty was at a premium, for the English revolution followed what became the standard pattern for such things: a dizzying cycle of changes.

The killing of a king was the beginning, not the end of the real struggle for power. It was followed a few months later by the declaration of a republic and the establishment of press censorship, as the republic became a military dictatorship. Parliament was dissolved – 'Take away that bauble' – and the dictator was given greater powers than the erstwhile monarch, but his attempt to establish a dynasty was frustrated by the incompetence of his son, unable to command the allegiance of his father's generals. They conspired to restore the monarchy, hoping for a grateful puppet, but their marionette (Charles II) proved an unexpected master of political guile, who capitalised on the wild popular rejoicing that greeted his return and managed to outmanoeuvre his opponents for the remainder of his colourful life.

The King's death provoked further plotting against his foolish heir (James II), which culminated in the latter's overthrow and replacement by his daughter and her stern but capable husband, William and Mary. Equilibrium was restored by limiting the powers of the Crown and the emergence of a two-party system – Whigs and Tories – which ensured that the oligarchs always took their turn in office. The authentic voices of democracy, briefly audible in the earliest days of the now despised republic, were vigorously silenced. They called it the Glorious Revolution.

All of which may have seemed like manifest destiny in England but caused consternation and chaos in Ireland, time and time again. The restoration of Charles II in 1660 was the first great shock to upset the applecart of Cromwellian confiscation, since dispossessed Catholic grandees demanded reinstatement, as reward for their loyalty to the exiled King. There was not enough land to go round. 'If the Adventurers and soldiers must be satisfied,' noted Ormond, and innocent papists restored, 'there must be discovery made of a new Ireland, for the old will not serve to satisfy these engagements.'[203]

Charles, however, was a realist. Knowing that he depended on the Protestant oligarchy of Ireland for the country's continued governance, he took steps to calm their fears – making a Declaration (November 1660) which formed the basis of the Acts of Settlement and Explanation of 1662 and 1665 – confirming the status quo, almost undisturbed, while providing some compensation for Catholic landowners whose lands had been confiscated. But Acts of Parliament were one thing and their interpretation another, for every disputed case had to be settled by the courts, and lawyers meant trouble.

In 1664, for example, Jane Devereux – 'alias Loftus, relict of Nicholas Devereux, of Balmagir, co Wexford' – wrote desperately to the King, saying that because she lived far from Dublin she was constrained to trust agents and counsel to put her claim to her late husband's estate before the Commissioners of Claims, which they had neglected to do until the deadline was passed, 'whereby your petitioner is likely to be ruined, unless by your Majesty's favour she may obtain a remedy herein. She has for the support of herself and her four small children only the jointure she claims, and prays that the Commissioners be directed to receive any claim which she puts in within four months.'[204]

Ballymagir (land of the hares) was certainly a prize worth fighting for, being at that time a moated mansion built around an old fortress tower, in the midst of the wonderfully rich grazing of its extensive salt marshes and meadows – for which it was later named Richfield – about halfway between the Hook and Wexford. It had belonged to the Devereux family for generations – they claimed to have arrived with Strongbow – but Nicholas Devereux sided with the Catholic Confederation during the civil wars and was sentenced to be transplanted to Connaught, along with thirty of his dependents. Ballymagir was seized by Cromwell's son-in-law, General Ireton, who made it his headquarters, and Devereux himself appears to have died in exile.[205]

These might have seemed formidable obstacles to its redemption, for a woman less well connected, or less determined, than his widow; but Jane was the eldest daughter of Nicholas Loftus of Fethard and her younger sister Eleanor was married to Ireton's secretary, John Cliffe.[206] She might well have won the day under Cromwell's rule and certainly did so under the newly restored King Charles, regaining full possession of Ballymagir for herself and her children.[207]

Then it was the turn of her father to fight for his own estates, when the newly established Court of Claims opened for business in Dublin, on 4 January 1666. Twelve days later, Nicholas Loftus sent an urgent note to his younger son Henry, who was stationed as an Ensign at Duncannon Fort. There is an extraordinary energy in the writing – you can hear the voice of the old man, his affection for Henry and his excitement about the impending appeal, as he makes provision for the necessary bribes (jewels for the judges) while taking a fatherly, fussy concern for the cleanliness of his son's shirts.

Hary,

bringe your three Diamond rings with you, the necklace and bringe all your writtings with you Concerninge what estate I have made you: bringe the deede I made on your brothers marriadge, the recovery I past of all my old estate to William Ball. Bring all things with you that may give full Satisfaction to all there demaunds, forget nothinge. Bringe your linning with you to have it made Cleane against you begin your journey. Pray God blesse you in all your designes. I am your most affectionate father

Nicho. Loftus

Fetherd 16 January 1666

Lett no man living knowe that you Intend for Dublin till I speake with you.

There was also an afterthought, conveyed to his servant who wrote it on the outside of the folded letter, for the old man needed some wine. 'Sr. my master would have none wine but white wine and desires you to borrow a good bottell that would hold a pottel and to fill it and send it home.'[208]

Henry's mission to Dublin was sufficient to convince the Court, and the Loftus lands on the Hook were confirmed under the Act of Settlement, by 'letters patent under the Great Seal of Ireland dated 13 August 1666.'[209] About 1,900 acres granted or otherwise acquired in Cromwellian times were added to the 2,500 acres that the family held prior to the civil wars, making a consolidated estate of 4,500 acres, plantation measure – equivalent to nearly 7,000 acres by modern reckoning. It was worth a few jewels and a clean shirt.

Nicholas Loftus himself lived for only a few months after this settlement was confirmed, and died at the age of seventy-four in October 1666, soon after making his will. You might have expected some sense of triumph, after so much turmoil, as he surveyed his windswept kingdom and made provision for his heirs, but in fact I am mystified by his apparent longing for oblivion – as if, at the end, he was lost – so that even his identity, his place in the world, was uncertain, and all the constructs of church and state meant nothing. 'According to his own desire [he] was buried on the North-side of the Chancel of the Church at Fethard, pursuant to the Directions of his last Will, dated 27 September that Year, whereby he ordered, that he should be buried in the Nightime, without any Ceremonies, Assemblies, or Mournings, but privately as soon as he should be dead; and desired his Wife and Children not to wear any Mourning for him.'[210]

But his wife was already gone, having died a fortnight before him, at the age of sixty-two. They lie together still, in the family vault at Fethard, a stone's throw from the ruins of his castle.

INTERLUDE

CHAPTER 15

The Gift of Tongues

Entering the Old City walls at Damascus Gate, I followed the covered bazaar (the Suq Khan es Zeit) through the heart of Jerusalem, climbed a flight of steps, wandered along a deserted alley to the Coptic monastery of St Anthony and turned through a half-open door.

Suddenly I found myself on the roof of St Helena's chapel, where a ragamuffin band of Ethiopian monks inhabits a shanty town of make-shift cells, built in the lee of ancient buttresses and ruined Gothic arches, shaded by half a dozen trees – including olives that are said to be cuttings from the biblical bush in which Abraham found the ram, which God permitted him to sacrifice instead of his beloved son. The Ethiopians were evicted from their original monastery by the Copts, long ago, in one of those jealous realignments of power and privilege between the six ancient Christian sects that share ownership of this confusing warren, the Church of the Holy Sepulchre, and they have camped here ever since, baked in the summer heat, frozen in winter. Now their devotions are constantly interrupted by groups of pilgrims carrying crosses, who process across the sloping stone roof that serves as the Ethiopian cloister, through a narrow door into the monastic chapel, down a dark flight of stairs into another chapel – dedicated to the Archangel Michael – and out into the light of day, in front of the main doors of the church.

I followed one of these groups, but found my attention caught by the ragged chant of the ancient Ethiopic texts, as the monks sang their liturgy in the bottom chapel, and by the dark eyes of a couple of Abyssinian nuns, gleaming from the shadows of their voluminous cloaks.

Then I went on my way into the church past the Stone of Unction (a fake, dating from 1810), past the Sepulchre itself (a hideous marble structure, held together by girders, which replaces the original tomb – destroyed by the Caliph Hakim in 1009), past the Coptic chapel at its rear and into another chapel, apparently abandoned to decay, where a solitary candle burned on a ruinous altar, below a Syrian icon so blackened by the smoke of centuries as to be utterly indecipherable. And I crawled into a clawhole in the rock, black and greasy from candle wax, which is claimed by the Ethiopians as the Tomb of Joseph of Arimathea.

Onward through a babel of ancient liturgies, pursued by processions of Catholic and Orthodox – Italian, French, Greek and Serbian – each trying to out-chant the others in the echoing vaults of this strange architectural palimpsest. I hurried past 'The Prison of Christ' (another smoke-blackened hole, which belongs to the Armenians) and down into the depths, through St Helena's chapel to the supposed Roman cistern – actually a later quarry – which is known as the Chapel of the Invention of the Cross. Here, according to legend, the True Cross is said to have been discovered by the Empress Helena, in the year 326.

Perhaps 'invented' is a better word, because this story (like so much else about the place) does not bear too much scrutiny – and there is another version, which claims that the original Invention of the Cross took place long before the Empress Helena's visit to Jerusalem, within a generation of the death of Christ. This account was discovered by my eccentric ancestor, the seventeenth-century Orientalist Dr Dudley Loftus, grandson of the great Archbishop. It was 'contained in a Bialogie of Eastern Saints' which had arrived in Dublin 'about five years since from Aleppo', and was 'written in a fair Estrangalar character, wherein the Aramaeans usually write matters of the most precious concern.'

I am quoting from Dudley's preface to his translation of *An History of the Twofold Invention of the Cross*, published in Dublin in 1686.[212] It is a bizarre compendium of oddities, which does much to justify the learned Doctor's reputation as a brilliant fool. A dedication in flowery Italian to James II's Catholic queen is followed by an odd, rambling introduction which begins by praising 'the present Bishop of Rome who (as is given forth) rates questionable Miracles as false Money, put in to fill the Bag,' and concludes by recommending the practice of signing with the Cross, while admitting 'that they who think the use of the Cross in Baptism superstitious, may be apt to exclaim against me, as Popishly inclined; but I, who have always followed the rule of the Italian proverb (*Fa bene e lascia dire*) need not apologise for what I think well done.' At the heart of these digressions is Dudley's robust defence of the literal truth of his ancient text: 'Such is the likelihood of the Narrative so well agreeing with the Consent and Approbation of other authentick writers, and the credit of the Author, so sober and grave in what he relates concerning this Subject, that I shall not need to argue for the Belief of what he delivers.'

What follows is a curious tale, which strains credulity to breaking point. It attributes the discovery of the True Cross to 'Patronica, wife of Claudius Caesar, whom Tiberius constituted the second of his Empire.' This remarkable woman – unknown to every reference work of classical biography – is said to have 'renounced the Heathenism of her forefathers', converted to Christianity, visited Jerusalem, forced the Jews to hand over the three crosses of Golgotha and identified the True Cross by challenging God to restore her Virgin Daughter to life. She then 'commanded that a great and stately Building should be raised over Golgotha, and over the Sepulchre.' In a subsequent reversal of fortunes the Christians were expelled from Jerusalem and the Cross recovered by the Jews, who 'digged it into the earth about twenty cubits', where it was hidden until 'Helen the Queen, and Mother of Constantine the Faithful Emperour, found it in the seventh year of the Reign of Constantine.'

Despite being embroidered with dramatic miracles, strange revelations and an almost convincing clutter of circumstantial detail, this extraordinary text was of insufficient length to make a decent volume, so Dudley added an appendix, totally unrelated in content to the rest, which he introduced thus: 'It is thought fit, as well for the satisfying of the curious, as for the filling up of blank paper, to give the following Account of the conversion of the Ethiopians, as it is found in Abulpharagius, his Ecclesiastical History.' This text is even briefer – no more than half a dozen pages – and tells how the Ethiopic Nation of Nubida was converted by Julianus, who 'remained for the space of two years, preaching from the third hour to the tenth, vested in a Linnen Surplice; he stood in the subterraneal Caves abounding with water, and baptized there; for there were not to be found pure waters above them.'

I love that image of a hidden spiritual oasis. It has the quiet ring of truth.

In the silent 'subterraneal cave' of the Chapel of the Invention of the Cross, I found myself thinking about the noisy confusions of legend and language, and about the descendants of those Ethiopian converts, stranded on the roof of St Helena's chapel, almost directly above my head. I was alone except for an old woman, prostrate in prayer in the far corner of the cavern. Then a slight, dark-clad figure appeared at my elbow, and muttered urgently in my ear, 'You must leave now. The Armenians are coming.' And come they did, bearded and robed, chanting their sacred texts with the vengeance of the righteous.

> And they were all filled with the Holy Ghost, and began to speak with other tongues, as the Spirit gave them utterance . . . and every man heard them speak in his own language . . . Parthians, and Medes, and Elamites, and the dwellers in Mesopotamia, and in Judaea, and Cappadocia, in Pontus, and in Asia, Phrygia, and Pamphilia, in Egypt, and in the parts of Lybia about Cyrene, and strangers of Rome, Jews and proselytes, Cretes and Arabians, we do hear them speak in our tongues the wonderful works of God.[213]

Seventeenth-century Orientalists were inspired by that famous reference to a community of biblical civilisations because they shared a belief, common to all the reformers, that European Puritanism was a return to Christianity's roots, which could be found in the burning visions of early Eastern sects. Dudley Loftus's nephew and biographer, Robert Gorges, quotes the great Archbishop Ussher – founder of Oriental studies in Ireland: 'he often affirming – that by his Acquaintance and Correspondence with some eminent persons of those parts, hee had discovered more primitive purite of Christian religion might bee got from the Easterne than the westerne books, the former having never been so corrupted by the heathen as the Westerne books had been by the degenerate Christians.'

The pursuit of such learning demanded men who combined the boldness of great explorers – as they mapped uncharted territories in an esoteric world – with the odd, intuitive genius of code-crackers. Their passion was to be discoverers – of texts and the keys to deciphering these texts, opening doors into strange regions of intellectual speculation. They were interested in time – when did the world begin? – and they were interested in space, extending eastwards the boundaries of religious philosophy and the map of cultural history. They were intellectual archaeologists.

Orientalists shared the mania for collecting which afflicted early explorers, like the horticultural enthusiasts who brought back roses from Persia and China, tulips from Turkey, and caused the strangest bubble in all of investment history, when fevered speculation in rare bulbs nearly wrecked the Dutch economy. Unlike the passions of these plantsmen, the enthusiasms of the linguists were obscure, and barely comprehensible to society at large. It was their ideas, not their acquisitiveness, which had far-reaching repercussions. In 1654, for example, Archbishop James Ussher decided from his study of the ancient texts that the act of Creation began at the extraordinarily prosaic moment of nine o'clock in the morning of 26 October 4004 BC. His biblical chronology was printed in the margins of the Authorised Version for more than two centuries after his death, presenting a vast moral obstacle to the evolution of scientific thought.

The interest in Eastern studies was strongest at the universities of Oxford, Dublin and Leyden – intellectual centres of maritime trading nations – and would often lead its devotees to long years of voluntary exile on the coasts of India or Asia Minor, Palestine or Syria, as chaplains to small colonies of English or Dutch merchants. Here they could learn the Eastern languages at first hand and begin to establish the network of agents and correspondents who supplied them with a steady stream of Oriental manuscripts, which dealt, for the most part, with philosophical or theological controversies of the utmost obscurity.[214]

Return to Europe meant a life immured in study, constructing grammars and dictionaries of long-dead languages and translating ancient texts, as the manuscripts continued to arrive from all corners of the East, overwhelming the tiny bands of dedicated scholars with the sheer weight of undeciphered learning. An Orientalist in Dublin at the end of the seventeenth century had at his disposal thousands of manuscripts collected by Archbishop James Ussher, eight hundred manuscript volumes assembled by Archbishop Narcissus Marsh, and thousands more accumulated by Trinity's Provost, Robert

Huntingdon, from all the corners of the East – vast, unsorted collections, for scholars to explore.

One such was Dudley Loftus. This wonderfully odd character was born in 1619, in the fortress luxury of Rathfarnham, 'a magnificent castle buylt by his great Grand father', the Chancellor-Archbishop. He was the third son of an enormous family, one of seventeen siblings and hordes of cousins. His father, Sir Adam, was 'Vice Treasurer of Ireland and one of the Lords of his Majesty's Cowncill in this Kingdom, [and] being of that Quality, kept the best Chaplaines hee could gett for the Education of his Sons' – the daughters were destined for marriage, and education was irrelevant. One of those sons was a prodigy, with a startling gift for languages, who raced ahead of the rest and was admitted to Trinity College Dublin, at the age of sixteen.

Among other feats of learning, Dudley appears to have taught himself Ethiopic without the aid of a grammar or dictionary, and 'before hee was twenty years old was able to translate neer as many languages into his mother tongue.' Such a linguist of genius was bound to catch the eye of Archbishop Ussher, who was 'an intimate Acquaintance of his father'. Ussher encouraged Sir Adam to send the boy to Oxford, as the prelude, he evidently hoped, to a career in the Church.

These details of Dudley's early life are recorded in a letter written many years later, on 25 July 1693, in response to a request for biographical information that arrived just as the old man 'was readie to take horse, on his provincial visitation of the primacie of Armagh.' Despite his age – he was seventy-four at the time – Dudley was impatient to be off and asked his nephew by marriage, Robert Gorges, to deal with the matter. The celebrated scholar departed on his journey while Gorges, eager to please, picked up his quill and began to write.[215]

He noted that Dudley enrolled at University College Oxford in 1639, was incorporated BA at Cambridge in the same year and 'intended to take the degree of Batchelor of Law' at Oxford, before finishing his brief career there as Master of Arts, in 1640. This helter-skelter progress through the great universities of England is typical of Dudley's impetuosity. Within a few weeks of arriving at Oxford he had written to Ussher, referring to a catalogue of Greek manuscripts that he had already sent his patron and an Ethiopic document that he was in the process of translating into Latin – and a few months later he was bored. He decided to explore the world. 'Leaving a good valuable piece of plate with the College, he returned to Ireland with a resolution to take leave of his friends, and to improve his study by Travells into forrain parts, but was prevented by the horrid rebellion of Ireland wch breake forth the 23 of Oct 1641.'

So this tall, gangly, beak-nosed intellectual, twenty-two years old, found himself commanding a garrison – responsible for defending his father's castle, 'a frontier to the Cittie of Dublyn, against the barbarous mowntaineers of the County of Wicklow' (the septs of O'Toole and Byrne). At the same time he was appointed with Dr Faithful Tate to take temporary charge of the college where he had been an under-graduate only three years earlier – for the Provost had fled to England – and a few months later was elected MP for Naas.[217] Life accelerated to match his sense of drama.

It was during these hectic times that Dudley married Frances Nangle and fathered the first of their seven children – but I have almost no sense of him in a domestic context. The only clue comes from a commonplace book of his historical jottings, compiled many years later. There is a page filled with a series of stylish signatures: Lettice Loftus, Lettice Boyd, Lettice, Lettice Loftus – the doodlings of Dudley's daughter and her older cousin, playing with their shared name. It's a tiny, affectionate glimpse of family life.[218]

Dudley held Rathfarnham against numerous attacks, as the character of the uprising changed and became a long and complex civil war. Bands of marauders roamed the neighbourhood, terrorising tradesmen and farmers, seizing their cattle and horses, while inhabitants of the castle lived under intermittent siege. At times of particular danger Rath-farnham was crowded with a motley huddle of refugees, which on various occasions included the caretaker of a local cloth mill – who saved his own life during a rebel assault by escaping through the mill sluice – and Ireland's first theatre-manager, John Ogilby.[219]

This fascinating Scotsman had arrived in Ireland in Wentworth's train, as tutor and dancing master to his children, and persuaded the Lord Deputy to create for him the post of Master of the Revels, on 28 February 1638. In this capacity, Ogilby built Dublin's first theatre in St

Werburgh Street – just down the road from the house occupied by Dudley Loftus's cousin, the Lord Chancellor, Sir Adam Loftus – where he staged a series of plays by his friend James Shirley and others by Beaumont and Fletcher, Middleton and Ben Jonson, as well as catering for more bloodthirsty tastes with displays of bear-baiting and cudgelling. On the outbreak of the rising, in 1641, his theatre was closed and Ogilby fled to Rathfarnham.[220]

He sheltered there for the winter and must have spent long hours in conversation with Dudley Loftus, when he wasn't poking his inquisitive nose into the organisation of Rathfarnham's defence. Ogilby supposedly had some military training as a member of Wentworth's guard of honour, but in typically melodramatic fashion he was almost killed by an explosion on 17 November 1642, 'upon his birthday [when] he scaped blowing up with pounder [gunpowder]' – according to Ashmole, who cast his horoscope.[221] I suspect that the irrepressible Ogilby had tried to make a firework, to celebrate his nativity, and had miscalculated the amounts. Eventually he returned to England, damaged and destitute, and recovered at Cambridge, where he 'became such a master of Latin and Greek, that he translated Virgil and Homer, [and] paraphrased Aesop's *Fables*' – inspired, it seems, by his friend the Orientalist. According to his own account, Ogilby's translation of Virgil was begun in Ireland, 'bred in phlegmatic Regions, and among people returning to their ancient barbarity.'[222]

For most of the next few years, the armies of the Catholic Confederacy confined the English settlers to a few pockets of Ulster and the south-east, and to the immediate neighbourhood of Dublin. Dudley had little choice but to remain at Rathfarnham. From his castle ramparts he could see the Wicklow hills – swarming with invisible insurgents – but Dublin was hidden from view, and there must have been times when he felt utterly cut off from the world, especially when it rained, or in the dense mists that often enveloped this seductively green landscape.

Dudley wrote a propagandist pamphlet and played an important role in negotiations between Parliament and Ormond, but for the most part stayed silent. His version of events, written after the Restoration, summarised eight years of civil war in a single sentence: '[He] continued in the vigorous defence of [Rathfarnham] till the Irish besieged Dublyn, at which time he and his Garrison were basely betrayed, by

Some who pretended to take sanctuary with him.' And even that terse detail may not have been true, as noted in a previous chapter.

But finally the war was over and Dr Loftus adapted, as he always did, to the new political climate. He presided over a court-martial, which sat for over two years in the aftermath of Cromwell's conquest, suppressing the remnants of rebellion with daunting severity.[223] And he was well rewarded – Deputy Judge Advocate of Leinster, Commissioner of Revenue, Judge of Admiralty, Master in Chancery. Each post carried a handsome salary and plenty of perquisites. There was a pension of 20 shillings a week for himself (and 10 shillings for his wife) which he was granted on Christmas Day 1651, and the sonorous sinecures which he was allotted four years later – Ingrosser of the Great Roll of the Clerk of the Pipe, and Chief Ingrosser of the Exchequer.

For a man of Dudley's interests all this was not enough, and somehow he found the time to spend long hours in scholarly study, preparing an Ethiopic version of the New Testament – complete with Latin translation – for Walton's *Polyglot Bible*. Dudley's original notes for this translation, dating from about 1654, survive in Marsh's Library, but his final manuscript version was not ready until two years later, when he sent it over to London in the care of another great Orientalist scholar, Dr Edmund Castell, who supervised its setting and revised the proofs.

The *Polyglot Bible* – published in 1657, dedicated to Cromwell – was a collaborative masterpiece of Puritan learning, with contributions from all the great Orientalists of the day, but it seems almost to have exhausted Dudley's interest in Ethiopic studies. He turned for light relief to translating an Armenian work of logic, and writing an introduction to Aristotle's philosophy – both in Latin – and he devoted his linguistic researches to Armenian and Syriac, continuing to publish translations from both languages until the last year of his long life.

'Yet notwithstanding his Learning, he was accounted an improvident and unwise Man; and his many Levities and want of Conduct gave the world too much Reason to think so.' Walter Harris's stern comment – in his 1764 edition of *The Writers of Ireland* – reflects the verdict of Dudley's contemporaries, but such a man was perfectly suited to the sudden change of mood that accompanied the Restoration. Impetuous, indiscreet, tending to overstatement, a lover of ceremonial and an instinctive player of parts, unable to resist the lure of a splendid phrase or the glance of alluring eyes, Dudley was in his element as the dour repressions of Cromwellian Dublin were swept away. And he found himself living at the heart of things.

His erstwhile acquaintance, John Ogilby, raced back from England to outmanoeuvre William Davenant for his old post as Master of the Revels, which he obtained on 8 May 1661, and immediately began to build 'a noble theatre' on the site of a former tavern at the corner of Blind Quay; where he took lodgings within a few yards of Dudley Loftus, alongside a mixture of grandees and booksellers. Thus was founded the famous Smock Alley Theatre, which opened on 18 October 1662 with a performance of Fletcher's *Wit without Money* – an entirely appropriate choice since the scenery was incomplete and the actors under-rehearsed, according to 'the matchless Orinda', Katherine Philips. Loftus, I feel sure, was in the audience.

He certainly survived and prospered, managing to retain all his estates and sinecures, and to add to them. Primate Ussher appointed his erstwhile protégé Vicar General of Ireland and Judge of the Court of Prerogatives and Faculties, ecclesiastical offices which he held for the rest of his life – though he was never ordained or notable for the Christian virtues – and he was also made Pro-Vice-Chancellor of the University of Dublin. In 1661 he was elected MP for Bannow, one of the family constituencies in Wexford, and thirty years later was listed as Member for Fethard.[224]

Dudley acted his roles with relish. As Vicar-General and Pro-Vice-Chancellor he was responsible for one of the first great ceremonies of the new reign, *The Consecration of the twelve Bishops in St Patrick's Church in Dublin* on 27 January 1661.[225] He organised a public procession through the city, starting at 7 a.m., to mark this restoration of the episcopacy and published a pamphlet to commemorate the event, lovingly listing every detail of ritual and precedence, in which he played so prominent a part. Two years later he gave the funeral oration in Christ Church for Primate Bramhall, and used the occasion for a formidable display of learning, covering a great deal of ecclesiastical history as well as the life and works of the deceased Archbishop, all of which was expressed in scholarly Latin and printed for posterity – thirty-eight pages complete with footnotes.[226] I find it all irresistibly soporific, but I suspect that his original audience may well have been jolted into life by the preacher's theatrical delivery, full of startling gestures and vocal swoops.

Even more surprising than his political accommodation to changing circumstances was Dudley's infection by the sensuality of fashionable society. At the age of forty-eight he fell foolishly and suddenly in love.

The woman concerned was Maria Plunket, who claimed to be an Italian of noble birth and a former lady-in-waiting to the Queen Mother, Henrietta Maria – but Dublin gossips suggested otherwise and Dudley's eighteenth-century biographer claimed that she was 'a Lady of Irish birth, whom the Doctor would have pass for an Italian, being educated in Italy. It was well known he lived in too great Familiarity with this Lady.'[227] What seems to be true is that she was half Dudley's age, married to one of the four sons of the Earl of Fingal – each of whom had been heavily involved in the rebellion of 1641 – and was already the subject of rumour.[228] Her bizarre and very public liaison with Dudley Loftus compounded that notoriety and has all the flavour of a Restoration comedy.

It was an extraordinary, helter-skelter affair. Within a few weeks of their first meeting Dudley had drawn up an agreement in Italian, dated 5 July 1666, which reads like a secret marriage contract – 'Signora Francesca Lucretia Plunketta' and 'Dudleio di Casa Alsata' [Lofthouse] promised to live as close neighbours and to visit each other until death. And he signed the agreement in the presence of witnesses, an unwise move.[229] Early the following year, as increasingly lurid accusations were aimed at his beloved, Dudley leapt to her defence and published *The Vindication of an Injured Lady*, which – as Walter Harris noted a century later – was 'written by him in her Name'.[230] A few months later it was over, when a friend wrote a letter to Dudley from England and 'suddenly, as when they raise the curtain at the new Theatre', he saw his mistress in her true colours. 'You have changed a furnace of love into an Etna of disdain.'

Dudley seemed all the more foolish because the blindness of passion had caused him to deny what was obvious to the world. As author of *The Vindication* he had poured scorn on Maria Plunket's detractors, 'who have opened their black mouths, or shewed their bad teeth against me.' Writing in her name he claimed that she was accused of being 'a

Stage-player', that she was maligned because 'a certain Learned Person is civilly treated' when he came to visit her, that she was supposed to have 'practiced witchcraft to gain some ends on the Person above-mentioned' and was 'a common Liar'. The Injured Lady was at particular pains to refute the gossip that 'because I was civil to a Person of merit and civility, therefore I had submitted to unchaste embraces,' and praised Dudley as 'an Illustrious Example of refined morality, and an extraordinary gentility'. Their innocent friendship was very different from 'the much more frequent visits which they [her accusers] receive daily from younger Gentlemen.' Finally – and here the language is unmistakeably that of Dudley in full flow as a preacher – Maria's detractors were urged to 'Retraction, Compensation, and a lowly penitent dejection of mind before God, which if they forbear to perform, they will not only render themselves hereafter hateful to their own imaginations, but also lyable to be cast headlong to the lowest and most painful tormentory of hell, which I pray God to prevent in his mercy.'

Unfortunately the learned Doctor appears to have been rash enough to refer his inamorata's persecutors to the archbishop's Consistory Court, hoping to clear her name. It had precisely the opposite effect, causing Maria Plunket to fly Dublin for London, so blackened by scandal that she was forced to adopt a new identity, as 'Lady Tesborough'.

Worse still, from Dudley's point of view, was that news of the scandal caused the authorities such concern that the draft of a warrant was issued by the King, for a commission 'to try Dr Loftus for the ecclesiastical offences alleged against him.' The warrant was 'disallowed by the Lord Keeper as illegal' but the evidence which it cited was hair raising, claiming that:

for the fulfilling of his fleshly lusts and carnal concupiscence with Maria Frances Lucretia Plunket [Dr Loftus] is alleged to have made very wicked and damnable contracts with her, (notwithstanding that he has been married for divers years) and has covenanted to live with her during both their lives or at least as near as he can to her – and to love her most constantly to the last gasp of his spirit, putting himself without any reservation into her power to order him according to her pleasure, and that he will never love another with so great affections nor touch any other woman against her will, promising, when he is free of his present wife, to give himself in matrimony to her.'

And so on, with increasing foolishness, to the end of a contract which Dudley 'has been so presumptuous as to commit into two several writings and has set his name thereto written in his own blood as also his seal in the presence of witnesses.'[231]

Exposed to the world as the ridiculous dupe of a dangerous and manipulative woman, Dudley turned in fury on the object of his passion and poured out all his bitterness in another pamphlet – *Lettera Essortatoria di Mettere Opera a fare sincera Penintenza Mandata Alla Signora F. M. L. P. fugita Excommunicata per Caggione delle Enormita de suoi Misfatti egrandissimi falli* (Exhortatory Letter Urging the Course of doing sincere Penitence, addressed to the Lady F. M. L. P., an excommunicated fugitive on account of the Enormity of her Misdeeds, and vast faults).[232] The text, like its title, was twice as long as the earlier Vindication, and pulled no punches.

I have heard that you have reached the distinction of being the greatest example of shameless arrogance in the world, an impudent publiciser of her own ignominies, saucy in her speech, lascivious in her dress, petulant in her gestures, puffed up by a foolish belief in her imagined excellence, immodest in her deportment, dissolute in her habits, filled with the wind of tumid arrogance, that your Ladyship, having lost the honour of modesty, having trampled on the flower of pure chastity, having broken the restraints of shame, has been moved to put her modesty on the public market, that you are so far prey to sensual brutishness, and to the licentious excesses of pleasure, that you have broken, in the face of the sun, your obligatory faith with your husband with many impure lovers, to whom, with disinterested love, you dispensed your delights, while you planted on your good husband the horns of cuckoldry.

Dudley rejoiced in her departure, claiming that 'nothing is heard in the streets but shrieking and yelling at every corner, "Plunket the whore, the brothel-lash, has gone away, and may she never return." ' He vehemently denied having received any greater favours from her 'than the condition of a most chaste nun was capable of conceding to me,' and also denied that the infamous contract between them signified what Maria Francesca Lucretia had apparently claimed – 'As for our being married to one another, that is a lie and a calumny unworthy of a response.' His protests are too vehement to be entirely credible and at one point, when upbraiding his former mistress for her folly, Dudley sounds as if he is speaking from his own bitter experience. 'The pleasures which are taken illicitly may be full of flavour before they are had, while they are hoped for, or when they are enjoyed; but when they have been had, they are certainly tearful and painful.'

These confessional outpourings are those of a man betrayed, ashamed of his folly. His mistress, it seems, had deceived him with younger men, including a mysterious 'person of quality – a vengeful man, too strong for me to oppose, though I must try to save my honour.' There was no question of charitable forgiveness for either of them. 'My just defence saved me from punishment and disgraced your ladyship. As for the person of quality, may his heart now break and be incinerated in the flames of anger. I do not want to triumph too much, but the attack of the person of quality against myself was not that of a good Christian.'

Christian mercy was far from Dudley's heart and there are times when you realise that he relished the role of thunderer, cursing the damned. He even admitted as much after a particularly lurid passage, when he depicted 'the horrors of the infernal abysses' with unseemly relish, like a medieval Doom painter. 'Those torments will be equally extreme and eternal; but I have enjoyed myself too much, I return to pick up the thread.'

As so often with this strange character there is a sense that the pleasure of playing a part was sufficient to shape his actions, however foolish. Dudley was a chameleon. With instinctive theatricality he slipped from one role to another as easily as he switched tongues. The Cromwellian Puritan metamorphosed into the Restoration Anglican, of Romish persuasion. The scholar became the soldier, the lawyer the preacher, the lover the fool.

Even his legal judgements express this emotional ambivalence. Two of those decisions concerned key issues of sexual politics and were published by Dudley in pamphlet form – it would be hard to find a greater contrast of language and sympathy.

The first was the famous judgement that Loftus delivered in 1669, *In the Case of Ware and Shirly*.[233] This was one of those notorious abduction cases, so common in Irish history, in which an heiress had been seized by an impoverished 'gentleman', raped and forcibly married.[234] All too often such affairs were hushed up. Public sympathy tended to be greater for the abductors than their wretched victims, and judges would often take the view that the women had provoked their fate, and must now make the best of their plight – ruthless colonial expediency expressed in sexual arrogance. But Mary Ware had the courage to take the matter to court and the luck to have her case tried by Dudley Loftus. Not only did he unhesitatingly condemn her abductor, James Shirly, but he went out of his way to dismiss the snide rumours which surrounded the case – as they do so often in rape trials today.

Hence it is that this Ladies condition hath been drawn into debate, and though some persons and they of honour and judgement, hold it as evident a truth, as that the three angles of a triangle are equal to two right angles, that she is no whit prejudiced by her late misfortune, yet others seem to be of the opinion, that she is thereby brought under the suspition if not the presumption of worse dispositions, and a greater facility of temptation, and that therefore she is notably damnified in her reputation. The latter opinion seems to me too severe & grounded upon a temporary surmise, not to be warranted by any principle of piety or rule of chastity – and if there be any difference between the state of her untoucht virginity, and her new confirmed chastity of mind, as to the valuation it is almost like that of the starrs in the firmament whose different magnitudes are not perceptible to the most clear seeing eye.

Let no man discharge upon her innocency the misapprehensions of his wild fancy or untamed wit, let no man make her Rape farther matter of discourse, but rather let that misfortune be hidden under the veil of perpetual forgetfulness, let the Garland of chastity remain unwithered on her brow, let her flowrish in an honourable reputation while the Defendant deserves to have his goods confiscate and his Memory banished out of the world: and let her vertuous mind enjoy the quiet of a serene conscience, whilst his black Soul is left during Divine pleasure to the dismal horror of midnight dreams, to the terrors of the law, and the dreadful apprehensions of the day of judgement.

You can hear the echoes of a great and theatrical preacher in every phrase, but there is also a sense of emotional engagement and moral outrage.

In striking contrast was Loftus's judgement in October 1676, when he was asked to consider the case of Katherine Fitzgerald.[235] She had been 'married' by the Archbishop of Canterbury to John, Lord Decies (later the 2nd Earl of Tyrone), when he was eight and she was twelve; but two years later, when Katherine was fourteen – and therefore legally of age – she repudiated her betrothal and married Edward Villiers.[236] The matter came to court and judgement was given against the bride, based on highly technical points of matrimonial law – but the crux of Dudley's argument was that Katherine's childhood betrothal could only be renounced or confirmed by her 'husband', when he too came of age, and that her own consent was irrelevant. As in the case of Ware vs. Shirly, you can sense the preacher behind the judge, but Dudley's language had lost all the emotional sympathy of that earlier case. His tone was dry, hard, unforgiving, and he took as his text one of the cruellest edicts of the Book of Deuteronomy: 'If a Damsel is betrothed to an Husband, and a Man find her in the City, and lie with her: then ye shall bring them both out unto the Gate of that City, and ye shall stone them with stones, that they die.'

That startling emotional volatility was apparent throughout Dudley's life. Unpredictable changes of mood caused him to be suspected of Papism at one moment, or Puritan fury the next. On 24 Nov 1671 John Brennan, Bishop of Waterford, wrote to Cardinal Barberini in Rome, praising the Vicar General as a man who was very helpful to Catholics.[237] But the following year Loftus challenged the Earl of Essex's decision to relax the rules regarding the oath of supremacy – in order to admit some Catholics into the administration of Ireland – and became embroiled in a long and furious row over changes imposed by the Lord Lieutenant, intended to make the Mayor and Corporation of Dublin more subservient to his wishes. Dudley declared the new rules to be illegal – 'destructive to the liberties of the City' – and took his opposition to such extremes that eventually Essex lost patience.[238] On 2 September 1673 he issued a warrant to the Constable of Dublin Castle, ordering him 'to take Dr Dudley Loftus into custody' – but imprisonment did nothing to calm the doctor's fury. On 23 October Essex wrote to the English Secretary of State, Lord Arlington, complaining that:

> Dr Loftus, who, as I told you, was a principal incendiary, is still in custody, and his carriage has been such during his imprisonment as I cannot find any motives to induce His Majesty to show him favour, and indeed, though of great learning, he is so very indiscreet and unfit for employment, as I am confident it would be a service to the kingdom to have him laid aside. I have herewith sent a draft letter for His Majesty's signature directing that Dr Loftus be struck out of the establishment, and Dr John Topham, already a Master in Chancery, be inserted in his place.

Dudley was dismissed from the civil administration, only retaining his place as a judge in the Prerogative Court.[239]

Increasingly it seemed that Dudley's heart had closed against the world, and language was the mirror of his mood. Having turned away from Italian – the living language of love – he rediscovered his passion for long-forgotten tongues, the dead dialects of scholarship. Loftus resumed his contacts with distant Orientalists, most notably with William Sancroft, Archbishop of Canterbury, with whom he exchanged arcane snippets of information concerning the manuscripts of Dionysus Syrius, Abul-Pharagius and Moses Bar-Cepha – and with the great Oxford Arabist, Dr Pocock.[240] Their correspondence began in 1676 when Dudley announced the safe arrival of 'a Chaldee priest', sent by Pocock, whom he kept in his household for the next two years, in order to gain a living knowledge of the Nestorian rituals and language. That initial letter led to a lengthy exchange, almost impossible now to comprehend, because both were fascinated by scholarly problems of the utmost obscurity.[241]

While scanning an ancient biography of Pocock for trace of these obsessions, my eye slipped and I read a paragraph which referred to another of the learned Doctor's correspondents, Dr John Moore, who wrote to him on 3 January 1685, asking: 'Whether there be more evidence, than the affirmation of the Arabian in Dr Wallis's Arithmetic, by Dr Pocock translated, that the Egyptian Oeba, which is believed to be the Epha, was the sixth part of the Egyptian Ardob, which was the cube of the cubit?' After which mind-boggling query some previous reader had neatly written in pencil, 'God knows!' Immediately next on the page was a reference to a letter from Dr Loftus, comparing 'the variations of Dr Huntingdon's Syriac Abul Pharaji from Dr Pocock's Arabic'. So it continued.

As Dudley buried himself in arcane scholarship, glossing the margins of long-forgotten texts, he resembled a strange leviathan, beached on the shores of modernity – expiring from the sceptical air that gave life to this brave new world. The history of that stranding is written in the minutes of the Dublin Philosophical Society, which was founded in the autumn of 1683.[242] On 26 October that year, 'Dr Loftus discoursed concerning Père Simon's Histoire Critique.'[243] A fortnight later, on 12 November, 'the Lord Bishop of Ferns [Narcissus Marsh] produced a discourse concerning sounds and hearing, and compared them in many respects to images and seeing, he offered many curious proposals for advancing one, as t'other is advanced by optic glasses.'[244] The minutes, always terse, are nonetheless fascinating for what they reveal about the varying degrees of interest excited by the different speakers. Dudley took as his theme a matter of immediate controversy. Père Simon had argued that the scriptural texts were often debased and could only be understood through the commentaries of St Jerome and other critics – an argument that was strenuously opposed by most Protestants, who emphasised the primacy of scripture alone and looked to the primitive 'uncorrupted' texts as the purest source of revelation. The debate was fascinating to theologians and textual scholars but evidently bored his audience, whereas Narcissus Marsh – who pioneered the science of acoustics – held his listeners spellbound as he delivered the first draft of his famous *Essay on Sounds*.

It was a defining moment in the transition between the medieval world of speculation, centred on theology, and the new religion of experimental science. A minority of the Dublin Philosophical Society clearly believed that 'Philosophical' meant what it had always done – loving wisdom, implying moral purpose – but most of the founder members took a secularist view, that it was knowledge not wisdom that concerned them, or perhaps that wisdom would come from knowledge.

Their interest was practical scientific enquiry. This, from the start, became a battleground.

The nub of the argument was about money. Dudley and his allies saw no reason for rules or subscriptions, since it cost nothing to meet together for the purposes of philosophical discussion. For the 'scientists' (or 'mechanics', as Dudley termed them) subscriptions were essential to fund the practical experiments which, in their view, were the main purpose for the new society's existence. The scientists won and their leader, Sir William Petty – the great surveyor of Ireland – got together with a couple of like-minded friends to draw up a set of rules, modelled on those of London's Royal Society, of which Petty was a founder member.

The new rules were adopted at a meeting in January 1684, probably acrimonious, although the minutes are silent on the matter. They began with a declaration that 'the Society is to be called The Dublin Society, instituted for the improvement of useful knowledge in nature' – thus eliminating further debate about the meaning of philosophy – and continued by ordering that 'every fellow at his admittance be obliged to pay nine shillings or two cobs [the name given in seventeeth-century Ireland to the Spanish silver dollar, or 'piece-of-eight'], and ever after during his continuance in the society a weekly contribution of a quarter cob, for the defraying of all public charges of experiments, letters etc and other conveniences that are to be purchased.' It was also ruled that any member who 'shall defame or abusively expose this society' would be expelled.

Dudley had already left – having condemned the proposed rules as the 'fetters and yokes of bondage' – and was busy composing the first of a stream of venomous satires, *A Letter to a person concerning the Society*, which he circulated on 29 January. He sneered that:

> your politic man [Sir William Petty] hath lately, notwithstanding the preoccupations and prejudices in many mens hearts conceived against him, by a serpentine subtilty insinuated himself into credit with some novices in mechanic learning at this time not exceeding the number of twelve persons, most of whom are ecclesiastics, and the rest physicians and gentlemen (diversely qualified) so far as to join with him in the erecting of a society of mechanics.

The dispute continued for months, increasingly bitter, often ludicrous, but Dudley had a point when he referred to 'the brabbling shop of their useless curiosities' – for the Dublin Society never achieved the high reputation of its English progenitor, being far too liable to marvel at wonders (a chicken with two beaks), give credence to bizarre theories (that fossil trees were a particular species which had grown underground), or waste time with somewhat simplistic experiments. His mockery of the 'mechanics' is not far off the mark, despite some serious and valuable work of practical scientific interest.[245]

They justified his scorn when new rules were added to the Society's constitution, at Petty's behest, in November 1684. Rule 7 stated that 'they be ready to entertain strangers and persons of quality with great and surprising experiments of wonder and ostentation' – science as entertainment for potential sponsors. Rule 8 purged the ranks of dissenters: 'That they were not to pester the society with useless or troublesome members for the sake of sixpence a week.'

Farcical though it now seems, this was the beginning of the technological age.

As Dudley grew older, he became a figure of fun, striding round Dublin like some gaunt bird of prey, tattered and reckless. General opinion agreed with the 'very satyrical Reflection made by a great but free spoken Prelate, who was well acquainted with him, "That he never knew so much Learning in the Keeping of a Fool."[246]

That was a fleabite compared to the mockery Dr Loftus faced on 11 July 1688, when the twenty-year-old Jonathan Swift gave first public utterance to the 'savage indignation' that eventually consumed his mind. The academic year at Trinity College Dublin had ended, as usual, with the formal ceremonies of Commencement (typical inversion of common parlance) and it was time for some light relief – the traditional students' satire. This was the annual opportunity for new graduates to tease their erstwhile seniors, but the boundaries of the fool's licence were uncertain. Swift, it seems, decided to test those limits.

He spoke through the mouth of a friend – John Jones, one of that year's graduates – before a rowdy throng of fellow students, free at last from their studies, who were crowded into the Hall, together with the Fellows, professors and local worthies. Jones began his oration in the strangely accented Latin of scholarly discourse – interspersed with a few light-hearted asides in English – and his listeners laughed. Gradually, however, heads began to turn and mouths to mutter, as wit turned to insult and scatological abuse was heaped upon his elders by a master of the art, for Swift's text was scandalous.

That furious disgust enabled 'Jacky' Barrett, one of Trinity's most eccentric scholars, to recognise the satirist's hand and to write a brilliant *Essay*, which was entirely devoted to confirming Swift's authorship of this infamous 'Tripos'.[247] As a great Orientalist, Dr Barrett wrote with fastidious disdain of the fact that 'Swift delighted in the composition of barbarous Latin,' but his main attack was on the satirist's muck-racking.

> Nothing is more observable in the true and undisputed productions of Swift, than the pains which he seems to take in raking together the most nauseous ideas, and dwelling upon the most indelicate images. See the description of a college steward, wherein one passage can only be parallelled for filthiness with the Lady's Dressing Room, or the poem of Strephon and Chloe, or the character Swift gives of Primate M[ars]h; in all of which the same filth occurs: – see also the place where the author undertakes to describe the breeches of the infamous Barnard Doyle.

The stink of those breeches can be smelt even now, and several such passages in Swift's tirade still have the power to shock, but I am more interested in the portrait that he provides of another of his victims, Dr Loftus. This sketch of Dudley in his old age is a strange mixture of cruel mockery and half-admiring wonder, the verbal caricature of a brilliant scarecrow 'with short feet and rhinocerous nose'. It is the only likeness that survives of this extraordinary man.

> *Salvus sit inter socios juniores cum pedi brevi et naso rhinocertis,* who by his own sermon of angles and triangles has thrice shown his smattering in the mathematics . . .

The reference to angles and triangles shows that Swift had read the Doctor's writings with surprising attention, and perhaps with greater sympathy than he expressed – but sympathy turned to scorn when Swift switched to Latin, and expressed his most scathing insults in the language of formal courtesy.[248]

> *He is a mighty doctor of Civil Law, but a Polygamist, toothless but a*

Polyglot; so full of learning that the characters of every language are clearly inscribed in the lines of his face. It is in vain, therefore, o reverend doctor, that the envious mutter, saying that now, worn down by old age, you do not understand the eastern tongues – for your countenance is truly the index of your mind. Again and again let him be hailed, our grandiloquent elder, whom the Muse has given the round mouth of speech.

Because of his looks and eloquence we name him Ulysses; for Ulysses was not handsome but he had the gift of tongues.[*]

> No Tartar is more fair, no Athenian better hung,
> Sol varnish'd o'er his face, and Mercury his tongue.

That was a particularly vicious jibe, in plain English, for mercury was the traditional treatment for syphilis.

For his height let us salute him as Ajax, for his scrawniness as Tithonus, for his shaking head as the palsied Priam, for his swiftness as Achilles and finally (for his giant shanks), as the Colossus.

Of their own accord they hasten, it is hard to restrain them, or to put it in English,

> With aukward gown tuck'd up, he Scow'rs along,
> And at each stride measures a parasang.[249]

'The decent obscurity of a learned tongue' was for Dudley and most of his fellow academics no more than a transparent veil, as Swift well knew, and he ended the third act of his 'Tripos' with a plea for forgiveness – for he seems to have hoped, against all the odds, that even the grossest of his insults would provoke no more than token punishment. 'I have not left myself one friend in the mansion of Unrighteousness. Dr Loftus will bite me, Mr Loftus and Mr Lloyd will nose me.'

Had the satire been directed against Loftus alone, Swift might well have got away with it, but a coalition of his victims proved more powerful than this elderly eccentric, and the echoes of their fury continued for decades afterwards. In 1752 that discreetly indecent moralist Samuel Richardson, the author of *Pamela*, wrote to Lady

---

[*] Sections of this text in italics are those that have been translated from the original Latin.

Bradshaw, repeating the still vivid gossip which he had garnered from 'the son of an eminent divine, a prelate who was for three years what is called his chum' – that Swift 'raked up all the scandal against the Heads of that University, that a severe enquirer and still severer temper could get together in his harangue. He was expelled in consequence of his abuse.' In fact Swift was suspended rather than expelled, but the authorities had their revenge, and he never forgave them.

The stings of student satire were, nonetheless, soon forgotten – for Ireland was once again the battleground for English politics. It was a time of confusion and terror, vividly expressed in Dudley's letter from Dublin to Lord Clarendon, on 16 December 1688.

> The fear of Death and love of life have been the two most active passions wherwth the minds of men and women have been agitated of late in this place, insoemuch that the best able to fly out are departed hence into England, and those who are unable for flight stay behind. How far either of them will be justified the event yett doubtfull, will hereafter declare, in the mean time those who have taken the safest course are reputed the wisest & I hope that our good God, who is protector of both will preserve them both in their goeing and Staying.[250]

Dudley himself remained at home, and his letter to the Jacobite Clarendon was studiously non-committal as to his own allegiance, while recording that 'The Protestants of Londonderry have shutt up their Gates' and 'the Irish Catholiques are very buisie in raising of men, designeing a very numerous Army.' He clearly hoped that some sort of reconciliation could be achieved between the Catholic King James and his Protestant son-in-law, William of Orange, but it was already too late, and their struggle for power had spilled over into an Irish civil war that would not conclude for another three years.

So Dr Loftus returned to his studies, apparently oblivious to the world. He burrowed through the vast libraries of texts at his disposal, continued his correspondence with Primate Sancroft and made Latin translations of the Syriac commentaries of Gregory Maphrino. On 14 October 1690 he wrote to inform Pocock that 'during the late troubles in Ireland he had translated eight Syrian liturgies into Latin, and the

Ethiopic liturgy, together with the ancient form of prayer used in the primitive Church for the cure of diseases.'[251] The fascinating minutiae of primitive rituals had filled his mind to the exclusion of all else.

Loftus's long-suffering wife died at their house on Blind Key in 1691 and he himself was increasingly feeble, but three years later, at the age of seventy-six, he once more scandalised the world. Though 'very much impaired in his Parts and Memory, [he] married a second Wife.' This was Lady Elizabeth Irwin, who, it is said, caused him 'nothing but trouble and discord' and proved a litigious widow.[252] Worn out by this final folly, Dudley 'died the Year following in June 1695, aged Seventy-seven, and was buried in St.Patrick's Church, Dublin, leaving behind a large Library of all Sorts of Books.'[253]

These included manuscripts in Arabic, Armenian, French, Hebrew, Italian, Persian, Russian, Syriac and Welsh – as well as seminal works of Irish history and language, compiled by Catholic priests. Despite his sometimes violent prejudices, Dudley had a breadth of interest and love of his land unmatched by most of his contemporaries.

That unique library was saved by Archbishop Narcissus Marsh, who is the likeliest author of the damning judgement on Dudley, which I quoted earlier: 'that he never knew so much learning in the keeping of a fool.' Marsh, too, was an Orientalist and a student of Irish history, but he was also a mathematician and scientist. This remarkable man devoted much of his wealth to the endowment of learning, and particularly to the preservation of books and manuscripts relevant to his interests – in pursuit of which he made it his business, after Loftus's death, to acquire the old man's manuscripts from his widow. Most of these are now in the Bodleian at Oxford – together with a large part of Marsh's own vast Oriental collections – but some of the most interesting remain in Dublin, at the wonderful public library that Marsh built at his own expense, next to St Patrick's Cathedral.

Here, in the quiet antiquarian atmosphere of a building which has remained almost unchanged since 1701, you can read Dudley's hand-writing, noting the slow evolution from the neat notes of a young lawyer through the excited scrawls of an impetuous scholar, to the shaky jottings of old age. Here is a catalogue of his library, written in a feeble hand the year after Swift's public assault on him. It includes nine different editions of the Bible in various languages, several works in

Hebrew and the complete writings of the Venerable Bede. Here too is one of the books from that library, a tiny Hebrew lexicon, impossible to read without a magnifying glass, which was printed in 1631 and has Dudley's signature on the title page. Here is a fourteenth-century psalter that some patient monk must have copied, three centuries before Dudley acquired it, and the few surviving pages of a fifteenth-century manuscript from Rievaulx Abbey, in Yorkshire, and a collection of Slavonic poems, and a medical *vade mecum – The Makyng of Medecines And ther Vertues, Taken out of the Fyve Bokes which Leonard Fuschius made to cure all diseasys* (1557), which includes a couple of recipes at the end, in Dudley's hand. And here, most celebrated of all, are two famous seventeenth-century manuscripts written by Irish priests – Geoffrey Keating's *History of Ireland* and Richard Plunkett's *Gaelic & Latin Dictionary*.

But far more interesting to me than any of these is the large leather-bound volume in which Dudley wrote his own *Annals Civil and Ecclesiastical relating to the History of Ireland*.[254] Nothing more clearly illustrates the fascinations of his magpie mind, so greedy for glittering trinkets, than this strange assortment of wonders, anecdotes and seemingly random snippets of information.

> 1556 This year thir appeared for many nights out of the north a starre wch did ghout [gush] like a Spoot [spout].
>
> 1560 This year was ye quart of Gascoyn wine for ye ob: [halfpenny] and ye quart of Ale for 2*d*.:ffarth and ye Peck of wheat for 50 testors.
>
> 1571 This year ye art of printing and casting, and Characters of ye Irish tongue began in Ireland in ye City of Dublin.
>
> 1582 Dr Sanders ye popes nuncio Died in a wood being half starved of a Cloudy flux. None could come hardly to him by reason yt ye wood was full of Briars & thornes, where his body was at Last become a prey to ye wolves.

And so it continues until 1629, when the entries stop – though the last date for which a page is provided is 1643, as if Dudley had been distracted and set off on another goose chase, and never returned.

The two wives of Adam Loftus, Viscount Lisburne.

RESTORATION & REVOLUTION

CHAPTER 16

A Tangled Web

At around three o'clock on the afternoon of Tuesday 10 February 1663, Dudley Loftus walked the few yards from his house on Blind Quay to the theatre in Smock Alley, founded the previous year by his friend John Ogilby. He was on his way to the first performance of a new play, a production of *Pompey* translated from the French by Katherine Philips, 'the Matchless Orinda'.

During her visit to Dublin Mrs Philips was taken up by the Boyles and wrote her translation while staying in the household of the Countess of Cork, where she became a favourite of her three daughters, the Ladies Elizabeth, Anne and Frances Boyle – 'the lovely Celimena', 'the adored Valeria' and 'Amestris'. Such fanciful names were typical of those given to the women – and a few favoured men – who were adopted by 'Orinda' into her Society of Friends, a coterie of mutual affectation not untypical of the times. Katherine wrote several loving verses to the Boyle sisters and an enchanting poem celebrating the bravery and gentleness of 'The Irish Grey-hound', as the huge wolf-hounds were then called. And then to amuse herself – and perhaps to impress her new friends – she translated a scene from the third act of Corneille's *Pompey*. This caught the attention of Lord Cork's politician brother, Roger Boyle, Earl of Orrery, who fancied himself as a play-wright and patron of the arts.

By some Accident or another my scene of Pompey fell into his Hands, and he was pleas'd to like it so well, that he sent me the

French Original; and the next time I saw him, so earnestly importun'd me to pursue that Translation, that to avoid the Shame of seeing him who had so lately commanded a Kingdom, become a Petitioner to me for such a Trifle, I obeyed him.'[255]

Orrery was determined to see the new translation staged in fitting style, so he 'advanc'd a hundred Pounds towards the Expense of buying Roman and Egyptian Habits' and persuaded the poet and duellist Earl of Roscommon – recently married to his niece, Lady Frances Boyle – to write the prologue, which called on the Lord Lieutenant, the Duke of Ormond, to show his favour. The classical restraint of Corneille's original was embellished with *entr'acte* songs composed by Katherine and set to music by various influential friends, with elaborate dances choreographed by the theatre's manager and former dancing master, John Ogilby. And an epilogue was provided by Sir Edward Dering, 'the noble Silvander', whose wife Mary had been a friend of Katherine Philips since they were at school together. With such a web of social interest, success seemed guaranteed.

By half past three in the afternoon, when the curtain rose on the first performance, the tiny theatre was crammed to bursting. The Lord Lieutenant and his wife, the Duke and Duchess of Ormond, their daughter Lady Mary Cavendish, 'the bright Policrite', and most of the leaders of Dublin society were seated in their boxes. Among numerous Boyles and their connections we can probably include Orrery's nephews, Adam Loftus and his cousin Richard Jones, with their glamorous young wives. Adam's mother, the redoubtable Dorothy Boyle, would certainly have been there, possibly accompanied by Adam's youngest sister Jane and her husband Robert Gorges – the future biographer of their eccentric uncle, Dr Dudley Loftus. Dudley himself would never have missed an occasion of this sort, but I doubt that he brought his wife. The Advocate General, Dr Pett, must certainly have found a seat, for he had composed the music to one of Orinda's songs, and most likely invited his friend Sir Nicholas Armourer – head of the King's Guard – who loved the theatre. And Sir Nicholas may have been accompanied by his Ensign, the hapless Bromley, who was killed in a duel a few days later by Adam Loftus. Most were connected, in one way or another, by kinship or money. Dublin was a tiny, incestuous world.

This tangled web of relationships was the basis of power, wealth and influence – and of a gaudy arrogance that stares out at us from the portraits of those times. It gave this small, close-knit class a sense of privileged immunity, however outrageously they behaved. But mapping those connections is like trying to plot several hundred intersecting lines in three dimensions – so I decided to select a few threads from the rest and trace their paths through the maze.

My own copy of Katherine Philips's *Poems* – including her translation of *Pompey* – is that which originally belonged to another Katherine, Lady Ranelagh, most brilliant of all the Boyles. She left her mark in the form of a wonderful seventeenth-century binding – black leather, intricately tooled and gilded. The book then passed to her granddaughter, Frances Jones, who inscribed her name on the endpapers, in her youthful, unmarried hand. But stamped in gold on the cover, oblivious to its defacement of the earlier binder's art, is the seal of her husband, Lord Coningsby. Each of these successive marks tells its own story.[256]

Let us begin with Lady Ranelagh, the seventh of fifteen children of Richard Boyle, the 'Great Earl' of Cork – and mother of Richard Jones, of whom more anon. It was in her eldest brother's household in Dublin that 'Orinda' stayed while translating *Pompey*, and it was thanks to a younger brother, the Earl of Orrery, that the play was staged. One of their sisters, Dorothy Boyle, had married Sir Arthur Loftus of Rathfarnham Castle – which brought his family into the vast network of Boyle cousinage. Their marriage produced a single surviving son, the impetuous Adam, and a string of daughters. The eldest of these girls, Letitia Loftus, married an English West Country landowner, Humphrey Coningsby, and bore him a son called Thomas, while the youngest, Jane, married Dr Robert Gorges of Dublin. One of Robert's nieces, Amy Gorges, married Henry Loftus of the Hook, while another, the tempestuous Barbara, was Thomas Coningsby's first wife. His second was Frances Jones, his cousin.

Between marriages, Thomas Coningsby conducted two notorious affairs. He briefly eloped with Frances Cecil (wife of his neighbour Lord Scudamore) before she was forced to return to her husband, at pistol-point. He then seduced another Cecil, Lady Scudamore's cousin Margaret, the young second wife of Richard Jones, Viscount Ranelagh (son of Katherine Boyle). Coningsby and Lady Ranelagh were found in bed together by her husband when he returned home unexpectedly – 'at which sight he said nothing, but withdrew very civilly, and went downstairs about his business.'[257] He was less civil a few weeks later, when Coningsby abandoned his new mistress for her stepdaughter, Ranelagh's daughter Frances Jones, whom he married in the teeth of her father's fury.

Triumphant in his conquest, Coningsby had his armorial seal stamped in gold on the covers of his new wife's books, including the copy of Orinda's *Poems* that lies beside me as I write. His motto *Vestigia Nulla Retrorsam* means 'There's no turning back'. As I deciphered those gilded words I was reminded of a darker version, from the lines of *Pompey*. 'Who fears a Crime shall ever be afraid, But he'll rule all, who dares all things invade.'

CHAPTER 17

The Golden Ball

Gallant, gambler, duellist and bounty hunter – Adam Loftus was the wild father of an infamous daughter. The history of his life is a series of dramatic snapshots, flashes in darkness, which ends in a sudden explosion.

Born around 1635, Adam was the heir to power and influence (grandson of another Adam Loftus, the Vice Treasurer of Ireland, and of Richard Boyle, the mighty Earl of Cork) and was saved by those connections, again and again, from the penalties of his own recklessness. But the family lineage was a mixed blessing – for Adam combined Loftus eccentricity and Boyle arrogance, to a dangerous degree.

His father's family was rich with oddities. Great-Uncle William 'died a Religious in Spain' and Uncle Dudley was the famously eccentric Orientalist, while another Dudley (Adam's cousin) broke resolutely through the family circles and 'married a Russia Lady' – which reminds me of that marvellous episode when Orlando courts a Russian princess on the frozen Thames and ditches his betrothed, 'one of the Irish Desmonds'. Even the dates are close, in the parallel world of Virginia Woolf's imagination. Adam himself seems like a violent cousin of that later Orlando, the Restoration courtier who caused Nell Gwyn to sigh, and 'walked through the house with his elk-hounds following and felt content.'

As for the Boyles, you need look no further than the family monument in St Patrick's Cathedral – a shrine to dynastic pride, in all its tasteless glory.

On 12 May 1657 Captain Adam Loftus was paid his bounty (a Treasury Warrant for £20) for capturing one of the most wanted of the Irish 'Tories', Daniel Kennedy, and cutting off his head – which he sent to Catherlough, where it was 'set up on the castle walls, to the terror of other malefactors'.[258] It's a brutal glimpse of a merciless war and its aftermath, the Cromwellian 'pacification' of Ireland.

There are parallels with the 'ethnic cleansing' of the Balkans. A programme of transplantation forced Irish Catholics from their homes, as ruthless 'Adventurers' (English or Scottish in origin, Protestant in religion) seized for themselves most of the valuable lands east of Connaught. Vast numbers of native Irish were uprooted to the poor, boggy west, and those who remained were reduced to beggary – divided from their masters by ancestry, religion and language. But the losers included powerful families, particularly the Catholic 'Old English' – dispossessed for their loyalty to the Stuart cause and determined on vengeance.

Their moment came, or so it seemed, with the Restoration of Charles II in 1660. The new King was known to be sympathetic to Catholics and many in Ireland expected him to recompense his friends for their sufferings on his behalf. There was a scramble of claimants for Irish property as every opportunist fought for royal favour. Royalists and Catholics evicted under Cromwell sought redress for their wrongs, while the Cromwellian incumbents of their estates were determined to retain possession – and there were countless accusations of hidden treachery. Protestant grandees like Adam Loftus needed swiftly to launder their allegiance.

Most of his relatives had supported Cromwell during the Civil War, despite their subsequent protestations of continued Royalist loyalty – but the family was too well entrenched for the new government to risk vindictive reprisals, and Charles II was a realist. When Adam's uncle, the Earl of Orrery, included his name in a long list of Irish gentry that he presented to the King with a request for specific pardon – over and above the general amnesty for those of dubious loyalty – Charles immediately agreed. On 30 April 1661 he ordered that, 'This pardon shall be enrolled in the acts of the Council and shall be favourably construed.'[259] Secure in his place in the world, Adam Loftus arranged to have himself elected Member of the Irish Parliament for the borough of Lismore – through the influence of Orrery's brother, the second Earl of Cork.

It was too good to last. On 25 February 1663 Winston Churchill (father of the first Duke of Marlborough) wrote to the English Secretary of State, Henry Bennet, with news that he clearly hoped might serve the latter's interests.

I am sorry to say that Mr Bromley, Sir N. Armorer's ensign, was killed last week in a duel by a Mr Loftus, a nephew of Lords Cork and Orrery. As the wound was under the left pap it is said that he did not meet with a fair adversary and was found with his sword in his scabbard. Mr Loftus' second [his cousin, Dudley Bagenal] was a worthy man. The estates of either are temptations to the friends of the deceased to prosecute.[260]

Churchill was one of the commissioners of the Act of Settlement of 1662, resolving the claims of those who had lost their lands during the Cromwellian confiscations. The Act was vague and its administration was necessarily a process of rough justice – which provided plenty of opportunities for men like him to act as scavengers for the great political vultures, such as Bennet. This man of influence, soon to become the Earl of Arlington, was avaricious for land and infamously corrupt – even acting as the King's procurer to further his own ends – and his cold, formal manner concealed a tenacious predator, on the lookout for rich pickings. As soon as he learnt of Adam's duel he tried to stake a claim to his inheritance, the valuable Rathfarnham estate.

One of Bennet's principal allies in Ireland was Colonel Richard Talbot, who later became Lord Lieutenant, as Earl of Tyrconnel. Talbot was a powerful Catholic and protégé of the King's brother James – who was determined to reverse the Protestant Ascendancy in Ireland by packing the government with Catholics and redistributing Protestant estates to his supporters, when any excuse could be found to do so – and Talbot was ruthless in pursuing this policy to his own advantage. He wrote regularly to Bennet, with details of valuable estates which his agents had discovered might be vulnerable to seizure for one reason or another, proposing to share the spoils in return for Bennet's assistance – but Rathfarnham, it seems, was beyond their reach. Talbot wrote on 25 March 1663 to warn the Secretary of State that powerful protectors were at work.

The Lord Lieutenant [the Earl of Ormond] has heard from you touching a grant which you said you had got, or were to get, of Mr Loftus' estate, and is sorry he cannot help you in it as Mr Loftus is nephew to the Earls of Cork and Orrery. I fear that opposition to it is here so great that it may prejudice you in the matter of Clanmalier's

estate, which is four times as great. I advise you to drop Loftus'
matter till you are sure of Clanmalier.[261]

Three days later Ormond himself wrote to Bennet, to warn him off.
Even if Loftus was found 'guilty to the degree of forfeiture', his estate
was 'so settled by conveyance and so charged with debts and portions,
and a jointure, that his interest is inconsiderable' – and in any case 'the
disobligation would extend to a huge alliance he has by his mother, who
is sister to the Earl of Cork.' Bennet was reluctant to take the hint,
forcing Ormond to write again, a month later, with the clear instruction
that Loftus 'should not be treated with undue severity, as he is a young
man'.[262]

Despite this protection, Adam himself was fearful of vengeance –
perhaps because he had indeed killed Bromley before the latter had a
chance to defend himself, or because the survivor of any duel was
liable to legal proceedings. He fled abroad – his name is included in a
list of Members of the Irish Parliament who were absent from Ireland,
in March 1664 – and it was not until early in January 1666 that a
memorandum was presented to the King on his behalf.[263] A few days
later Charles II formally ordered that Adam be discharged 'from being
burnt on the hand for the manslaughter of John Bromley' and that 'his
recogizances, which have been estreated to the Court of Exchequer in
Ireland, shall be cancelled and released to him.'[264] The threat of
forfeiture, or worse, was finally lifted.

Emboldened by his return to favour, Loftus decided to push his luck
and petitioned the King for payment of £2783 6s. 9d. that he claimed
had been owed him by the English government since 1652.[265] It took
a daring man to demand a Cromwellian debt from the perennially
mortgaged monarch – there is, alas, no record of the royal response –
and 'Addy' compounded that recklessness when he came to Court with
a huge, brindled wolf-dog, spoiling for a fight.

The tale is told in a letter from Lord Conway to his brother-in-law,
Sir George Rawdon (who managed Conway's estate in Ireland) dated
London 29 October 1667.

We had yesterday an unfortunate passage. Addy Loftus brought an
Irish dog to fight with a mastiff before the King; the Irish dog had all

the advantage imaginable, and dragged him 5 or 6 times about the ring, so that everybody gave the mastiff for dead; all men were concerned as if it had been their General, yet at last the Irish dog run away; I lost my money; and afterwards the King called me to him, and said he would lay £500 that neither I nor all the men in Ireland could bring an Irish wolf dog that would not run away. I pray speak with my Lord Dungannon about it, for tho' I will not upon any man's confidence venture so much money, yet I am willing to go my share, and I am sure the King will lay it. I pray speak with my Lord Lieutenant, and know what dogs he hath, and enquire amongst all your friends, for I would fain recover the credit of our country.[266]

You can hear the aristocratic drawl in every word; in the familiar reference to 'Addy' Loftus, the enthusiasm for blood sports, fever for gambling. Conway continues his letter with the latest political gossip, plus a note about some crates of trees, plants and seeds that he is sending back for his garden at Lisburn, having paid £14 for the lot. It is the authentic voice of courtly society, of which 'Addy' was a dashing habitué.

So too was Adam's wife, the daughter of Lord Chandos, whose portrait by Lely was reproduced as a popular engraving – the image of a Restoration beauty of uncertain morals. Lucy Loftus was 'somewhat remarkable for her gallantries' (according to my great-uncle Jack) and Lucia, the only surviving child of her marriage to Adam Loftus, was even more disreputable. Lacking any pretensions to real beauty – she inherited the Loftus nose – Lucia was sufficiently alluring to attract the wicked Thomas Wharton, whom she married, and a succession of high-born lovers. Like mother, like daughter.

Adam, at any rate, seemed somewhat loosely attached to his wife and was devoted to the pleasures of the chase – wherever he found them. On 7 May 1671 the strait-laced William Aglionby wrote to Lady Paston, while on a tour of France as tutor to her son: 'Saumur swarms with English; there are my Lady Holland with Adam Loftus and my Lord, Sir Robert Atkins and his lady, a coach and six horses, a pack of hounds and half-a-dozen stable horses, and divers other private gentlemen.'[267] The sense of disapproval at such an ostentatious entourage is compounded by the hint that Loftus was accompanying Lady Holland as her acknowledged lover, with the complaisant acquiescence of her husband – or perhaps I am reading too much into a careless conjunction of words.

By the middle of the following year Adam was back in Ireland, recruiting for a regiment commanded by the King's dashing but unreliable bastard, the Duke of Monmouth, to serve in France. Monmouth was a dangerous claimant to the throne (the choice of many who feared the Catholic succession of the King's brother James) and to be his friend tempted royal disfavour, but Adam's extraordinary luck continued to hold, for it was the King himself who wrote to the Lord Lieutenant, ordering him to 'give all needful warrants to Capt. Adam Loftus for raising 500 volunteers, for the Duke of Monmouth's regiment, as also for their marching, quartering and transportation to Dunkirk.'[268]

Only his relatives, it seems, disapproved of him – for about this time, in a letter from Rathfarnham, he mentioned a severe family affliction. His aunt, the Puritan spinster Grizzel, had died on 9 February 1672 – so scandalised by Adam's behaviour that she wrote a will which bequeathed only minor trinkets to a host of relatives and left the valuable bulk of her estate to her minister, Mr Isaac Smith. As for the King, he was blind to Addy's faults. On 24 October 1674 he appointed Loftus to be 'Ranger and Master of the Game of Phoenix Park, near Dublin, and of all the King's Parks, Forests, Chaces and Woods in Ireland' – a pleasant sinecure, which he held for about a year.[269]

But Grizzel was right to disapprove, for Adam's friends were a rackety lot – courtiers and aristocrats, linked by an intricate web of kinship, whose habits were fashionable, arrogant and expensive. Among the most shameless was Adam's cousin Richard Jones, Viscount Ranelagh, one of the greatest embezzlers of a corrupt age. In 1671 this amazing con man persuaded King Charles to let him take complete personal charge of the state finances of Ireland – collecting the revenues and paying the bills, and making further cash payments to the King. He wisely honoured the last part of his agreement, but left a string of debts and deficits that wrecked the Irish finances. Ranelagh's 'undertaking' ended in 1675 but the clamour for explanations pursued him for years afterwards, to no satisfactory result – and somehow this slippery fraudster managed to pull the trick again, on an even bigger scale, when King William appointed him Paymaster General of England in 1691. He stole £70,000 from the Treasury, but once again escaped prosecution.

Ranelagh was a gambler, whose patronage was dangerous, but Adam was his cousin's crony. He shared in the spoils of office and he shared his patron's enemies, as the stakes were raised – for the gossip, scandal and politics of life at Court were increasingly shadowed by fear, as ruthless opportunists used the so-called 'Popish Plot' to denounce their political foes. Rumours of a Catholic conspiracy to kill the King, massacre Protestants and bring James Duke of York to the throne multiplied out of control, generating a mood of mass hysteria. Many innocent men were convicted on perjured evidence and summarily executed – almost all were part of that small, intimate circle that 'Addy' knew so well.

At first Ranelagh seemed strangely unconcerned at the fate of his friends. He wrote to his cousin Viscount Conway, in July 1679, announcing that he had finally signed his version of the accounts for his Irish enterprise and was off to Dublin, to confront his detractors on the spot. 'Loftus has promised to accompany me, and we heartily wish you were idle enough to go with us. To-morrow Sir George Wakeman will be tried, and yesterday Langhorne was executed, dying most resolutely.'[270] A few days later he mentioned that 'Wakeman and four others were acquitted yesterday, at which the Queen is well pleased' – but continued (almost in the same breath) to discuss his journey to Ireland, which he intended to break at Ragley, Conway's estate in Warwickshire.

> I hope I shall have both your coach and your company [to the port of Chester] and, when you are so near that happy country of Ireland, I heartily wish your good nature may carry you further if for no other reason, at least to show Gwyn [cousin of Conway and royal courtier] how much our country is better than his. Loftus tells me that he will bear me company, but I am afraid the boxes and dice of London will detain him.[271]

But it was Loftus who left for Ragley while Ranelagh was detained at Court – by matters more grave than the seductions of gambling. As he told Conway in an agitated note, scribbled at midnight on 27 August, the King was dangerously ill. 'Should he miscarry, which God forbid, it would not be safe to be away.'[272] The news alarmed Adam Loftus, who sent a morose letter to his patron, but the crisis passed and Ranelagh set off for the West Country, stopping on the way to write a cheerful note to Conway. 'I intend to dine with you at Ragley tomorrow, where I hope to find Squire Loftus in better humour than when he wrote to me. The King is finely recovered but does not yet go out of his chamber.'[273] Adam and his cousin set off for Ireland, where Ranelagh scandalised the world by living openly with his mistress, 'Cocky' Wright, while defying his enemies to prove the frauds alleged against him, as if invulnerable.

But Loftus himself was suspected of financial misdeeds and was summoned back to England in January 1680, to answer charges before the Board of Green Cloth.[274] He wrote to Conway with the latest news, clearly apprehensive. 'Lord Ranelagh and his miss make much discourse in Dublin, more than his undertaking. He meets with many rubs, and I apprehend he will be extremely uneasy in his great concerns. Great things are threatened and I fear some will fall heavy.'[275] Adam was relieved when he learnt that the affair with Cocky Wright was over, but the parting was painful, for she left Ranelagh with an infection, which detained him in Dublin. Lacking his patron's protection, Adam decided to avoid the intrigues of Court. 'Mr Loftus and his fair lady are settled for this season at Kew. Lord Ranelagh would fain come over, for the Irish air is not good for his health, as 'tis said to be at present, and Mistress Wright has left him, but the hands of the physicians are still upon him and, I fear, shackle him too fast.'[276]

Adam may have chosen to lie low because he had lost the confidence of powerful friends, in the feverish atmosphere provoked by Titus Oates and his fictitious 'Popish Plot'. Sir Richard Newdigate, Chief Justice of the King's Bench, was one of those accused of involvement in the Plot and wrote to Conway on 28 September 1680, 'miserably tormented with the toothache' and indignant at 'the abominable foul play' that he had recently suffered. 'Notwithstanding all the malicious contrivances of my adversaries, my innocence was vindicated, the particulars of which I will, the first opportunity acquaint you with, as well as our transactions relating to Mr Loftus, who has receded from all his own proposals.'[277] There is no explanation, but a few weeks later it was alleged that 'a Mr Dalton, an Irish Papist, [who] was or had been steward to one Esquire Loftus' had 'tampered with Madame Cellier in suborning perjury about the plot.'[278] Suspicions alone were sufficient to damn greater men than Adam, in those dangerous days.

Was he a rogue or a rascal, unreliable scamp or treacherous opportunist? It's impossible now to answer. Whatever the truth of the matter, Adam retired to Ireland and sulked, because the fall from favour had cost him his dearest dreams; he was still a 'Mister', not a Lord. But yet he schemed, and when Conway was appointed Secretary of State for the North, early in 1681, Adam staked his claim. On 22 February he wrote from Rathfarnham, offering his congratulations and asking a favour.

> If ever I was ambitious of any title of honour, you were the first that proposed it to me and by your recommendation to the late Treasurer I had been successful, had not the revolutions of times and persons been so extraordinary. Last summer I revived my pretensions and had the Duke's assurance that the King had granted my request and that I might depend on it, whenever I pleased, but then you may remember on what a sudden the Duke [the future King, James Duke of York] went to Scotland and in what confusion affairs have been since.[279]

Loftus was disgruntled, because 'I see letters every post of Irish honours granted, as lately to Lord Wotton and a younger son of Lord Anglesey,' and he was prepared to back his case with cash. 'I know you will not be displeased in effecting this proposal, if another friend of yours may be obliged, who in his way may forward this design, I mean your friend Progers, to whom I engage myself to present 500 *guineas* on the accomplishment.'

Once again, nothing came of it; so Adam consoled himself with a second marriage. On 16 April 1681 Francis Gwyn had written to Ormond with the news that 'Mr Loftus's wife is lately dead in France,' and shortly afterwards Adam was betrothed to Dorothy, daughter of Patrick Allen. She was stylish, seductive and probably rich.

Finally, after all, the accession of James II brought Adam his heart's desire, for the new King purchased allegiance at the cost of honours.

Loftus was 'advanced to the Peerage by Privy Seal, dated Whitehall 5th January 1685, and by Patent, the 29th of that Month, by the Titles of Baron of Rathfarnham and Viscount Lisburn; and had a pension of £300 a year on the military establishment, commencing 1st January, 1687.' Conway may well have played some part in this ennoblement, judging by the title that Adam chose – for Lisburn was Conway's Irish estate.

Loyalty lasted little more than a year, as the new Viscount Lisburn (like most of the Protestant Ascendancy) welcomed the 'Glorious Revolution' and the accession of William of Orange. He wrote immediately to the new King, claiming that he had always served his cause and 'been so many ways persecuted for doing so' – and requested that he might be appointed Minister to the French Court.[280] The plea went unanswered, but Adam supported William in the Irish wars and commanded a regiment of foot at the taking of Carrickfergus, on 28 August 1689. Military life perhaps took second place to the pursuit of pleasure, for a confidential report, after the review at Dundalk in October 1689, claimed that 'the Col. puts himself out very little and in an extravagant style. He is also too fond of his bottle.' Adam nonetheless served with distinction at the Battle of Aughrin, in July 1691, and at Limerick, on 15 September, he met his fate.

A contemporary *Diary of the Siege of Limerick* records his end.

We continued all this day to Bomb and Batter the Town, and made the Breaches so wide, that we could plainly see into the Town, which looked Ruinous. The Enemy made much Sod-works, and a very deep Trench or Ditch with Pallisadoes and Stockadoes, yet the Men continued impatient to Storm it. About 3 this afternoon the Lord *Lisburne* was unfortunately killed by a Cannon Ball from the Town, as he was coming out of his *Tent*, which he had placed in the *Trenches*. This Evening our Cannon were thrice discharged, and our Army made several Vollies, in Demonstration of their Joy for the great Defeat given to the *Turks* by the *Emperours Forces*. This night we again Fired the Town, which burnt furiously for two hours.

Another eyewitness was the Rev. George Story, chaplain to Thomas Gower's regiment of foot, who published his *Impartial History of the Wars in Ireland* in 1693. Here is his account.

That Afternoon my Lord *Lisburne* then upon Duty with his Regiment, to the Left of the Great Battery, his Lordship having laid himself down to rest in a little Trench-Tent, just in raising up was unfortunately shot by a great Gun from one of the Enemies Batteries; being a Man of excellent Parts, and who had shewed himself very diligent and forward upon all Occasions, since the beginning of this War.

Yet another history of the siege (written by a Jacobite sympathiser) tells us that Adam 'was a remarkable zealot for the Prince of Orange' and claims, with evident satisfaction, that 'the cannon ball cut his head clean off.'[281]

None of these contemporary witnesses mentions the dying words attributed to Adam, ninety years after the event, by the eighteenth-century genealogist John Prestwick, who was employed by a Loftus descendant to embellish the family tree. Prestwick wrote what his patron wanted to read: that Adam was a Protestant hero, who died gloriously and was honoured on the field of battle.

He was Encouraging his brave men with these remarkable Words. SOLDIERS! AS WE FIGHT UNDER GOD FOR THE DEFENCE OF OUR RELIGION AND LIBERTY SO LET US CONQUER OR LIKE MARTYRS DIE, IN THIS GLORIOUS CAUSE. By Order of the Great King William his body was ordered to be placed in the Middle of the Field and over which he caused a Royal tent to be pitched, which was hung with Mourning and garnish'd with Military Ensigns and other tokens of Honour. Here the Corpse lay in State and after a proper time was removed to the City of Dublin and buried 28th September 1691 in St Patrick's Cathedral.

Alas for truth. The Great King William was far away in England when Adam rose from his 'little Trench-Tent' and was silenced by a cannonball, at three o'clock in the afternoon. There was no dying speech, no royal tent hung with mourning, no lying-in-state in the middle of the field of battle. But something stranger than Prestwick's fiction was recorded a few years after Adam's death by the eccentric London bookseller, John Dunton, who visited Rathfarnham Castle and was prompted to note down 'what I have been told of the late Lord Lisburn.'[282]

That lord, who was the first of his family that was ennobled, in his younger days when the heate of youth perhaps made him doe things not verie accountable for on some occasion (tho I think nothing could be a just one), struck his father, as they say, on his head and made him bleed. The old gentleman wiped his blood with his handkercheif and long after, on his death bed, left his son the cloath stain'd with the blood his hand had drawn from him. No doubt but twas a verie mortyfieing legacy. And this same son who was after made a lord, at the last siedge of Limrick, had his head and one hand, as he was putting on his crevat in his tent dasht in peices with a cannon bullet. You may make what inferences you please from this true story but for this unfortunate lord, he was lookt upon here as a true English protestant and of as much if not more dareing bravery than any nobleman shewed in its cause. He was buried in St Patricks, and I was assur'd by one of the auditors that the late Arch-Bpp of Dublin who preacht his funerall sermon (for no funeral ever shewed so much pomp in Dublin as his) did say that the cannon ball first gently kist his hand and whispering him in the eare sayd Great Sir you are no more; and had it been a golden ball he had deserved it.

And then, even stranger, the instrument of his death did indeed become a golden ball, for 'His friends gott the bullett, that had killed him, to be guilded, and to be hung over his tomb in the Cathedral church of Dublin dedicated to St Patrick the apostle of that kingdom; and this to stand a monument of his good affection and fidelity to that usurper. A folly in Grain!'[283]

'In grain', ingrained, everlasting – that mysterious phrase has a curiously appropriate lineage, for it derives from the dried bodies of cochineal insects, resembling grains, which produced the most durable of scarlet dyes, bright as blood. And the once-gilded cannonball, ingrained with rust, hangs there still, suspended over Adam's grave.[284]

CHAPTER 18

On the Hook

The Parish of Hooke is a narrow tract of land, jetting southward into the sea, surrounded with great shelves and Rocks; upon the uttermost point whereof stands a high tower called the tower of Hooke, which is made use of now as a light-house to direct ships into ye River of Waterford and Rosse. The soyle within this Parish of Hooke is good lime and stone ground: it yields good wheate and excellent white pease and good pasture, and is naturally inclined to yield furrs, but noe trees of any kind will grow there except preserved with great cost and art, by reason of ye sea winds, and bleake situation. The Parish belongs at present to Henry Loftus Esqre who has *repaired ye old Mancion House there*, lying on the East shore of ye River of Waterford, aforesaid, and added other considerable buildings of lime and stone thereunto, and inclosed his gardens with high stone walls to preserve some fruit trees newly planted there, and dwells in that house now. It was formerly called 'Redmond's Hall' from ye old proprietor, it is now called Loftus Hall. Mr. Loftus is now building a key for fishing boats, on the East side of ye said tract of land or pen-insula neere a place called ye Slade.

ROBERT LEIGH OF ROSEGARLAND, 1684[285]

That limestone quay, built by Henry Loftus, continues to shelter the tiny harbour at Slade but the old *Mancion House* was demolished in the nineteenth century to make way for a vast, gloomy pile, which dominates the horizon for miles around. Little now remains of Henry's building work except the 'high stone walls' that once protected his fruit trees, the dry-stone walls that still enclose the fields and some of the tall granite piers, topped with massive balls, that marked the avenue to the house, the gates of the deer park and the entrance to the demesne. It was here, at Portersgate, that Henry proclaimed his ownership, engraved in stone for all to see: 'Henry Loftus of Loftus Hall, Esq. 1680.'

There is a sense of proud satisfaction in those words, the mark of a man who outlived seven brothers and four nephews to inherit this windswept promontory, which he gradually transformed into a richly productive estate. The same inscription identifies a portrait by Garret Morphy, which Henry commissioned to celebrate his new house. Morphy painted him wearing one of those 'monstrous Perrucqs', fashionable at the time, and it is only when you recover from its absurdity that you notice the elegant cut of his grey coat, the brilliant scarlet of his fur-lined cloak, the casually knotted linen scarf about his neck and the face of a man who could preserve his dignity even when crowned with a mountain of ringlets. Absorbed in his steady stare, I forget the wig and recognise the strange familiarity of those determined, slightly melancholy features. The eyes, the eyebrows, the mouth; gazing at Henry's face seems more and more like looking in the mirror. That beaked nose, grander than mine, has recurred in every generation of the family, before and since.

Henry Loftus was forty-three when his portrait was painted, but looks older. It is hard to recall that this Protestant grandee, master of his blusterous kingdom, was once the young Ensign 'Harry' whom his father summoned in haste to have his linen washed at Fethard Castle before setting off for the Court of Claims in Dublin. That madcap dash with a bundle of title deeds and a small bag of diamond rings and other jewels – 'things that may give full Satisfaction to all there demaunds' – secured the family estates from rival claimants. When old Nicholas Loftus died a few months later, exhausted by a life of struggle, his sons inherited the Hook.

Three were left, for the rest died young. The eldest, Sir Nicholas, took over his father's castle at Fethard, 'that was the Bishop's seate formerly'.[286] Henry installed his wife and their three young daughters in the smaller and much more domestic castle of Dungulph, which stands in a relatively sheltered position, facing south across its garden, and is the only one of these old fortified houses that is still occupied as a family home. John, the youngest, unmarried brother, most probably lived at Kilclogan, which his grandfather Dudley had acquired in 1590.

Apart from those three castles and their estates, most of the family lands on the Hook were those that 'Nicholas Loftus the Elder did for very valuable considerations purchase from several Adventurers and

Soldiers', and then placed in trust to provide 'a competent maintenance & livelihood for his second son Henry Loftus & for his children, he having disbursed the money of the said Henry Loftus in the said purchases.' Henry may have advanced his first wife's dowry to finance the acquisition of these lands – for the eventual benefit of their children – but the original deed of trust provided for Henry's elder brother, Sir Nicholas, to enjoy their use in his lifetime. Nicholas relinquished that right shortly after their father's death, and made a second deed, giving Henry immediate control of most of the southern Hook: 'Castles, houses, Edifices, messuages, mills, Cottages, Lands, Tenements, meadows, pastures, ffeedings, Comons, woods, underwoods, ffirs, waters, watercourses, and all other hereditaments whatsoever.'[287]

Henry the Accumulator – it became a lifelong habit. Over a period of fifteen years, between 1669 and 1684, he acquired nearly five hundred acres in the barony of Bantry, in the neighbourhood of New Ross. His second marriage, in 1688, added more lands in Wexford belonging to his new wife, and in 1703 he was able to purchase all the lands in Fethard that the Loftus family did not already own. Both his brothers died before him, leaving Henry their heir. Harry was king of the Hook.

It was a wild place, far from the seedy glamour of the Restoration Court or the social and political intrigues of Dublin and London. Those were the haunts of Henry's dashing cousin, 'Addy' Loftus, for 'Addy' was always in motion, a moth to the flame, chasing mistresses, titles or glory. Henry was a man of very different temperament. He stayed in the same place all his life, accumulated land, built things that were useful, planted trees. And he seems to have loved the Hook, despite the 'sea winds and bleake situation', mentioned by Robert Leigh.

Leigh himself described with relish the 'abundance of Salmon, which is barrelled up yearly and sent to Spaine,' the 'codds, Gurnetts, Whiting and other sea fish', and the 'Lobsters, Crabbs, Prawnes and Shrimpes' – not to mention the delicious oysters harvested by Henry's neighbour and cousin, Sir Caesar Colclough. And he sniffed the breeze like a hound as he listed the pleasures of the chase. 'The Country about New Ross is good for hunting and hawking, there being good riding and plenty of game, especially hare, Phaisante, Grouse, and Partridge, and too many Foxes. The aire is excellent, good, cleare and sharpe, and begets a good stomach.'[288] That abundance of fish and game is now no more than a memory, but the sharp sea air – gusty and brisk – is still the taste of the Hook. Vast skies and the smell of salt – it's hard to leave such a place, once you become addicted.

That was certainly true of Henry Loftus, whose abiding concern was the slow, laborious work of rebuilding the prosperity of an estate that had been devastated by civil war and long years of neglect. He made a deer park adjacent to Loftus Hall, to compensate for the fact that red and fallow deer, formerly abundant, had been much depleted in the wild and were 'almost destroyed, as well as the woods', and a rabbit warren was constructed near the lighthouse. He built the harbour at Slade, to shelter the numerous fishing boats that harvested the wealth of the sea; constructed the superb dry-stone walls that divided his demesne into large fields, and the long retaining wall and cliff-edge path that protected the western boundary of his estate from the ravages of the waves; made slipways and moorings in those little western coves; remodelled his house, 'added other considerable buildings of lime and stone thereunto', and planted his fine walled garden.[289] He made beautiful stone gateways to his gardens, his park and his fields, and he developed the old red sandstone quarry at Harrylock, near Templetown, as a source of millstones, water troughs and window frames. The land itself was revitalised with the application of seaweed and lime – quarried and burned locally – and the limekilns, too, were lined with red sandstone.

One of Henry's closest allies in the renovation of his estate was his relative by marriage, William Mansell, to whom Henry leased the old castle of Slade and its surrounding farmland, in 1685. Mansell came from an English West Country family that had acquired an estate in Wales, on the Gower Peninsula. He supported Charles II's illegitimate son, the Duke of Monmouth, in his rebellion against King James and fled to Ireland following Monmouth's defeat and execution, because his wife had inherited a half share of her father's lands in County Wexford and his own family had Irish connections. He was made welcome by Henry Loftus (whose eldest daughter Jane married William's cousin, Thomas Maunsell, in 1694) and built a new life in a place that must often have reminded him of the sea-girt Gower.

Mansell brought with him from Wales a reputation as an eccentric and was believed to converse with the devil, a rumour that he seems to have enjoyed. He was in fact much interested in astrology and astronomy, and spent hours on the roof of Slade Castle, gazing at the stars, but he was also an entrepreneur ahead of his time, and shared Henry's passion for construction. Mansell soon abandoned the castle for a comfortable farmhouse that he built nearby, together with a fine range of stone outbuildings, and then embarked on a series of improvements that transformed the village. A row of neat new houses for his labourers was built facing the harbour, where Mansell constructed a second quay and a saltworks – which was housed in a solidly built stone range with corbelled stone roofs. A machine that he invented, powered by the wind, was said to have been used 'for the carriage of coals' – imported from Mansell's former homeland, Wales – but more probably was designed to pump seawater into the great vats where it was boiled with rock salt shipped from Cheshire. This 'salt on salt' technique produced a fine product, suitable for domestic use as well as for the Newfoundland fishery that was supplied from Waterford harbour. Mansell is also reputed to have built a clock that ran for thirty-eight years, outlasting its maker, and to have 'introduced shoes and stockings among the peasantry', who became so well clothed that a saying was current in Ireland, 'As smart as a Slade man'.[290]

All in all, I have a sense of peace, rising prosperity and increasing social ease, before the 'Glorious Revolution' destroyed, once again, the hopes of religious toleration.[291]

Henry Loftus was married for the second time on the eve of that Revolution, to a woman who was as much a product of the Restoration as his first wife, Amy Gorges, had been of the Protectorate. Amy was a Protestant from the North, whom Henry had wed in 1658, when both were very young. Her father was governor of Londonderry and her family had been related to the Loftuses for generations. They tended to be army men or ministers of the church, with the occasional black sheep. A silver rosewater dish, engraved with the arms of Loftus and Gorges, was made in Dublin to celebrate their wedding. It is a thing of Puritan beauty, lovely in its simplicity.

Ann Keating, who married Henry Loftus in January 1688, was a woman of very different stamp. The elder sister of William Mansell's wife, Susan, she was the daughter of Henry Crewkern of Exeter (a Captain of Dragoons who fought in Ireland and died at Carlow in 1665, having acquired more than a thousand acres in County Wexford), and widow of Oliver Keating, of Ballibar House in County Carlow. Keating had served in the civil wars under Ormond, whose tenant he was in County Kilkenny, and came from a family with long-standing connections on the Hook. The Keatings were Catholics and proud to be Irish – Oliver's forebear Geoffrey Keating had written a Gaelic history of Ireland – which provokes me to speculate about Ann's own sympathies. She is unlikely to have been have been a Catholic but was certainly accustomed to the intermingling of Catholic and Protestant, Irish and English, which characterised County Wexford prior to the Penal Laws. And she seems to have been a woman of strong character, entirely at home in the country, quite unlike the fashionable Protestant heiresses preferred by Henry's Dublin cousins.

Something of that force of personality is evident in the marriage settlement that she signed on the eve of her wedding to Henry Loftus. After reciting the catalogue of Henry's landholdings (2,408 acres in Shelbourne barony and 1,106 acres in Bantry barony, County Wexford, 955 acres in Queens County and 182 acres in County Carlow) the deed makes provision for a decent income to be paid to Ann, after Henry's death, and then includes a schedule of her personal estate, 'by her valued, taken and herein made'. Ann was about twenty years younger than her fifty-year-old husband, but she brought to her marriage a resolute independence of spirit and a dowry of goods and chattels that reminds me of the Irish epics.

Three hundred twenty and five sheep. Thirty four head of black cattle. Six horses vallued att Twenty two pounds. One hundred and twenty ounces of plate, besides a large Silver tankard, and a Silver Salt, being hir childrens, vallued att Thirty Pounds. Seaven Goathere bedds with boulsters, pillows, bedscloathes, curtains &c and hangings suitable, vallued att Twenty one pounds. Six peeres of Arras hangings, with one dussin and halfe of Turkyworke chaires, fourteene leather chairs, tables and carpetts, vallued att Forty five pounds. Five pairs of holland Sheets, with twelve pairs of pillowberes, vallued att Eighteen pounds. Twenty pairs of Flaxen Sheets, with twelve pairs of pillow-beres, besids coussones [cushions], Thirteene pounds. Furnaces, brasse, pewter, iron utensills and the like in brew house and kitchine; vallued Forty pounds. Table linnen &c vallued att Ten pounds. A

The Chancellor-Archbishop Adam Loftus. Fur-lined cloak, red-soled boots and
embroidered purse for the Great Seal of Ireland are the marks
of wealth and high office – but so, too, is his guarded, watchful gaze.

The Loftus Seal Cups, made from the silver matrix of the Great Seal of
Ireland. That on the left is dated 1593, 'Adam Loftus beinge then Lord
Chancelor . . . in which yeare he builded his howse at Rathfernan.'
That on the right was made in 1604, 'After the Death of The Blessed
Queene Elizabethe The Moste Blessed Prince That Ever Raigned.'
Missing its original 'steeple'.

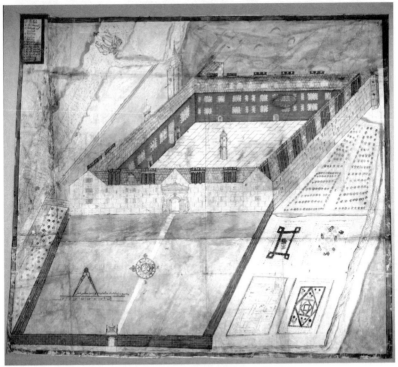

(*above*) 'The fayre head'. Sixteenth-century drawing of the skull and antlers of a giant Irish elk, which had been dug out of a peat bog near Dublin and were displayed by Archbishop Adam Loftus at Rathfarnham Castle.

(*below*) Birds-eye view of Trinity College, Dublin, shortly after it was founded in 1592.

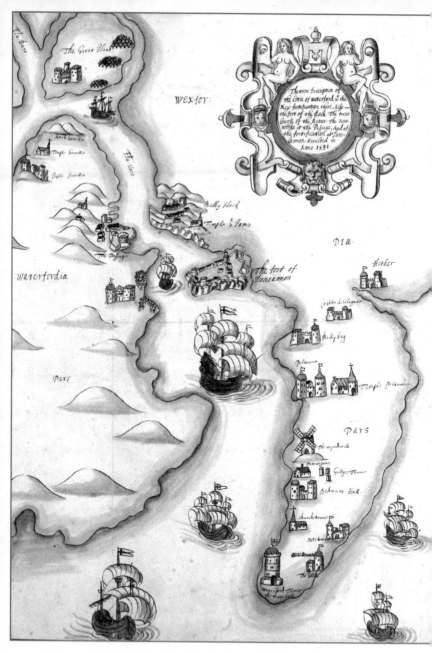

'The trew Discription' of the Hook, County Wexford, drawn by Francis
Jobson 1591 (detail). It shows the the Hook peninsula dotted with castles,
including Redmans Hall (later Loftus Hall) and the great Tower of the
Hook guarding the entrance to Waterford Harbour.

(*above*) Slade Castle, the Hook, County Wexford – the best surviving example of the Anglo-Norman castles on the Hook.

(*below*) Birds-eye view of the Hook tower and peninsula, *c.*1685. The view exaggerates the height of the tower, but shows its state as an operating lighthouse.

Hook Tower at the Entrance of Waterford.

(*above*) The portraits of Nicholas Loftus of Fethard and his wife Margaret (*née* Chetham), may originally have been a single canvas, as indicated – probably painted as an icon of mourning for King Charles I, shortly before his execution in January 1649

(*below*) This somewhat fanciful image depicts an attack by the parliamentary forces on Redmond's Hall (later Loftus Hall) in 1642.

(above) Walton's Polyglot Bible, 1657, detail.

(below) Dr Dudley Loftus's manuscript catalogue of his library, compiled in 1689, detail.

Henry Loftus of Loftus Hall. Painted in 1680 by Garret Morphy shortly after Henry moved into the former Redmond's Hall, which he renamed Loftus Hall. The 'monstrous perrucq', elegant grey coat and fur-lined cloak – evidence of wealth and privilege – are combined with a simple linen scarf, symbol of Irish nationalism.

coach, a Close, wooden vessells &c in brewhouse, barns, Stables, severall houses &c; Chests, drawers, boxes, looking glasses &c vallued att Twenty pounds.

Even more intriguing than this mad medley of livestock and silver, goat-hair beds and Turkey work chairs, bedlinen, furnaces, boxes and looking-glasses, is that this formal alliance between the great landowner and his practical bride seems to have been the case of a man marrying his mistress. The first of their two sons, named Nicholas after his grandfather, was born in 1687, before his parents were wed.

Their marriage coincided with a series of political upheavals, as years of makeshift compromise under Charles II were succeeded by a much more determined programme of Catholic preferment under King James, implemented with the utmost rigour in Ireland by his new Lord Lieutenant, Tyrconnell. James may well have preferred a more even-handed approach but Tyrconnell was resolute in appointing Catholics to command the army, the judiciary and local government. In pursuit of that policy he revoked the charters of most Irish towns and issued new ones in the King's name, as a means of substituting his own Catholic nominees for the Protestant merchants who dominated local corporations.

New Ross received its new charter on 5 March 1688, and fêted its arrival with extraordinary pomp. The gilt-framed charter sparked bonfires of celebration wherever it passed on the road to Ross, and was greeted at the town with 'the sound of Drums, ye harmonious noise of Violens, ye voices of virgins, and the Musicall straine of pipers,' not to mention 'the new Mayor – Patrick White Esq., a person of commendable presence, mounted on a stately Gray gelding, attended by fifty proper comely young men, all decently clad in white, marching before him to the soveraigne's house.' Then came the local notables, with their relatives, servants and dependants, 'exceeding in all about three thousand persons'. They were met by 'angelicall young virgins, carrying in their hand a Laurell, gilt with gold, consisting of about Sixty in number, the best men's children of the Corporation, very richly clad and decently dressed, dancing a part with themselves, with a garland, valued at twenty Guineas, and musick playing for them.'[292]

There followed a five-hour ceremony for the swearing in of the new mayor and corporation, after which everyone adjourned, exhausted, until nine o'clock the following morning, when 'the Mayor having a glasse of wine in his hand, drank a good health to ye King,' and another day of feasting and celebrations began.

The new corporation was still a mixture of Catholics and Protestants, as it had been before, but a Catholic mayor replaced the Protestant sovereign, Nathaniel Quarme – and the burgesses felt encouraged to adopt a clear, partisan agenda. Their first, symbolic action was to order 'the bell in the Town Hall to be given back to Father Anthony Mulloy for the Franciscan Abbey of New Ross, formerly deprived thereof by Oliver Cromwell.' Their second, a week later, was to set out for the Hook, to proclaim their rights to the ancient lighthouse that guarded the approach to the harbours of Waterford and New Ross.

The owners of the Hall had long claimed Hook Tower – which was built more than four centuries earlier, as a beacon to guide shipping to Ross – but traditionally leased it to the Corporation of Ross. The lighthouse had fallen into disuse during the civil wars and for some time afterwards, but was repaired by Robert Readinge in 1671 – since when the burgesses had come to regard it as their own. Eventually, on 12 March 1688, they decided to test that claim.

The mayor and burgesses 'went up along to the lamp on the top of the said Tower, the Mace bearer with his mace, and the Mayor with his Rodd,' to declare their ownership of the Tower and seven acres of land. Soon afterwards they met 'with Mr. Thomas Loftus, son and heir of Sir Nicholas Loftus' – while 'Thomas White, water bayliffe' led another group of burgesses that 'went by water with Collours flying along to Redmonds Hall, to proclaim their right and priviledge of the Corporation to the river from Enisteoge to the said Tower.'[293]

This incident was a small flurry, more show than substance, to which Henry responded by asserting his own right to the Tower, without confrontation, but it was one of a series of measures that unsettled the Protestant landowners, aggravating their sense of insecurity. The reference in the Corporation's minute books to 'Redmond's Hall' was in flat contradiction to the judgement of the Court of Claims, twenty years earlier, and to Henry's renaming of the place, in 1680. It contained an implicit challenge, reclaiming the old pattern of landholding against the Protestant 'usurpers'.

Giving context to this local drama was the accelerating upheaval in English politics, as James II blundered into the revolution that brought his son-in-law, William of Orange, to claim the throne. William arrived in England in 1688 and James fled to France. In March 1689 (exactly a year after the Corporation of New Ross had staked its claim to Hook Tower), James landed on the south coast of Ireland, with French assistance. And so the fighting began again – and did not cease until more than two years later, after the Siege of Derry, the Battle of the Boyne, the Battle of Aughrim and the Siege of Limerick, where Adam Loftus lost his head.

One of James's first actions, on landing in Ireland, was to call a Parliament, packed with Catholic supporters. So effectively was the election managed by Tyrconnell that Catholics were returned even in areas where Protestant landowners traditionally held sway. Many of those landowners had fled to England and others, like Henry Loftus, stayed quietly on the sidelines, making no attempt to exert their usual influence. Jacobites were 'elected' for all the pocket boroughs on the Loftus estate – two army officers for the estate village of Fethard, a relative of the Mayor of New Ross and a Dublin crony of Tyrconnell for the ruined towers of Clonmines, and a couple of Catholic grandees for the cabins and marshes of Bannow. These were the Commissioner for Revenue, Francis Plowden, and a noted divine, Dr Alexis Stafford, who was shortly afterwards appointed by King James as the first Catholic Dean of Christchurch in more than a hundred years.

The new Parliament had a short life, but significantly increased the stakes for both sides by passing an Act of Attainder that declared 2,000 individuals to be traitors to King James and their estates forfeit to the Crown – liable to confiscation and redistribution had the Jacobite cause prevailed. Inevitably it provoked a comparable response from their enemies, with William of Orange declaring, after the Battle of the Boyne, that none of the landowners who opposed him would be pardoned for their 'rebellion'. Both sides, once again, were fighting for their land.

The hysteria of those intolerant proclamations was in marked contrast to the quiet common sense that finally ended the war, when the Jacobite forces at Limerick surrendered to William's Commander-in-Chief, General Ginkel. The peace treaty agreed by Ginkel, on 3 October 1691, and signed by the Lords Justices on the Crown's behalf, promised that William and Mary would use their 'utmost Indeavours that the same should be ratified and confirmed in Parliament.'[294] Had that happened, the subsequent history of Ireland might have been very different, so it is worth pausing for a moment to consider what the Treaty contained.

The first of its provisions, permitting the Jacobite forces 'free liberty to go to any Country beyond the Seas, with their Families, Household-stuff, Plate and Jewels,' was honoured in full. The 'Flight of the Wild Geese' took thousands of Irish to France, to serve in the army of Louis XIV. For those who remained, however, the promises of Limerick were comprehensively broken, including the famous guarantee of religious freedom.

> That the Roman Catholicks of this Kingdom enjoy such Privileges in the Exercise of their Religion as are consistent with the Laws of Ireland, or as they did enjoy in the Reign of King Charles the Second and Their Majesties (as soon as their Affairs will permit them to summon a Parliament in this Kingdom) will endeavour to procure the said Roman Catholicks such further Security in that Particular, as may preserve them from any disturbance upon the account of the said Religion.

Property rights were protected for Jacobite 'rebels' in the counties of Limerick, Cork, Clare, Sligo and Mayo, to 'hold, possess and enjoy all and every of their Estates of Free-hold and Inheritance' as they had in the reign of Charles II. Likewise the right to bear arms for personal protection: 'Every Nobleman and Gentleman shall have liberty to ride with a Sword and Case of Pistols if they think fit, and keep a Gun in their Houses for the Defence of the same, or Fowling.' And there was a clause preventing legal recriminations for actions taken by either side 'for any Trespasses by them committed during the Time of the War'.

I have drawn my summary of the Treaty of Limerick from the remarkable contemporary account provided by George Story, a regimental chaplain in King William's army and 'an Eyewitness of the most Remarkable Passages' of the war, whose conclusion deserves to be quoted in full.

> What means soever may be used for the procuring of Unity, or Settlement, in a Countrey, Men must at the same time be careful not to deface and dissolve the Bonds of Christian Charity; nay of humane Society, since acting to the contrary, is but to dash the second Table against the first; and so to consider others as of this or that Persuasion, and to treat them ill upon that account, is to forget that they are Men; and indeed to me it seems full as unreasonable to destroy other People, purely because they cannot think as we do, as it is for one man to ruine another, because the outward Figure and Shape of his Body is not the same with his own.

That clear, courageous expression of tolerance, by a Protestant partisan, is a fine riposte to those who try to excuse the subsequent betrayal of the promises of Limerick by arguing that different times make for different judgements, or claim that ambiguities in the drafting of the treaty explain the failure to ratify it in Parliament. That Story's words went unheeded is true but was not inevitable, and the blame for what followed rests squarely on the shoulders of the great Protestant landowners. Fear of civil war and determination to ensure that never again could Catholic rebels challenge the Protestant Ascendancy caused them, step by step, to approve a code of penal legislation which deprived their Catholic neighbours of all the rights that the treaty had been intended to protect, and many more.

That process began with the first Irish Parliament of William's reign, in 1692, an assembly of the victors. Among those 300 newly elected Protestants (all Catholics having been debarred from sitting in the Irish House of Commons) was the aged, eccentric Orientalist, Dr Dudley Loftus, representing the family's borough of Fethard, and Henry Loftus – who had chosen to represent Clonmines, one of the loveliest ghosts of a medieval town. Across the estuary from Clonmines was another fictitious borough, long abandoned – 'for on the east side, towards the town of Bannow, where the ancient passage was, and ships used to come in, it is now a perfect dry strand.'[295] A few cabins in Bannow nonetheless returned two Members of Parliament, Nathaniel

Boyse and John Cliffe, who were elected under the auspices of the Loftus family. This was the beginning of that elaborate system of parliamentary patronage and borough management that became such an important feature of social and political life in eighteenth-century Ireland.

The 1692 Parliament sat for only a few months but made its mark by challenging the right of the English House of Commons to initiate Irish finance bills and by refusing to ratify the terms of the Treaty of Limerick. There was also an unsuccessful attempt to restrict the right of *habeas corpus* to Protestants alone. The signs were ominous for the future.

Having stayed on the Hook during the recent wars, without taking sides, Henry Loftus seemed reluctant to identify himself with this new sectarian intolerance, preferring to straddle the social and religious divide. A clue may be found in a letter that he wrote from Loftus Hall in May 1693, when laid up with 'a humer fallen into one of my leggs'. Henry's usual doctor had been unable to cure him, so he asked his local minister, Rev. Williams, to send another, recently arrived physician to provide a second opinion. And then he added a postscript, asking Williams to notify Edward Smith of New Ross and James Keating of Maylerspark 'that I have by last post writt to Dublin about Pastor Booths Subpena, & I will take care that noe advantage be gott against them, as I doe for my Selfe.'[296] Booth was a Protestant divine who had evidently gone to law against Smith (the Sovereign of New Ross, presumably a Protestant), Keating (member of an old Catholic family, related to Henry's wife) and Loftus himself. Though the facts are obscure it seems probable that Booth's action was aggressively sectarian, which Henry was determined to oppose.

His passion, in any case, was not for politics in the wider sense but for his family and his estates. A month after his letter to the Rev. Williams, 'Henry Loftus and Ann his wife' signed a long legal document – the final stage in the conveyance of the Loftus lands on the Hook to them and their heirs, from Henry's brother Sir Nicholas. So strong was Henry's desire to safeguard these lands in the Loftus family that every foreseeable contingency was described, every possible male heir identified, and their succession determined. And finally, there was an admonition to future generations.

Henry doth hereby lay a charge upon and recommend to his male Children and the heires male of their bodyes, as they Expect his blessing and the blessing of the Lord who hath commanded Children to obey their parents, that they presume not to destroy the settlement hereby made upon the name and family of the Loftuses, [and] that the Inheritance of the same and of every part thereof may continue in the name of the Loftuses so long as any of the name shall be living, notwithstanding any distance of Relation whatsoever.[297]

That instinctive attachment to landed property, combined with a fear of dispossession by their Catholic predecessors, was the strongest unifying force in the second, much more carefully managed Irish Parliament of King William's reign, which was elected in 1695 and sat intermittently until its mandate expired with the King's death in March 1702, two weeks after he was thrown from his horse when it stumbled on a molehill. Henry Loftus was once again returned for Clonmines and his brother Sir Nicholas succeeded Dr Dudley Loftus as one of the members for Fethard. Both were presumably present when Parliament passed the first of the notorious Penal Laws, banning Catholics from educating their children abroad, from bearing arms and from owning a horse worth more than £5 – a particularly mean-minded measure that served no political aim save social humiliation. Two years later, Catholic bishops and clergy were banished from Ireland and the intermarriage of Catholics and Protestants was made grounds for disinheritance. It was the vindictiveness that George Story had feared – 'to destroy other People, purely because they cannot think as we do.'

I find it hard to imagine that Henry Loftus could have voted for these measures, even though I am constantly reminded of the more recent examples of sudden intolerance, among former friends and neighbours, in the ruins of what was once Yugoslavia. His wife had been married to a Catholic, his neighbours included Catholic 'Old English' families with whom he had long been on easy terms and his father had been a Royalist in the civil wars of the 1640s – all of which suggests that Henry and his brother Sir Nicholas (unlike their grand Dublin cousins) were instinctive Tories. In the Irish context that meant more than the English archetype of choleric country squires, high-church traditionalists. They may have been perfectly happy to curse the Pope and all his works, but for long-established rural Protestants, such as the Loftuses, this went hand-in-hand with a degree of Catholic tolerance and deep suspicion of Protestant dissenters. They supported the pragmatism of William III and were opposed to the much more fiercely Protestant line of the Irish Whigs (fashionable grandees who moved easily between Dublin and London). And there was often a strain of what would later be called Nationalism – a hatred of English interference in Irish affairs.

The key test was the Treaty of Limerick. Tories tended to support the Articles as a practical settlement, likely to calm recent antagonisms, while Whigs were bitterly opposed. The Whigs even tried to impeach one of the original signatories to the Treaty – the Lord Chancellor Sir Charles Porter – whom they accused of showing too much favour to Catholics. Their first attempt was frustrated by the dissolution of the 1692 Parliament but the attack was renewed, with fierce determination, in 1695. Porter was only saved by a convincing plea in his own defence and the strong support of the country Tories, including Henry and Nicholas Loftus, who voted in his favour.

This polarisation of politics was aggravated by English determination to treat Ireland as a colony, and to exact economic revenge for its Jacobite 'rebellion' a decade earlier. Two unrelated instances in 1698 provoked numerous Irish landlords to share a sense of nationalist outrage. One arose from a dispute between the Bishop of Derry and the London Company of Adventurers over the ownership of large estates in Ulster, which the Bishop had won on appeal to the Irish House of Lords, but lost when its English counterpart overturned the verdict and ruled that the Irish house had no jurisdiction. The other was a bill passed by the English Parliament, in February 1698, preventing the export of Irish woollens to any country save England. It was a blatant piece of protectionism, instigated by English wool merchants, fearful of being undercut by Irish competitors. Widely circumvented by smuggling, the Act nonetheless had huge symbolic significance.

The combination of those events provoked the publication of an apparently inoffensive booklet, *The Case of Ireland's Being Bound by Acts of Parliament in England, Stated*. This may be one of the dreariest titles ever published but its appearance in 1698 caused a political storm – and gave rise to a subsequent myth that it was burned by the public hangman. Reading its densely argued pages reveals the reason, for its author,

William Molyneux, set out to prove that Ireland was not and never had been bound by the Acts of England's Parliament – it shared a King but not a government with its sister nation. 'That Ireland should be Bound by Acts of Parliament made in England, is against Reason, and the Common Rights of all Mankind.' This became a key text for Irish 'patriots', opposed to English meddling in their affairs, and a precedent for the 'nationalist' politics of the United Irishmen, a century later.

Neither Henry Loftus nor his brother Nicholas stood for Parliament after William III's death, but Henry's son, another Nicholas, represented Fethard (and subsequently Clonmines) between 1710 and 1714. Nicholas made himself so unpopular with the Whigs that by the end of Anne's reign he was included on a 'blacklist' of Tories, whose re-election was to be opposed at all costs. So strong was the family interest in Wexford, however, that he defied his opponents and abandoned a safe seat in one of the Loftus boroughs to stand instead for the county, which he represented until he was ennobled, as Viscount Loftus of Ely, in 1751.

It was under Queen Anne (and to a lesser extent George I) that the worst of the Penal Laws were implemented by men who took delight in serving their revenge cold. Catholics were deprived of the franchise and the right to hold any public office, and of most of their rights to own or acquire land or pass it to their children – and those children, indeed, were encouraged to convert to Protestantism, by which means they were legally entitled to deprive their parents of everything they owned. Thus it was that three quarters of the population became an underclass, effectively unrecognised in law, owning less than 15% of the land of Ireland (and that the worst land), impoverished and demoralised – comparable in their circumstances to the mass of the peasant class of mainland Europe but utterly unlike their neighbours in England or their Protestant masters in Ireland itself.[299] These were the foundations on which the Protestant Ascendancy built its beautiful houses and the basis on which they lived such intemperate lives that they still fascinate us, and seem to demand forgiveness, like spoilt children.

And, of course, their childish fears were real – since every act of repression bred the reverse, in an endless cycle of sectarian distrust, and the Jacobites dreamed of victory, long after their cause was lost. As late as 1707, Henry Loftus had to request that a contingent of a sergeant and twelve men 'be detached out of Major General Fitcomb's Regiment, from Waterford or Duncannon Fort,' to guard Loftus Hall at a time of local disturbance, caused by recruitment for the Old Pretender, James Stuart, who was preparing an invasion of Scotland, with French help.[300]

European politics were always more complex than most Irish Protestants comprehended (the Pope, as it happened, supported King Billy at the Battle of the Boyne) but the fear of a Catholic league against the Protestant kingdoms of Britain had real substance, and that cartoon bogeyman, the Pope of Rome, was a force to be reckoned with; hence the deep, abiding dread that loyal Catholic subjects could be turned overnight into fanatical rebels, by papal edicts of excommunication and deposition. That fear lingered long, in unexpected corners, and I found one of its purest expressions in the Corporation Book of Bannow, the Loftus pocket borough that was little but a stretch of sand. 'The Oath of a Burgess of Bannow', recorded in 1713, was administered to a dozen dependants and relatives of the Loftus family when they took office, their sole function being to 'elect' whichever friends Henry Loftus decided to appoint for the next Parliament. After declaring his loyalty to the Crown, each Burgess solemnly swore the following.

> I doe sweare that I doe from my heart abhor & detest, & abjure, as impious and hereticall that damnable doctrine and position that persons excommunicated or deposed by ye Pope or any authority of ye court of Rome may be deposed or murdered by their subjects or any other person whatsoever; And I doe declare that noe Foreign Prince person prelate State or potentate hath or ought to have any jurisdiction power Supremacy or authority Ecclesiastical or Spirituall in this Realm soe help me God.[301]

It sounds like a prayer, muttered by a child, to ward off the devil in the dark.

Henry Loftus died when he was nearly eighty, in 1716, and was buried in the family vault, at Fethard Church. Twice married, he fathered six children, accumulated great estates and lived through so many troubles that he learnt to keep his counsel. I have a sense of physical energy and passion, constrained by the austere Protestant ethos of his upbringing. Such constraints were thrown to the winds by his heir.

CHAPTER 19

Lilliburlero

The devil has all the best tunes, even if he has to steal them. How else to account for the fact that a Flemish setting of the psalms, published in Antwerp in 1540, jumped across the sea to England where it became a 'Quick Step', and then jumped again, to Ireland, as an anti-Jacobite anthem, so lively and catching that 'the whole army and at last the people, both in the city and country, were singing it perpetually. And perhaps never had so slight a thing so great an effect.'[302] And finally it leapt again, into the pages of *Tristram Shandy*, as an echo of that gentlest of men, Uncle Toby, whose answer to every argument, or to 'any thing that shocked or surprised him', was to whistle 'half a dozen bars of *Lillabullero*.'

'Lilliburlero' is irresistible – a rollicking, rousing romp of a song that careers through a dozen verses to its unexpected conclusion, when it turns upside down all that has gone before. As the final jaunty chorus dies away, you realise that the engaging Irish brogue and Catholic Jacobite words are all a sham, and that this is an Orange marching song, a triumph for King Billy. *Lèro, lèro, lilliburlèro, lilliburlèro bullen a la*. That dancing refrain is itself a coded message, for it conceals the Gaelic watchwords used by Irish papists during the massacres of 1641, but strings them together in a way that can be heard as a Protestant chant, celebrating the Orange lily: *An lile ba léir é ba linn an lá* (the lily was triumphant and we won the day).[303]

The author of those words (and the devil who stole the tune) was a witty, wicked Whig, Thomas Wharton, who claimed thereby to have 'sung a deluded prince out of three kingdoms.' Wharton's support for the Protestant succession eventually gained him a string of titles and lucrative offices, including his appointment as Lord Lieutenant of Ireland, but his lack of principle earned the even more remarkable distinction of a character assassination by Swift, unmatched in its vitriol. Devoting an entire pamphlet to the task, Swift skewered Wharton as a man 'without the Sense of Shame or Glory, as some men are without the sense of smelling – He is a Presbyterian in Politicks, and an Atheist in Religion; and he chuses at present to Whore with a *Papist*.' Describing his victim as a habitual liar, whose lies were 'sometimes detected in an Hour, often in a Day, and always in a Week,' Swift claimed that his thoughts were 'wholly taken up between Vice and Politicks'.[304]

To which Wharton might have replied that one thing led to another. The political triumph of 'Lilliburlero', for example, culminated in October 1691, when the siege of Limerick ended with a defeated Jacobite army sailing into exile. One of the last casualties of that siege was Adam Loftus, Viscount Lisburne, who lost his head to a cannonball a fortnight before peace was signed, leaving his daughter Lucy as the sole heir to his estates, worth £5,000 a year. Three months later, in January 1692, Tom Wharton was spotted by his brother Goodwin at a ball at Kensington Palace, dancing with his 'new mistress', Lucy Loftus. And then, in July, they were married.

Lucy entranced Wharton's friends – one of whom described her as 'the witty fair one' – and their appreciation was recorded in a salacious toast at the Kit Kat Club, within a few years of the marriage. By then, it seems, her favours were shared, and Wharton was synonymous with 'whore', as she passed from hand to hand.

> When Jove to Ida did the gods invite
> And in immortal toastings pass'd the night,
> With more than bowls of nectar they were blest,
> For Venus was the Wharton of the feast.

Other contemporary descriptions are less enamoured: 'Unfeeling and unprincipled; flattering, fawning, canting, affecting prudery and even sanctity yet in reality as abandoned and unprincipled as her husband.' Lucy and Tom were certainly well matched, for Swift claimed that Wharton 'bears the Gallantries of his Lady with the indifference of a *Stoick*, and thinks them well recompensed by a return of Children to support his Family, without the fatigue of being a Father.' It left him more time for his Papist mistress.

The first of those children, a boy named Philip, was born six years after the marriage, on Christmas Eve 1698 – but Wharton seldom visited the nursery and seemed very melancholy, according to his sister Mary. Perhaps he was contemplating the child's paternity. Two daughters followed at long intervals, in 1706 and 1710, spaced either side of Wharton's notoriously debauched period as Lord Lieutenant of Ireland. And gradually their mother's face (that had once seemed 'so gay, so sweet, so gentle and agreeable') came to resemble a bird of prey, as everything faded except her prominent eyes and long Loftus nose. Twenty years of married dissipation had taken their toll, as Swift wrote gleefully to Stella, in February 1712: 'I saw Lady Wharton, ugly as the devil, coming out of the crowd [from the Queen's concert] all in an undress.'[305] But Lucy and Tom stayed together, against all the odds, and she could present a brave face when occasion demanded. The following year, for example, she appeared at her husband's side on the hustings at Aylesbury, stylishly political, with a tuft of wool in her hat to demonstrate Whig support for the trade that had once been the foundation of England's prosperity.

The election was lost but the reign of George I, beginning the following year, saw Tom Wharton made a marquis and granted a large government pension. A few weeks later his sixteen-year-old son eloped with and secretly married the poor but virtuous daughter of a general, provoking a fury that led to Wharton's death – which prompted a Tory rival to exclaim, 'there goes another great atheistical, knavish, republican, Whiggish Villain.' Lucy survived him by two years, and was buried at his side. On his other side, it is said, was buried his favourite mistress.

Lero, lero, lilliburlero, lilliburlero bullen a la. As in the song, there was a twist at the end. Young Philip Wharton outdid his father in profligacy, squandered his vast fortune, and proved a political turncoat. 'A godson of William III, he accepted one dukedom from George I and another from the Old Pretender' and eventually became a Catholic, to secure a Spanish bride. He ended his days abroad, bankrupt and abandoned by his Jacobite friends, and described by Pope as 'the scorn and wonder of our days'.

'Lilliburlero', too, has been transformed. The song that inspired an army, chased a king off his throne and soothed Uncle Toby was until recently (for some mysterious reason) the theme tune of the BBC World Service. Needless to say, it has now been replaced by a jingle.

Fig. 1. A Lighthouse on an Island or Head-
land, to direct Ships in the Night
A, the Grate B, the Lightman stirring the Fire.
C, a Crane to land the Coals.

Fig. 2. A Porcupine to clear old Bars.

NICHOLAS

CHAPTER 20

The Extinguisher

As you head south down the Hook, across an increasingly flat and treeless landscape, two simple shapes dominate the bleak horizon – the horizontal block of Loftus Hall and the vertical stump of Hook Tower. The present version of Loftus Hall is a vast hulk from the end of the nineteenth century, but the massive lighthouse has stood as a landmark to travellers on land and sea for eight hundred years.

> There is a Towre called ye Tower of Hooke standing upon the mouth of ye River of Waterford, on a Cape of land running into ye Sea, which hath formerly been maytained for a Light House, and used to be white-limed for a Land Marke by day, and to have a great fire kept on the Topp thereof for a marke by night for Shippes to shun those sands, shelves and rocks, which do lye neere the same: for want of ye maintenance of which, severall ship wracks have lately been on those Coasts to the discouragement of Marchants, Seamen and others.[306]

When Colonel Rudgeley petitioned for the restoration of the Hook light, in 1657, the 'great fire' had been extinguished for most of the previous decade, during the turmoil of the civil wars and their aftermath. Rudgeley requested, 'in the behalfe of ye seamen and mariners which traffique upon ye coast of Waterford, and other harbours, that a certeyne Rate may be sett upon every Tun [of shipping] for ye maintenace thereof' – but it was not until Robert Reading repaired the beacon in 1671 that the Tower of Hook once more served the purpose for which it had been built, five hundred years earlier.

It was then (and remains) the oldest operating lighthouse in Europe, possibly in the world. A fifth-century monk called Dubhán (St David's uncle) was the first to keep a beacon fire on the black rocks of Hook Head, but the present tower was built at the beginning of the thirteenth century, on the orders of William Marshall, Earl of Pembroke, who founded the port of Ross. Dubhán's successors (the Augustinian canons of Churchtown) were given responsibility for looking after the new beacon, and were housed in cold cells within the thickness of the tower's massive walls. They took turns to feed the flames, and gradually consumed every tree for miles around.

The town of Ross held Hook Tower from William Marshall's successors, by feudal tenure, and a custom arose whereby the sovereign and bailiff came once a year to assert their rights to the foreshore and the beacon, shooting an arrow from the headland into the sea. But tenure was never ownership, and rent was paid. In 1411, for example, a jury recorded that the sovereign and Community of Ross held 'the Tower of Hooke, and 12 acres of land close by' from Thomas Mowbray, 'by the service of 18d. a year'. Ownership passed to the Redmonds (who took as their crest a fire beacon), and then to the Loftus family, who acquired the Redmond Hall estate from 'several Adventurers and Soldiers', in the 1650s. By then the Tower had fallen into disuse, as noted in Rudgeley's petition, but following its restoration, the New Ross burghers became increasingly determined to assert their claim to it. Their chance came with the granting of a new town charter, in 1688, and the corporation decided that 'money be raised out of the revenue to pay for getting the clause in the charter about the tower of Hooke.' The new mayor's revival of the old custom of shooting an arrow into the sea at Hook Head was part of that campaign to establish ownership.

All of which came to nought when James II was defeated, his charters annulled, and the Protestant grandees re-established their influence over local politics. And New Ross was further punished by England's economic vengeance on Jacobite Ireland, for it was omitted from the list of ports permitted to export wool to England in the notorious Act of 1698; whereas neighbouring Waterford (with which it shared an estuary) was one of the privileged few. It was not until 1705, in the reign of Queen Anne, that this injustice was put right, when the English

Parliament passed 'An Act for making the Town of *New Ross*, in the County of *Wexford* in the Kingdom of *Ireland*, a Port for the Exporting Wool from *Ireland* into this Kingdom.'

A year earlier, in 1704, the Queen had passed all responsibility for Irish lighthouses to the Revenue Commissioners, who prepared a report which indicated that the Hook light needed urgent repair.

> *Waterford*. The lighthouse at the Tower of Hook of this harbour is 140 steps to the top, and above that a large oval lanthorn, glazed, very much in want of repair, and to make the light serviceable an alteration should be made in the light or lanthorn wherein the light is kept. The lighthouse stands in the most convenient part of the harbour's mouth, and was formerly kept by Henry Loftus, Esq., who employed a person who was a smith, and allowed him only 12 barrels of coals yearly to keep up the light, which was no manner of use. It is the opinion of the most knowing men of those parts that the light once put into sufficient repair could not be kept with less than 200 barrels of coals every year, at a cost of 30l., and that 40l. per annum should be given to a careful person to look after it, with two servants to blow up the fire.

So an estimate was compiled for 'the repair and alteration of the lanthorn at Hook Lighthouse, lyme for pointing and ruffcasting the outside of the tower, and other mason's work about the lanthorn and battlements, also 140 foott of glass for the lanthorn, iron for the great bricks for the breast of the lanthorn.'[307] And then, when the tower was freshly repaired, white-limed and gleaming, a new lease was signed.

> Henry Loftus did in the year 1706 Demise unto John Kent, then Collector of Waterford, for the use of Her Majesty, her heirs, etc., The Tower of Hook, on which the light was kept for the use of all Shipping trading to and from the several Ports of Ross and Waterford, and other ports of this Kingdom, together with that part of the said Tower where a stock of coals had been kept for the use of the said Light House, and also a passage for carrying the said coals to the said Tower, for the Term of 21 years at the yearly Rent of £11 sterling.[308]

Henry was glad to be relieved of his responsibility for maintaining the light – hence the modest rent – and this new arrangement went unchallenged for the rest of his life. But his son and heir, the headstrong Nicholas, was determined to agree better terms when the lease expired in 1728. He demanded a twentyfold increase and took drastic action when the port authorities refused to negotiate, by threatening to put out the light. Increasingly ominous announcements appeared in the *Dublin Gazette*.

> Whereas it hath been ever since the 4th day of July last advertised that the Light which was kept in the Light House commonly known by the name of the Tower of Hook, being in the Estate of Nichs. Loftus Esqr, would be lett out on the 20th of this instant August.
>
> Now this is to give Notice to Sailors, Merchants, Traders, and all others whom it may concern, that the said Nicholas Loftus will continue the said Light until the 29th day of Sept. next and no longer. Dated this 20th day of August [1728].
>
> *Sd.* NICHO. LOFTUS[309]

Needless to say this threat provoked a huge furore, and petitions to the Lords Justices of Ireland from Edward Elsmere, Collector of the Port of Ross, and from 'Aldermen John Porter and Thomas Gledstanes, merchants, in behalf of themselves and other Traders of this City, and of Capt Stewart and Capt Ellis in behalf of themselves and many other Masters of Ships trading to and from this Kingdom.' Elsmere claimed that the proposed new rent of £200 per annum was 'infinitely more than the Tower is worth, the former Rent of £11 being in the opinion of such as know the place more than the Vallue.'[310] The seamen spoke with foreboding of 'the sudden Approach of this Winter'.

Recent historians have tended to assume that matters were finally settled with a modest rental increment, but family legend tells of a more drastic outcome – whereby Nicholas acquired his nickname, the Extinguisher. It is said that winter storms, no light and some wrecked ships brought the commissioners to a radical change of heart. This unreliable memory was surprisingly confirmed by a document that I found hanging in a dark passageway at Mount Loftus, which proved that a new twenty-one-year lease was eventually signed by 'his Majesty's Hon Commissioners', backdated to 25 March 1728, when the rent for 'the Tower of Hook, for the purpose of Erecting and keeping up a Light House thereon,' was increased from £11 to £120 per annum. The

Extinguisher may not have achieved the full extent of his demands, but certainly won his point.

Many years later, when that lease expired, Nicholas again requested an increase – but this time there were no threats; perhaps because he was old and had lost his fire, or perhaps because the memory of his previous actions was so burned in the memory of all concerned that coercion was needless. Whatever the outcome of that negotiation, the Hook light was never again extinguished.

But a light that mariners look to for safety may also be a lure for pirates, and in the decades that followed there were repeated sightings of French privateers off Hook Head. Sometimes they left empty-handed, as their intended prey hugged the shore or slipped into harbour and safety, but on other occasions guns were fired and prizes taken while the lighthouse keeper peered through the gathering dusk, helpless to intervene. And then the privateers would sail into the darkness, setting their course home from the beacon on Hook Tower.

There is an unexpected postscript to this story, long lost to memory but preserved in the cramped columns of a couple of eighteenth century newspapers.[310A] In September 1761, when he was old and grand, Nicholas Loftus was presented with a silver box by the citizens of Cork, granting him the Freedom of the City: 'In Testimony of his Lordship's great Humanity and Benevolence, in saving several Ships and their Cargoes that were stranded on his Estate in the County of Wexford, without any View to Salvage or private Interest. An example worthy Imitation.'

The Extinguisher, it seems, was now a hero.

CHAPTER 21

The Present State of Ireland

In 1758, to celebrate his seventieth birthday, Nicholas Loftus had his portrait painted – an apparently conventional image of a florid man with a big nose, wearing a plain grey wig, a black coat and a linen scarf. Look closer. That very plainness of dress contains a coded message, for this was a man whose social position is clearly conveyed by the inscription on a folded letter – *the Right Honble Nicholas Lord Visc. Loftus, Ireland –* which lies on a couple of large books, on a table beside his chair. And one of those books has its spine turned towards us, equally clearly labelled, *Present State of Ireland.* This, too, has a hidden significance.

Both inscriptions were intended to be read, and both provide important clues to the sitter's social and political identity. The first is unambiguous, a statement of name and (recently acquired) rank which contrasts quite deliberately with his lack of ostentation, but the second is more surprising – for the title on the book is that of a small but fascinating pamphlet, printed nearly thirty years earlier, not the large quarto volume implied by the artist. *The Present State of Ireland consider'd* was published anonymously in Dublin in 1730 and again, later that year, in London – in a composite edition, sandwiched between two much more famous tracts.[311] One was Thomas Prior's *List of the Absentees of Ireland, and the yearly value of their estates and incomes spent abroad,* and the other was Dean Swift's *A Modest Proposal for preventing the children of poor people being a burthen to their Parents or the Country –* each of which had appeared separately the previous year. Prior's *List of Absentees* claimed that Ireland was being ruined because more than £600,000 was sent abroad every year to absentee landlords in England, many of who also benefitted from Irish government sinecures. He listed the guilty parties, with a figure supplied for each, of the 'Yearly Value of their Estates spent abroad'.[312] Swift's *Modest Proposal* was his most savage satire, suggesting that the poor of Ireland should fatten their babies, as food for the rich. Both pamphlets were versions of the same argument, that the rich (the Protestant Ascendancy) exploited the poor, and in the process wrecked the economy on which their own prosperity depended.

Prior made the point unequivocally.

> There is no Country in *Europe*, which produces, and exports so great a Quantity of *Beef, Butter, Tallow, Hydes* and *Wool*, as *Ireland* does; and yet our common People are very poorly cloath'd, go bare-legged half the Year, and rarely taste of that Flesh-Meat, with which we so much abound. We pinch our selves in every Article of Life, and export more than we can well spare, with no other Effect or Advantage, than to enable our Gentlemen and Ladies to live more luxuriously abroad.

That theme is repeated in the lucidly argued pages of *The Present State of Ireland*.

> That our *Absentees* are one great Cause of all our Misfortunes cannot be deny'd; they annually draw *immense Sums out of the Kingdom, none of which ever returns*.
>
> If I have 1000*l. per Ann.* and Annually lay out 200 in *foreign consumable Commodities, necessary only to Luxury, I am one fifth part an Absentee*, let me live where I will.
>
> What good Clergy-man, that goes into the Pulpit to exhort his Audience to Acts of Charity, setting forth the Rewards of those, who *feed the Hungry or clothe the Naked, whereby a Treasure is laid up in Heaven*, would not rather appear in an *Irish Linnen Band*, and thereby help to maintain and employ the *Poor of this Kingdom*, than in a *Cambrick* one, which only enriches a *Flanderkin*; or would not rather dispense with the Roughness of an *Irish Stuff Gown*, and do thereby a Service to his *Country* and *Countryman* by whom he is supported, than to indulge in an *Italian Mantua Silk*, or *Paduasoye*, to the real Prejudice of both?

The publication of this anonymous work, in the same volume as two related pamphlets by Prior and Swift, was of great political importance at the time and provoked much speculation as to its author. It has sometimes been attributed to Swift (but there seems no good reason why it should have remained anonymous when *A Modest Proposal* was acknowledged) and often to Prior, to whom the same objection might apply. The language seems livelier than Prior, less bitter than Swift, and *The Present State of Ireland* may perhaps have been written by one of the landed gentry, close to the circle of friends who founded the Dublin Society – 'for improving Husbandry, Manufactures, and other useful Arts' – the year after it was published. Possibly by Nicholas Loftus, given the way that it figured in his portrait, when he was old and grand.

Whether or not he wrote it, Nicholas was a strong supporter of Irish manufactures and seems never to have had much time for foreign luxuries – or indeed for luxury of any sort. A long-standing opponent of English meddling in Irish affairs and a Trustee of the Linen Board (an industry close to Prior's heart), Nicholas was also well acquainted with the founders of the Dublin Society.[313] Two of them, Dr William Stephens and Dr Francis LeHunte, came from Wexford families and several of LeHunte's relatives were regularly returned to Parliament for the Loftus boroughs on the Hook – as were prominent members of the Society such as William Tighe and Abel Ram. Nicholas himself joined the Society in the year of its foundation, and remained a member until his death, in 1763.[314]

It was Thomas Prior, the great opponent of absenteeism, who brought the Dublin Society into being and held it together through dogged application. Though it met in the Philosophical Rooms of Trinity College, the Society was shaped by the practical, utilitarian approach of its prime begetter, and thereby proved attractive to enlightened landowners such as Loftus, who attended his first meeting less than four months after the Society's foundation, on 14 October 1731. He may have been lured there by his Wexford friend, Dr William Stephens, whose *Dissertation on Dyeing, and several materials made use of in dyeing and particularly Woad*, was read by its author to the assembled group – after Prior himself had presented a paper on *The best Method practised in Hampshire in the Culture and Management of Hops.*[315]

That apparently haphazard programme was consistent in its resolute practicality, and in this sense typical of the Society's early years. When Nicholas Loftus next found time to attend a meeting, four months later, the topics discussed included the making of cider, the draining of bogs and the manuring of land. It was all quite literally down to earth, utterly unlike the speculative concerns of his great-uncle Dr Dudley Loftus and the founders of the Dublin Philosophical Society, half a century earlier. That practical ethos persisted, even when the Dublin Society became a fashionable forum for the Ascendancy grandees and their successors, and its major social event, the Dublin Horse Show (founded in 1864), is grounded in agricultural history.

For Nicholas Loftus, such practical concerns were given added force by his own, unconventional perspective on Irish affairs. Shortly after *The Present State of Ireland* was published, he had begun an affair with his Irish housekeeper, Mary Hernon, which continued for the rest of his life and produced the two sons whom he favoured over his legitimate offspring, to the scandal of the world. He sent both boys to be educated at Kilkenny College and then to Trinity College Dublin, and procured for them commissions in the army. The elder son, Edward Loftus, was married the same year that his father's portrait was painted, to a minister's daughter with a large inheritance in County Tyrone, and was provided by his father with an estate in County Kilkenny that Nicholas had acquired from a spendthrift ne'er-do-well.

That complex experience of Irish identity, legitimacy and the obligations of landownership was in a sense prefigured in *The Present State of Ireland*, for the Right Hon Lord Viscount Loftus was someone whose own habitual dress had something of the modesty of an *Irish Stuff Gown* but was accustomed to order his tableware from Dublin's grandest silversmith, John Hamilton. And this was also the man who decades later scorned the violent drunkenness of his eldest son and the indolent self-esteem of the drunkard's younger brother, to leave all his personal possessions (and a valuable estate) to the boy who most deeply shared his father's love of the land, the illegitimate child of a Protestant Ascendancy grandee and his Irish Catholic mistress.

That favourite son was himself the author of two brief publications. One was a pamphlet, 'to assert my honour' against what he saw as the insulting condescension of his grand legitimate brother, and the other was a letter, published in *The Proceedings of the Dublin Society* – 'On the Culture of Potatoes'.

CHAPTER 22

Captain Freney's Blunderbuss

One of my strongest childhood memories is the cool weight of Captain Freney's blunderbuss, a big, bell-mouthed weapon that stood in the corner of a corridor at Mount Loftus. Wonderful in itself, the blunderbuss gleamed with legends – of Freney the highwayman, the Extinguisher's accomplice. There was talk of a bet, of cabbage stalks, of holdups on the back avenue – fantastic stories that everyone knew to be true. And there to support these fables was the thing itelf: the butt engraved with a peer's coronet and a flamboyant initial 'W' (for Lord Waterford), and the barrel with a single word, 'Kilkenny'. Stolen by the gallant Captain, long ago.[316]

The highwayman is handsome, ironic, swathed in a dark cape and gallops through the night on a magnificent black stallion – while the burglar is somewhat stupid, wears a striped vest and leaves through the window with his sack of swag. Both are champions of the dispossessed, robbing the rich but friends of the poor. Even the criminals themselves, violent and dangerous men, have often conspired to propagate these myths, acting their parts as if on the stage.

This was certainly true of 'Captain' Freney, most notorious of the 'Tories, Robbers and Rapparees, out in Arms and on their Keeping'. That swaggering phrase is taken from one of several proclamations declaring him an outlaw, with a reward of £100 for anyone who brought him to justice, and the promise of a free pardon if they happened to kill him while doing so.[317] Short, scarred by smallpox and missing the sight of one eye, Freney cut no physical dash but his memoirs are full of daring exploits, cynical wit and acts of unexpected gallantry. He had worked his way up from pantry boy to butler in the service of the Robbins family of Ballyduff, but quit in order 'to follow my Pleasures – and delighted in nothing but Hurling, Horse-racing, Gaming, dancing and such like Diversions.' He then tried to make a living with his wife, keeping a tavern in Waterford, but was prevented by 'several Gentlemen of the City'. Whereupon he took to the road, with a sort of wild boldness.

Mounted on his bay mare Beefsteaks (that afterwards 'died of the staggers'), Freney robbed on the highway in broad daylight, and then surprised the gentry at night when he burst into their bedrooms and seized the gold from under their pillows. He never seemed afraid when outnumbered and often returned their purses to those who convinced him of their need. When he fell sick his remedy was that of a hero – half a pint of brandy – and somehow, despite going heavily armed with pistols and blunderbusses (which he fired with gusto when in danger), he never killed anyone at all.

One of the best stories is that told by John O'Keefe, who met him when he was old in a pub in Kilkenny.

> This man was the once remarkable and indeed notorious, bold Captain F—, of whom were made ballad-songs. He was the audacious and resolute leader of the Rapparees. When a General with a troop of horse went to take him prisoner, Captain F— called out, and said he would surrender, if the General would ride up to him alone; the other complied; the Captain placed his pistol to the General's breast, and took from him his purse and watch, in view of the whole company of soldiers.[318]

But beneath the romance of these tales is a harder, seedier reality, a sense of corruption and betrayal at all levels of society. Freney makes this plain from the very beginning of his *Life and Adventures*. The book is dedicated to the Earl of Carrick, who heads a short but glittering list of subscribers, including Sir Ralph Gore, Chum Ponsonby, John Croker, Joseph Robbins and the Provost and Vice-Provost of Trinity College, Dublin. Freney thanks Carrick for saving his life, by interceding to obtain 'the King's most gracious Pardon', and then refers to his Lordship's efforts to abolish 'that Notion and Scheme of Protection, which had for so many Years prevailed in the County of Kilkenny, and was the real source from whence the Practice of Horse, Cow and Sheep-stealing, and House-breaking sprang, and continued so long in the County.' Lest anyone fail to grasp what this implied, Freney explains that robbers are encouraged in their ways, 'when they hope and expect that by the disposing of Part of the Fruits of their

Rapine, to certain Persons, will be a probable Means of escaping that Punishment which they justly merit by their Crimes.'

Freney kept a reckoning, and noted the price of protection with a fierce sense of injustice. Early in his life on the road he stole a gold watch from Colonel Palliser, in County Wexford, which he gave for safe keeping to his principal accomplice, the sheep-stealer James Bulger. 'When Bulger came, I asked him what he did with my Watch, he said he was obliged to give it and several other valuable Things to a Gentleman, without whose Interest he would not remain in that neighbourhood.'

When two of Freney's gang were captured in 1748, 'I went to the house of one George Roberts, [who] said he had a Friend who was a Man of Power and Interest, that would save either of them, provided I would give him Five Guineas.' After a certain amount of haggling Freney handed over 'a Plate Tankard, value Ten Pounds, a large Ladle value Four pounds, with some Table Spoons.' At Kilkenny Assizes, the following spring, the 'Man of Power' exercised his influence over the jury to ensure that both robbers were acquitted. Towards the end of his tale Freney identifies Roberts as 'a Justice of the Peace's Servant, who by his Master's Permission, corresponded with me on very particular Terms'. The 'Man of Power' proves to be the same mysterious 'Gentleman' who had demanded a gold watch and 'other valuable things' from James Bulger, but he is never named, and was evidently too powerful to prosecute.

The thieves were equally corrupt, and frequently betrayed their friends in the hope of a large reward. Freney himself had many a close escape from being 'set' by members of his own gang and every outrage that he perpetrated raised the odds against him. After five years in constant danger, James Bulger grew fearful. He 'dream'd, that the Soal of his Shoe fell off, which he said was a bad Omen, and desired me to quit the Road that Day.'

Soon afterwards Freney and Bulger were caught in an ambush. Freney saved his friend's life when he was wounded, but Bulger shot the sheriff as they made their escape. It was a fatal mistake.

With the authorities hard on his heels, Freney made several attempts to negotiate an outcome that protected his closest associates at the cost of naming men like George Roberts, who were key agents in the

'Scheme of Protection'. But Bulger's killing of the sheriff meant that this was not enough to strike a bargain, so finally (and by his own account reluctantly) the 'Captain' turned King's evidence and betrayed his entire gang, to save his neck.

The end of his narrative is littered with corpses, as nine men were tried and hanged. Freney himself had hopes of a subscription organised by Lord Carrick, 'in order to enable me with my family to quit the kingdom – however the gentlemen of the county refused to subscribe, and that scheme came to nothing.' So he turned to writing and produced a bestseller, which was published to the world in 1754.

Freney's subsequent career was a classic example of poacher turned gamekeeper, for he was appointed 'county keeper' (probably by the influence of Lord Carrick), 'and was of use in preventing those outrages, of which he himself was once the most daring ringleader and per-petrator.'[319] Finally, on 3 September 1776, he became a supernumary tide waiter at the port of New Ross, responsible for boarding ships as they docked, to prevent the evasion of customs duties. He was paid £5 a quarter and held the job until his death, on 20 December 1789. His long-suffering widow, the ever-resolute Ann, survived him.

Those skimpy details are all that anyone seems to know of the later life of this once famous highwayman. But we have our own family legend of Captain Freney, which I learnt as a child from my father, and he from his – who was told it when a boy at Mount Loftus, by old people in the neighbourhood who had heard it from their grandparents, who were witnesses.

This is how it goes. Nicholas Loftus met a heavily indebted land-owner, John Eaton, and challenged him to a horse race, with £6,000 to the winner. It was a furiously close-run thing and they were neck and neck at the finish, but Lord Loftus claimed victory as he leaned forward and touched the tape with his whip. Eaton objected, so Loftus agreed to race again on condition the stakes were raised, and that Eaton wager his estate in County Kilkenny. Loftus won and claimed Mount Eaton for his own.

But Eaton refused to surrender his lands. He hired two Dublin prizefighters to patrol the demesne, one armed with a pike, the other with a musket, and barricaded himself in his house – where he sat with loaded pistols, swearing to shoot the first man that entered. So Loftus enlisted the help of Ireland's most notorious highwayman, 'Captain' Freney, who had recently retired from his trade but was feared throughout County Kilkenny as the 'one-eyed man with a bay mare'.

Loftus and Freney approached Mount Eaton just as the farm labourers were knocking off for their midday break. Eaton was a mean employer so when the Extinguisher promised the men a week's holiday they did nothing to raise the alarm, and one of them was sent into the fields to fetch two of the largest cabbages that he could find. Armed with these unlikely weapons, Freney crept up to the house and then, screaming like a banshee, used the cabbages to smash through the windows. The terrified Eaton took the cabbage stalks for blunderbusses and was tied to a chair before he had time to recover his wits. Loftus followed Freney though the wreckage of splintered wood and broken glass, carrying his silver-mounted pistols, and took possession.

Eaton was allowed to stay on as a farm tenant, living in the ruins of Drumroe Castle, while Nicholas moved into the main house, which he renamed Mount Loftus, and hired Freney as his butler. On at least one occasion the 'Captain' is said to have reverted to his former ways, slipped out after dinner and robbed the guests on their way back down the avenue. The proceeds were shared with his master.

It sounds too fantastic to be true, a romantic Irish invention – and yet . . .

Freney's blunderbuss somehow survived at Mount Loftus, and the legend of the cabbage stalks seemed too absurd, too random, to have been invented. There was even a precedent, for it was said that when serving Mr Robbins of Ballyduff, Freney robbed his master's agent as he returned one evening from collecting the rents of the tenants – and was forced to improvise, using a thick cabbage stalk to mimic a pistol.[320]

The clincher came later, when to my astonishment I discovered among a bundle of old deeds the original affidavit of a man called Garret Drake, who was employed to serve a court order on John Eaton, at the end of January 1763. Full of crossings out and corrections, this amazing document was evidently written in haste – as Drake blurted out his report a couple of days after the attempt, still shaking from fear.

On the thirtieth day of January I went to John Eaton's dwelling house at Mount Eaton in the County of Kilkenny, & on the next day made enquiry in the Neighbourhood whether Eaton was at his house or not, and was there informed that John Eaton was then at home, & did not stir abroad, for fear of being Served with some order or process, and that no person but his own Servants would be permitted to go in the house, & that he had two Servants or Men employed by him to Guard the Doors of his House to prevent any Person from having Access to him.

On Tuesday the first day of February I went to Eaton's house early in the Morning and continued the whole day about the house but could not get access to Eaton or entrance into the House, & about Eight o'Clock at night, under the protection of the night, I got near the Parlour window and saw Eaton in the room by the assistance of the Candles which were lighted therein but could not get access to him.

On Wednesday the second of February before day light in the Morning I again went to Eaton's house and Continued about the house till about four o'Clock in the afternoon, during which time I could not get any access to him, and about that Hour, two Persons armed, one with a Gunn, the other with a Hanger [sword], came out of the House & came up to me & asked me where I came from, & told me, if I was a bailiff or person who came from Lord Loftus to serve any order, that I should never go back alive, and finding that Eaton secreted himself and kept armed men to prevent this order from being served on him, and also hearing from several persons in the Neighbourhood, that Eaton kept himself concealed, & that there was no possibility to serve him personally with the order, I returned to Dublin.

And I believe it will be Impossible for Lord Loftus to have Eaton personally served, or even a Copy of the Order left for him at his House: and that if any person employed by Lord Loftus should attempt to do so, that He will be in Danger of his life, Eaton having, as I was informed in the Neighbourhood of his House, provided himself with Pateraras [pistols] & other fire Arms, and declared he would destroy any person who should come upon such business.[321]

The original writ that Drake tried to serve also survives, demanding that Eaton pay 'five hundred & fifty seven pounds Eight shillings & Eleven pence with Interest' to Lord Loftus, as ordered by the court the previous November.

As I pieced together the rest of the story I realised that this dramatic incident was only one stage of an enormously long legal process, which had begun a decade earlier and went through numerous twists and turns before it was finally settled. But hidden within the thicket of legal jargon – in a pile of bills, deeds and writs – were clues to the truth behind the family legend of how Mount Loftus was won.[322]

That legal trail began on 25 October 1752, when Articles of Agreement were signed by John Eaton and his Wexford neighbour, Lord Loftus. Eaton contracted to sell his estate in County Kilkenny, for a price that was calculated in the usual fashion, at twenty-one times net rental income. This amounted to just over £8,000 for 1,675 acres, plantation measure (approximately 2,700 acres by modern reckoning), plus 'mountain land not surveyed'. The estate was heavily encumbered with debt, so Eaton agreed to convey the lands free of all charges or mortgages, on the basis that Lord Loftus should 'apply the purchase money in discharge of the incumbrances affecting the same, as far as such purchase money should go,' and that any outstanding creditors would have their claims secured by Eaton on his other lands in the county. Loftus also agreed to lease back the heart of the estate to Eaton and his heirs, at a fair market rent. All of which caused endless litigation in the future but seemed, on the face of it, fairly straightforward.

But here is a possible scenario that makes sense of the legend and explains Eaton's reluctance to go through with the deal. Having lost an enormous sum of money at a game of hazard with Loftus, Eaton was unable to pay and grudgingly agreed to swap that unenforceable gaming debt for a contract to sell his estate. I tend to discount the horse race, which is probably an accretion from some later retelling of the tale (in which the Extinguisher was confused with his grandson, another Nicholas, who bred racehorses) but I do believe in the wager. For one thing is manifestly clear: that Eaton was never a willing seller – he did everything he could to hang on to his lands, come what may.

Loftus was equally determined to enforce the contract. Immediately after the agreement was signed he 'lodged money in the hands of his Bankers with Directions to his Agents to call for and pay John Eaton's Creditors as fast as he could settle with them, which John Eaton promised should immediately be done.' The bulk of the purchase money (£7,800) was handed over within a matter of weeks, and Loftus had his lawyers prepare the deed of Conveyance for Eaton to sign, but the latter 'made frivolous objections in order to avoid executing them.' Nicholas went to court to compel him to account for the rents and profits of the lands that he agreed to sell, but Eaton took years to answer. Judgment was finally given in favour of Loftus, but then there was need to resurvey the lands and to draw up yet another account for all the moneys paid or due, and the case was moved to another court, and so it continued for years on end and nothing was finally settled.

At some point Loftus managed to gain effective control of much of the estate but Eaton held on to the valuable core of Mount Eaton and Powerstown, for which he never paid a penny's rent. The Extinguisher's claim for the accumulated arrears continued to mount and several of Eaton's largest creditors (including his widowed mother and his younger brother Charles) remained unpaid. Charles Eaton engaged in constant lawsuits to secure his claims, but Lord Loftus was determined to protect his own interests ahead of any other claimant – 'availing himself of the privileges of Parliament as a Peer, he sometimes promised his assistance and sometimes withheld it, & John Eaton was always adverse and gave every opposition in his power.' The lawyers themselves seemed in no hurry for judgment, but were content with repeated delays, while the fees racked up.

In 1762, ten years after the original agreement was signed, it was calculated by the Court of Chancery that Eaton owed more than £8,000 to his various creditors, including £557 to Lord Loftus. An order for Eaton to pay this debt was served on his housekeeper, Margaret Rinney, and his attorney James Connor, but the man himself evaded the process servers – so another writ was issued in January 1763, and Garret Drake set off for Mount Eaton.

When Drake returned and told the tale of Eaton barricaded in his house 'with Pateraras & other fire Arms', and with armed ruffians to protect him, the Extinguisher finally lost patience. He obtained a further judgment, dated 12 March 1763, ordering Eaton to pay up within a fortnight, and seems to have decided to serve the writ himself, with the help of Captain Freney. One way or another, the septuagenarian Lord gained the upper hand, and then, having seized possession of the house, Loftus was determined to prevent any attempt at re-occupation by Eaton and his henchmen. So Freney was employed as bodyguard and butler, resuming the life in service that had been his for so many years, before he took to the road.

His Lordship was then unstoppable. He employed the most determined professional sequestrators, Messrs French & Hygatt Allen, to secure the rents of all of Eaton's tenants and to seize and sell his cattle. Mr French's account for their services makes plain that this was no easy matter, and that they 'served upwards of 160 copies of sequestration on the Defendant's estate in the counties of Wexford and Kilkenny & Sequestered the same & also his stock of Cattle, being very dangerous and Troublesome for each Sequestration.'[323]

With his entire rental income in the hands of his rival, his cattle sold and his house occupied, Eaton capitulated, and at the end of November 1763 he signed the formal Conveyance of the Mount Eaton estate. A few days later, on 3 December, Lord Loftus transferred the lands to the trustees of his son Edward's marriage settlement, as he had promised to do five years earlier. He had finally achieved his objective.

But that hard-fought victory seems to have drained the last of the old man's energy. Exactly four weeks later, on the eve of the New Year, he died at his house in Dublin, having bequeathed this fine estate in County Kilkenny and all his personal possessions to his favourite illegitimate son, my 'four greats' grandfather, Edward Loftus. Among the silver, china and family portraits, the piles of deeds and bills, the accumulated debris of a lifetime, was a stolen blunderbuss.

I am struck by how similar they were, the lord and the highwayman. They lived by their own codes, for better or worse.

CHAPTER 23

A Scandalous Settlement

If any of his enemies had happened to wander down Capel Street, in Dublin, on New Year's Eve 1763, they might have fancied they heard a thunderclap and smelt a faint whiff of sulphur – for Old Nick was dead. Lord Viscount Loftus of Ely had finally expired. After seventy-six years of turbulent life, the Extinguisher was extinguished.

Earlier in the century Capel Street had been one of the most fashionable places to live in Dublin, but fashion moved elsewhere and the street became more commercial. Numerous shops and workshops supplied elegant fixtures and fittings for the stylish houses that speculators like Luke Gardiner were building in Henrietta Street (where Lord Loftus's eldest son had bought one of the grandest, in 1755) and Sackville Street (where his Lordship's favourite illegitimate son lived in the 1760s) and throughout the ever-expanding city. Nicholas himself was much more modest in his tastes, or perhaps you could say that he was settled in his ways, for he continued to rent accommodation in Capel Street, at No 47, as he and other members of his family had done for more than twenty years. The house belonged to Richard Moore, 'upholder', who was paid seventy guineas 'for Lodging' after his Lordship's death and carried on his business as upholsterer and cabinet-maker in workshops at the back of the yard. Lord Loftus most probably occupied the tall, panelled rooms on the first floor.

It was here that he died, early one Saturday morning at the tail end of the year, after a short illness. He had been cared for by 'two Nurse Tenders', attended by various Physicians and supplied with medicines by Edward Croker, Thomas Savage and Mr McMullin, Apothecaries. And when he was dead, Catherine Donevan, washerwoman, was employed 'for Washing Blanketts' and other laundry, as the tidying up began.

Lord Loftus must have wanted to be buried with his ancestors, in the family vault at Fethard, because his body was taken on the slow journey to County Wexford. There were payments 'for Watching the Corpse on the Road', to 'the Smith for Shoeing Horses', to 'Helpers for attending the Horses' and to 'Servants that went with the funeral to the Country'. Richard Moore seems to have supplied the coffin (his 'Bill for funeral' was £28), the Undertaker charged £50 and John Dillon provided five guineas' worth of candles. The funeral service was conducted by the Rev. Thomas Burrowes, who was one of his Lordship's tenants on the Hook. John Byrne supplied '1½ hundred of Oysters' and charged 13s. 4d. 'for Ale to the Cook', while various merchants delivered copious amounts of wine, to refresh the mourners. Five shillings was paid to the 'Pastry Cook for Baking Pyes'. The servants at Loftus Hall had their wages settled in full and £100 was distributed among 'the poor of the Parishes of Hooke, Fethard and Templetown, agreeable to the Will of Lord Loftus'. And then there were the lawyers' fees – more than £650 in total.

Those details, and others equally evocative, are recorded in a settling of accounts between Sir Edward Loftus and his brother Captain Nicholas, six years after the event.[324] This wonderfully clear document shows that trunks full of papers were removed to Edward's house within days of his father's death, and that an inventory of their contents was taken on 6 January 1764 in the presence of his Lordship's heirs and executors. There was a bundle of promissory notes for the rentals due from all his tenant farmers, including the Catholic priest Thomas Broaders (who later became famous for exorcising the ghost of Loftus Hall) and his Protestant counterpart, Rev. Burrowes. Outstanding debts ranged from modest amounts owed to Lord Loftus's butcher, Lewis Tarrell, and his ironmonger, O'Brien, to the jointure due to his estranged widow, Lady Loftus, and the pension to his mistress, Mrs Hernon.

When 'Mary Hernon my Servant' (who was also the mother of two of his children) looked 'in Lord Loftus's desk' she found thirty-two guineas and a further '10 pieces of Gold' which the executors deemed to be worth five guineas. She retained fifteen guineas for herself and handed over the rest to her eldest son, Edward Loftus. She also learnt, as perhaps she already knew, that his Lordship had provided for her in his will, with an annuity of £150 for the rest of her life – more than sufficient for decent comfort. And Mrs Hernon had her own house, as is evident from the note of a payment for looking after it, while she was helping to clear things up at Capel Street: 'Allowed Wm Shee for Care of her house upon Lord Loftus's Death, £1 15*s.* 6*d.*' [325]

These were small settlements – nothing to perturb his heirs – but the Extinguisher died as he lived, in defiance of the world's opinion, and the heart of his will caused a scandal, as a Wexford gossip wrote to Lord Arran, on 7 January 1764: 'The whole Talk of this County turns on the Destination Ld. Loftus has made of his Fortune, the reflections on it I need not trouble your L^dship with, Dublin is full as censorious I doubt not as the County of Wexford, but it gives me pleasure, my Lord, to reflect that some of his Rank take care to set a far better Example & need not dread the Reproaches of any, when they shall be no more.'[326]

The author of that letter, Eyton Poutts, was an egregious toady and a man of witless judgement, who also claimed (quite falsely) that 'By the Death of Ld Loftus, all the [political] Interest of his Family in this County, as it was entirely personal, I presume dies with him'; but he was certainly right about the scandal. By a codicil to his will made five months before his death, Lord Loftus did all that he could to favour his 'reputed or natural sons by Mary Hernon' over his legitimate heirs.[327]

That scandalous settlement was the last of a series of increasingly radical afterthoughts, embodied in several private memoranda and three successive codicils, as the Extinguisher became increasingly disillusioned with his legitimate sons.[328] The girls had been well provided for, with £3,500 settled on each when they were married, but the most valuable family estates were destined for their brothers, whose weaknesses were all too apparent. The eldest, Nicholas, had achieved sudden wealth through his marriage to an heiress from the North, but his fits of drunken rage drove her to an early grave and he persecuted their only son, whom he locked away from the world. His brother Henry was more amiable, but full of his own self-esteem, which stretched beyond his means and provoked much mockery. But Lord Loftus loved his bastards – particularly Edward, his favourite 'Ned', for whom he had purchased a commission in the army, arranged a good marriage and given his name and coat of arms.

He appointed the illegitimate Edward as one of his executors, to ensure that his wishes were fulfilled, and made him the main beneficiary, in so far as he was able. The Loftus Hall and Ballymagir estates had already been settled on his eldest boys when they were married, but his

Lordship altered the terms of those settlements to ensure that if they had no surviving male heirs the inheritance of each reverted to their illegitimate younger brothers. More damaging still, he charged the Loftus Hall estate with the sum of £2,000 – payable to Edward – and Ballymagir with the same amount, to be divided between his 'natural sons'. Edward Loftus was confirmed in his possession of 'The Estate I bought from Mr John Eaton' in County Kilkenny, plus some valuable leasehold lands in County Wexford, and was left 'all my Plate'. His brother, yet another Nicholas, got the 'Lands of Cool, Tinnock and Ballygow'. And 'the rest of my personal Estate and effects, of what nature or kind soever' was shared between them, without so much as a teaspoon to any of his Lordship's legitimate sons or daughters.

Henry was particularly annoyed that his own expectations had been diminished by the codicil, since the charge of £2,000 on the Ballymagir estate had originally been arranged for his benefit and he could ill afford to pay such a large sum to his illegitimate siblings. So he struck a deal with them. They agreed to renounce their claim to the £2,000 and he promised to ensure that Edward would be returned for one of the family boroughs at the next parliamentary election. They kept their side of the bargain but Henry broke his – which provoked a typically Irish 'affair of honour', as the headstrong Edward challenged his half-bother to a duel. But that is a story for a later chapter.

Despite those burdensome charges and the scandalous preference given to his bastard sons, Lord Loftus might well have argued that his legitimate heirs had little to complain of. His last will and testament was part of a complex network of property arrangements, including a series of marriage settlements that provided valuable estates for each of his sons and substantial dowries for his daughters. There was sufficient for all, and there was no great tally of debts. It is true that his Lordship still owed Mr Cotton King a large sum of money for an estate in Wexford that he had purchased but never paid for, but the income from those lands exceeded the annual interest on the debt, and Nicholas believed that 'to sell it again will bring £1,000 profit.'[329] As for the rest, the 'Inventory of the Effects of the late Lord Loftus' showed that his Lordship was wealthy enough to have loaned £2,000 at 5% interest to John Sheppard and a similar sum on the same terms to Sir William Parsons, which together with other amounts due to him totalled £6,783.

Once all the bills were paid there was more than £4,000 to be divided between Sir Edward Loftus and his brother, Captain Nicholas. Not cash of course (Ireland was chronically short of cash, for most of the eighteenth century) but the accumulated total of promissory notes and other future obligations to pay. In spite of his apparent recklessness, Lord Loftus never wasted his estate with riotous living. His extravagance was limited to lawyers' fees, and that was an Irish habit.

One of the few clauses of Lord Loftus's will that remained untouched by any subsequent codicil was his determination that all future heirs to his estate, however remote, must 'take and use the name of Loftus', or forfeit their inheritance. That imperative to preserve the family name and birthright, come what may, was expressed in the most detailed computation of the remote pathways of genealogy. His Lordship's children, legitimate and illegitimate, their male heirs, the line of male descent through various cousins, the 'reversions' through daughters and granddaughters – every eventuality that his attorneys could conceive was plotted and planned. But all this careful and expensive forethought was thrown into confusion by a 'trial for idiocy', which became one of the longest and costliest cases in Irish legal history. Once again, it was the lawyers who had the last laugh.

THE

CASE

O F

Edward Loftus Esq;

AINFUL as the tafk muft be, to trouble the Public with diffentions of a private nature, I find myfelf under the difagreeable neceffity either of fo doing, or of lying under an imputation, of all others the moft grating to a gentleman. My fole view in this is to affert my own honour ; and, fortunate fhould I efteem myfelf, could I gain this important

point,

AFFAIRS OF HONOUR

CHAPTER 24

Portraits of a Marriage

My gaze flickers from the fluttering black ribbons that tie his hair and encircle her throat, to the scribbles of white chalk on his cravat, his buttons, the lace of her cap, to the soft, barely formed contours of their young faces, and finally to their eyes – as he looks at her and she, somewhat reserved, glances at me.[330]

The eighteen-year-old Thomas Hickey drew Edward and Anne Loftus in 1759, at the beginning of their married life – only three years after having graduated from the Dublin Society School, where he was 'much noticed as a boy for his amazing likenesses in chalk'.[331] So the artist was even younger than his subjects and that sense of youthful immediacy and sympathy is very evident in these lovely grisaille portraits. Edward's face is eager, thoughtful but open, while Anne looks more serious, slightly uncertain, a girl determined to be a woman. She may perhaps be pregnant (their first child was born later that year) and already, despite her youth, I can envisage the day when she would complain because she was sometimes mistaken for her husband's mother.[332]

It's not so much a question of looks as of character: a northern, Protestant caution, curbing the frank impetuosity that Edward expressed all through his life; for Anne was the only daughter of the Reverend Paul Read, a wealthy clergyman from County Tyrone, while Edward was the illegitimate son of a scandalous father and his Catholic housekeeper. Her inheritance was the carefully husbanded accumulation of Protestant planters, while his had been won in a bet and secured with the help of a highwayman. And they say that she became somewhat haughty, famously proud of her small hands and feet, while Edward was open and easy with all. But however disparate their backgrounds and temperament, this was a marriage of affection, which endured for a lifetime. He never took a mistress – rare exception to the family tradition – and they died within months of each other, half a century later.

It was also, inevitably, an alliance of interests, nicely balanced on both sides. Anne's relatives were solid, prosperous, northern Protestants, nothing grand. Her father was a Read, her mother a Hamilton (whose second husband was Dr Ferguson) and her uncle was Alexander McAulay – all good Scottish names, careful with their cash. Edward's ambiguous illegitimacy, by contrast, had the aristocratic stamp of old money, political ramifications, a devil-may-care insouciance. He was educated at Ireland's best school, in Kilkenny, and then spent a year or two at Trinity College Dublin – along with many who later became famous in Grattan's Parliament – before his father bought him a commission in a fashionable regiment, Lord Conway's Horse.[333] He was married to an heiress, 'elected' as MP for one of the family boroughs and granted his father's arms, 'with proper distinction'. In 1766 Edward was awarded an honorary doctorate by Trinity College and appointed Colonel of the Wexford Militia. Two years later he was made a baronet, and served as High Sheriff of County Tyrone, the first of several occasions. In 1784, a year of high political drama, he was High Sheriff of County Wexford.

Social status was backed by landed wealth, which both enriched and troubled them for much of their married life. Anne Read's dowry of 5,000 acres in County Tyrone was not hugely profitable but seems to have been worth about £400 annually when they married. Added to the rent roll of the Mount Loftus estate in County Kilkenny and various other lands there and in Wexford (at least £600, plus 'a couple of fat Hens out of every House or Cabbin'), this was a decent income to start their life together – and it grew much larger.[334] Partly this was a matter of inheritance – outliving their relatives – and partly a consequence of the growing agricultural prosperity of Ireland towards the end of the eighteenth century. Their total landed revenue grew to more than £4,000 per annum.[335]

But their outgoings also rose, probably as fast as their income. They built a tall new house at Mount Loftus, in County Kilkenny, 'finished in an elegant manner', and enclosed its large demesne with a high stone wall. Gardens and orchards were planted with 'the choicest kind of fruit trees', the fishponds, pigeon house and rabbit warren were 'all well stocked' and the park was adorned with 'beautiful Deer'. But it seems that country life was too boring or too expensive, and when he was made a baronet Sir Edward decided to let Mount Loftus and to live for most of the year in the heart of fashionable Dublin, at his house in Sackville Street.[336] The young couple travelled frequently to England and may also have contemplated a tour through France and Italy, but there is no evidence that they ever went there, save a marker stuck in a guidebook that Edward inherited, a year after their marriage.[337] And then, as their family grew larger, they spent more of their time in the country, returning to Mount Loftus and enlarging the old fortified manor at Richfield, in County Wexford, which Sir Edward inherited on the death of his half-brother Henry. They lived well – Anne loved the theatre and life in both Dublin and Kilkenny was extremely social – but their children proved expensive as they grew older.

Almost as costly as their children were the lawyers, for litigation was the constant habit of fashionable society, played for even higher stakes than were usual at the card table or the racetrack. Arguments about ownership and inheritance often dragged on for decades in a game of bluff that became a war of attrition. It was an Irish compulsion, seemingly inescapable. So the man in Hickey's portrait – frank, engaging, impulsive – is often hidden from view by the piles of briefs, bills and deeds, which survive as the all too evident debris of a life of lawsuits.

A clue to these seeming contradictions is Edward's illegitimacy, and the fact that his mother's status – Irish, Catholic, a servant – placed her beyond the pale of social recognition. Though his father's favourite son, he was repudiated by the half-brothers whose support he counted on for advancement, scorned as 'Ned Hernon'. All of which seems to have fired his liberal instincts and turned him into an enlightened landlord, supporter of Napper Tandy and leading protagonist in the Kilkenny Assembly of Volunteers – but also made him determined to defend his rights, whenever he saw a chance to increase his property or enhance his standing in the world. It was a question of honour.

Early in their married life there was some sort of dispute with Anne

Loftus's relatives about her inheritance, but the main, ongoing litigation was the old battle with the former owner of Mount Loftus (as Mount Eaton was now renamed) and his numerous creditors.[338] The matter dragged on for years, but was was finally resolved when Sir Edward's half-brother Henry died, in 1783. As heir to the pastures of Richfield, on the coast of County Wexford, Edward was wealthy enough to come to a settlement. It cost him over £4,000 but enabled him to secure the remainder of Eaton's unsold lands in County Kilkenny to add to his estate at Mount Loftus. Part of the deal was that he should settle his opponents' legal costs, but the bill eventually submitted by Eaton's attorney John Hobson (fifty-five pages of resentment, totalling £784) went unpaid. It was long after the principal litigants were dead and Edward's own charges, from various lawyers, were troublesome enough.

Many of these concerned a much more public battle, involving vast estates, extraordinary cruelty, allegations of madness and enormous bills, which began in 1767 with the death of the elder of Edward's half-brothers, the monstrous Nicholas, and was finally decided by a single vote in the Irish House of Lords, on 2 May 1775. The case of 'the Ideot Earl' is too strange and lengthy a saga to summarise here (you must wait for another chapter) and Edward was not directly involved in the lawsuits – but he was certainly interested in the outcome. Had things gone differently, he would have stood to inherit the valuable Loftus Hall estate, on the Hook. So he incurred huge costs as a series of expensive lawyers kept a watching brief on his chances and their clerks sat in court, transcribing the evidence.

That expense went unrewarded, but the Richfield inheritance meant that Sir Edward's estate was nicely consolidated in County Kilkenny and County Wexford, and he felt less and less inclined to journey north to look after his wife's property in Tyrone. Eventually they decided to sell, and first to go were the lands leased from the Bishop of Derry.

Two Castles, one hundred Messuages, one hundred Cottages, fifty Lofts, one hundred Gardens, one hundred Orchards, ten Mills, twenty Pidgeon Houses, three hundred acres of Arable Land, two hundred acres of Meadow, two hundred acres of Pasture, one hundred acres of Wood and Underwood, one hundred acres of Furze Heath and one hundred acres of Moor Marsh.

Those neat round numbers suggest the rigorous order of Protestant plantation, with each cottage having its carefully measured plot of garden, farmland, wood and bog, but the value of this estate had much declined. It was sold for £2000.[339]

Far more valuable was Lady Loftus's estate in Drumnabeigh, which by now was yielding 'a clear yearly income or profit rent of six hundred and fifty four pounds,' but its disposal proved unexpectedly complicated. Several of the crucial deeds had gone missing and it took four years, from 1798 to 1802, before all the legal formalities could be resolved and the sale completed, to 'Patrick Plunkett of the City of Dublin Esquire, Doctor of Physic'. So long drawn out was this process that at one point Sir Edward's lawyer, James Orr, had to negotiate with 'Mister Waters for borrowing three thousand pounds', to tide Sir Edward over. Orr himself waited so long for his money that he added a grumpy note to his bill, requesting payment within a month, 'otherwise I shall proceed for the Recovery thereof as the law directs.'

Emerging from the dusty language of that pile of legal transactions I turn with relief to Sir Edward's household accounts, which lovingly record the purchase of a 'monstrous turbot' or a plate of fresh mushrooms, and I relish his delight in the small details of daily life, the sensual pleasures of seasonal produce, the care of his numerous dependants. I read the pamphlet that he wrote, in defence of his honour, or the passages that he underlined in a political tract, urging social justice. I remember the stories that I was told as a child, of his impulsiveness and generosity, his wife's hauteur and practicality, their lovely country houses and their madcap children. And I look again at Hickey's portraits.

Their gaze spans the centuries.

CHAPTER 25

The Ghost of Loftus Hall

'On a dreadful stormy night as the small family sat by the large log fire in the Hall, with the wind screeching in the gloomy corridors, a loud knocking was heard at the outer gate.'[340] Thus the story begins, in classic style. It's set on the Hook, in 1765, when Charles Tottenham (brother-in-law of Nicholas Loftus, the wicked Earl of Ely) was living at the Hall with his second wife and his youngest, unmarried daughter. She was named Anne after her late mother, Anne Loftus.

The waves were crashing on the black rocks below the house, hurling spray into the night, when a servant announced the arrival of a young gentleman who had lost his way in the storm. The handsome stranger was pressed to stay, and soon held his listeners spellbound with tales of his travels. Anne was smitten.

In the evenings they played cards and sometimes, when the fire was ablaze, the men slipped off their boots under the table. The stranger partnered Anne as they won every game, night after night, until the moment when she dropped her cards in excitement, and they scattered on the floor. As she bent to retrieve them Anne saw to her horror that her partner had a pair of cloven hoofs. She screamed, then fainted, and the devil shot through the roof in a ball of fire, with a noise like thunder.

Anne was carried to the tapestry room, where for some months she lay in a state of pitiable terror, until eventually she died. And the hole in the ceiling through which the stranger vanished resisted all attempts to repair it – a gaping monument to his memory.

Thus far this is a classic ghost story, a tale for stormy nights by a good fire, but myth blurs into history. It is said that 'the devil continued to disturb the household with shrieks, screams and other frightening noises' until eventually the staunchly Protestant Tottenham could stand it no longer and turned in desperation to Canon Broaders – the Catholic parish priest who was a tenant on the Loftus Hall estate. 'By various forms of exorcism' Broaders is supposed to have confined the devil to the tapestry chamber (where Anne Loftus had died) and 'the Tottenham family were ever after very kind to him, to the day of his death.' The story is given added credence because the priest's tombstone was supposedly inscribed with this unusual epitaph.

> Here lies the body of Thomas Broaders,
>   Who did good, and prayed for all,
> And banished the devil from Loftus Hall.[341]

But the devil was imprisoned in the tapestry chamber, not banished from the Hall, so no one was put to sleep there unless every other room was occupied. Occasionally there was little alternative and a wretched guest might be awakened by 'growling noises, like that of a dog', as something heavy fell on the bed and 'the curtains were ripped back and the bed-clothes pulled to the floor.' Others reported seeing the tall figure of a woman, 'dressed in stiff brocaded silk' and carrying a fan, who glided towards a closet in the corner of the room, silent in the moonlight. It was not until the old Hall was demolished in 1871 that the haunting ceased – but the shivering continued, for the vast mansion that replaced the seventeenth-century house was itself so gaunt and chill that the family abandoned the place. Loftus Hall was eventually sold to a community of Rosminian nuns, whose numbers declined year by year, until seven of them were left to rattle their bones within the vast empty rooms – so cold that they, too, could take it no longer. 'The electricity bill for the poor creatures' last two months' residence [in 1982] was reported to be over £700, and even then they were probably only getting the temperature up to freezing point.'[342] The house stood abandoned; the devil had won.

In the visitors' centre at Hook Lighthouse you can now buy a video of *The Legend of Loftus Hall* (a 'drama-documentary' of 'the greatest Ghost Story in Irish history'), presented as a lurid fable of oppression and retribution. Loftus Hall is described as 'built on misery, persecution and sadness. A blood stained site which down the centuries witnessed many murderous atrocities . . so unholy as to warrant a visit by the devil.' Of course this is nonsense, a crude caricature, but there is indeed something hidden in the story that hints at family unhappiness, the uneasy relation-ship of Protestant landlords and Catholic tenants, and a sudden shock, never fully explained. Those hidden meanings are hard to catch, too subtle to be heard against the noise of propaganda (the sacred myths of Irish history), but they may be closer to historical experience.

CHAPTER 26

The Said Late Earl

A young man, partially crippled and of notoriously strange temperament, sat in a wheeled chair in the large, flagged hallway of Dr Mosse's Lying-in Hospital in Dublin. Agitated by the unfamiliarity of his circumstances, the invalid began to laugh, with high-pitched intensity, and with bony knuckles he violently rubbed his long nose, until the pale ivory glowed pink.

I know the shape of that nose, the sound of that laugh. I know who upholstered the young man's chair, and who made his wig. I know the names of his servants and lawyers. And I know that it must have been the invalid's uncle who calmed his laughter, before speaking to an official of the Chancery Court, standing guard on the back room.

The door was opened, revealing a long table piled with hats and surrounded by curious faces. Fearful 'that the unusual Appearance of so many Hats on the Table might alarm or Disturb his Nephew, who he Sayed had weak Nerves,' Henry Loftus requested that they be cleared away, before returning to the hall and taking hold of the handles of that wheeled chair. Resolutely, steadily, he propelled his nephew into the back room.

Thus it was that on 24 January 1767, Nicholas Loftus Hume, second Earl of Ely, appeared before the commissioners and jury appointed by the Court in Chancery of Ireland, for his personal examination. His Lordship was effectively on trial, for a crime unknown to common law but of supreme importance to his relatives: 'The Question before them was, whether the Lord was an Ideot or of unsound Mind'.[343]

For several days beforehand, an excited throng of fashionable Dublin society had crowded into a large, elegant room at the front of Dr Mosse's famous hospital, which had been commandeered by the commissioners for the 'Publick Examination' of witnesses in the case. It was already a *cause célèbre*, having all the right ingredients for melodrama: a young, sickly nobleman, rescued by his scheming uncle from virtual imprisonment and a life of appalling horror; a cruel, dissipated and recently deceased father; the tragic mother, who had died of a 'miscarriage, occasioned by a fright', when her son was only two; and a disputed inheritance, enormous wealth.

Property and the obsession with property coloured the outlook of all those present, except the central character himself, whose sanity was now on trial. For many it seemed that Lord Ely's 'ideocy' lay less in the strangeness of his behaviour (he was, after all, very rich) than in the fact that he was not 'Capable of making a contract or bargain or understanding a common Deed of Conveyance'.

What no one disputed was that the defendant had long been shut away from society, was of a nervous disposition, easily upset by crowds, and that his physical sufferings had left him greatly debilitated. So the commissioners agreed to examine Lord Ely in private, with only the jury present, together with his uncle Henry Loftus (for the defence), his accuser George Rochfort and a few court officials and legal counsel. When they filed out of the public hearing into the 'back room' of the hospital and closed the door behind them, they left a frustrated crowd to imagine the invisible drama.

I, too, had often speculated on what was said. The outcome was known and summaries of the proceedings existed, but I could find no surviving transcripts of one of the most scandalous and fascinating trials of its age. The words of the witnesses, the testimony of the accused, all seemed lost.

Then an elderly cousin died and four tin boxes of family papers arrived on my doorstep from Ireland. Slowly I sorted my way through wills and codicils, marriage settlements and deeds, account books and fragments of diaries. I lingered so long on so much that was fascinating that it took me weeks to discover the manuscript book, bound in grass-green vellum, which lay at the bottom of one of the boxes. As soon as I opened it I was spellbound.

Here, in all its immediacy, was the story of that famous trial, and the life of trials of Lord Ely ('the Said Late Earl'), written in the bold copperplate hand of a legal clerk over two hundred years ago. It was astonishing: 218 folio pages of thick, handmade eighteenth-century paper filled with the depositions of twenty-four witnesses, copied for my 'four greats' grandfather, Sir Edward Loftus, when proceedings were reopened after Lord Ely's death. Together with this book, I found a collection of other documents relevant to the case, including a bundle of affidavits and the record of the personal examination of Lord Ely himself, on that cold day in January, 1767.

Now, as I write, I am surrounded by these documents, vivid with the voices of the past.

It was one of the longest court cases of the eighteenth century and concerned the sanity of the heir to an enormous fortune, the only child of Nicholas Loftus, 1st Earl of Ely (who owned thousands of acres in Wexford) and Mary Hume, the heiress to huge estates in County Fermanagh.

The boy's father 'was a Man of strange Disposition, and uncommon Violence of Temper', who seems to have provoked his wife's early death, when their son was a child of two. The boy was so traumatised that for many years he was unable to speak or to do the simplest things for himself. This in turn provoked his father's disgust, for he abandoned the child to his grandmother and then, when he was twelve, sent him to live in the household of a man called Richard Moore (one of the most fashionable furniture makers in Dublin) where he himself lodged when in town, before acquiring his own house in Henrietta Street. There are poignant testimonies of the men who worked for Moore, telling how they fed the teenager mustard, to make him splutter; and 'of his speaking a great many vile and bawdy words, which he said Richard Moore's workmen taught him'; and of seeing him gazing out to the street, 'with a small bit of paper tied to a string, flying it out of the window like a kite'.[344]

As Nicholas approached his eighteenth birthday, his father became concerned that rumours of his insanity were provoking his maternal relatives to legal action, to prevent him inheriting the Hume estates in Fermanagh. So the Earl removed his son to the seclusion of Clermont House, in County Wicklow, where he was hidden from view and treated with appalling severity. Nicholas reached his majority in 1759 without any knowledge of the fact or its consequences, or that his father had arranged for him to be elected as MP for one of the family constituencies, to frustrate legal action. He himself, the wicked Earl, enjoyed the wealth that was rightly his son's.

It was only later, when the case came to court, that the terrible story was told. Here, for example, is the testimony of a housemaid, Cordelia Fawcett, who was hired to look after Nicholas, in 1762. She was twenty years old and earned seven guineas per annum.

I gave him Physick by the Directions of his Father every second Morning to prevent his being able to come to Town to attend a Commission [Nicholas was being poisoned so that he could not appear for a legal examination in Dublin, as demanded by his maternal relatives].

I saw his Father about two or three times a week treat him very cruelly and beat him severely with Ratans and with a Switch, and I often saw his Father break Ratans to pieces over him. I saw the streams of Blood running down his back and I washed his back with Brandy to prevent its Mortifying. I thought that his father was Mad at Times and that he would then beat every Body about him.

This savagery was compounded by those employed to teach Nicholas to read and write – the Reverend Needham and a house painter called Cuvillie – each of whom believed that education could be beaten into the young man by brute force. Nicholas lost the use of his legs, was confined to a wheelchair and suffered from scurvy. And so it continued, until his father suddenly died and the young man's uncle, Henry Loftus, appeared as his saviour.

Nicholas was whisked away to Dublin, to a life of unexpected luxury. He was attended by the best physicians, Doctors Robinson and Quinn, who testified their surprise that despite being 'a Man of exceeding weak Nerves, easily agitated and thrown into confusion', the young Earl 'never answered Foolishly or Sillily and that he had a sense of decency, cleaness and neatness, and that he seemed to have a strong Desire to oblige.'

That biddable nature was, of course, a boon to his uncle Henry, who was able to act in his nephew's name in claiming his mother's fortune, which enabled him to acquire the old Loftus estate at Rathfarnham and undertake major improvements and alterations to the Castle. One of those employed on this work was the house painter, Cuvillie, despite the fact that to Nicholas (his former pupil) he remained a terrifying ogre. Henry was even prepared to invoke Cuvillie as a bogeyman, to curb his 'easily agitated' nephew, as witnessed by John McDermot, 'Wigmaker and Hair Dresser', who visited Nicholas in his uncle's house, in April 1767, accompanied by his assistant, James Hanby.

I waited upon him for the purpose of trying on a Wigg but I was afterwards detained whilst my man shaved Lord Ely. The operation of shaving the Earl of Ely was interrupted three or four times, each time by means of him laughing. James Hanby could not safely shave his face whilst he was laughing, so he stopped shaving him and Henry Loftus desired the Earl not to laugh and told him that the man could not shave him whilst he laughed. Hanby having gone on with shaving his face, Lord Loftus laughed out in the same manner as he had done before.

This incident was repeated twice more, until finally Henry lost patience.

He went to the door of the Room and opened it and called out, Cuvillie, Cuvillie, come in, and thereupon the Earl cried out Ah don't let him in I will be a good Boy I will laugh no more, and thereupon he was quiet and desisted from Laughing and gave a heavy sigh, upon which Henry Loftus asked him what ailed him to which he replied Ah Sir you have Lowered my Spirits and Henry Loftus sayd I am very sorry for that my Lord but you hindered the Man from shaving you. And James Hanby then finished shaving him.

Clean-shaven, dressed in an extraordinary blue velvet coat with gold frogging and enormous cuffs of leopard fur, and wearing one of McDermot's wigs (cunningly designed to look like natural hair), his Lordship posed for his portrait. And sometimes, to please the crowd, he was driven around Dublin in his carriage, like royalty, or an automaton. These formal displays were intended to prove that he was as 'normal' as the average Irish lord – not, some might think, a very high test of sanity. But alone at home he was teased and maltreated by his servants, until word of it reached his uncle, who sacked the offenders.

So life continued, in a daze of wealth and comfort, and perhaps of loneliness, but this startling change of fortune came too late. Worn out by decades of cruel treatment at the hands of his father, the 'Ideot Earl' slowly sickened. Eventually Henry took him abroad, to Spa, hoping for a cure. They stayed for a few weeks, while Nicholas took the waters and Henry acquired a few baubles to decorate Rathfarnham Castle. And then, when it seemed clear that the invalid was dying, they returned to Rathfarnham, where Nicholas signed a will, leaving all his great wealth to his uncle Henry.

A few days later he was dead, at the age of thirty-one.

CHAPTER 27

To Assert my Honour

No young fellow could *finish his education* till he had exchanged shots with some of his friends or acquaintances. The first question asked as to a young man's respectability and qualifications (particularly when he proposed for a lady-wife) were, "What family is he of?" – "Did he ever *blaze*?"[345]

Jonah Barrington's account of the eighteenth-century 'fire-eaters' is frequently dismissed as wild exaggeration – but the facts suggest otherwise. The passion for duelling became a sort of frenzy, particularly in the '70s and '80s, when literally hundreds of duels were fought, often for the most trivial of reasons.

Earlier in the century such encounters had been less regulated by recognised codes of honour and many were little more than drunken brawls, fought with swords in taverns. Casualties were high. But the increasing fashion for pistols meant that duels became less dangerous, with only about a third of combatants being killed or wounded. A direct hit from a pistol shot could well be fatal, especially given the primitive state of surgery and the likelihood of infection, but pistols were seldom accurate and often misfired. In such cases most duellists were persuaded by their seconds that honour had been satisfied, rather than continuing to blaze away until one of them was incapacitated.[346]

What one eighteenth-century Irishman referred to as 'that damn'd thing called honour' was the excuse, all too often, for these touchy explosions of male vanity, fuelled by port or brandy. But there were also duels of a different sort, the expression of long-standing grievances, many of which were political in origin; and as politics became more exciting duels became more frequent, especially at the time of elections. These had been rare occurrences earlier in the century because the Irish Parliament was only dissolved on the monarch's death – a strange state of affairs, which persisted until the passing of the Octennial Act in 1768, limiting Parliament's life to eight years. There was an election

when George II came to the throne, in 1727, and another after his
death in 1760 – but in the three decades between those dates political
life in the constituencies was almost at a standstill, except for the
occasional by-elections to replace Members who died or were ennobled.

This meant that gaining control of parliamentary seats at the
beginning of the new reign was all-important, for it gave the borough
magnates uninterrupted influence during the King's lifetime, with all
the jobbery and wealth that flowed from such patronage. As a result,
the great landowning families competed fiercely for dominance of the
parliamentary boroughs, sometimes with violent consequences. The
most extraordinary of these political feuds was that between the Flood
and Agar families for the control of a single seat in County Kilkenny.
Their bitter battle lasted for more than a decade, involved the most
ruthless chicanery and resulted in the deaths of three men, before
culminating in two duels between the leading Patriot, Henry Flood,
and his opponent James Agar. In the second of those encounters, in
1769, Agar was killed.

'An election was held to return two members of Parliament for the
Borough of Clonmines in the County of Wexford on 9th May 1761.'
Thus the record begins for what my great-uncle Jack described as 'a nice
little family party'. There were seven electors – including Nicholas and
Henry Loftus, their brothers-in-law John and Charles Tottenham, and
three other dependants of the Loftus family: James Boyd and the Trench
brothers – Samuel and John. 'Henry Alcock of Wilton and Charles
Tottenham of Tottenham Green Esquires [married respectively to Mary
and Elizabeth Loftus] were duly and unanimously elected and returned
Burgesses to serve in the ensuing Parliament for the said Borough.'[347]

The cynical formality of those proceedings was typical of the closed
circle of influence whereby the borough magnates such as Viscount
Loftus fixed the infrequent elections. The Extinguisher controlled a
handful of seats in County Wexford, including the classic 'rotten
boroughs' of Clonmines and Bannow (almost uninhabited villages of
medieval ruins). He exercised that influence with discretion, bartering
political power for ennoblement, and was otherwise content to take a
back seat in the scramble for place and honours – but his family could
count on parliamentary seats as a matter of right. His legitimate sons,

Nicholas and Henry, his sons-in-law Charles Tottenham and Henry Alcock and his distant cousins, Thomas and Henry Loftus, all benefitted from the old man's favour. Such patronage even extended to Nicholas's favourite bastard, Edward, who was returned for Jamestown, in Queens County, during the bitterly contested election of 1761, thanks to his father's influence over their cousins at nearby Monasterevan. But the Extinguisher died two years later and Edward had to fend for himself.

By 1767 it was clear that the Octennial Bill would be passed and an election was imminent. Edward could no longer rely on the support of his Monasterevan cousins and was forced to look elsewhere for a parliamentary sponsor, so he turned to his half-brother Henry. The latter was by then in effective control of all the family boroughs in Wexford (through his dominance of the nominal head of the family, 'Nicholas the fool'), and thereby commanded at least eight seats in the Irish House of Commons, which made the 'Loftus Legion' one of the most powerful groups in Parliament.

Edward claimed that Henry had promised him, some years earlier, 'that whenever a dissolution of Parliament should take place, he would return me for a seat in one of the family boroughs' – and had good reason to believe that he was owed this pledge. Edward and his illegitimate brother, Captain Nicholas, had curried favour with Henry after the Extinguisher's death by renouncing their claim to the large sum of £2,000 which had been left them in their father's will, charged on Henry's Wexford estates, and had subsequently supported him in a bitter contest for political influence with his fierce-tempered elder brother, the Earl of Ely, and against another 'person in power', discreetly unnamed. These tactics were sufficient to win promises of a parliamentary seat from the ambitious Henry, but the pledge was made to be broken. 'The advancement of his fortune, by the death of Lord *Ely*, immediately deprived him of all memory of his best friends, at least of me. He then openly threw off the mask, and at once renounced all acquaintance with me.' Not only did Edward fail to secure the expected nomination for election but Henry contrived to have him and his brother replaced as Burgesses of Fethard and Clonmines, thus depriving them of any influence in the selection of candidates for these boroughs.[348]

Such political manoeuvres were not unusual, but Edward was

persistent in his claims. He wrote on 16 February 1768 to remind Henry of his promise, and wrote again a month later. Neither letter, nor numerous subsequent messages, provoked an answer until Henry finally scrawled a note on Tuesday 29 March, denying any promise or obligation with the sneering comment that 'it would have been *shameful* to have been represented by you.' The added bitterness of social rejection spurred Edward to fury. He replied by return. 'I hope you'll recollect yourself by twelve o'clock next *Thursday*; at which time I hope and expect to hear from you.'

This was an unambiguous challenge, but Henry was determined to avoid a duel. At the appointed time 'On *Thursday* morning, *March* the 31st, between the hours of eleven and twelve' Edward Loftus was waiting at home in Sackville Street when 'Mr Sheriff *Boyd* came to my house, and informed me, in the presence of Major *Waring* (who happened accidentally to be with me upon a visit) that the Lord-Mayor did, by him, bind me over to the peace.'

Edward wrote to Henry the following day, expressing 'my surprize at being put yesterday morning under an arrest, by the Sheriff of *Dublin*, upon the presumption that I had called you to account, and that an affair was to be determined immediately between us.' This was a disingenuous pretence, to preserve the legal niceties. Major Waring had certainly been there the day before to act as Edward's second in the anticipated duel; but there was little that either could do to pursue the matter except to remind Henry of the promise that he had made, 'to bring me in for a seat for one of the Family Boroughs,' and to announce that 'if that promise be not immediately fulfilled, I shall lay before the Public the whole transactions that have passed between us.'

The question of legitimacy, social as well as genealogical, was at the heart of the matter. Edward had been granted his father's name and coat of arms, but was illegitimate by birth and was scorned by the half-brother whose sudden rise in fortune had made him doubly pompous; Henry reminded everyone of Edward's parentage by calling him 'Ned Hernon'.[349] Honour and respect were at stake. A man of honour knew that his name counted for something in the world, relied on certain privileges and sinecures, could expect his share of patronage and the ability to dispense patronage in his turn. These were the measures of respect. By denying his brother a share in the family's political inheritance, Henry had attempted to erase the claims of kinship, and he compounded that offence by refusing to meet him in a duel.

Edward's standing in society was dependent on satisfaction, so he turned pamphleteer; *The Case of Edward Loftus* was his substitute for pistols. Elegantly printed at his own expense (Dublin, 1768), it was written to 'convince the Public of the propriety of my conduct and demonstrate the black ingratitude which has been returned to a constant and uniform series of the most friendly and affectionate actions.' In publishing his quarrel to the world, Edward acknowledged that it was painful 'to trouble the Public with dissensions of a private nature' but claimed that, 'I find myself under the necessity of so doing, or of lying under an imputation, of all things the most grating to a gentleman. My sole view in this is to assert my own honour.'

Within three months of the aborted duel, Edward had consoled himself with a baronetcy, which may have been purchased at the going rate but magically transformed his social status. Later, it is said, there was some question of raising him to the peerage, by claiming the succession to brother Henry's earldom; but this was vetoed by the ever-practical Lady Loftus. 'We are very well off as baronets, but would be very poor lords.' Honour, it is clear, had its price.

CHAPTER 28

Count Loftonzo

In my hand lies a gold medal. One side is boldly embossed with the seated figure of Hibernia and the motto of the Dublin Society, *Nostri Plena Laboris* ('filled with our labours'). The other is engraved, somewhat unevenly, with a Latin inscription that records its presentation to Henry Loftus, Earl of Ely, in 1773, for 'cultivating a mountain'. It weighs exactly an ounce.[350]

I found this small treasure almost by chance and then I hunted for its history. The minute books of the Dublin Society, of which Henry's father was a founding member, provided the first clue. On 4 March 1773 it was formally resolved by the Society 'That a Gold Medal be presented to the Right Hon Henry Earl of Ely, for 30 Acres, 1 Rood and 3 Perches of Mountain, which he caused to be reclaimed in the County of Dublin, since August 1768, and which has now a promising Appearance of rich Pasture, the Grass being from 6 to 9 Inches high.'[351] But where was this mountain?

I discovered that some time in the late 1760s Henry Loftus had acquired a large house with wonderful sea views in the parish of Dalkey, a few miles south of Dublin. He promptly renamed it Loftus Hill and decided to 'improve' the small estate. Barren rock was blasted with explosives and covered with cart-loads of good soil, turning unproductive land into grassy meadows. Trees and shrubs were planted, a new road was cut around the hill and a wall was built to mark the boundary with his neighbour, Sir Oliver Crofton. But Crofton was a wild and feckless man – he had killed an opponent in a duel – and he ordered his servants to throw down Loftus's new-built wall. Henry appealed to the Irish House of Commons, claiming (as Member for Bannow) that such insults constituted breach of parliamentary privilege. The House found in his favour and Crofton's servants were arrested. Finally, when the grass was rich and long, he was presented with a gold medal, for cultivating his bare mountain.

The story demonstrates all the characteristics for which Henry was often mocked – grandiose self-importance, expensive habits, frequent demands for political favour and a love of honours – but it also reveals the one great quality that even his contemporaries acknowledged: 'an unbounded passion for improvement and a skill equal to that passion.'[352] With the death of his nephew (the 'idiot Earl') in 1769, the new Lord Loftus at last had the resources to express this passion to the full. After a lifetime as the younger son – modest prospects, little honour – Henry was suddenly rich, titled, a man of influence. Along with his vast inheritance (the Hume estates in Fermanagh, the Loftus lands on the Hook, Rathfarnham Castle near Dublin) Henry was heir to the 'Loftus Legion'; favoured relatives and friends 'elected' as MPs for the family boroughs in County Wexford. His wealth gave him the means, Rathfarnham the opportunity and parliamentary representation the motive to transform an Elizabethan castle into a magnificent setting for hospitality, display and political intrigue.[353]

Rathfarnham had already been modernised by its previous owners (Archbishop Hoadley and his son-in-law, Bellingham Boyle) and was no longer the dark fortress built by Adam Loftus in the sixteenth century. It had acquired tall Georgian windows, a grand staircase and a new kitchen wing – and had also acquired a ghost, according to family legend.[354] There were fine gardens, a beautiful well-wooded park and 'a great many fishponds, where is the largest carp ever I saw in my life' – as Lady Anne Connolly wrote to her father in 1733.[355] But this was not enough; Henry wanted to refashion everything in the latest taste and was impatient to get started.

Within a few months of his nephew's death he was pestering Sir George Macartney, the Chief Secretary, for permission to import two or three plates of French looking-glass – 'as they make them of a larger size than is made in London' – and he decided to employ two of the most fashionable architects of the day to transform the house and embellish the garden.[356]

Sir William Chambers and James 'Athenian' Stuart were chalk and cheese. Stuart had never worked in Ireland but was famous for his pioneering book on Greek architecture and through such diverse projects as classical temples at Shugborough Park and magnificent interiors for Spencer House in London. He combined a passion for the primitive vigour of the Doric order with a love of movement, lightness and exquisite colour. Chambers, by contrast, preferred Classical Rome to Ancient Greece and was very much the establishment choice: rigorous, sometimes dour, in his formal brilliance. The 'Casino' that he designed for Lord Charlemont, just outside Dublin, was a building almost without purpose save its perfect symmetry.[357]

Initially it seems that Stuart was commissioned to design a suite of family rooms on the south side of Rathfarnham while Chambers was allocated a couple of grand reception rooms on the north.[358] Stuart at least ensured that he was properly briefed, but Chambers stayed in London awaiting further instructions. His earliest surviving letter to Loftus (22 April, 1770) was a tetchy request for measured plans of the rooms and their situation, and directions on 'how you wish me to have them fitted up', in response to a message from Henry complaining that nothing had happened. It was not until months later that his designs were dispatched, by which time the first phase of Stuart's work was already well in hand. We know this because the young Lady Shelburne paid a call with her husband in August 1770.

> We found Lord Loftus and Miss Munroe his niece at home. She is a celebrated Beauty and very deservedly so, she walked about ye shrubbery with me and showed me a flower garden that is making for Lady Loftus and when we came home sent for a harper to play for us. Lord Loftus walked about with my Lord and showed him his Improvements. The house was an old one of which only the shell is preserved and some of the rooms within he is fitting up after the designs of Mr Stuart's. There is a great deal of French cabinet work and Lord Loftus showed me several fine pieces of his turned ivory which he bought from Spa and other expensive toys.[359]

Those 'expensive toys' may have allowed Lady Shelburne a moment of superior disdain, but she was certainly impressed. Having a harper on call to entertain your guests was a sign of princely magnificence – even when used as a stopgap for conversation.

The sequence of rooms that Stuart designed on the first floor of the castle gives a tantalising flavour of Rathfarnham's former glory. The small drawing room may have lost most of its original features, including the grisaille wall decorations shown in the background of a family portrait by Angelica Kauffmann, but the breakfast room next door still has a lovely ceiling in Stuart's favourite greens, framing roundels of fat cherubs masquerading as the four seasons, while a small, near-perfect cube – the 'Gilt Room' – glitters with brilliant combinations of gold, cream and delicate sea-green, highlighting the symbols of the gods that circle the ceiling.

But that, for the moment, was that. Stuart was overwhelmed with commissions, and Lord Loftus was left to deal with the prickly Chambers, who remained determined to undertake his designs at a distance. His initial commission was for the ground-floor dining room and the ballroom above – both of which had been enlarged by constructing a semicircular bay on the east of the castle, flooding them with light from tall windows in the curvature of the bow.[360] By the time that Chambers got around to his designs, the decoration of the dining room may already have been completed – the lovely plasterwork of the earlier ceiling was extended into the bay, and the walls were apparently lined with a Chinese or 'Indian' paper – so his main concern was with the large ballroom, which he proposed to embellish with decorative pillars at the junction between the original rectangular space and the new apse. Lord Loftus, of course, wanted these to be splendid – scagliola or marble – but Chambers pointed out that the floor would not stand the weight and they would have to be made of wood. He complained that the workmen were careless and did not read his instructions, and grumpily enclosed his bill.[361]

That cantankerous attitude must have tried Henry's patience, but Stuart was impossible to pin down and there was more to be done on the main floor of the house – most notably the long-planned gallery. Chambers responded with three packets of designs, but most were never executed or else were severely modified, for at the last minute Stuart returned to the task and devised a scheme that Loftus liked better.

The result, with atmospheric appropriateness, is a house in two halves, reflecting the character of their designers. Stuart's south-facing rooms are light, wonderfully elegant, with particularly original plasterwork that reminds me of Japanese fans and the recently rediscovered 'Orientalism' of Palmyra. Elegant door-cases – framing doors of Cuban mahogany with intricate fittings – and a subtle brilliance of colour contrast quite markedly with the more severe formalism of the north-facing rooms attributed to Chambers. But I think it must have been

Chambers who designed one of the finest features of Rathfarnham: the
lovely external staircase, linking gallery to gardens. On the south side of
the castle, held within the clasp of two massive corner towers, this
double flight of stone curves down in a perfect semicircle, suspended in
the air. As you open the glass door from the gallery and step outside,
you seem encouraged to pause to admire the view, before descending
with delight to the ground.

'As far as the eye can reach there is nothing but wide green open or
shaded lawns and woods of chestnut, beech, elm and every variety of
tree. On the river facing the house is a picturesque mill-wheel, and a
pretty bridge carries one safely across the stream to an old mill house.'
Such was the view until the grounds of Rathfarnham were sold for
speculative development, in 1914. Now, alas, that vast and handsome
demesne has shrunk to a plain municipal lawn surrounded by meanly
designed dwellings, crowding out the vista that formerly stretched
without interruption to the distant blue of the Wicklow Hills. And the
Roman triumphal arch that Lord Loftus commissioned as a grandiose
gatehouse to the castle, near a new bridge over the River Dodder,
lingers in melancholy isolation, severed from its park by a housing
estate, on the edge of a busy road.[362]

For a sense of what it was like centuries ago, I must depend on the
eyes of others – on William Jones who painted a large landscape of
Rathfarnham in 1769, or Angelica Kauffmann who showed a glimpse
of the gardens in the background of a family portrait, and on the
eighteenth-century visitors who described the place in their letters and
diaries. They praised the 'beautifully stuccoed, gilt and painted' ceiling
of the porch, the 'elegant paintings and China Vases,' magnificent
mirrors and furniture that once adorned the castle, and the gardens –
with their hothouses, ripening exotic fruit, and the ice house, filled in
winter when the lake was frozen. And the aviaries, menageries, fishponds and pavilions that formerly dotted the grounds.

I like to imagine being caught in a sudden shower in that eighteenth-
century landscape, and dashing back into the house through a small
door at ground level that leads to a tiny lobby, giving access to the
private staircase that Henry used, when slipping outside from his bedroom. There, if you glance up, you can see what still gives pleasure
today: a delicate stucco wreath of mistletoe. That must have been

Stuart's work, a piece of delight – and I wonder how many kisses were snatched beneath its pale berries. Upstairs on the next landing, between the gallery and the dining room, is Chambers' riposte: a neoclassical miniature on a grand scale. For here is the head of Apollo, and radiating to the corners of the ceiling are the rays of the sun, his symbol.[363]

I also wish that I could have ridden with Lord Loftus to his country retreat on Mount Pelier, up in the hills to the south, near the source of the River Dodder. Henry's notion of rural simplicity was of course grander than most – the façade of his 'hunting lodge', outbuildings included, extended to more than a hundred yards, and the house itself, though relatively modest in size, was more than a rural cottage. Tall, well-proportioned rooms with stuccoed ceilings and marble fireplaces were flooded with light from bay windows that commanded beautiful views to Dublin and the sea, with Rathfarnham Castle in the middle distance. Above the front door was the Loftus crest – a boar's head, carved in stone – and flanking the house were large arched gateways, surmounted by huge stone balls. Long wings stretched on either side of these arches, containing servants' quarters and stables, and at each end stood a square, three-storey tower with castellated walls and Gothic windows.'[364] Henry named the place Dollymount after his favourite niece, Dolly Monroe.

And then, if his Lordship felt inclined, we might have travelled south again, to the Hook. There we could have viewed the work that he put in hand, following the survey of the Loftus Hall estate that he commissioned from Richard and Charles Frizell in 1771. As well as making the most beautiful maps of every field and farm, the Frizells had added detailed notes on the condition of the soil, exposure to the wind, suitability for crops or pasture, quality of the tenants and opportunities for improvement. They extolled the 'Dignity and Grandeur of the situation, the richness and fertility of the Land, being all inclosed with Lime & Stone Walls, the great plenty of fish, wild Fowl, Pigeons and Rabits at all seasons,' and the 'pleasing prospect' of the demesne, overlooking 'the Ships at Anchor in the Harbour, as well as all that sail in and out.' Even now, more than two centuries later, I can sense the pleasure it must have given Henry Loftus to read those words, while relishing his great fortune.[365]

*

But this life of splendour concealed a hidden terror, for his Lordship's glory was built on the quicksands of a disputed inheritance, and he lived in constant fear of losing half his wealth – the Hume estates, bequeathed him by his nephew. The nephew's maternal relatives, the Rochforts and the Humes, had mounted a powerful legal challenge to that inheritance, hoping to prove that the 'idiot Earl' had been incapable of making a valid will, and they had powerful allies. Several times they had come close to success and it looked increasingly likely that the final appeal, to the Irish House of Lords, would be determined by the narrowest of margins, influenced as much by ties of kinship and political allegiance as by the legal arguments on either side.[366] That fear of disinheritance was compounded by vanity and by the expensive ambitions of Henry's wife. She dreamed of a grander title, political influence, social coronation.

Knowing those fears and playing on that greed, the much-loathed Deputy, Lord Townshend, had no hesitation in exploiting the situation for his own ends. Townshend was determined to break the power of the great political 'undertakers' on whom Dublin Castle had long depended for the passage of government business – the grandest of whom was Loftus's cousin John Ponsonby, the Speaker of the House. The Viceroy wanted to replace that established system of favours given and patronage received with a looser network of corruption, under his direct command. To achieve this aim, every vote was vital – and Loftus controlled his 'legion' (at least eight Members of Parliament elected through his influence), which had hitherto voted as Ponsonby saw fit. But Townshend was unscrupulous. His stick was the threat of ruin – that Henry's cause would be lost when it came to the House of Lords – and his carrot the promise of preferment: an earldom at least and maybe more.[367]

Still Loftus hesitated, for Ponsonby had proved a generous patron in the days when Loftus was poor, and to betray his kinsman would earn the scorn of half his friends. It was his wife, a foolish and determined woman, who made him turn. For at this critical moment, in the autumn of 1770, Townshend became a widower, and Lady Loftus took it into her head that all her social ambitions would come to fruition if she could manoeuvre the Viceroy into marrying her niece, the beautiful 'Dolly' Monroe. Driven by this mad dream, against every sense of decency or reality – Townshend was a cynical rake of forty-six, Dolly was seventeen – she made her desires abundantly plain and Townshend played along with her. He took to visiting Rathfarnham at frequent intervals, and went so far in his apparent courtship of Dolly that she was persuaded to throw over her acknowledged suitor, Hercules Langrishe.

Langrishe – who was also a widower, and only a few years younger than Townshend – always spoke of Dolly with tender respect, but soon had his revenge on Lord Loftus and his ambitious wife. He began by publishing a couple of open letters to his Lordship, as rumours started to circulate that Henry had agreed a secret deal with the castle. 'The present Viceroy must infallibly, within a few months be removed; and upon the first change you will find your folly; despised by your friends, renounced by relations, cast off by Government, and hooted at by a nation.'[368]

All of which was to some extent hypocritical cant – for there was not much to choose between the corruptions of Ponsonby's gang of 'Undertakers' and Townshend's cynical intrigues, and Langrishe himself was no political virgin. He held a succession of official sinecures, voted with the government when it benefitted him to do so, and eventually proved vulnerable to bribery of the most straightforward sort, accepting £15,000 from Lord Castlereagh not to vote against the Union. But he was at least a wit – and so, when plain words had no effect, he turned to satire. His *History of Barataria* originally appeared in the *Freeman's Journal*, in the spring of 1771, and was subsequently enlarged, with contributions from Flood and Grattan, as a scandalously successful book, which mocked the pretensions of 'Count Loftonzo' while exposing the corruptions of Townshend's Viceroyalty.[369] Ireland was transposed to Barataria – the village over which Sancho Panza was given brief dominion, in a famous episode from *Don Quixote* – Townshend became Sancho and everyone else was assigned a suitably Spanish pseudonym. Here is an extract.

As to the Countess, her imagination was on fire! – it already presented to her, her niece, the incomparable Dorothea, crowned Vice-queen of the island of Barataria; her Lord Loftonzo distinguished by all the coronets of his ancestry; and the deputyship of the island conferred on him, at the departure of Sancho. Every thing was accomplished in her ardent mind; and sports and pastimes – tilts and tournaments – dance and festivity, were proclaimed throughout the Castle and the forests of Rafarmo.[370]

Those glorious expectations were captured in a vast family portrait, painted by Angelica Kauffmann in 1771. It is unexpectedly revealing. The setting is lovely – an interior at the castle, with a view to the garden – and the iconography is evocative of the Holy Family, but the overall impression (glances, gestures, relationships) is curiously uncertain. Henry and his wife pose majestically in the scarlet and ermine robes of the Irish peerage as an Indian page hovers nearby, carrying a tasselled cushion on which rest the coronets of the newly created Earl and Countess of Ely. The servitude of this 'young black boy from the Malibar coast' – who is said to have accompanied a gift of ostriches to Lord Loftus – is echoed in the lowered head of Dolly Monroe, standing on the left of the picture, to whom Henry draws our gaze as he glances with somewhat tentative affection towards his unsmiling wife. Dolly is the sacrificial lamb, soon to be anointed, and her sister Frances, seated at a keyboard, plays the role of John the Baptist, as she points to the words of a song. But the traditional text of sacred imagery (*Ecce Agnus Dei*) has been replaced by a warning, for the music lies open at an aria from a popular opera, *La Buona Figliuola* ('The Good Girl'), which begins: 'Away, away, Sir, I will allow no one to touch me'.[371]

That sense of unease was prophetic. As soon as Lord Loftus voted with the government he was rewarded with the promised earldom, but Townshend ceased his courting. The wretched Dolly became the butt of Dublin gossip as the Viceroy transferred his attentions to her cousin, Anne Montgomery – who was also, as it happened, a niece of Lady Loftus – and the wits of Dublin laid huge wagers as to which of these two young beauties would be the next Lady Townshend. The Viceroy himself was in no hurry to come to an altar, and dallied with Anne as he had with Dolly. Eventually he became so deeply unpopular with the Irish power-brokers that the ministers in London decided to recall him, and he embarked for England, closely pursued by Miss Montgomery's brother, a noted duellist. Before they reached London, Townshend was forced at sword-point to issue a formal proposal of marriage to the girl whom he had jilted; and those who had wagered on this outcome are said to have won a total of £20,000. Her unhappy rival, Dolly

Monroe, met a happier fate – for she was married in 1775 to William Richardson of Richhill Castle, a thoroughly decent man who seems to have loved her.

If the new Lord Ely was disappointed he made no show of it – but turned instead to his favourite pastime, improvement. By 1770 he had decided that his town house in Cavendish Row no longer matched his new social status, and leased an undeveloped plot of land close to the fashionable heart of the city, in what was promptly named Ely Place. Within a few months he commenced construction on a thirty-six-roomed mansion.[372] As with so many Dublin houses, magnificent interiors are hidden behind a plain brick façade, but the sheer scale of what remains – dominating its setting, as it faces down Hume Street towards St Stephen's Green – is quietly impressive, and the site originally included a coach house, stables and other outbuildings, as well as a spacious garden. Now, when you step inside the hall and gaze at the life-size statue of Hercules who guards the astonishing staircase (embellished with scenes of his Labours), you can still experience something of the force of that former glory, despite the institutional furnishings and pious knick-knacks, and an ugly office block that covers most of the old garden. Almost every room is decorated with exquisite plasterwork, embellished with a carved marble fireplace and entered through a door of 'panelled West Indian mahogany, with silver handles and lockplates, pierced and chased'.[373] The grate of one of those fireplaces is framed in silver and the mantel of another is adorned with a carving of Hercules asleep, sprawled on a boar's hide, with its bristling head tucked beneath his arm – a reference to the family crest. Everywhere you look there is evidence of the handiwork of Dublin's finest craftsmen. It was all enormously expensive, somewhat over the top and rather splendid.

This marvellous house was completed only a year or two before Henry's wife fell ill – and she died in 1774, having scarcely had time to display herself in its setting. With his 'passion for improvement' it seems inevitable that Lord Ely's second wife, whom he married the following year, was young, beautiful and socially well connected. Reynolds painted a full-length portrait of the new-wed couple, walking together in a garden, magnificently dressed. They look like father and daughter, as he introduces her to her new domain and she steps forward into adult life – Anne Bonfoy, exploring her role as Countess of Ely. A few years later, in 1778, they went to a masquerade ball on St Patrick's Eve and acted a different story, with Lord Ely dressed as a hermit and his wife as a washerwoman; and about the same time she posed as Hebe, goddess of youth, for a likeness in pastels by Hugh Douglas Hamilton. That play-acting streak survived Henry's death, for his dashing widow transformed a room at the top of Ely Place into the 'attic theatre', where her friends would gather for amateur dramatics.[374]

Anne and Henry may have been well matched, for he, too, seems to have spent his entire life posing as someone other – the man he wanted to be and never quite was. As a younger son he had lived on hand-me-downs and leftovers, dependent on men like Ponsonby for a modest sinecure or a government pension for his wife. It was not until his brother died that he finally took centre stage, as the saviour of his maltreated nephew and then his heir. So all his resources were spent on constructing the framework of a grand and civilised life. He built himself a series of magnificent stage sets, acquired the clothes, the titles, the attributes of a great man, and was renowned for having his books bound with princely splendour, but I wonder whether he ever read them. Like the hunting lodge that he built in the hills, Henry seemed all front and little depth, and lacked the force of character to play a major role in the drama of Irish politics. He was sometimes the buffoon, often ignored and left little trace on the history of his times. But for all his pomposity and the weakness that allowed him to be manoeuvred into shameful stratagems by his first wife, he was essentially good-natured. And his 'unbounded passion for improvement' was worth a great deal more than the cynical games of those who mocked him.

Even the mockers were dazzled. So many curious members of the gentry applied to visit Rathfarnham that Lord Ely had to organise a weekly opening. Silver tokens were struck, embossed on one side with his Lordship's coronet and the words 'This ticket to be left at the Porters Lodge' and on the other 'This Ticket admits four persons to see Rathfarnham on Tuesdays only'.[375]

The last decade of Henry's life was one of quiet satisfaction. 'Count Loftonzo' was forgotten and the Earl of Ely basked in social approbation, which culminated in his appointment as one of fifteen founding Knights of the Order of St Patrick, intended to be Ireland's equivalent of the Garter. He received the news in Bath, in a letter from his younger cousin William, who was an aide to the Lord Lieutenant. Henry replied with unctuous affection, reminders of favours given and self-important claims regarding his own part in the invention of the new order, so long mooted and so often postponed – 'what is called A Will of the wisp, or an imaginary Phantom, for men to follow'. He wrote with sublime self-esteem that 'my Peerage and my Consequence ought to place me' in the first rank of the new Knights, and claimed that eight years earlier he had been 'recommended to his Majesty for the Red Ribbon [Order of the Bath], Which I declined accepting of, as This Order for Ireland, was then in Agitation, and offered to me, which I prefer'd.' But then, just as pomposity reached the limits of absurdity, Henry concluded his letter with this delightful postscript: 'If you do not find an opportunity very soon of sending me a few Bottles of high toasted Snuff from Mc.Donnald, I must enclose My Nose to you in a letter, for tis now as great an inconvenience to me, as a house would be without Furniture.'[376]

That cheerful joke – which echoes Henry's passion for furnishing lovely houses – now reads with special poignancy, for this is one of his last surviving letters. When the Knights of St Patrick paraded in their blue robes before their inaugural dinner at Dublin Castle, on 17 March 1783, Henry was absent. His health had begun to fail and he stayed in Bath, 'taking the waters', hoping to recover.

A few weeks later, on 3 May 1783, an unexpected visitor called at Rathfarnham Castle and was admitted to the house, perhaps having explained that he was a distant cousin of Lord Ely. It was John Wesley, the founder of Methodism, who may have hoped to impress upon his Lordship the vanity of worldly things – but Henry was in England, and close to death. Wesley's description, recorded in his journal, is that of a prophet of doom.

> It may doubtless vie in elegance, if not in costliness, with any seat in Great Britain, but the miserable master of the whole has little satisfaction therein. God hath said, 'write this man childless'. For whom then does he heap up these things? He himself is growing old.
>
> And must he then leave this paradise? Then leave
> These happy shades, and mansions fit for gods?[377]

Five days later Henry Loftus, Viscount Loftus, Earl of Ely and Knight of St Patrick, died at the Circus in Bath.

CHAPTER 29

Receipt for a Person in Love

Lying on the table beside me is an eighteenth-century account book, unbound, almost in tatters, which formerly belonged to the Creaghs of Dangan, forebears of one of my great-grandmothers.[378] The frayed leaves of that household ledger cover the years 1780 to 1789 and contain a shopping list, an inventory of *House Linnen* and an election ballad, alongside the daily details of income and expenditure; *6 Couple of Turkey @ 20d. per Couple, Cash paid Thomas Nihill to buy a watch £1 2s. 9d.* Scrawled at the end, in a faded flourishing hand, is this extraordinary prescription.

> *A Receipt for a Person in Love*
> Take 1 pound of Consideration 40 Drachms of indifference
> 5 Ounces of Discretion & 9 Grains of patience Boil all
> these together in a Bottle of Water of Content keep Stirring it
> With the Ladle of Hearts Ease put therein two or three handfuls
> of light hearted flowers in their full bloom and a great
> Deal of the balsam of who cares eat the Bread of
> Sprightliness Drink of the Liquor of chearfulness sitt by the
> fire of comfort & lie on the bed of ease take a Draught of
> this two or three Mornings fasting & you will have a
> complete Cure

The cure was evidently incomplete because the writer added a post-script, suggesting a more cynical remedy to satisfy urgent desire. A few crucial words have disappeared, where part of the page was torn out by some subsequent reader (scandalised at his ancestor's indecency?), but sufficient is left to guess at the transaction that is implied.

> Or give the following note if you love a woman
> I Promise to pay Pretty Dame a Certain Sum [*of Money*]
> By which means She must be paid and Let me [— *her Coney*][379]

The words in brackets are my restoration, based on a bawdy hunch.

Coney means rabbit, but it also has another, sexual meaning – pungently implied by Thomas Dekker in *The Virgin Martir* [1622]: 'A pox on your Christian cockatrices! They cry, like poulterers' wives, "No Money, no coney".'

A Receipt for a Person in Love has the authentic bitter-sweet flavour of eighteenth-century Ireland and its clever, impetuous children, with their vivid delights and obsessive infatuations, acted out within the charades of adult civilisation. Fashionable society might dance to capricious codes and move with elaborate artifice, but its compulsions were intemperate – duelling, drinking, gambling, litigation and making love. All of which was shaped by an unexpected liaison of irresistible sensuality with heartless indifference.

The implicit colonialism of aristocratic sexuality (women as a subject people) had a particularly local flavour for the Anglo-Irish Ascendancy. Protestant grandees married within their own class, for reasons that had as much to do with property as social ease, and contracts of marriage were ratified by the family lawyers in treaties of laborious complexity – but the men took their pleasure where they found it and their mistresses, for the most part, were Catholic. Across that boundary of legitimacy there were no rules, and the victims had scant redress.

At the margins of privilege, amongst the landless Catholic squireens, such tensions were extreme. Insistent on their gentility yet barred by the Penal Laws from any genteel profession (or even from a decent education), these idle, improvident 'buckoons' subsisted on pride and dreams, in which savage sexuality was entwined with visions of wealth. They dreamt of heiresses and their abduction.[380]

On the night of 14 April 1779, there was a violent battering on the door of a house in Graiguenamanagh, a few miles from Mount Loftus, across the river Barrow in County Carlow. The wood splintered, the door gave way, and half a dozen men with blackened faces stumbled upstairs, carrying flickering storm lanterns and an assortment of weapons. They burst through the barricaded door of a bedroom where the widowed Mrs Kennedy and her teenage daughters (who had come to the town for a ball) were huddled in terror with their host, James Neale. Threats were uttered, the girls were seized, and the gang disappeared into the night before any pursuit could be raised.[381]

Shortly afterwards there was an unexpected announcement in Finn's *Leinster Journal*. 'Married. A few days ago, Mr Gerald Byrne of Ballyine in the County of Carlow, to Miss Kennedy of Waterford; And Mr James Strange, of Ullard, in this country, to Miss Ann Kennedy of Waterford.'

Among other things the announcement concealed was the fact that the double marriage was conducted at night, under extreme duress, and was followed by a double rape, in the endlessly repeated pattern of Irish eighteenth-century abductions. There were even abduction clubs, or so it was widely rumoured, whose members would select a victim from available local heiresses, choose her future husband by lot from among their number and aid him in taking her by force. It was always by night – sometimes in alliance with gangs of Whiteboys, who terrorised the countryside in the name of patriotic resistance – and frequently went unpunished. The combination of a sense of shame (her reputation ruined) and of binding legality (the sacred wedding contract) might be enough to cause the wretched victim to submit to her fate and persuade her family to hush up the circumstances. Even if the case came to court it was hard to secure a conviction, for there was widespread popular sympathy with the perpetrators of such crimes. Their disregard for the law was somehow conflated with heroic defiance of colonial injustice – and there was a strange, pitiless scorn for their victims, as if the women should be glad that the men risked their necks to obtain them.

All such emotions were magnified when the daughters of the widow Kennedy were seized in Graiguenamanagh. For one thing, they were very young – Ann was fourteen, Catherine a year older. Although it was not unusual for Irish girls to be married at fifteen, their age provoked an extensive hue and cry which led to their rescue, as their captors were trying to smuggle them out of the country on a boat bound for Bordeaux.

Attention then focused on the abductors, who escaped when the girls were rescued and got as far as Wales before they were arrested on 6 July 1779. A wave of popular sympathy accompanied them on their long journey from Carmarthen to Carlow, and thence to the courthouse gaol in Kilkenny. They, too, were young – Garret (whose name had been misprinted in the *Journal*) was twenty-two, his friend James two years younger – and they acted with the bravado which their roles demanded. They inserted a notice in the newspapers, offering the sincere thanks of Garret Byrne and James Strange, 'gents', to the High Sheriff and the Sub-Sheriff of County Carlow for their polite behaviour during their confinement there, and to the volunteer officers for the genteel manner in which they were conducted from Carlow to Kilkenny, and they dressed in style, in the new clothes that their families brought to them in prison.

Most emotive of all, in making this a test case of public opinion and legal morality, were the ambiguities that surrounded the relationship of the abductors to their victims. Garret was a cousin of the Kennedy girls and had been a welcome visitor prior to the kidnapping. He and James Strange had frequently danced attendance on Catherine and Ann at the local assemblies and were generally assumed to have been courting them, although it was known that their mother had grander plans for her beautiful daughters. The question that dominated debate and formed the crux of the trial was how far the girls themselves had encouraged the squireen's advances, or even (it was said) been complicit in their own abduction.

That trial finally came to court on Friday 14 October 1780, after the sisters were persuaded to give evidence against the accused.

The judge was none other than the Attorney General, 'Copper-faced' Jack Scott, a man of complex passions, well versed in the labyrinths of sexual intrigue. He had married two heiresses – the first of them secretly, against the will of her family – and a cousin of his second wife was the long-standing protector of Dublin's most celebrated madam, Peg Plunket. 'Mr Justice S—' is listed in Peg's memoirs as a guest at her most extravagant 'masquerade', and later, when he was dead, she referred to him without pity, as 'a man of diabolical memory'.[382]

The Attorney General was looking for a conviction and determined on an exemplary sentence, but the bill of indictment had first to be approved by a grand jury. The foreman of that jury was Sir Edward Loftus, a local landowner of upright reputation and liberal convictions, whose task was unusually bitter, for he knew the defendants well. Garret Byrne lived at Ballyline House, near Borris (just across the river from Mount Loftus) and the Stranges even closer, at the entirely Catholic village of Ullard. Whatever their faults, these were mitigated by the frustrations of a life that was bounded by the Penal Laws. Whatever their actions, they were members of his own social circle, the gentry. And now, whatever the consequences, Sir Edward had to live with his decisions, in the intimacy of his immediate neighbourhood. But the evidence was overwhelming and after a short delay he returned to the courtroom with the grand jury's approval of the bill. The case could proceed.

The arguments in court took all day, as the prosecution gradually demolished the evidence of the defence and forced Garret's sister to admit that she had forged two letters, supposedly from the Kennedy girls, which had seemed to prove their compliance in the affair. The following morning Lord Justice Scott delivered his summing-up. 'If this abduction is suffered to pass with impunity, there will be no safety for any girl and no protection in the domestic peace and happiness of any family.'

Despite this explicit direction the jury took two hours to reach a decision, as tension mounted in the courtroom. Finally they returned with the inevitable verdict, guilty – but their foreman added a strong recommendation for mercy, in view of the abductors' youth. Scott ignored that plea, and pronounced sentence of death.

Six weeks after the trial, despite public appeals for mercy, Garret Byrne and James Strange were hanged, together with James's brother Patrick, who had been convicted as an accomplice in the affair. Convention demanded that the victims wore their finest clothes as they walked from Kilkenny Gaol to the place of execution, guarded by three hundred Highlanders. Byrne was dressed in 'a Pomona-green Coat', James Strange in light blue and his brother in mulberry, and 'each of them had a white Sattin Waistcoat and Breeches. At the awful Hour of Death they supported a manly Fortitude and Composure that did them Honour.'[383]

Their funeral took place the following day, Sunday 3 December 1780, and an immense crowd followed the coffins on the journey to Ullard and Kiltinnel. The road passed through the Hare Park of Mount Loftus, and the cortège paused to rest on the summit of a hill near the house, where (according to my great-uncle Jack), 'the people called down maledictions upon Sir Edward and his family.' They were looking for a scapegoat (in the absence of the judge) and they blamed the foreman of the grand jury for failing to save their sons.

This prophetic curse had classic symmetry, as a mirror of the victims' doom. Three young men had died without heirs to their name, so Sir Edward's own three sons must suffer the same fate, leaving no male heir to inherit the Loftus name and the Loftus estates – and thus it was, for the curse in effect came true.

The Kennedys, too, were damned for their 'cruelty', in the harsh judgement of popular opinion. Both made loveless marriages and lived wretched lives. Catherine was haunted by Garret's memory, as was her superstitious husband who saw his ghost everywhere. She became grossly fat and fell into despair. Ann's husband ran through her modest fortune and then cast her off. She died in miserable poverty.

Society never forgave them, and its verdict was summarised in the press. 'At the same time that we acknowledge the Propriety of the Law and the necessity of its rigid Execution, in a County said to be more remarkable for such Outrage than any other part of the Kingdom, yet it should be remembered the unhappy culprits were not vulgar Ruffians, but Gentlemen of irreproachable Characters, of equal Birth and Connection with their Prosecutors [and] that matrimony preceded the Consummation of the Fact.'[384]

Abduction and rape could be excused, it seems, as long as the perpetrators were gentlemen. This, in all its bitterness, was their receipt for love.

CHAPTER 30

The Angelic Miss Phillips

'The Angelic Miss Phillips' and her friend Elizabeth Loftus were heroines of my youth, whose tales were told whenever I visited my cousins at Mount Loftus: Anna Maria the actress, with whom Nicholas Loftus (Sir Edward's eldest son) had a love affair; and his sister, sad Elizabeth, who never recovered from seeing her rebel lover's head impaled on Wexford Bridge in 1798. But these romantic memories were faded and somewhat deceptive, like the delicate charm of their pale oval portraits: Elizabeth glancing sideways, pensive, apparently weighed down by the ramparts of dark hair, piled on her head; Anna Maria more vivid but playing a part, while supporting a strange little ewer, balanced on a tray.

I saw them then as adults – freighted with memories, conscious of their past – because that is what I had always believed, and it took decades to discover that these portraits were made in 1778, when the girls were fifteen and sixteen respectively. That was eighteen months before Anna Maria's first appearance on stage – at Drury Lane in London, starring in the opera for £6 a night – and twenty years before the Wexford Rising. Confronted with the evidence, those previously sophisticated ladies suddenly became teenagers; perception transformed as my eyes adjusted to new-found facts. Elizabeth's air of wistful memory was simply the gawkiness of youth, not inconsolable mourning, and Anna Maria's wide-eyed gaze was tinged with impatience at a pose that seemed increasingly absurd, the longer she held it.

What prompted this revelation was the discovery of another pastel portrait, of an elegant society lady who appeared in some strange way to have been Anna Maria's role model – the same colouring and clothing, the same striped ribbon twined through her hair, and carrying the same ridiculous ewer. I came across it in an auction catalogue, described as 'Portrait of Lady Loft as Hebe, Goddess of Youth' (cup-bearer to the gods) but it turned out to be a likeness of the young second wife of Henry Loftus, Earl of Ely. It was drawn some time between 1775, when they were married, and 1779, when the artist – Hugh Douglas Hamilton – set off for Rome.[385]

That the young Countess of Ely should be flattered as the goddess of youth is no mystery, but how did it come about that a friend of her niece Elizabeth was portrayed by the same fashionable artist, in an identical pose? This seemed even odder when I considered that Elizabeth's father, Sir Edward Loftus, had come close to fighting a duel with his half-brother Henry, the noble Earl, a dozen years earlier. I felt sure there was a prank behind these portraits.

To begin with, I considered the picture frames. Lady Ely is surrounded by a delicate, gilded oval, the rim carved with a wreath. The frame is identical to numerous examples for aristocratic clients of Hamilton and must have been made in London, where the artist was based at this time. The much more substantial and rustic frames for Anna Maria and Elizabeth suggest a provincial origin, possibly Kilkenny – and family tradition has it that their portraits were done when Anna Maria was staying at Ullard House, a couple of miles from Mount Loftus.

Then I remembered that Sir Edward's youngest son, born in 1777, was named Francis Hamilton Loftus – and it occured to me that Hugh Douglas Hamilton, who was Irish, could have been related to Sir Edward's wife (whose mother was a Hamilton) and might have stood sponsor at the baptism of their son. It seemed likely that the artist returned to his native country to say farewell to his friends – before setting off for Italy – and may have visited Mount Loftus at the same time that Anna Maria was staying nearby, on the way to see her Irish cousins. Whatever the reason, Hamilton drew her portrait in Ireland.[386]

'In these her youthful days Miss Phillips was very lively, and to her family and most intimate friends frequently displayed a great share of comic humour.' Hamilton responded to that spark by dressing her up in the same guise, with the same props, that he had recently used for her friend's fashionable aunt, as the Goddess of Youth. It would have been a private joke at the pretensions of Henry Loftus and his new wife, who lived a life of princely splendour, far removed from the bustling family household at Mount Loftus. Place the two likenesses side by side and it is immediately evident that one is of a poised, socially aware adult, conscious of our gaze, and the other of a mischievous, down-to-earth teenager, unsuited to her role – but Hamilton could indulge his sense of fun, safe from recriminations, because he knew that the portraits would never be compared. It was only through utterly improbable circumstances that his joke was finally rumbled, more than two hundred years later, when the Countess came face to face with the actress.

Behind the joke lies a love story, for on the back of Anna Maria's portrait an impetuous declaration lies hidden: 'The Angelic A. M. Phillips'. The writing is the unmistakeable scrawl of Nicholas Loftus – but this was his adult hand (recognisable from the Stud Book in which he recorded the details of his beloved racehorses), not that of the nineteen-year-old boy who fell for this precocious girl, so many years earlier. It seems to prove, as legend tells, that this was more than a passing passion – I can almost hear him sigh as he remembers.

Anna Maria was certainly worth a sigh. Never truly beautiful but intensely alive, resourceful and amusing, she had learnt to disregard convention as one of the six children of Peregrine Phillips – a radical lawyer and political pamphleteer who was imbued with republicanism by his French mother and by Benjamin Franklin, during a boyhood spent in America. Raised in such a household, Anna Maria had a mind of her own, but she also had an open heart.[387]

When she returned to London and became a star at Drury Lane, I suspect that Nicholas chased after her, for she is said to have become his mistress. He must certainly have been in the audience when Anna Maria returned to Ireland a few years later – to storm the hearts of others at Dublin's Theatre Royal, in Smock Alley. There was talk of an elopement. And it is at this point that a parallel story begins, which may be the truth behind those family memories or may be a rival romance, echoing the original, much as her portrait does, mimicking the guise of another.

The Smock Alley Theatre was 120 years old when Miss Phillips arrived to perform there. Structural collapse and violent riots had caused it to be rebuilt several times during the previous century, but it remained a ramshackle and exciting place. The boxes were frequently crammed with Protestant grandees and their Catholic courtesans, rubbing shoulders with the more sober members of Dublin society, while up in the gallery and circle was a noisier throng of tradesmen, including some of the most radical elements in the city. The pit was a parade ground for the fashionable sprigs of the Ascendancy, dodging a bombardment of oranges from the gods as they sprawled on the benches and ogled the beauties. It was noisy, smoky and hot, with the smell of innumerable candles giving a warm, waxy base to the rich aromatic mixture of powdered wigs, perfumes, posies, oranges, seldom-washed flesh and plenty to drink.[388]

Excitement bordering on mayhem was the essence of eighteenth-century theatre. The dramatic stock-in-trade (bawdiness, sentimental songs and cynical wit) made a dangerously explosive mixture when crammed into the tiny space of such a rickety playhouse, infecting the audience with anarchy; it took a brave man to be manager of Smock Alley. One of the most famous, Thomas Sheridan, discovered this to his cost in 1747, when his attempts to impose some measure of discipline at the theatre provoked a riot in the house and pamphlet warfare on the streets. Seven years later he tried again and 'was driven from this theatre by public tumult, consequent on his bravely protesting against insults offered by some of the audience to certain actresses.' Sheridan's successor, Richard Daly, took such episodes in his stride. He treated the Smock Alley actresses as his private property and fought a string of duels with all who provoked him.

Daly would have been quite unfazed by the wild scenes that greeted Miss Phillips at the opening of her Dublin season, in 1783. The house was packed, for the actress combined the fatal allure of youth, vivacity and wit. Her previous visit, a year earlier, had been announced by extravagant puffs in the local press and provoked a great deal of bad verse and protestations of love from half the chancers of the town; and now, it seemed, the fever was worse. One of her admirers sent a series of hysterical letters to the victim of his obsession – and when she ignored him, went to Smock Alley on the first day of her run, determined to impress her. As Miss Phillips was about to go on stage this wild and apparently dangerous young man rose from the throng in the pit, brandishing a pistol, and threatened 'like a despairing maniac' to shoot the actress and then himself, because she refused to love him. He was arrested and led away by 'officers of justice', while the house erupted in pandemonium. I suspect that this was a stunt organised by Daly himself, to publicise Anna Maria's appearance, but real life in eighteenth-century Dublin had a bewildering tendency to echo the dramatic prototypes, and the pistol may have been loaded.

Likewise with biography, formulas shaped the facts. Maria Young's *Memoirs* of the actress, published soon after her death, were clearly based on the private papers of her heroine – but the instincts of a romantic novelist constantly subvert what was in any case a remarkable story. Her breathless prose makes it all seem like fiction. Here, for example, is Mrs Young's account of a love affair in that dramatic Irish summer, shortly after Miss Phillips had escaped from her would-be assassin and fallen into the arms of a more desirable suitor.

> He loved her with the purest and most disinterested affection; he was ardent and sincere in his professions; he thought, and with reason, that she was formed by nature to grace the highest station, and formed the resolution of raising her to *his*. They were both under age; he was the heir to a great fortune and title; his father, of course, had high matrimonial expectations for him; but love, all-powerful love, overcame his filial duty, and triumphed also over hers.[389]

In the face of parental disapproval the lovers had no hesitation in taking the well-worn path of theatrical convention. Accompanied by her brother they eloped, and tried to persuade a Catholic priest to marry them – 'but the moment he declared his name, the priest refused to marry him without the consent of his father. Another was tried; but his name was too well known in the kingdom for any priest to marry him, as he was under age.' So they set off for Scotland, pursued by the avenging Furies of family respectability.

As in all the best chase movies the denouement came suddenly, just when you thought the lovers had got away with it. They had reached the coast, found a boat that would take them and were waiting to go on board, 'when, behold, the father of the young gentleman, accompanied by Mr. Phillips, arrived at the inn with numerous retinue! All hopes of concealment and escape were at an end; the house was surrounded: the two fathers entered the room, where the lovers were lamenting their fate; and their situation is easier to be conceived than described.'

Mrs Young's pen is in full romantic flight, scattering punctuation marks like confetti; but finally she comes to the coda.

Mr. Phillips was not a rich man; he was adorned with no title, but that of *honourable man*, who disclaimed the idea of his daughter stealing herself clandestinely into a family who would consider the alliance of an heir with an actress as a disgrace. He had observed the young gentleman's attachment; but as the season of her playing in that kingdom was nearly over, he hoped absence would obliterate the impression his daughter had made on so youthful a heart, as he never suspected that she would take the step she did, and was extremely surprised and alarmed at the disappearance of Miss Phillips and her attendant, for he knew not, at first, that his son was of the party; and guessing the lover with whom she had eloped, he went immediately and informed his father, who, highly applauding the honourable and disinterested conduct of Mr. Phillips, set out with him in pursuit of their fugitive children with all possible expedition, and overtook them just in time to prevent their marriage – to rend two hearts asunder which pure affection had united, and to destroy at once all the bright prospects of conjugal felicity which mutual love had promised; and this was effected by a high sense of family dignity on the side of one parent, and the innate principles of true honour on the side of the other.

After which extraordinary sentence (nearly two hundred words long) even Mrs Young has to pause for breath, and ends her paragraph.

Anna Maria was taken to England and put in the care of a respectable elder sister. She returned to the stage at Drury Lane in a performance of the new season's hit, *The Double Disguise*, which provoked a rival actress to deliver one of the show's liveliest songs in a particularly 'pointed and arch manner' – and to do so again when it was 'universally encored' by a delighted audience.[390]

> Each pretty young miss, with a long heavy purse,
> Is courted, and flatter'd, and easily had:
> She longs to be taken for better or worse,
> And quickly *elopes* with an *Irish lad*.

The daring of the elopement, the two fathers united in concern for their children, the anguished innocence of the lovers – in most essentials it feels like a romantic version of the much-repeated story that I learnt as a child. Nicholas may not have had quite such glittering prospects as Mrs Young describes, but was the heir to comfortable wealth and his father's baronetcy – and the Loftus name was sufficiently well known in Ireland to cause any Catholic priest to balk at a hedgerow marriage, though neither party was under age. But perhaps, like the portrait's twin, this is a parallel tale, a deceptive echo of the one I know so well.

In any case, life went on. A few months after her return to England Miss Phillips became Mrs Crouch, having been married secretly (and in some haste) to a naval lieutenant, Rawlings Crouch, shortly before giving birth to a child, who died two days later. Who, I wonder, was the child's father?

As her celebrity increased, Anna Maria commissioned portraits by the best-known artists of the day, including George Romney who painted her in 1787. The tilt of her chin, line of her mouth, large eyes and unruly hair – this is recognisably the adult version of the teenager in Hamilton's pastel. And once again, there is a mischievous story behind the image, for Anna Maria is shown with a musical score in one hand while the other is clutched to her heart, holding the chain of a miniature portrait – which may be that of her husband, whose ship sails away in the background, but looks suspiciously like the tenor, Michael Kelly. For by this time, as was well known, Mrs Crouch was living in a *ménage à trois* which also included Kelly – one of Mozart's unexpected friends, who had recently returned from Vienna after singing in the first performance of *The Marriage of Figaro*. She soon abandoned her husband and lived with this cheerful Irishman for the rest of her life, despite various flings on the side, including – it was rumoured – with the Prince of Wales. And she returned regularly to Ireland.

On Tuesday 3 December 1793, for example, the *Hibernian Magazine* announced 'Mr *Kelly* and Mrs *Crouch*'s first night of this season, with the farce of the *Divorce*'. I like to imagine that Nicholas Loftus was in the audience and that afterwards they talked together of their youth. Anna Maria had been permanently scarred when her hackney carriage overturned a few months earlier and he was plumper than when they first met, but neither was the type to acknowledge such setbacks. She turned her best profile to the light, and he was dressed in the latest fashion, in a waistcoat made from the 'orange and pink striped sattin' that he had recently purchased from Ann Smyth, woollen draper of Dublin, at thirteen shillings per yard.[391]

Anna Maria died of an 'internal mortification' at the age of forty-two in Brighton, on 2 October 1805, and was buried according to her own instructions, wrapped in a woollen shroud 'neither flounced nor trimmed', in a plain black coffin, with a few simple prayers. Michael Kelly erected a monument to her memory in the churchyard.

A more poignant memorial is that which Nicholas kept near him for the rest of his life, and which hangs in the room where I write: the likeness of his first love.

Lady Jane Lofters 8 Cavendish Row Rutland Sqr
S Dublin

59
HIGH STR? WORCESTER.

68
PICCADILLY, LONDON.

Bo.t of H. & R. Chamberlain
Porcelain Manufacturers
by Special Appointment
To their Royal Highnesses

THE PRINCE REGENT, PRINCESS CHARLOTTE OF WALES & ROYAL FAMILY.

45 ✓	60 Table plates			
24 ✓	24 Soup "			
24 ✓	24 Small plates			
18 {	4 Dishes in 10. 12 & 14			
	2 " 16. 18 & 20			
6	6 Square dishes & Covers			
2 ✓	2 Round Soup Tureens & Stands			
4 ✓	4 Sauce & Stands	715	105	
1-1 ✓	1 Sallad & 1 Drainer			
	a Complete Desert with			
	Vase Cream Basket			
	1 Complete Tea Set No 623	10. 10		
	1 Instantaneous Light with Candle			
	1 Bottle of	1 11. 6		
	Package	1. 4		
	£118 " 5. 6			

Compared

INTERLUDE

CHAPTER 31

City of Rogues

Eighteenth-century Dublin was a city of extravagant folly and savage humour, where crooks and grandees, whores, clergymen, journalists and wits consorted together in violent intimacy, against one of the most elegant civic stage sets in Europe. Close by, backstage, were the dark and densely overcrowded alleys and tenements of the poor, stinking and riddled with disease.

The fashionable world was narrowly focused. Clustered around College Green were Parliament House, Trinity College and Daly's Club, the most luxurious gambling den in the city. A short walk west, down Dame Street, led to the Castle, the Royal Exchange and the Smock Alley Theatre; a leisurely stroll south was Peg Plunket's famous brothel, known as the 'Pitt Street Nunnery'. The wealthy young bucks spent much of their lives in this neighbourhood, gambling at Daly's, whoring at Peg's, or parading along Beaux Walk, the north side of St Stephen's Green.

Of all the habitués of this stylish microcosm, few were more stylish than Sir Edward's distant cousin Dudley Loftus (seagoing yacht, showy carriages, pet monkey, private sedan chair, expensive house, aristocratic wife) and none was more extravagant than his friend Buck Whaley. The Buck was described by his brother-in-law, Valentine Lawless, as 'a perfect specimen of the Irish gentlemen of the olden time – gallant, reckless, and profuse, he made no account of money, limb, or life, when a bet was to be won, or a daring deed to be attempted.'[392] Elected to the Irish Parliament at the age of eighteen, he spent most of his time at Daly's next door, or holding 'midnight orgies' at the house where he kept his inordinately expensive mistress. 'But soon growing tired of this manner of living, I conceived a strange idea of performing, like Cook, a voyage round the world.'[393]

Whaley commissioned a ship to be built, at a cost of £10,000, and boasted of his plans to his cronies, until 'one day at dinner, with some people of fashion at the Duke of Leinster's,' he undertook an extraordinary wager, which made him famous. 'The conversation turned upon my intended voyage, when one of the company asked me to what part of the world I meant to direct my course first, to which I answered, without hesitation, "to Jerusalem." This was considered by the company a mere jest; and so, in fact, it was.' Half his friends were of the opinion that Jerusalem didn't exist, the other half were certain that the Buck would be unable to find his way there. The provocation was irresistible. 'I instantly offered to bet any sum that I would go to Jerusalem and return to Dublin within two years of my departure. I accepted without hesitation all the wagers that were offered me, and in a few days the sum exceeded twelve thousand pounds.' As the wagers continued to mount the Buck was persuaded by his long-suffering stepfather that the upkeep of mistress and ship was more than his purse could stand. He reluctantly sacrificed both. The order for the vessel was cancelled ('for a small compensation to the builder, who, I understand, afterwards sold her to the Empress of Russia'), and his mistress was packed off to London with a modest annuity.

Free of all encumbrances but determined to depart in style, Whaley persuaded Dudley Loftus to lend his yacht for the first leg of the voyage. On 20 September 1788, the day appointed for his departure, the Buck led a colourful procession of servants, animals, creditors and friends through the streets of Dublin to George's Quay – where 'Loftus's fine ship' lay waiting, ready to set sail. The curious gawped and a contemporary balladeer recorded the occasion for posterity.

> [Ruffians cleared the way] as Whaley debonair,
> Marched forward with his Bear'.
> Then came French valets two and two
> By garlick you'd have smelt the crew.

A huge black dog, a baboon and Whaley's lapdogs (in their own striped carriage) were followed by the ship's owner.

> In phaeton and six, high rear'd,
> Dudley Loftus next appeared:
> A monkey perched was by his side,
> Which looked, for all the world, his bride.

Friends, relatives and assorted hangers-on were waiting at the shore, including one who loved a spectacle – 'Peg Plunkett on her horse, Was surely there of course.'[394] Another face in the crowd was that of the radical polemicist James Napper Tandy, who was standing, as it happened, close to one of his many political enemies, 'the Boxing Bishop', William Beresford. When Beresford trod on his toe, the excitable Tandy 'lent his Grace a clout, And so they boxed it out.'

Jerusalem Whaley won his bet, after a dangerous journey, and even managed to make a profit on the adventure; 'the only instance in all my life before, in which any of my projects turned out to my advantage.'[395] But on his return to Dublin, Whaley rapidly resumed his old ways, 'so that in a few years I dissipated a fortune of near four hundred thousand pounds.'

The Buck's boon companions on his road to ruin were two of Dublin's most unscrupulous rogues, the 'Sham Squire', Francis Higgins, and 'Copper-faced' Jack Scott, Lord Clonmel.[396] Higgins was a government informer and scurrilous hack (proprietor of the *Freeman's Journal*) who acquired his nickname by marrying an heiress under false pretences. She is said to have died of grief but he went on to acquire a fortune through various disreputable means. Clonmel was the notoriously corrupt Chief Justice who had sentenced Strange and Byrne to death for the abduction of the Misses Kennedy. The two of them were responsible for numerous mischiefs, and were rightly reviled by their contemporaries, but one of the stories of their villainies has an entertaining ending, which summarises the unique character of Ireland at this time.

Higgins and Clonmel launched a ferocious persecution against 'The Man of Ireland', John Magee, patriotic proprietor of the *Dublin Evening Post*, who had exposed their corruptions in his paper. Magee was imprisoned on several occasions at the 'fiat' of the Chief Justice, until the House of Commons declared the whole process unlawful. He then happened to come into some money and determined on a spectacular revenge.

Clonmel had acquired a country house in Blackrock, south of the city of Dublin, and spent a fortune on the gardens, of which he was inordinately proud. Magee bought a field next door, called it Fiat-hill and advertised a series of entertainments there, culminating in the Grand Olympic Pig Hunt, to celebrate the birthday of the Prince of Wales. Thousands turned up on the appointed day – 'the entire disposable mob of Dublin of both sexes' – lured by the promise of free whiskey and plentiful entertainment. They were greeted by asses in scarlet judicial robes, and dogs dressed as barristers, in gowns and wigs; as well as 'dancing girls, grinning hags,' a variety of games and plenty to drink.[397]

Peg Plunket was there and so, too, was Valentine Lawless, later Lord Cloncurry, who links all the strands in this story in the most apposite way: he was brother-in-law to Lord Clonmel and to Buck Whaley, as well as a cousin to the 'Buck' Lawless who had been Peg's keeper in the 1760s. He was also a political radical who had argued vehemently for Magee's release and was present on Fiat-hill as a friend of the 'Man of Ireland'.

According to Cloncurry, when the party was in full swing Magee released a number of strong, squealing pigs, 'with their tails shaved and soaped – and announced that each pig should become the property of any one who could catch and hold it by the slippery member.' The drunken horde, in pursuit of the terrified pigs, crashed through the boundary hedge and ran rampage over Clonmel's garden, utterly destroying it and panicking the Chief Justice into precipitate flight to Dublin Castle, where he announced that the country was in rebellion and pleaded with the Viceroy to suspend habeas corpus.[398]

There was of course a coda. John Magee was rashly married in a brothel to an 'impure' with whom he was besotted. He set her up with a house on College Green and another at Blackrock, provided her with a carriage and servants, and squandered about three thousand pounds on her in a couple of months. Magee then had a revulsion, as violent as his original passion, gave his wife a beating and turned her naked out of doors at two o'clock in the morning. Mrs Magee took refuge with Peg Plunket – who noted that 'she became extremely troublesome, and was besides too fond of the native,' i.e. whiskey – until she was taken away by Buck Whaley 'in order merely to have it to say, that he had Mrs Magee, the Woman of Ireland, in keeping,' and perhaps as some obscure form of revenge on poor Magee himself, for the antics at Fiat-hill.[399]

Many of these lives, so strangely intertwined, can be read as moral fables, ending in retribution. It almost seems as if there was a compulsion to mimic the stereotypes of contemporary fiction – or perhaps it is simply that the literary conventions, which now seem so artificial, were closer than we grasp to common experience.

John Magee ended his days in the Hospital for the Insane, which had been founded by the bequest of Dean Swift. Buck Whaley 'was stabbed in a fit of jealousy by one of two sisters to whom he was paying marked attentions,' and died at the age of thirty-four on his way from Liverpool to London, after years of exile from his creditors on the Isle of Man. Peg Plunket came to a bitter end, after being robbed and raped by footpads. 'Copper-faced' Jack Scott died on the eve of the Rising of 1798, leaving a scandalous diary that his family unexpectedly published, as an act of posthumous revenge.

As for that consummate survivor, Francis Higgins, his name was universally reviled for his part in the betrayal of Lord Edward Fitzgerald, leader of the United Irishmen, just before the Rising that Fitzgerald alone might have led to a successful conclusion. Higgins attempted to expunge the memory of his infamy by leaving most of his fortune to charity and by arranging for 'a fulsome epitaph' to be carved on his headstone, but this merely provoked the fury of the mob. The tomb was destroyed shortly after his death and he lies in an unmarked grave.

And Dudley Loftus? This elegant descendant of a famous archbishop lived for a bright moment, reflected in the glory of his friend, and survives in the rough verses of the ballad of Jerusalem Whaley, perched on his phaeton with a monkey by his side. His possessions were those of a man of wealth and his friendship with the Buck suggests a degree of dissipation, but I know him best through his wife, Lady Jane (daughter of the Earl of Arran), because sometimes I eat off her china.

Four plates survive from the enormous service that she ordered in 1814 from H. & R. Chamberlain of Worcester, seven years after

Dudley's death. The border is palest lilac blue, with circles and arabes-
ques of gold leaf, interspersed with hand-painted sprays of flowers and
with a posy of flowers in the centre – restrained, rather French, very
elegant. And Lady Jane's name is indelibly fired on the back of each
plate, in crimson copperplate script. It was a purchase of great luxury.[400]

Lady Jane could well afford this extravagance. She lived in one of the
most fashionable streets in Dublin, at No 8 Cavendish Row, and she left
more than £20,000 at her death in 1831, in addition to her 'House &
furniture, Wine & Books', and her share in her late husband's estate.
There were generous bequests to each of her army of servants (who
received between one and four years' wages), 'Trinkets' to her 'children,
Grand Children & Friends,' and 'the Madeira in Cavendish Row I leave
to Wm Henry Mangan, who is Married to my daughter' – but the bulk
of her wealth was divided equally between her daughters, Kitty and
Betsy. Jane was careful with her money, for all the cash was invested in
3½% government stock and she left specific instructions that her heirs
were not to tamper with it; 'above all I wish them to Avoid Speculation.'
It was the voice of caution from one who had lived through an era of
perilous extravagance, enjoyed herself and survived.[401]

This story has an epilogue – a strange, rattling echo of Lady Jane's
prudence. For there was another Jane Loftus, her relative, and another
fortune, less carefully hoarded; and a mad sister who went naked or
dressed in red handkerchiefs, a musical parrot, and gold coins spilling
from the pages of unread books. It seems like a tale of Georgian Dublin,
with all its reckless follies, but this one took place in the first year of
Victoria's reign.

Jane and Martha Loftus were the unmarried sisters of Dudley,
whom they long outlived. They shared a house in Fitzwilliam Square
where they camped in increasing squalor until eventually, in 1838,
Martha's sanity was challenged in court. She was seventy-eight years
old but refused to sleep in a bed and lived entirely in the drawing
room, which she also used as kitchen. She 'frequently appeared naked
at the windows, or scarcely clothed at all when going into the street,
or driving about town in a jaunting car,' and 'she caused a number of
red pocket handkerchiefs to be stitched into a gown.' Her sister Jane
'was also deranged'.

Her parrot dined off the same plate with her; and fancying that a musical instrument has been invented on which parrots could play, she importuned the music sellers to procure it for her favourite polly. In boxes, kept near the large fires always burning in her chamber – a very dirty one – large sums of money were found and other property to an enormous extent. Debentures [were] discovered, on which unclaimed interest had for many years been accumulating. Bank of Ireland notes for £500 each and bonds for £600. Coins, plate, gold watches and other valuable property thrust between rags, book-leaves, and concealed amidst dirty vessels and clothes, about the apartment.[402]

The jury found them insane but this miserly extravagance – soiled and threadbare – was the crazed mirror image of the world in which these sisters were raised, the city of rogues.

SHADOW OF THE CASTLE

CHAPTER 32

The Volunteer Banners

As a child of seven, on my first visit to Mount Loftus, I was shown the Grattan banners. They were unwrapped with great solemnity by my cousin Bettina Grattan-Bellew and were spread on a long table, which supposedly was that from Grattan's Parliament. I had no idea what all this meant or even who Grattan was (except that he must have been some sort of ancestor of Bettina's husband), but I was entranced by the beautiful black silk banners, painted with green and silver wreaths of shamrock, surrounding the word IRELAND lettered in gold, and adorned with pink and silver scrolls bearing strange messages: FREE TRADE, LEGISLATIVE RIGHTS ESTABLISHED, JUDGES MADE INDEPENDENT, A Limited inftead of a Perpetual Mutiny Bill. The size of the banners, the feel and rustle of the lustrous silk, the richness of the painted wreaths and scrolls – everything combined with the mystery of their meaning to give me a sense that they were magical. And even now, having learnt their history, I know that this was true.[403]

The natural state of Ireland is civil war, or so it often seems. In that sense, at least, the eighteenth century was an aberration. The first half saw crop failures and famine and the second half increasing civil disturbance – as violent local gangs sought revenge for their poverty – but this was, nonetheless, a time of growing prosperity and relative peace. That deceptive calm, the moment of tranquillity before the storm, is dreamily suggested by a report in Finn's *Leinster Journal* in the summer of 1779, announcing that Sir Edward Loftus's gardener had produced a giant mushroom weighing 6lbs 4ozs, with a stalk nine inches in girth. It was the wonder of the locality, and crowds flocked to see it.[404] But this extraordinary fungus was one of the last uncomplicated marvels of a turbulent year. For Sir Edward and his family, 1779 was the beginning of the long political journey that led, with numerous fits and starts, to the disasters of '98.

It was a particularly bad time for the terrifying nocturnal raids of the Whiteboys, who roamed the land under cover of darkness; robbing, maiming horses and cattle, terrorising the neighbourhood. Their grievances ranged from tithes to a more generalised sense of poverty and exclusion from the land, and their targets included the Protestant gentry, Catholic farmers, priests, adulterers and informers. The kidnapping of the Kennedy sisters by Garret Byrne and James Strange in April that year, may well have been accomplished with Whiteboy help, and their activities were so bold throughout County Kilkenny that a number of their victims were provoked into retaliatory action.

Sir Edward Loftus, as one of the magistrates for the county, raised a posse of his neighbours to hunt down the marauders, with such success that eventually the Whiteboys sued for peace. He won the trust of their leaders whom he persuaded to surrender together with their weapons, on promise of an amnesty – but his fellow magistrates reneged on the deal and several of the Whiteboys were tried for offences committed prior to their arrest. One was sentenced to death. This provoked a formal protest from Sir Edward, who accused his brothers on the bench of having shamefully broken faith.[405]

Even among those who were tempted to such arbitrary abuses of local power there was a growing sense that it was time for political reform and that the opportunity had come. Much of the British army was tied up in America, including most of the Irish garrison, and the example of the American Revolution provoked furious constitutional debate. The English government was on the defensive and Ireland was unprotected. Suddenly, in the autumn of 1779, bands of Volunteers were formed throughout Ireland – led and equipped by the Protestant gentry but increasingly open to others from the oppressed minorities: Dissenters in the North and Catholics (eventually) in the South. The Volunteers were ostensibly raised for the country's defence against a possible French invasion and for the maintenance of civil order at a time of great unrest, but they were also, unmistakeably, a flamboyant expression of Irish nationalism and Irish identity, closely linked to Henry Grattan and his fellow 'Patriots'.

They presented a formidable threat to English authority. By the end of 1779 there were more than 40,000 Volunteers under arms, and at the height of their activities there may well have been twice that number. Though loudly protesting their loyalty to the English Crown, the bands were in no way adjuncts of the English army. They elected their own officers and their assemblies provided the perfect forum for political agitation – which frequently found expression in a language of radical protest that was almost indistinguishable from the outbursts of native Irish nationalism. Consider, for example, this stirring 'republican' anthem, which was in fact a marching song of the Volunteers.

> No laws shall bind us
> But those we frame ourselves;
> The English now shall find us
> As free as they're themselves.
> The Irish Volunteers my boys
> Have wed the glorious Cause;
> And will, with many hearts and hands
> New-model Poynings Laws.*

Sir Edward Loftus was determined to play his part in these exciting events and decided to convert his informal posse of Whiteboy hunters into a band of volunteers. Meeting at Goresbridge, on 12 December 1779, they agreed to form 'a troop of Light Horse to consist of 40 independent Gentlemen to be called The Barrow Rangers – for the Defence of the country at large against the attack of an Invading Enemy [and] the preservation of the peace in our immediate district.' As with the local hunts (with their distinctive buttons and coloured coats) the Barrow Rangers were determined to make a brilliant show, with a uniform of 'Scarlet faced with Black, Gold Buttons, Gold Epaulets, White Cloth Waistcoats, and Buff Belts', and the panoply of a full regiment – colonel, lieutenant, cornet, adjutant and paymaster-treasurer. The necessary drills were to be combined with the pleasures of a dining club, stimulating political debate, but the Rangers also constituted a

---

* Poynings Laws made the Irish Parliament subservient to that of England.

genteel protection racket. Having agreed to apply to 'the Resident and Absentee Gentlemen of property for further subscription' they 'resolved that we will never lend any Assistance for the protection of Persons or Properties of any who refuse their support to the Association.'[406]

Finally, as with all committee meetings, it was time for the vote of thanks. 'Resolved that the thanks of the Corps be presented to Sir Edward Loftus Bart, our Colonel, for his unwearied diligence and spirited activity in restoring Tranquillity to this Barony, as by his exertions he not only induced the principal leaders of the Whiteboys to surrender themselves but their arms also.'

The ardour that inspired this and other similar declarations was sufficient to overcome the extraordinary inertia of colonial politics. The Volunteer bands joined into regional and national associations, and were prepared to back their demands for reform with vigorous demonstrations. The fact that these protests provided a splendid opportunity for bombastic display in no way diminished their attraction – on the contrary, the Volunteers swaggered for the public and for posterity, firing their cannons and muskets to frighten the ladies, who gasped with well contrived horror as their heroes paraded to impress them.

Francis Wheatley was on hand to capture their likenesses, which he incorporated in a series of memorable paintings. The first of these depicted the parade on King William's birthday, 4 November 1779. *The Dublin Volunteers meeting on College Green* is packed with the excitement of those times – gaudy uniforms, clouds of gun smoke, great flags in bright colours and a crowd of fashionable onlookers leaning from the windows, like boxes at a theatre, or perched precariously on the leads of the roofs. Among the Volunteers it is possible to recognise the Duke of Leinster (brother of Lord Edward Fitzgerald, one of the leaders of the 1798 Rising), Luke Gardiner (vastly prosperous developer of Dublin) and the young Napper Tandy, whose radicalism was not yet sufficient to cause his banishment.[407]

Wheatley's most interesting canvas was painted a few months later and captured the crucial moment when the demands of the Volunteers achieved the political momentum necessary to launch the process of reform. It showed Henry Grattan delivering his famous speech before the Irish House of Commons, on 19 April 1780, as he moved the resolution 'That the people of Ireland are of right an independent nation and ought only to be bound by laws made by the King, Lords and Commons of Ireland.' This, too, was a highly theatrical painting, showing the stalls packed with MPs and the gallery crowded with spectators, as Grattan took centre stage.[408] Expectations ran high and the debate lasted through the night but eventually, around half past six in the morning, the exhausted House lost its nerve and the motion was indefinitely adjourned.

Grattan's eloquence had failed to win the crucial vote but the influence of his speech was such that it encouraged a process of increasingly radical debate, both inside and outside Parliament. The old longing that Ireland might be a nation, free of English control, was given specific shape in dozens of Volunteer resolutions and numerous political pamphlets, arguing the case for legislative independence. These were no longer phrased as pleas for justice but as urgent demands for rights – a shift of language that echoed rising confidence. In the process of these debates a strange transformation could be seen, as Sir Edward Loftus and others like him, the decent Protestant gentry, emerged as political radicals. For a few hectic, optimistic years, they played their part in what they hoped would be a peaceful revolution, as the Volunteer assemblies came increasingly to express the popular will, in a way that Parliament had never done.

The militant nature of their demands frightened the English government into taking notice and the initial response was to resort to the usual tactics, relying on wholesale bribery or threats to circumvent the need for action. There was also an attempt to bring the Volunteers under English control by turning them into a force of militia, subject to army discipline – but this only seems to have inflamed matters, as the new Viceroy discovered to his cost when he arrived at Dublin Castle in December 1780. Lying on his desk, amongst a heap of petitions from office-seekers, was a long, anonymous and menacing letter, which seems also to have been circulated in manuscript among the Volunteers, judging by the copy I found among the papers of Sir Edward Loftus.[409]

Disguised as *Brutus* and claiming that he wrote as 'an Irishman – totally uninfluenced by party', the author referred to 'the Iron hand of Oppression', 'British Tyranny' and 'the Spirit of Irish Freedom,' before launching into a paean of praise for the Volunteers: 'an example of National Virtue not to be paralleled in the Annals of ancient History.' Such virtue was compared to the perfidy of the English in continuing to frustrate the promises of free trade for Ireland and the iniquity of a Perpetual Mutiny Bill, by which army discipline was enforced without annual scrutiny by Parliament. Brutus then referred to the rumours that the new Viceroy had been instructed to 'use every argument and every artifice' to turn the Volunteers into a militia force.

> Can the folly or Idiotism of a Minister Suggest that 100,000 Virtuous Independent Citizens Conversant in the use of Arms, and able to afford the expense of Cloathing and Accoutring themselves, and Laying up Stores of Ammunition, and providing Ordinance and every other Military aparatus necessary for enabling so Numerous an Army to act on the offensive or Defensive, as Circumstances may require, can I say, even Human Imbecility suppose that such an Army could become the Venial Janizaries of the most Venal and Corrupt Administration that ever disgraced the Annals of Britain? Had your predecessor in office pursued those plans, which it is said the Ministers of Britain had Concerted, and were determined on, Ireland would ere now have been Convulsed and Shook to its Centre, and Steady opposition to such alarming measures would have ended in the last Awful appeal to the great disposer of Human Events, to direct their arms to the public protection and Common Defence.

The Volunteers had been ready to take up arms against the English government – 'This Kingdom [was] in a State of Smothered War.'

> Should your employers ask what it is that will satisfy the Irish, tell them nothing short of an absolute Free Trade, a Mutiny Bill of our own, a repeal of Poynings Laws, a new Habeas Corpus Act, an Act for making our Judges Independent of the Crown, and a renewal of the Declaratory Act that the King Lords and Commons of Ireland are only Competent to make Laws to bind Ireland.

The writer's choice of pseudonym evoked a famous classical precedent, immediately evident to his educated readers. Lucius Junius Brutus was the founder of the Roman Republic – the man who rallied opposition to the Etruscan kings of Rome after Prince Tarquinius raped Lucretia, most virtuous of Roman wives. The original story combined a sermon on republican rectitude with a myth on the theme of colonial exploitation, the rape of the land – and it was certainly read as such in eighteenth-century Ireland. Hibernia / Lucretia was the suffering victim and the English King's Viceroy was the wicked Tarquin, which meant that anyone adopting the disguise of Lucius or Junius or Brutus – all of which were used to conceal the authors of various nationalist tracts – proclaimed himself the champion of incorruptible republican virtue, the defender of a downtrodden people.

But who were the people? The language of 'patriotism', as expressed in Brutus's letter, reflected complex ambiguities about what it meant to be Irish. A century earlier most Protestant settlers would have described themselves as English, even those whose families had been established in Ireland for several generations. Now, almost without exception, the Protestant gentry thought of themselves as Irish, a quality they shared with the Catholic majority, and regarded the agents of English government as 'colonial' intruders. But nationality and citizenship were two different things, and rights in Irish citizenship varied enormously. Despite the gradual relaxation of the Penal Laws, Catholics were still excluded from mainstream politics; they could not stand for Parliament and they could not vote.

Less noticeable, but nonetheless real, was the effective disenfranchisement of large numbers of Protestants, either because they were women or because they were poor, or because of the bizarre arrangements that applied to the election of representatives for the 117 boroughs which returned three-quarters of the Members of Parliament. The crowded City of Dublin (with a population approaching 200,000) was represented by two MPs, elected by a limited franchise of a few thousand voters. The ancient village of Bannow (which 'retains only the name, being totally uninhabited') also returned two Members to the House of Commons, as did each of the neighbouring boroughs of Clonmines and Fethard, all of them 'elected' by a dozen burgesses who were servants or dependants of the local grandee – Sir Edward Loftus's half-brother, the Earl of Ely.

Being a Member of Parliament was a symbol of status and provided access to the system of patronage. Status was a matter of theatre, of rhetorical gesture – like so much else about Irish politics – but patronage was the key to advancement. Almost every honour and office, every promotion in the army, the judiciary or the church was a reward for services rendered or the price of continued loyalty. This gave the aristocratic borough-mongers their power but it also made them ultimately dependent on the English Viceroy, the greatest patron of all. A determined Viceroy, cunning in the uses of corruption, could always expect to win sufficient votes in Parliament and frustrate the clamour for reform.

The practiced rottenness of this corruption provoked a sense of dispossession, which divided the modest country gentlemen and the Protestant tradesmen of Dublin (the rank and file of the Volunteers) from the great aristocratic 'interests' and their cliques of dependents, but which prompted other coalitions. To the growing consternation of the power-brokers, Volunteer demands to share in the political process echoed the long campaign for representation by the maltreated masses of Ireland – Catholics and Dissenters – prefiguring an alliance that eventually gave birth to the Society of United Irishmen.

As the clamour for reform mounted, even the political magnates such as Lord Ely came to believe that the momentum for legislative independence was irresistible and that their own best interests might well be served by allying themselves with the Patriots and the Volunteers, but they were faced with the continued intransigence of the English government. It was not until March that the logjam finally broke, when the resignation of the English Prime Minister, Lord North, led to a Whig administration under Rockingham, vastly more favourable to the demands of the Irish patriots.

Three weeks later, on 16 April, Henry Grattan rose from his sickbed to address the Irish House of Commons, knowing that his hour had come and that 'every heart [was] beating with expectation.' Pale but inspired, he spoke from the floor of the House with the certainty of victory. 'I am now to address a free people . . . I found Ireland on her knees, I have watched over her with an eternal solicitude; I have traced her progress from injuries to arms, and from arms to liberty . . . Ireland is now a nation; in that new character I hail her, and bowing in her August presence, I say, *Esto perpetua.*'

*

'Grattan's Parliament' was heralded as a turning point in Ireland's relationship with England, the moment when its claim to legislative independence finally proved irresistible – and patriotic enthusiasm was so extreme that the man himself was voted £50,000 to purchase the estate of Tinnehinch, where he lived out his days in glory. But even more persuasive than Grattan's words may have been the force of arms to which he referred so delicately in his speech – for outside on College Green (but visible in the minds of everyone crowded into the Commons) was an assembly of Volunteers from all over Ireland, their artillery pointed at Parliament. Over the largest cannon they had draped silk banners (black for mourning) which were beautifully painted with the slogans endorsed by Volunteer companies throughout Ireland, in the best attempt yet seen at popular democracy, distilling the hopes of a nation oppressed.

Those same banners were later presented to Henry Grattan in thanks for his apparent victory, and were unrolled for me nearly two centuries later by my cousin, who spread them on the table which she claimed was that which had appeared in Wheatley's picture, covered in a baize cloth and piled with books, at the focus of the parliamentary stage.

But the theatre of politics proved, yet again, to be a matter of smoke and mirrors. Though each of those demands was enacted during the life of Grattan's Parliament, each was cruelly frustrated – by the rival ambitions of 'patriot' politicians and their clumsy tactics when negotiating with the English government, or the corruption of the great political magnates, or the cunning of the colonial administration. The exalted hopes of reform were smothered by English inertia and Grattan himself came increasingly to seem irrelevant – a mere windbag of rhetoric who justified John Fitzgibbon's caustic comment, that 'the recollection of Mr Grattan's splendid periods is but a slender compensation for poverty and the most absolute dependence on Great Britain.'[410]

Grattan's declaration of Ireland's legislative independence had actually increased the value of parliamentary boroughs to their aristocratic 'owners'. Having lost the right to amend Irish bills in the English Parliament, Dublin Castle was now entirely dependent on the corrupt manipulation of Irish parliamentary votes for the passage of government legislation. It was claimed by Wolfe Tone, in the aftermath of 1782, that 'borough stock rose like that of the South Sea; a seat which would, the year before, fetch in the market a bare £1500 was now worth £2000; and, on an emergency, perhaps £3000. The Minister on his part scorned to haggle; he saw that if gentlemen were obliged to pay such high prices on the one hand, it was but reasonable they should be reimbursed on the other.' It was equally clear that genuine parliamentary reform would render such seats worthless and make English control near impossible, thus destroying the political economy on which the wealth of most great families ultimately depended. Grattan himself was a protégé of this system and his instinctive reaction to continuing Volunteer agitation was typical of his coterie: he described the Volunteers, his erstwhile allies, as 'the armed beggary of the nation'.[411]

Without the support of the Protestant magnates on the one hand, or the Catholics on the other, the Volunteers were powerless; and after the return of British troops from America (following the Treaty of Paris in 1783) they could no longer justify their role as defenders of the realm. The English government, reinvigorated under Pitt, could afford to ignore them.

As the impetus for reform weakened, there was a last effort to rekindle the passions of the heady spring of 1782, led by Napper Tandy. An energetic demagogue with a large nose and an attractive, impractical optimism, James Napper Tandy was a Dublin tradesman who first came to public notice by his attacks on municipal corruption. With his brother George he was prominent in the campaign to boycott English goods, and was one of the first to join the Volunteers, becoming a captain of artillery – which must have pleased him greatly, given his lifelong love of flamboyant uniforms and impressive noise. In the spring of 1784 Napper Tandy helped organise a series of 'aggregate meetings' in Dublin, bringing together all those interested in the cause of parliamentary reform. He was trying to drum up support for a National Convention, to be held later that year, and in pursuit of that aim wrote in June to the high sheriffs of every county, urging their help in persuading the local gentry of the need for political action. Sir Edward Loftus – as High Sheriff of County Wexford – replied from Mount Loftus on 9 July 1784.

I have the honour of receiving your favour of the 24th June, which should have come earlier to hand, but that it was directed to Wexford; nor was it forwarded to me until Wednesday last.

I will be so bold to say there is no person who has more at heart the purport of your application than I have – I am this instant setting out for the County Wexford, & shall lay your letters before the principal Gentlemen there, who, I doubt not, will cooperate with the Aggregate Body in every salutary measure.[412]

Most of the county sheriffs responded to Napper Tandy's initiative with much less enthusiasm, but Sir Edward summoned a meeting of the 'Gentlemen, Clergy and Freeholders of the County of Wexford', on 16 August, which passed strong resolutions in favour of Irish Preference and Parliamentary Reform, and appointed five Delegates to represent them at the proposed National Convention.[412A] When that Convention eventually got under way, on 25 October 1784, it was attended by 'a much respected peer, Lord Powerscourt, four baronets, several volunteer colonels, an archdeacon and respectable country gentlemen,' and there was a strong contingent from the north, including the radical physician William Drennan – but it was hard to escape the impression that this was the mere rump of an Association which only a year earlier had seemed on the point of storming Parliament to enforce its demands.

A sense of betrayal had replaced old optimism, as former allies deserted the cause. When Sir Edward attended a meeting of the Kilkenny Congress, in February 1785, it was shortly after one of their local MPs had implied that 'Miscreants' responsible for 'the most dreadful nightly outrages' in the county were incited by those same 'Citizens and Volunteers' now assembled in Congress. The delegates declared their 'Attachment to our Sovereign and Affection for our Sister Kingdom', and their commitment to constitutional reform, but deplored 'the extraordinary and unprecedented Doctrine of Attachments' – a mechanism whereby the English government tried to interfere with Irish finance bills. No one was listening.[413]

A few months later, in April, the National Assembly of Volunteers met in Dublin for what proved to be the last attempt at enlisting the nation's support. They voted for a similar plan to that which they had agreed two years earlier and Henry Flood once again tried to introduce these measures as a reform bill. It was rejected by the House of Commons, after a long debate during which the instincts of the Protestant ruling class were only too perfectly summarised in a speech by the fair-weather patriot and wit, Sir Hercules Langrishe.

> The honorable gentleman says the people demand Reform. The mob may demand it, but not the people – When a man talks of the voice of the people, he means the voice of those who echo his own. Personal equality of representation, the only equality that I can conceive, would be a pure democracy, and in a country like ours, where the democracy does not profess the religion of the State, a democracy subversive of the laws and the constitution. [414]

And that was that. As William Drennan so beautifully described it, the hope of reform was like 'a balloon left in the clouds – now precipitating from audacious height into vast vacuity.'[415]

Grattan's Parliament had allowed the Ascendancy to indulge in a mirage of revolution – exalted language, heroic gestures, the posture without the pain. An intrinsic belief that words are the equivalent of acts has shaped the habit of Irish mythmaking for centuries past, entwined in the cycles of bitterness and betrayal that form the pattern of Irish history. It is clear to me now that those lustrous silk banners of 1782 were indeed magical, but their magic was the deceiving, shape-changing sort. These were not the flags of a famous victory, as I had been told and many still believe, but funeral palls, painted with the epitaphs of hope.

CHAPTER 33

Five Miniatures

In 1790 six members of the Loftus family had their likenesses taken by Mr Thomason, silhouette painter, in his cluttered shop at 25 South Great Georges Street, which ran alongside what had once been the eastern perimeter of Dublin Castle. Thomason advertised 'PERFECT LIKENESSES In Miniature PROFILE. Taken by *I THOMASON* on a peculiar Plan & reduced to any Size, which preserves ye. most exact Symmetry & animated Expression of ye. Features superior to any other Method. Set in elegant gilt frames at 6s. 6d. only.' He also claimed to cause minimal inconvenience to his sitters – 'Time of Sitting from Ten to Two & from Two to five in the Evening, when each Person is detained 2 Minutes only.' Such prodigious facility must have been aided by the use of a *camera obscura* or comparable device, which enabled Mr Thomason rapidly to trace a shadow cast on paper. 'He keeps ye. Original Shades & can supply Those he has once taken with any Number of Copies.'

I know these details because five of the miniatures survive – elegant silhouettes, painted on fragile gesso ovals.[416] When I first came across them (in the house of a cousin) one was broken, one damaged and all the frames had been attacked by woodworm. There was no indication of the artist's identity and there was even some confusion about the sitters. Each miniature was inscribed with a name on the back, but the writing was in two different hands, seemingly of different dates. So I took them to a restorer who was trained in paper conservation and asked her to remove the backing papers, hoping for some evidence of origin or identity.

Kim Leyshon gazed at them silently as I shuffled the family group on her workbench: Sir Edward and his brother the Colonel (illegitimate sons of Viscount Loftus of Ely); Sir Edward's wife, Lady Loftus; and two of their sons, the dashingly expensive Nicholas and the idealist Lieutenant Edward – looking like the Colonel's twin in his cockaded hat, except that the Colonel's jowls are heavier, his nephew's profile more eager. 'They have the same nose,' she remarked. 'They're lovely.'

She rang me in excitement a few weeks later, to announce that she had discovered the artist's advertisement, pasted on the back of each gesso panel, beneath the paper ovals inscribed with the sitters' names. Those names themselves became much more legible when she had done her work and it was possible to establish that three of the inscriptions were contemporary with the miniatures and were written in iron gall ink, while the other two had probably been added in the nineteenth century, but covered faint traces of the earlier handwriting. And so, layer by layer, we discovered their history.

To begin with, I learnt about inks. Every household used to make its own ink, from a recipe passed down in the family or culled from one of those books which contained instructions on everything from how 'to make a very fine Sweet Lamb or Veal Pye' to 'A certain Cure for the Bite of a Mad Dog'. The usual way, in the eighteenth century and earlier, was to boil oak apples (galls) in order to extract tannin and gallic acid, and mix the resultant liquid with iron, in the form of ferrous sulphate. Some recipes called for the addition of human urine. This pale iron gall ink oxidises as it dries, turning a dark black, but it can also be corrosive and may eat into paper over time, causing endless headaches for those whose task it is to conserve ancient manuscripts.

Thus much I learnt, but a lingering curiosity caused me to consult a small fat volume, bound in red leather: Sir Edward Loftus's copy of *The Treble Almanack* for 1804. Part 3, *Wilson's Dublin Directory*, lists every tradesman of that city, with details of profession and address – eighty-five closely printed pages, nearly 4,500 names. I lost myself immediately, revelling in the incongruous combinations (Bookseller, Stationer and Hatter; Jewellers and Madeira Wine-merchant) the surreal congruities (Benj. Disrael, Stockbroker & Lottery Office-Keeper) and the bewildering variety of trades. The directory lists makers of Billiard Tables, Muffins, Umbrellas and Stays; manufacturers of Tiles & Garden Pots, Buckles & Buttons, Helmets, Girth-webs, Water-closets and Watch-glasses. There were Quill Dealers, Anchor-Smiths, Flour & Whiskey factors, Stone Cutters and of course numerous Brewers, including Arthur Guinness, Brewer & Flour Merchant, at No 1 James's Street. Further down the same street was Samuel Healy, Electrifying Machine maker.

There were half a dozen manufacturers of harpsichords, two or three makers of pianofortes, and you could have ordered a trumpet, French horn or pedal harp direct from a specialist craftsman. Or you could have taken any one of these tradesmen to court, by choosing a lawyer from the separate lists of Dublin's litigious army – 1,500 attorneys and 800 barristers, perhaps half of whom practised their profession.

But no one sold ink. I bought an earlier edition of the *Almanack*, for 1791, almost contemporary with the date of the miniatures. Once again I immersed myself in lists of names and trades, but still I could find no one who made ink or claimed to sell it. So Mr Thomason must have made his own, or delegated the work to an apprentice. And the apprentice was not an expert, because the ink faded – causing two of the original inscriptions identifying the sitters to be overwritten in a later hand, when they became illegible.

Those names were inscribed on oval sheets of paper, which seem originally to have been tinted blue-grey – perhaps by James Dunn, the 'Paper-stainer' who lived across South Great Georges Street at No 70 – but the colour has almost entirely faded. The paper itself must have been made in Dublin, by one of a dozen papermakers (two of them women) who were clustered just south of the River Liffey on Cook Street, Bridge Street and Usher's Quay. It was handmade – the first British paper-making machine was built by the Foudrinier brothers, in 1803 – and it was made from cotton and linen rags. Paper from wood pulp did not become a commercial reality until the mid-nineteenth century.

The next layer is the treasure. Stuck to the back of four of the gesso plaques was Mr Thomason's advertisement – a fine rococo design, embellished with swags and foliage. I learnt that the plate for this tradesman's label was engraved by Shillito of Leeds, from whom Thomason had purchased labels since he first set up as a miniature painter, in Manchester in 1786. It was the second version that he ordered following his move to Ireland in 1790, and he used this design from July 1790 (when he realised that the market could stand higher prices than first advertised) until the end of 1791, when he moved premises to Capel Street.[417]

The gilt oval frames and their domed glasses were supplied by a specialist such as Joseph Allsebrook – the 'Frame-smith' of Bow Street, north of the river – or possibly bought much closer to hand, at Lawrence

Crowe's Artists and Mechanicks Warehouse in Golden Lane. The frames are made of wood but each has an embossed metal rim, which forms the decorative moulding. Fitting snugly within the frames are the original ovals of domed glass, full of agreeable imperfections – a hair from the glassmaker's eyelashes appears to have fallen onto the surface of one of them – but skilfully shaped and with round rolled edges. All, that is, except one, for Lady Loftus was evidently dropped long ago. The metal crown of her frame was dented and the original glass was broken. A replacement was provided, almost indistinguishable from the others, but its edges were cut to fit, not rolled during the making.[418]

One task that may not have been subcontracted was the making of the plaques themselves. Like making ink, this was traditionally a job for an apprentice, but it demanded much greater skill. The procedures were essentially those described in Cennino Cennini's *Il Libro dell' Arte*, written in Florence in the fifteenth century.[419] A thick base was made of *gesso grosso*, unslaked plaster of Paris mixed with rabbit-skin glue. This was allowed to dry and then a layer of much finer *gesso sotile* was added, made with slaked plaster and powdered chalk, for extra whiteness. The workshop must have been filled with the sweet and rather sickly smell of the gluepot, warming in the ashes of the fire, and the acrid dryness of chalk and plaster. But the results were surprisingly durable, for so fragile a material. 'They're very well made,' said Stephen Wells – the frame restorer – as he peered through thick glasses at the gesso ovals. 'I doubt whether they would last two hundred years without cracking if made today.' And then I remembered that eighteenth-century Dublin was renowned for the skill of its plasterers, one of whom – Timothy Lawless, 'Plaisterer and Stucco-worker' – lived within a few minutes' walk from Thomason's studio, in Bride Street.

This agreeable sense of simple techniques, using everyday materials to construct something fine and good to look at, is even more strongly present when I consider the pigment that Mr Thomason used to silhouette his 'shades'. It was simple lampblack, the making of which Cennini described thus.

Take a lamp full of linseed oil, and put it, so lighted, underneath a good clean baking dish, and have the little flame of the lamp come about to the bottom of the dish, two or three fingers away, and the smoke which comes out of the flame will strike the bottom of the dish, and condense in a mass. Wait a while; take the baking dish, and with some implement sweep this colour, that is the soot, off on to a paper, or into some small dish; and it does not have to be worked up or ground, for it is a very fine colour.

Once again, I should like to imagine that this was a task for an apprentice, in between making ink, mixing gesso and pasting Mr Thomason's engraved advertisements onto the back of the framed silhouettes, in the hope that the sitters' friends might find their way to South Great Georges Street to have their likeness taken, in no more than two minutes. But I have to admit it is more probable that the artist simply popped across the street, to Gabriel Beranger, 'Pencil and Colour-man'. And Beranger in turn would have bought his supplies from Patrick Hynes, 'Lampblack-manufacturer of Hammond Lane'. And so filled was the city with specialists that I have come to doubt the existence of an apprentice at all. Thomason had no need of one and quite probably could not afford one. If he was married, his wife made the ink; if not, he must have scrounged it from a neighbour.

Those neighbours were crammed together in a jumble of trades and professions. Thomason himself lived above the shop of Dennis McOwen, Starch and Hair powder manufacturer, and most of the other houses in South Great Georges Street were in multiple occupancy. Number 55, for example, was inhabited by an Umbrella-maker, Cabinet-maker, Glover and Shoemaker – one of nine in the street. Next door was even more crowded, with another Shoemaker, two Clockmakers (one of whom also made watches), a Sadler, Tobacconist and Stonecutter. Several houses had a shop below and lodgings above, many of which were occupied by attorneys, who seemed to prefer living in collegiate proximity with one another. Two clergymen lived on opposite sides of the street. One shared a house with a Printer, an Army Agent and a lawyer, the other lodged above a grocer's shop.[420] Three bakers, one confectioner and a French cook; five brushmakers, four hosiers, two booksellers, a Pawnbroker, an Apothecary and three upholsterers; the list goes on and on. It was an incredible hotchpotch of humanity, which must have overflowed onto the pavements whenever the weather was fine. The street was like a bazaar – I am reminded of India.

History tends to analyse the past, separating common experience into its constituent parts and thereby destroying the confused reality of the moment. But taking those silhouettes apart, dissecting them layer by layer, revealed the small but fascinating details of their making – an accumulation of trades and techniques, smells and textures, which told me more about everyday life in eighteenth-century Dublin than anything I had read or seen. The process of discovery itself was like taking a walk through those elegantly shoddy streets, brushing against the crowd of passers-by, peering into the shops, sniffing the air, surrounded by noise and activities which are now much more distant from us, because things are bought and sold and delivered in circumstances far removed from the process of manufacture, let alone craftsmanship. Eighteenth-century economic activity was in many ways as specialised as ours, but it all happened close at hand, was mostly done by hand and involved a network of tradesmen who knew their customers. What we have lost, more grievous than the loss of common skills, is the sense of economic life as a social web, connecting different levels of society in an evident, tangible community. Only in rarefied ways – or by reading Pepys – can we recapture what used to be the immediate texture of experience, before the Industrial Revolution turned everything topsy-turvy.

CHAPTER 34

1798. A Family Divided

As they emerged into the busy street after having their shadows fixed by Mr Thomason, the five members of the Loftus family would have been assailed by all manner of smells – leather and bread and hair powder and mud – but they may not have noticed the strongest odour of all, unwashed humanity, because it was the constant background to everyday life. Much subtler, hard to catch, was the persistent scent of revolution – but if Lady Loftus had popped into one of the booksellers in South Great Georges Street, to purchase the latest novel, she might well have found it lying next to a bundle of radical pamphlets. For 1790 saw the first trickle of what soon became a polemical torrent.

It began mildly enough in April that year, with an anonymous pamphlet – *A Review of the Conduct of Administration during the Seventh Session of Parliament*. Despite its dull name, this was a vigorous attack on parliamentary corruption by an unknown author, Theobald Wolfe Tone, who soon became famous. [421] November saw the publication of *Reflections on the Revolution in France* by the Irish orator, Edmund Burke 'poured forth in the copious fury of near four hundred pages,' according to Thomas Paine, who replied with his own most powerful pamphlet, *Rights of Man*, in March 1791. And then, in August, came Wolfe Tone's *Argument on behalf of the Catholics of Ireland* – a founding text for the Society of United Irishmen. The battle had begun.

Fifteen years earlier, in 1776, Paine had inspired hundreds of thousands of Americans to a belief in the republican cause when he published a short but extraordinarily influential tract, *Common Sense*. The success of that revolution demonstrated the ability of determined men, with a vision of liberty, to throw off the yoke of a colonial power. It was a lesson that had incalculable resonance in Ireland but more immediate impact in France, and hence – because the bogey was on the doorstep – in England. Even the liberals took fright at the French Revolution of 1789 and their spokesman was Edmund Burke, who had been one of the few prominent political figures to declare for American Independence, but was shocked by events across the Channel. Burke's *Reflections* were a brilliant defence of property, tradition and oligarchy but alienated his more radical admirers and and provoked Paine's passionate exposition of a republican state. *Rights of Man* was dedicated to George Washington – in the hope 'that you may enjoy the Happiness of seeing the New World regenerate the Old' – and was an instant bestseller in Ireland, running through seven Dublin editions in little more than a year.[422]

It is hard, now, to sense the extraordinary power of the written word in a pre-televisual age, and to feel the almost shocking force of Paine's plain speaking, compared to the long, complex, beautifully ordered phrases of Edmund Burke – described by Paine as 'music in the ear, and nothing in the heart.' In *Common Sense* Paine had declared that 'Government, even in its best state, is but a necessary evil' – and now, in *The Rights of Man*, he expanded on this theme. 'Lay then the axe to the root, and teach government humanity – It is an age of Revolutions, in which everything may be looked for.' All of which was too much for the authorities, who recognised as clearly as did Paine that the revolutions in America and France threatened all the old certainties. They indicted the pamphleteer for seditious libel, forcing him to flee to France.

In eighteenth-century Ireland, Paine's message was given added force by the unresolved context of political and social relationships between the mass of the Irish Catholic population, the local Protestant Ascendancy and the imported government of England. The most striking expression of these colonial divisions, the Penal Laws, now provoked renewed debate, as the language of radical politics was applied to the long-running battle for religious and social emancipation.

A few months after the publication of *Rights of Man*, a Presbyterian woollen draper had dinner in Belfast with a young Protestant lawyer from Dublin. The draper was Samuel Neilson, head of a secret committee of political radicals, and his guest was Wolfe Tone, the son of a prosperous coachbuilder, whose most recent pamphlet had urged Catholics and Presbyterians to join together in the fight for enfranchisement and political reform.

Tone was warmly welcomed by Neilson and his revolutionary friends in Belfast, and the result of that dinner party was the formation, in October 1791, of a new political organisation, the Society of United Irishmen. The Dublin branch was established a month later. The inspiration for the new Society, implicit from the start, was the French Revolution, and there was always the hope of French support, but the language of liberty had been learnt from Thomas Paine. The Society of United Irishmen was the political incarnation of his beliefs.

There was another, less evident ingredient in this powerful cocktail of republicanism, religious emancipation and the struggle for social justice. While most of Paine's contemporaries were appalled by his radicalism there were others – at all levels of society – who read his words with exultation and one, Mary Wollstonecraft, who leapt ahead of him, into territory where even Paine himself might have felt uncomfortable. This former governess to one of the great families of the Ascendancy had been spurred by Burke's attack on the French Revolution to publish her own *Vindication of the Rights of Men* – a year before Paine's more famous pamphlet, which she may have inspired – and she followed it with an even more brilliant essay, *Vindication of the Rights of Woman*. The startling fact of a woman daring to engage in public political debate was accentuated by what she wrote, for her words were utterly at variance with the prejudices of polite society. Mary Wollstonecraft scorned any notion of 'the *divine right* of husbands' and expressed with cogent simplicity the irreconcilable problem that lay at the heart of the monarchical view of marriage. 'A king is always a king – and a woman a woman: his authority and her sex stand between them and rational converse.' Her aim was equally clear – 'I do not want [women] to have power over men; but over themselves.'

The implicit republicanism of such arguments ought to have had powerful resonance in Ireland, where the female figure of Hibernia (bearing the staff and cap of Liberty) had come to express the complex political aspirations of an increasingly radicalised patriotic alliance, but the moment swiftly passed. Women's rights had scant chance of rational discussion in an atmosphere when every hope of peaceful reform was blocked by mounting fear of change. That fear was the product of shock – for the violence of the French Revolution, on England's doorstep, caused panic even amongst those whose first response had been to cheer the dawn of freedom. All the courts of Europe suddenly felt under threat and so too did the landed classes on whom their support depended. Liberal concessions to reasonable political demands now seemed like the first stages on the road to annihilation, or fuel to feed the fire of revolution, and every proposal was stalled by protective self-interest. That dangerous inertia proved more incendiary than action itself, for the flames of radical protest continued to burn, hidden from view, and eventually blazed into the terrible conflagration of 1798.

The five children of Sir Edward and Anne Loftus came of age in this world of revolutions, inspired by the slogans of the Volunteers, the high hopes of Grattan's Parliament, the achievement of American Independence and the fury of the French *sans-culottes* – in an Ireland when, for an illusory moment, all seemed possible. I am reminded of my own family, five siblings of the '60s. But for us, and possibly for them, the real revolution, liberating and urgent, was in our own expectations, our hopes and our loves. Upheavals in the wider world formed a backdrop to the more immediate dramas of their own lives, as the old certainties of marriage – alliance of property, breeding of heirs – were challenged by claims of the heart, unsettling, intrusive. This is the deeper, subtler confrontation that demanded new forms of expression, novels and opera, and nothing more perfectly expresses those tensions than *Cosi fan Tutte*, which was written in 1789, a few months after the storming of the Bastille. Da Ponte's cynical libretto echoes the fierce frivolity of the *ancien régime*, with its emphasis on women as social and sexual objects, while Mozart's music – filled with the ambiguities of romantic love – is the overture of modernity.

In that same year of revolution, Edward Loftus, home on leave from his military duties, met and fell in love with a Catholic Irish girl, Mary Carroll. He was his father's namesake, his second and favourite son; she was the daughter of a farmer and shopkeeper in Goresbridge, a village on the River Barrow about three miles from Mount Loftus.[423] In earlier times this might have been a ruthless story of seduction and abandonment, in the casual colonial way, but it seems that Edward married her, in a secret and illegal ceremony conducted by a Catholic priest. Lady Loftus regarded the whole thing as a scandal and refused to recognise the marriage, but her son ignored the conventions of family and society and the following year, while her husband was quartered in Carlow, Mary gave birth to a daughter.

At the beginning of 1791 Lieutenant Loftus was ordered to Dublin, expecting to be sent abroad. He made his farewell in style – riding down Goresbridge Street at the head of his troop, with the infant Mary Loftus on the saddle before him – and he gave his wife a miniature, to remember him by. Framed in gold and guarded within a red leather case, it is a talisman of their love. On the back, ringed by an oval band of Waterford blue glass, are two locks of hair and the remains of a delicate scroll of seed pearls that once formed the twined initials MC and EL, for Mary Carroll and Edward Loftus. Her hair is pale, a honey blonde, and you can sense the weight of her tresses. His, finer textured, is darker, with a hint of chestnut. On the front is Edward's portrait, in the uniform of the 4th (Royal Irish) Dragoons, his uncle's regiment.[424] His pale, rather serious face has lost some of the eager boyishness of earlier portraits and he seems thinner, with the beak of his nose more pronounced. His eyes gaze at the viewer with a distant, melancholy air.

Perhaps he was already ill – for two months later, unable to return home, Edward died 'in the barracks of Dublin', on 25 March.[425] His body was brought back to Mount Loftus by his uncle Nicholas and he was buried in the family vault, in Powerstown churchyard.

Mary Carroll (she never bore the name Mrs Loftus) survived him by forty years and resolutely brought up their daughter as a Catholic, in the face of strong disapproval from most of the family. Edward's uncle, Colonel Nicholas, offered to adopt his great-niece, on condition that she was raised as a Protestant, but Mary Carroll refused. The Colonel continued to give the child presents and persuaded Lady Loftus to look after her, if not perhaps to love her. It was Edward's youngest sister, Elizabeth, who took the girl to her heart, adored and defended her through all the troubles to come.

Sad, intelligent Elizabeth, most mysterious of her siblings. She left no letters or papers of any sort, and few clues to her character – except the memory of her, in much-told tales, and her signature in a battered copy of Sterne's *Sentimental Journey*. It is the first Dublin edition, dated 1768, but the binding has been repaired and several pages are frayed and dog-eared, and for that very reason – because it has been loved and used – there is something more essentially Sterne-like about this survival of time's vicissitudes than if it were crisp, clean, immaculate and unopened. I read it entranced with Elizabeth in mind, because Sterne's sensibility matches my image of her, a combination of gravity and impulsiveness – in his case more impulsive, in hers more grave. She may have lacked the wildness of his wit but she suffered, I think, from the sudden starts of passion that he described with such tender sympathy. 'When the heart flies out before the understanding, it saves the judgement a world of pains.'

Elizabeth, it is said, allowed her heart to fly out, in defiance of the social conventions, for when she was in her thirties she fell for a man nearly twice her age, a Wexford neighbour, Cornelius Grogan of Johnstown Castle. Wealthy, liberal, unmarried, Grogan seems to have returned her affection – they may even have been engaged – but he was an old man who tended to vacillation. His sympathies were generous – he joined the United Irishmen – but when it came to the point of action he had to be dragged. Dragged he eventually was, and played his part in the Wexford Rising as commissar for the rebel forces. Eventually he was captured, tried by court-martial and summarily hanged on Wexford Bridge.

Knowing nothing of her darling's fate, Elizabeth was driving into Wexford with her mother shortly after the end of the fighting, when she was confronted by Grogan's bloody head, impaled on a spike above the courthouse gate. That terrible confrontation left no space in her heart for further passion. Elizabeth devoted herself to the upbringing of her niece, and to gardening, and died a spinster.

But I am leaping ahead of my story and need to turn back.

The Society of United Irishmen tried initially to achieve change by constitutional means, building a coalition of membership that included the obvious names like Napper Tandy, but firmly based on a strong network of minor gentry and prosperous tradesmen, town and country, Protestant, Catholic and Presbyterian. They formed committees and sponsored meetings to enlist the support of potential allies, up and down the country. One such was Sir Edward Loftus, who belonged to the liberal wing of Wexford politics, unlike his grand cousins at Loftus Hall who were bastions of conservatism. In fact they had become much more fiercely 'loyalist' since the death of Henry Loftus in 1783, whose estates and titles had descended to a nephew, Charles Tottenham of New Ross. Tottenham changed his name to Loftus but remained unwavering in his devotion to Property, Protestantism and anti-Popery. Sir Edward, by contrast, sympathised with the aims of the United Irishmen even though he never, as far as I know, became a member of the Society. But he joined the Whig Club of Dublin in 1790 and was an active participant in its reformist offshoot – the Friends of the Constitution, Liberty and Peace – which included among its supporters most of the Wexford gentry who subsequently played leading roles in the events of 1798.[426] The Friends may have adopted their name in homage to their French equivalent, but as that revolution turned increasingly violent they were at pains to emphasise that Liberty and Peace were mutually dependent. They feared – as did Pitt – that if political reform were further delayed in Ireland, the Irish Catholics would seek the support of the French to assert their rights, hence their willingness to agitate for urgent and radical change.

Those fears were heightened in January 1793 by the news that the King of France was on trial for his life. Pitt, Edmund Burke and Henry Grattan joined forces to persuade George III to accept with good grace a petition from the Catholic Committee of Ireland – and to inform the Irish Parliament that 'His Majesty trusts that the situation of His Majesty's Catholic subjects will engage your serious attention.'

For the Friends of the Constitution, this was the moment of hope. On 11 January – the day after the King's message was delivered in Dublin – Sir Edward Loftus helped convene 'a meeting of the Freeholders and Inhabitants of the County Wexford,' to urge their support for reform. After firmly declaring 'that the people of this Country are peaceable and quiet; & we know of no seditious practices therein, nor do we see the least shadow of, or tendency to, Riot or Tumult in this County,' they passed a string of punchy Resolutions, identical to those agreed three weeks earlier, in Dublin.[427]

That the Representative part of our Legislature is not derived from the People by that free & general election which the fundamental Principles of our Constitution require, & the state & condition of this Nation would warrant.

That the fundamental Peace & Welfare of Ireland can only be

established by a radical & effective Reform in the Commons House of Parliament & that this object once obtained the people ought to remain content and grateful.

That we will by all constitutional & lawful means promote a radical & effective Reform in the Representation of the People in Parliament, including persons of all Religious Persuasions; & that we rely on the Wisdom of Parliament to grant such reform.

But Wisdom needed goading, so Cornelius Grogan chaired a second meeting of the Friends, a fortnight later, which issued an unambiguous broadside addressed 'To the People of Wexford' – using capital letters to emphasise their demands. 'NO PALLIATIVE WILL BE SUFFICIENT TO FEED AND KEEP ALIVE THE PRESENT MORBID SYSTEM OF REPRESENTATION' – nothing less was needed than 'A RADICAL AND EFFECTUAL REFORM IN PARLIAMENT, INCLUDING PERSONS OF ALL RELIGIOUS PERSUASIONS.'[428] It was a message that Parliament chose to ignore.

That failure of constitutional protest provoked the United Irishmen to become increasingly radical and revolutionary. In May 1794 the Society was suppressed and vanished underground, splitting into small cells to minimise the consequences of betrayal by numerous government informers. It also became less clearly associated with the urban middle classes of Dublin and Belfast. Some of its new leaders were aristocrats and gentry with political connections in England, America and France, but its membership spread very much further, deep into the roots of rural discontent. It could even claim members among the rank and file of the armed forces. And Irish politics became ever more strongly polarised because a violent nationalist movement, the Defenders, initially formed to fight the new, aggressive Protestantism of the Orange Order, began to stockpile arms and established close links with the United Irishmen. The Defenders marked the beginnings of the transition from a middle class or aristocratic movement, largely constitutional, to a wilder, more populist, Catholic and deep-rooted revolution. They certainly frightened the authorities and in 1796 *habeus corpus* was partially suspended.

In December that year a French fleet carrying 15,000 troops and the tireless Wolfe Tone arrived off Bantry Bay and only failed to land because of stormy weather and poor seamanship Had it been otherwise, history might have been very different. Throughout 1797 and into the following year there were numerous arrests, including almost the entire Leinster leadership of the United Irishmen, but the hidden organisation of the Society and its allies continued to function and there was an escalating sense of imminent danger, which caused the government to invoke the Insurrection Act. By the spring of 1798 there was such widespread restlessness and unease that it was plain to all that a rising was imminent, but despite the best efforts of an army of government informers it was still unclear when and how it would happen. Martial law was proclaimed on 30 March, and Ireland was declared by the Privy Council to be in a state of rebellion, though none had yet taken place.

It was at this anxious time that a witty barrister from Dublin went to Wexford for the spring assizes. Sir Jonah Barrington seems to have viewed the onrush of events with a strange mixture of detachment and passionate concern. He was a 'patriot' – which meant a stalwart champion of the right of Ireland to control its own affairs – but he was also a 'loyalist'; a Member of Parliament, King's Counsel and holder of 'a very handsome office' in the government's employ. Fortunately for posterity, this inveterate gossip noted down anything that amused or interested him, and eventually edited those notes into a fascinating and arbitrary collection of tales, 'to wear away the long and tedious winter evenings of a demi-invalid'. [429]

Few stories more vividly convey the strange and dangerous flavour of those times than Barrington's famous description of a dinner party in Wexford to which he was invited by Lady Colclough, who was 'a near relative' of his wife and of half the company that evening – all of whom seem to have assumed that Sir Jonah was sympathetic to their cause or, if not, would honour the bonds of kinship. But nothing could have been further from the truth. Barrington was shocked by the conversation around the dinner table, and as the evening wore on became convinced that 'by plunging one step further, most of my relatives and friends would be in imminent danger.'

In a rash effort to reassure him, Bagenal Harvey 'who had been my school-fellow and constant circuit-companion for many years, laughed, at Lady Colclough's, at my political prudery; assured me I was totally wrong in suspecting him; and insisted on my going to Bargy Castle on the ensuing Monday.' At first all went well.

> The entertainment was good and the party cheerful. Temple freaks were talked over; the bottle circulated: but, at length, Irish politics became the topic, and proceeded to a length of disclosure which utterly surprised me. The probability of a speedy revolt was freely discussed, though in the most artful manner, not a word of any of the party committing themselves. I found myself in the midst of absolute though unavowed conspirators.

Within a month, the most serious rising in a hundred and fifty years had broken out, led by those same respectable Protestant gentry. With the exception of Barrington himself and two other guests, 'every member of that jovial dinner party was executed within three months and on my next visit to Wexford, I saw the heads of Captain Keogh, Mr. Harvey, and Mr. Colclough on spikes over the court-house door.' No other witness gives such a casual flavour of the violent intimacy of civil war – especially when we know what Barrington himself was keen to conceal: that he gave the names of those conspirators to the government.

One of them, perhaps not present that night but a friend and neighbour of them all, was Cornelius Grogan, the man to whom Elizabeth Loftus is said to have been engaged.

On 19 May 1798 Lord Edward Fitzgerald, the intended leader of the Rising, was arrested in Dublin and mortally wounded – but five days later the long-feared rebellion began. It was a sporadic and ill co-ordinated affair. There was a brief and rapidly aborted attempt to seize the streets in Dublin, and a short-lived uprising in County Meath. Ulster was slow to start and the rebels there were mostly Protestants or Dissenters and lacked the fire of Catholic nationalism. After losing their first engagements, they soon laid down their arms. It was in the South-East, and particularly in Wexford, that the Rising took hold, with a determination that was more than matched by its savage repression.

Even before it began, the land was filled with terror. Thousands of poor cottagers hid themselves in the countryside as British troops arrested and flogged anyone suspected of conspiracy, and burned their cabins as they searched for arms. And the gentry, too, had cause for alarm. Sir Edward Loftus was warned by one of his servants, shortly before the Rising, 'that the climate at Mount Loftus might not suit him,' and took his wife and younger daughter south down the River Barrow, to the family estate at Richfield, in County Wexford. Secluded in the southern marshlands, hidden from the main routes to war, it proved a haven of relative calm as the rest of the county was over-whelmed by violence. But he must have felt a shock of apprehension when the news reached him that the insurgents had occupied Wexford, on 30 May, and declared it a republic. And his elder daughter Mary found a much more dangerous refuge as she headed north, up the River Slaney from her home near Enniscorthy, and arrived in Carlow.

> In the midst of all this terror and confusion, there was a Protestant clergyman, a Mr Cary of Mount Finn, in the County of Wexford, obliged to fly with all his family, wife, children and servants, and take refuge in Carlow, to save their lives. Mrs Cary was the daughter to Sir Edward Loftus of Mount Loftus in the County Kilkenny, and sister to Lieutenant Loftus of the Ninth Dragoons, who were quartered in the town, and as all the family dealt with us for their saddlery goods and had a particular friendship for us, they took up their lodgings in our house.[430]

The narrator is William Farrell, a member of the United Irishmen, whose brother-in-law Andrew Fitzgerald kept the finest saddler's shop for miles around and was on excellent terms with most of his Protestant customers. But Farrell's own life was in danger, for Carlow had recently been the scene of fierce fighting and was now the centre of equally ferocious reprisals. As he himself records, the task of the authorities was made easier because many of the insurgents – and others who supported the United Irishmen but never joined the rebellion – had, before the Rising, cropped their hair in a style inspired by the French revolutionaries. So every 'croppy' was rounded up, on the basis that they had to prove their innocence to excuse their haircut.

As for the Loftus sons, Nicholas and Francis, both were in the army. Francis, the baby of the family, was the first to encounter the rebels in arms. As a young lieutenant of twenty-one he was stationed in Carlow when, very early in the morning on 25 May, a large but ragged force of

ill-armed country boys, led by Michael Heydon, stormed into town.
Perhaps 'stormed' is an exaggeration – 'crowded' may be nearer the
mark. Heydon was 'so confident in the assistance of the United men
that were in the Yeomen Militia and even the ninth Dragoons who, he
was certain, would run armed to join him the moment he entered town,
and so blinded with the hopes of victory, that he would listen to nothing
else.'[431] But the untested rebels fled for their lives when the troops
opened fire, and those who escaped being shot in the streets hid themselves in nearby houses – where some were burned alive by the enraged
soldiers, together with any inhabitants who happened to be trapped
there. Others were dragged from their hiding places and bayoneted or
shot, or hanged on gateways and signposts. And then the arrests and
reprisals began, as dozens of men were stripped and bound to the
infamous triangles, on which they were flogged with the cat o' nine tails
until they informed on their friends, or died.

Farrell's description of the sadism is frightening to read, even now,
and the reality must have been dreadful for Mrs Cary when she arrived
in Carlow to seek refuge, a day or two after the rebel attack. But she and
her brother Francis Loftus were able to play their part in saving one of
the intended victims, for Farrell himself was arrested soon after the
Carys crammed into lodgings at his sister's house. There came a day
when everyone else in his cell was taken, one by one to the yard, to be
beaten – but somehow he was spared, thanks to 'the interference of a
Protestant gentleman, Lieutenant Loftus of the Ninth Dragoons, as
afterwards I knew to a certainty.' But the reprieve was only temporary,
for Farrell was suddenly taken to Leighlin Bridge, to be publicly flogged
and executed. His sister, Mrs Fitzgerald, insisted on accompanying him
there and then returned to Carlow where she passed a sleepless night
before rising early, when she 'filled the house with lamentation.' Her
cries were overheard by Mrs Cary, who asked what was wrong.

'Oh, ma'am, enough is the matter with me! This unfortunate boy is
to be destroyed to-day in Leighlin Bridge and if they'd shoot him
itself, I wouldn't think so bad of it, But to make a public spectacle of
him, to mangle his flesh and sacrifice him, oh, I can't bear it!'

'Be patient, my dear Mrs Fitzgerald, be patient; God Almighty is
good,' said the kind-hearted lady; 'and who knows what may be

done? Who knows if I can do something myself? I will go off this moment to Colonel Mahon and see what can be done.'

She ran immediately to the door and seeing one of the Ninth Dragoons going by, she called out, 'Soldier, soldier, come here!' The man came immediately. 'Do you know Lieutenant Loftus?' said she.

'I do, ma'am.'

'Well he is my brother and you must come up with me to the barrack; I want to see Colonel Mahon.'

So off they went to the Colonel, who was not yet dressed. But Mrs Cary was a determined woman and refused to leave until he agreed to come with her to see Mrs Fitzgerald, 'where she made him sit down and write a letter in my favour to Colonel Rochfort, who commanded at Leighlin Bridge.' William Farrell's sister 'took a chaise and set off in full speed' and arrived just in time to save him.

This story ended well, and thus was exceptional. The memory for most was of cumulative horror – a mess of conflicting and ambiguous loyalties, heroism and treachery and brutal cruelty. However fragmentary those stories, they were also typical, in that almost no one at the time had more than a glimpse of the whole, and the synthesised narratives, written afterwards, were always in some sense false – clearer, less random than the confused experience. The most authentic memories may be those summarised in vivid images, indelible but momentary flashbacks.

Such were the anecdotes recorded by Rev. James Hall, when he travelled through Ireland about a dozen years after the Rising.[432] He went to New Ross, where one of the bloodiest battles was fought in its narrow streets, on 5 June 1798. The rebel army numbered at least 10,000 men, commanded by Bagenal Harvey, but the troops defending the town had the advantage that their attackers were channelled and constricted through steep lanes, which rendered them terribly vulnerable to the blast of cannons and musket fire. Despite enormous casualties, the rebels pressed on over the bodies of the dead, and almost won the town before the defenders rallied and counter-attacked, and drove them out again. Horrendous tales were told of the burning of houses in which the wounded had been placed for refuge or others had fled to escape, the shooting of women and children who happened to be in the way, the mass graves and the dumping of bodies in the harbour, the indiscriminate killing afterwards of any man found on the road to Wexford who was not wearing the red coat of a British soldier. And of pigs feeding on corpses when the slaughter was done. But what the women of New Ross remembered with a shudder, 'even now, when the danger is over,' was 'seeing from their windows hundreds of wounded horses, running through the streets, dragging after them their fallen riders, and trampling the dead and the dying.'

That shocking memory, recorded by Hall, was one that the women must have shared with Nicholas Loftus, who was a captain in the Kilkenny Militia, commanding a light company of that regiment at the Battle of Ross: 'Which engagement the detachment of skirmishers under his command, had the distinction of commencing, repulsing the rebel vanguard, but falling back before the main body of the rebel army, after bivouacking on the ground which they had won on the night of the 4th June.'

This brisk account, probably a quotation from his commanding officer's dispatches after the battle, is all that has survived in the family archives as a record of those events. No mention of the horrors of the following day, and none of his own experience. It is almost as if the collective family memory of 1798 was such a conflicting mixture of emotions, so painful, that they preferred to leave it in silence. But Nicholas did speak of these things to the Rev. Hall, many years later, and told him that 'instead of the 500 people, given out as killed on both sides, more than three times that number were slain.'[433] He may also have been the witness who told of the things that he could not forget, which the clergyman recorded with such tender sympathy – the Catholic woman shot as she sat, hiding a pike; the old woman shot and then decapitated by a hussar's sabre; rebels bayoneted as they tried to hide in chimneys; roads strewn with the dead. And then, strangely poignant, that 'Hares, rabbits, partridges, grouse and other animals, alarmed at the tremendous burnings, fled the country, and have not yet returned.' This sharp, huntsman's observation somehow expresses a sadness that was otherwise inarticulate.

Francis Loftus, meanwhile, had returned from Carlow to the rolling hills of Kilkenny, near his home. He was assigned to the staff of General Sir Charles Asgill, who was charged with suppressing the rebellion in that county, and he found himself serving alongside his grand relative,

Lord Loftus, whose detachment of the Wexford militia formed part of Asgill's forces. The early days of the Rising had seen a string of insurgent victories, at Oulart Hill, Enniscorthy and Wexford, when they still believed that the rest of Ireland was in arms and they would soon link up with allies from further north. But a growing recognition that they were now alone was followed by the disaster of New Ross, the convergence of British troops to crush the Rising in Wexford and the proclamation of martial law. For Francis, however, this was a period of relative calm. He may have been engaged in chasing after rebel bands as they crossed the River Barrow into County Kilkenny but he saw little real action until the end of June.

The focus of events was in the South-East, where thousands of insurgents were massing on Vinegar Hill, just outside Enniscorthy. This steep vantage point, commanding a view for miles around, was where the 'croppies' had gathered from the first week of the insurrection and where they now made a stand, as their enemies closed in. And it was here, on 21 June, that an army of desperate men, armed with pikes and blunderbusses, was comprehensively defeated by the artillery and musket fire of the English forces. One of the English commanders at this battle was General William Loftus, a professional soldier who was a distant cousin of Sir Edward.

Afterwards, as they retreated, a large column of insurgents under the command of Father John Murphy headed north and crossed into County Kilkenny at Goresbridge. Here and for the next few days they were harried by Asgill's forces but a pitched battle was avoided until eventually, after turning back from their northward march, the rebels once more crossed the river at Goresbridge and camped for the night of 25 June on Kilcumney Hill, just to the east of the town. Early on the following morning, before his exhausted prey had woken, Asgill attacked with his artillery and drove them from the hill, with considerable casualties. And then, as was the habit of the English army, the slaughter was multiplied as the troops set upon and butchered 'the people of the adjacent country who had not joined the insurgents nor left their homes, and the whole district was looted by the soldiery.'

I am quoting from an account written by Sir Edward Loftus, presumably based on the eyewitness testimony of his son Francis. He also noted that 'on this occasion the rebels came to Mount Loftus and took all the wine and ale in the house. One of them fired a shot at Lord Loftus's picture and the bullet made a hole in his finger.'[434] But Sir Edward seemed much less angry about the depredations at Mount Loftus than the savagery of the English troops.

So this was also, I feel sure, a time of hard, unspoken divisions in families such as ours, when small differences of outlook, prejudice or allegiance were sharpened and deepened by experience. And thus, at the end, there was silence. This huge convulsion left almost no trace in the family archives. No letters, no journals, nothing except the record of a few bare facts, a couple of stories and the witness of others. Elizabeth Loftus was left with the memory of a severed head, spiked and sightless in Wexford; Francis with the ferocity of the troops in Carlow and the sight of slaughter on a lovely hillside near his childhood home; Mary with the nightmare of savage reprisals from which she had saved a man she knew, though she knew him to be a rebel; Nicholas with the horror of fighting from house to house up the narrow streets of New Ross as the dead and the dying filled the gutters with blood, and the sight of horses – which he loved – trampling human flesh; Sir Edward with the death of all his liberal hopes; and his wife Anne with the unresolved discord between her own relief – that the rebellion had failed – and the possibility that some of her family might have preferred it to succeed. It was a bitter legacy.

I began with Wolfe Tone and I should like to close with him, but this fascinating, engaging and ultimately heroic man was shadowed to the end by his rival and parody, the irrepressible Napper Tandy. So my story has a tragic and a comic postscript.

Tone never gave up – not even after the failure of what so nearly was his greatest triumph: the French invasion fleet of 1796. Despite the changing political climate in France he battled on to persuade the sceptical Bonaparte to launch another armada – but Napoleon had his eye on richer prey and was preparing to invade Egypt. Tone's influence was in any case on the wane, partly because Napper Tandy (recently arrived from America) attracted a rival revolutionary court as he lorded it in Paris, while Tone was diligently serving as an officer of the French army, in Le Havre. But eventually, when news of the Rising reached France, Tone was recalled to Paris and a new expedition was authorised –

or rather three separate expeditions, departing in clumsy succession, when the rebellion had already been crushed.

The first 'invasion fleet' comprised three ships carrying a thousand troops under General Humbert, which arrived off County Mayo on 22 August. Humbert won an unexpected victory – known as the Castlebar Races, from the speed with which the English ran away – and proclaimed an Irish Republic, but surrendered when the rising of the masses that he had been led to expect proved no more than wishful thinking.

The second attempt pushed wishful thinking to the limits of farce. It consisted of a single frigate, the *Anacreon*, under the command of Napper Tandy, wearing the uniform of a French general and entrusted with the command of a small body of Irish refugees, intended to form the nucleus of an army in Ireland. Tandy was no longer the energetic campaigner who so inspired Sir Edward Loftus in 1784, but had become almost a caricature of himself – showy, boozy and indiscreet. After the *Anacreon* left port on 4 September he lowered the morale of all on board by endless bouts of gloomy drinking, and his melancholy was exacerbated when they reached the island of Rutland off the coast of Donegal, to discover that Humbert had failed and the rebellion was ended. Having scattered a few fantastic proclamations, calling upon Irishmen 'to strike from their blood-cemented thrones the murderers of your friends' and 'to wage a war of extermination against your oppressors,' Tandy drank himself senseless at the home of the local postmaster and had to be carried back on board. His companions also re-embarked and the ship set sail. On the way home they had a skirmish with a merchant ship, 'during which Tandy sat on deck with a pint bottle of brandy, directing operations.'[435] Yet somehow he arrived in Hamburg, safe and sound, where he was promptly arrested.

A third French expedition – ten ships, carrying nearly 3,000 men, including Wolfe Tone on board the flagship *Hoche* – left Brest in mid-September. Tone fully expected the venture to end in disaster, and wrote to his wife that 'he knew his life was gone'. The British, fore-warned, tracked the invaders as they approached the Irish coast and attacked on 12 October in the midst of a storm. Tone commanded a battery on the *Hoche* throughout the battle, but the ship was eventually overpowered and he was captured.

Despite wearing the uniform of a French colonel, Wolfe Tone was shackled like a common criminal and taken to Dublin where he was charged with treason before a court-martial presided over by General William Loftus. Tone made no attempt to deny the charges but used his moment in the dock to express his last political testament. He talked eloquently of 'the connection between Ireland and Great Britain as the curse of the Irish nation' and his conviction 'that, while it lasted, this country could never be free or happy.' But when he began to explain why he had sought French help, 'to rescue three millions of my country-men,' General Loftus interrupted, and asked Mr Tone to confine his remarks to the case against him.

Tone then spoke of his service in the French army, the dangers that he had suffered and the sacrifices that he had made. 'I have left a beloved wife, unprotected, and children whom I adored, fatherless.' He stressed that the recent horrors in Ireland were not of his making – 'Atrocities, it seems, have been committed on both sides. I do not less deplore them; I detest them from my heart.' And finally he concluded: 'I have spoken and acted with reflection, and on principles, and am ready to meet the consequences. Whatever be the sentence of this court, I am prepared for it. Its members will surely discharge their duty; I shall take care not to be wanting in mine.' This speech 'was pronounced in a tone so magnanimous, so full of noble and calm serenity, as seemed deeply to affect all its hearers, the members of the court not excepted' and silence reigned in the hall.

Then Tone made a final request, that as an officer of the French army he should be shot by firing squad, rather than hanged. General Loftus promised to submit this appeal to the Lord Lieutenant, together with a copy of Tone's speech to the court – and indeed he did so. But the request was refused and Tone was condemned to hang. On the morning of 12 November, when he was due to be executed, Tone was found in his cell with his throat cut by his own hand. He lingered for a week until he overheard the surgeon say that if he attempted to move or speak, he would die. 'I can yet find words to thank you, sir,' whispered Tone. 'It is the most welcome news you could give me. What should I wish to live for?' And with that he expired.

Napper Tandy, meanwhile, managed to delay his return from Hamburg by almost a year through protracted legal and diplomatic wrangling, until eventually he was handed over to the British and brought to England, in October 1799. The following month he returned in captivity to Ireland aboard *HM Packet Loftus*, which was stationed at Holyhead for the conveyance of mail to Dublin – the same speedy ship that had conveyed Buck Whaley on the first stage of his journey to Jerusalem eleven years earlier, when it was owned by Dudley Loftus. Some of Whaley's luck rubbed off on the old rebel, because the ferocity of revenge that destroyed Wolfe Tone had by then subsided and the legal proceedings against him took a more leisurely pace. He was tried, acquitted on a technicality, rearrested, tried again and condemned to death – but it was proposed instead that he should be transported to Botany Bay. Eventually, when peace with France was concluded with the treaty of Amiens, Tandy was released at the behest of Napoleon, and returned to a hero's welcome in Bordeaux, in March 1802, where he proceeded to father a child with his French housekeeper before dying the following year at the age of sixty-six. It was a *coup de théâtre* that no one but this flamboyant – and slightly ridiculous – revolutionary could possibly have achieved.

CHAPTER 35

A Dishonourable Union

Lord Loftus, Lord Loftus,
Your head large and soft is,
And not overloaded with brain.
You're a vile, sulky mule,
Between knave and fool,
And your name's on the peerage a stain.
You a beggar of late,
On a sudden grew great
By Ely's great bounty and will.
A peerage you got,
But what of all that,
You remain the same dirty dog still.[436]

Charles Tottenham, who inherited the Loftus estates on the death of
his uncle the Earl of Ely, was a man of no discernable principles save
Protestant prejudice, vanity and greed. He took the name of Loftus and
was made a baron on the promise of political support for the government, but provoked the verses quoted above when he betrayed that
allegiance during the Regency Crisis of 1789. Pitt was trying to prevent
the Prince of Wales becoming Regent in more than name (during the
madness of King George) while the Prince and his political cronies, led
by Charles James Fox, were conspiring to bring about a change of
government. Tottenham saw the political crisis as a chance to sell his
parliamentary votes – 'the Loftus legion' – to the highest bidder.

As it happened the crisis passed – George III recovered his sanity –
and nothing came of these manoeuvres, save that Charles Tottenham
Loftus, Baron Loftus of Loftus Hall, was made Viscount Loftus of Ely
and joint Postmaster General – his price for renewed support. The
Lord Lieutenant grimly remarked that 'it will no doubt be found very
difficult to prevail on His Majesty to confer honours on Lord Loftus,
and so far to reward his treachery,' but one of the great political

magnates had to be bought, and Loftus was deemed less likely to engage in further double dealing than the alternative, Lord Shannon.[437]

Such greed seemed all the more inexcusable since his Lordship was, by his inheritance, an enormously wealthy man. The Loftus estates in County Fermanagh, at Rathfarnham and in Wexford amounted to 47,000 Irish acres with an annual rent roll of £22,000, and the Tottenhams themselves were a long-established and prosperous family, owning much of New Ross.[438] But Lord Loftus was, by general esteem, a man of bone-headed arrogance, for whom enough was never enough. Within less than five years he managed to extract further concessions, being made Earl of Ely and Knight of St Patrick, in 1794.

The Rising of 1798 and its fierce repression proved to such men that all their prejudices were justified – that the mass of the Irish population was composed of ingrate savages, who could never be coerced except by ruthless severity. It was also the turning point that caused the English government to conclude that the continued existence of a Parliament in Dublin fed the aspirations of Irish nationalists, even to the point of rebellion. And so the decision was taken that Union was the only answer, cost what it may.

In such circumstances, the smallest cry for liberty could provoke an extreme reaction; and thus it was one summer evening, not long after the Rising had ended. As 'Lord Ely, the High Sheriff and other gentlemen of the county, were retiring after their wine from the Grand Jury,' they heard a young maidservant singing at the window of her mistress's house, in Wexford.

> As the song sounded to their loyal ears of a rebellious tendency, it was thought advisable to demolish the fragile parts of Mrs Lett's house-front without delay; and, accordingly, my lord, the high sheriff and their friends (to preserve the peace and protect the constitution from such traitorous maid-servants), forthwith commenced their laudable undertaking; and stones being the weapons nearest at hand, the windows and the warbling maid received a broadside, which was of the greatest utility to the glazier, and had well-nigh put fees into the pockets, not only of the surgeon, but of the sexton and coroner likewise.

Somewhat to everyone's amazement, his Lordship, the High Sheriff, and others of the drunken party were brought before the court. Jonah Barrington was appointed to defend Lord Ely, but his Lordship decided to cross-examine the maidservant himself.

> 'Now, girl,' said he, 'by the oath you have taken, did you not say you would *split my scull open?*'
>
> 'Why, then by the virtue of my oath,' said the girl, turning to the judge, 'it would not be *worth my while* to split his scull open, my Lord!'
>
> 'Ha! ha!' said Lord Ely, 'now I have her!' (wisely supposing she made some allusion to a reward for killing him) 'and *why*, girl, would it not be worth your while?'
>
> 'Because, my Lord,' answered she, 'if I had split your Lordship's scull open, – by virtue of my oath, I am sure and certain I should have found little or nothing inside of it!'
>
> The laugh against the noble Lord was now too great to admit of his proceeding any further with his cross-examination: he was found guilty and fined.[439]

Incidents such as these, combined with his own instinctive prejudices, inclined Lord Ely to support the administration's efforts to pass the Act of Union, abolishing the Irish Parliament and substituting direct rule from Westminster – but he was determined to extract a high price. And he knew, as did the government, that every vote would count, for the arguments against such a move had been vehemently rehearsed and were strongly supported by a clear majority of Irish MPs and peers. The only argument in favour, for those who might be bought, was outright bribery. So the government set aside the enormous sum of £1.5 million, to achieve this end.

The price of a parliamentary borough (for the owners of those abolished under the Act) was set at £15,000. Lord Ely was paid £45,000 to compensate him for the loss of the boroughs of Fethard, Clonmines and Bannow, a total of six parliamentary seats, but he also controlled the borough of Wexford, which elected two members to the Irish Parliament and was due to return a single member to Westminster, under the Act of Union. The government claimed that one seat in Westminster was worth two in Dublin, but Ely was persistent, and was also determined to secure for himself a seat in the English House of

Lords. So eventually, after protracted negotiations that necessitated a letter from William Pitt to support private promises made by the Lord Lieutenant, the Earl of Ely was made a Marquis (in the Irish peerage) and Baron Loftus, in England.[440] Even that was not enough, for his Lordship managed to secure promises of lucrative preferment for his two sons – one succeeded his father as Irish Postmaster General, and was appointed Teller of the Exchequer and a Commissioner of Treasury, while the other was made Bishop of Clogher, a diocese that possessed 27,000 acres of land. And his cousin, General William Loftus, was given a sinecure colonelcy worth £1,597 a year, and the Lieutenancy of the Tower, worth £745.[441] All in all, it was probably the most expensive deal agreed with any Irish peer, in the most comprehensively corrupt purchase of votes ever undertaken by the English government.

The Act of Union was passed in the sad spring of 1800, and came into force on 1 January 1801. Many promises were made but few of them came to much and the most important – Catholic emancipation – was shamefully broken, because George III would have none of it. Ireland became a backwater: poor, divided, forgotten.

Power, prestige, influence and patronage had been centred on Parliament and the Castle, and both now lost their function. The elegant Parliament House was taken over by the Bank of Ireland and the Castle became little more than a barracks, for the Viceroy moved to Phoenix Park. Deprived of all that gave its political and social life vivacity and meaning, Dublin rapidly decayed. Fewer grand houses were built, few remained occupied, and property prices halved. The streets became dirtier, the beggars more numerous, their plight more extreme.

The Marquis of Ely lived for five more years before dying at his mansion in Ely Place – whereupon his widow moved to Bath and the house was sold.[442]

And my five-greats grandfather, Sir Edward Loftus? Like so many others of his class, he gave up his Dublin house and lived entirely on his estates, pursuing the life of a gentleman farmer. For him, at least, this was a time of quiet enjoyment.

No 4 will open Bed locks No 4 & 7
No 1 opens THE 1. 2 & 3

TOWN AND COUNTRY

COMPLETE No 5 put to well bound Pocket Book

Family Account-Book,

[illegible] For the YEAR 1808, Loftus

IMPROVED BY INTRODUCING

ADDITIONAL LINES IN THE ACCOUNTS,

TOGETHER WITH OTHER NEW AND USEFUL MATTER,

Rendering it altogether more simple and easy to keep an exact, yet concise REGISTER of every Article made use of in a Family; or by a private Individual;

THE WHOLE JUDICIOUSLY ARRANGED

On Fifty-Four Ruled Pages of fine Writing Paper,

Each containing the Names of the Articles, and Seven Columns for the Expences of the Week; likewise ample Room for Memorandum Appointments, Engagements, and with distinct Tables at Bottom, in order to know the total Expence of each Week:

Also, among others equally Valuable and Useful,

Tables and Intelligence highly interesting to every prudent and economical Person in the United Kingdom,

1. A correct Chronology of remarkable Occurrences since 1743.
2. A complete List of Commercial Stamps, Bonds, Notes, Bills, &c.
3. Observations on Longevity, and the Art of Preserving Life.
4. Fifty-four Ruled Pages for Accounts, Observations, and Memorandums.
5. General Table for the Expences of each Week in the Year.
6. Hints relative to Bed-Rooms.
7. Treatment of Burns.
8. Treatment of Scalds.
9. Observations on Debility.
10. An Abstract of a Report of the College of Physicians, on Vaccine Inoculation, lately laid before Parliament.

BEING THE MOST COMPLETE, USEFUL, AND INTELLIGENT PUBLICATION OF THE KIND HITHERTO PRINTED.

LONDON:

Printed for B. CROSBY and Co. Stationer's-Court; and LANGLEY and BELCH, No. 173, Borough High-Street; And sold by every Bookseller, Stationer, and Newsmen in the United Kingdom.

To be continued Annually.—Price 2s.

No 1 will open 1. 2 and 3 .. No 4 will open padlocks No 4 and 7. No 5 put to the well bound large pocket Book

MOUNT LOFTUS

CHAPTER 36

The Gentleman Farmer

Visitors to England at the end of the eighteenth century might rail at the food, the inns or the state of the roads; but they were astonished at the evidence of rural prosperity. A German, Carl Philip Moritz, was regarded as a dangerous member of the vagrant poor – or simply mad – when he undertook a walking tour of England in 1782, in a country where 'the poorest of them would rather sit on the outside of a coach at the risk of breaking his neck than go for a stretch on foot.' At Sunday service in the village of Nettlebed he noted that, 'All the farmers I saw here were dressed in good cloth and good taste (not as ours are, in coarse smocks)' and as he walked from the village towards Oxford he felt he was in paradise. 'My journey was an uninterrupted stroll through a great garden.'[443]

That sense of a pastoral idyll was echoed, quite consciously, by England's painters – by Gainsborough, Constable and Morland, for example – and was given definitive visual expression by Stubbs, in his *Haymakers* and *Reapers* of 1785. Serene, rational and perfectly composed, these views of the land and its bounty, the gentleman farmer and his well-clothed labourers, were propagated through engravings to become embedded in the imagination, as archetypes of a national dream.

Such images were far removed from the experience of the rural poor, dispossessed by enclosures, subsisting in the most precarious manner, harassed by vagrancy laws and dependent on the uncertain mercies of Poor Law relief, locally administered with varying degrees of ruth-lessness. Most feared of all, for those with nowhere else to turn, was the workhouse. I still remember the dread of that word to Suffolk farm workers, fifty years ago, when they referred to what had long since been converted into the Blythburgh Hospital for geriatrics but still retained, in local memory, all the terrors of a nightmare.

Rural poverty and the harshness of its consequences were, nonetheless, patches of darkness in an altogether sunnier picture. Prosperity in England was rising throughout most of the eighteenth century and the view that visitors recorded – of sturdy, beef-eating countrymen and the rolling richness of English farmland – was, for many, the evident, solid reality.

The Englishman abroad painted a very different picture of what he saw there. He was astonished at the scrawny, underfed destitution of rural France and Germany and he was shocked, as were other foreigners, by the wretchedness of Ireland. Rising agricultural prices brought rising rents, which enriched the landlords but left the Irish peasantry as colonial victims, dependent on the pig and the potato. Time and time again contemporary observers spoke of a demoralised, dirty and often drunken population, clothed in rags and living in hovels.

The blame, as often as not, was attributed to absentee landlords and their notorious middlemen, and to a great extent this was true. 'There are too many possessors of great estates in Ireland, who wish to know nothing more of it than the remittance of their rents,' claimed the English agriculturalist, Arthur Young, and he was equally scathing about England's colonial policy. 'The entire administration of the colonies has been commercial. It was that baleful monopolizing spirit of commerce that wished to govern great nations, on the maxims of the counter. That did govern them so; and in the case of Ireland and the Indies does still govern them so.' He even spoke, with prescience, of 'the hazard we now run of losing or ruining Ireland'. But English folly and greed was not enough to account for the lamentable state of agriculture, in a land where 'every country gentleman is by necessity a farmer,' so Young set out on a series of journeys to discover the facts.

He progressed from one grand house to the next, enjoying the 'unbounded hospitality' of the 'gentlemen of Ireland,' which 'left me under few difficulties in gaining intelligence' – but Young also made it his business to talk to numerous 'common farmers' and 'cottagers', from whose 'ease or oppression, a multitude of conclusions may be drawn.' The result was a 'register of experiments and repeated observations' for his readers to 'compare, combine and draw conclusions from them. To men thus scientific, too many facts can never be published.' But just in case his Irish readers were insufficiently 'scientific' to deduce the answers for themselves, 'I have ventured to recommend several courses of husbandry, as improvements upon what I found them practising, and have given directions how they should be performed.' The key to it all was 'turneps'.

I am quoting from Young's *Tour in Ireland*, which he published, with some difficulty, in 1780. Four hundred Irish gentlemen had subscribed their names to this publication but many of those subscriptions proved worthless, 'there being 100 of my receipts in gentlemen's hands in Ireland, of which the most repeated applications have not been sufficient to procure me any account whatever.' So the book appeared without some of the engraved plates that Young had promised, and the author lost 'a sum to me considerable'. Despite these difficulties, Young's *Tour* was widely read and highly influential. It reinforced patriotic demands for free trade and identified 'scientific' agriculture with political reform – to be recognised as a model landlord became the new paradigm for those, like Sir Edward Loftus, who were prominent as Volunteers. Major Nicholas Loftus, his brother, was one of those who subscribed (and paid) for a copy.

Young's influence in fact survived, for a number of unexpected reasons, long after the disbandment of the Volunteers, the carnage of '98, the Act of Union and the death of Irish politics. When the capital echoed with absence, after 'the quality' had fled to London or retired to the country, it was there, on their estates, that those who remained in Ireland found their social stage. For some this meant little more than the usual round of hunting, shooting and social engagements, but others discovered a better role, as enlightened gentleman farmers.[444] 'Scientific agriculture' provided wonderful opportunities for social competition. When I read Sir Edward's letter to The Dublin Society in 1806, *On the Culture of Potatoes* – 'the red apples are strongly recommended, as also the minion cup; red noses did wonderfully well' – I am reminded of the announcement, twenty-five years earlier, that his gardener had grown a giant mushroom, which all his neighbours gawped at.[445]

Progress, nonetheless, was lamentably slow. 'Passed through a land of misery, where I would not have given sixpence for the whole apparel of any man, woman or child whom we saw along the road.' Thus wrote an anonymous Englishman, in his *Journal of a Tour in Ireland, in 1804*.[446] Even in Kilkenny – 'a beautiful town, where the inn is clean, the breakfasts comfortable, the streets handsome' – he noted in disgust 'the nineteen beggars which we counted at the coach door.' This confident English tourist managed to cram the whole of Ireland into four weeks and a brief pamphlet. It took two years and more than 750 pages for William Tighe to explore a single county, Kilkenny, and produce the vast, fascinating report which the Dublin Society had commissioned from him, and which it published in 1802.[447] Tighe's *Statistical Observations* confirmed the evidence of poverty but provided a much more varied picture, because he was interested in everything – geology and natural history, agriculture, social conditions, schemes for improvement. Tighe recorded the traditional incantations made by country people when picking medicinal herbs, commented on the utility of feeding sheep on a diet of Jerusalem artichokes, learnt everything there was to tell about the Kilkenny coal mines and filled a large appendix with plans for new canals.[448] And he visited local members of the Dublin Society, including Sir Edward Loftus, whose curiosity matched his own.[449]

When he arrived at Mount Loftus – which he described as 'commanding a most extensive prospect' – Tighe immersed himself in geology, for this was the exact spot where granite met limestone, in the parish of Powerstown.

The granite varies in shades of grey, red and yellow, and in the fineness of its grain, though none is very course. The best is raised in a quarry at Mount-Loftus, which is a beautiful stone of a light yellow cast, fine-grained and compact. It is mostly used in single stones for gate posts, nor can there be any kind handsomer or more durable, nor at the same time cheaper; a pair of gate posts costing lately but one guinea.

Near the extremity of the granite district, Sir Edward Loftus has discovered in his demesne, pieces of a very fine, deep red and compact Jasper embedded in yellow clay, in the northern declivity of a granite hill. At the foot of this hill, and here only, does the limestone approach close to the granite. Gneiss sometimes adjoins it; specimens of which containing schörl crystals, one third of an inch in diameter, have been found near Mount-Loftus.

Limestone was essential for balancing the acid soil of much of Ireland, and its presence on the Mount Loftus estate was a valuable commercial resource.

At Powerstown lime is sold by the barrel of four bushels for 16d. Farmers from the county of Wexford come here to purchase lime, and draw it home 25 or 30 miles, over mountain roads, and through difficult passes, as the Scollagh gap near Mount Leinster. Near Gowran 120 barrels are commonly put on an acre, and more by the rich farmers.

Ownership of his own quarry allowed Sir Edward to be liberal in his use of lime to improve what was already, according to Tighe, 'Some of the finest soil in this part – An excellent wheat-soil, consisting of a clayey loam, mixed with stones' – and he took advantage of this good fortune to experiment with several different strains of wheat.

One bearded variety called velvet wheat produces a grain very beautiful to all appearance. Sir Edward Loftus had this year a field partly sown with it, and partly with a remarkable kind of wheat, the seed of which came a few years ago from a southern climate: it is distinguished by the largeness of its husks and the great size of its grain, which is nearly double that of the common wheat.

Tighe was so taken with this variety that he begged a little from Sir Edward, in order to try it for himself.

He was also impressed with the Mount Loftus cattle, which included 'some fine beasts of the old large, long horned English breed, that were imported many years ago,' and in general gives the impression of a beautifully managed demesne, something of a model. But the value of Tighe's study is that he analysed the circumstances of the poor as well as the rich, providing a detailed breakdown of the cost of living for day labourers and brisk summaries of life on a tenanted farm. Two of his examples, drawn from farms of similar size on Sir Edward's estate, demonstrate the range of possible outcomes, from a life of modest decency to one of wretched squalor.

Both farms were in Powerstown, on land that was let at 26 shillings an acre. The larger (twenty-two acres, on a thirty-one year lease) was tenanted by a farmer who managed to keep a cow, three horses and three goats (but no pig) and cultivated seven acres of wheat, three of barley and two of potatoes. 'No meadow, the farmer buys a small quantity of hay at the rate of seven guineas per acre; he keeps his horse chiefly for the purpose of drawing flour to Dublin, at the rate of 2s 8d per hundredweight: the ground has been tilled from time immemorial and produces from five to seven barrels of wheat and from thirteen or fourteen of barley per acre.'

Those were good yields and the farmer must have made a decent living, well above the poverty line, but his earnings as a haulier were threatened by the success of the Barrow 'navigation'. This lovely, rushing river – which shaped the eastern edge of the Mount Loftus estate – had recently been transformed, through a series of locks, into a navigable waterway for barges laden with goods, all the way upstream from the port of Ross, in the South, until the river was linked to the Grand Canal, which led to Dublin. Tighe notes that the toll per ton on the Barrow was a penny per mile, plus lock fees, which undercut all other forms of transport.

The other, smaller farm that Tighe describes at Powerstown, of eighteen acres, seemed burdened with disadvantages. There was no lease (hence no security) and it was held by a partnership of two brothers, who had to pay a tithe of about £4 per annum. '*Stock* 2 horses; neither pig nor goat.' The brothers cultivated six acres of wheat, one of barley, one of oats, four of potatoes.

> They have a fallow of about four acres every second year: no meadow, buy an acre [of hay] at the rate of £6; for ploughing fallow borrow two additional horses; the horses sometimes get the potato skins, and a few potatoes for food, and occasionally some furze tops. The two brothers with a son and a daughter perform the whole work of the farm; the men were ragged and their houses miserable; the crops of wheat and oats were excessively bad; and a small piece of ground *let out* three years ago, had scarcely a covering of grass.

This picture of wretchedness combines the seeming incompetence of those particular farmers with the lack of incentive to invest in improvements, which Tighe believed was at the root of rural poverty. He argued passionately for the security of long leases, at stable rents, and equally vehemently against the injustice of tithes, which not only forced the Catholic Irish to pay for Protestant clergymen but penalised success, since the tithe – as a tax on income – took more from farmers who managed their land well. He also urged the landowners themselves to invest in their estates, as a matter of self-interest – particularly in improving the cottages of their labourers and tenants, and providing schooling for their children.

Those concerns were shared by an enlightened English clergyman, the Rev. James Hall, who undertook his *Tour through Ireland* in 1808/9 and was so concerned at what he saw that he warned his readers of escalating rural unrest. 'So poor are many of the people, that they have not so much as a chair, table, or stool in the house; their seats are made of platted straw, or rushes, and, sometimes, stones, set round the fire, with round coils of platted straw by way of cushion.' [450]

Poverty was moderated by rearing livestock, but this was a means of providing some small income for the family rather than to enrich their own diet.

> One help towards the support of families in these cabins is, that they buy a pig or two, soon after it is weaned, for about ten shillings each; and, having fattened them for a year or so with the peelings and refuse of potatoes, they sell them at two or three guineas each. As much as possible, too, they rear geese, ducks, turkeys and the like, which they dispose of to good advantage.
>
> Though all animals live not only about, but literally in the house with the family, the hog seems most at home, and at his ease. At breakfast, dinner, and every meal, he draws near the board, squats on his hams like a cur, and grunts his request. The master and mistress give him the peelings and the worst potatoes. In fact he breakfasts, dines, and sups with his master.

Hall seems a more careful and accurate observer than most English tourists, and the picture he paints is not one of unmitigated gloom. When this curious clergyman came to the neighbourhood of

Goresbridge, on the River Barrow, he recorded a very different state of affairs. 'Having gone into a variety of cabins and farmhouses in the county of Kilkenny, I found some of the inmates enjoying happiness amidst extreme poverty.' Hall enquired as to the cause and was told by an Irish woman that it was all to the credit of a local landowner, a great farmer, who devoted his time to improving his property. The name of this paragon was Sir Edward Loftus, 'who lives in the vicinity, is kind to all his tenants, and gives every body, that applies for it, work, of some kind or other.'

> I afterwards found what the good woman said of Sir Edward was true; that he is at much pains to increase the number of dependents; that he generally lives on his estate; that he has procured a local schoolmaster to teach the children of the poor, and allows him a house and some acres of land: in a word, that his tenants are happy. Were all the landed proprietors to do as Sir Edward does, there would be no fear of a rebellion.

And then, as was his habit, the clergyman extracted a moral from this edifying story.

> The practice of the generality of people of the best taste, it is to be owned, is directly against Sir Edward's conduct; but when it is considered that this practice of theirs proceeds rather from a compliance with the fashion of the times, than their own private thoughts, the objection is of no force. It is of no consequence for the absentees, and landed proprietors, who live in England and at a distance from their tenants, and the poor Irish, to say that they pity them. Pity of itself is but poor comfort, and unless it produces something more substantial, is rather more troublesome than agreeable. To stand bemoaning the misfortunes of our friends, without offering some expedient to alleviate them, is only putting them in mind that they are miserable.

I sense Sir Edward's own sentiments behind these words, the echo of an evening's conversation at Mount Loftus where, it seems clear, the Rev. Hall was welcomed for the night, as he was at most of the other great houses at which he called on his travels. Even in his old age Sir Edward retained a radical streak, expressed in an enduring concern for the day-to-day practicalities of life on his estate and the well-being of his numerous dependents.

Most of the records of that estate were lost when the house went up in flames, in 1934, or vanished in other, haphazard ways. What survives is a random assortment of evidence, which I scan for clues. A battered edition of Gibson's *Farrier's Guide* is filled with anatomical engravings and remedies for equine ailments, and a bookmark slipped between the pages of an old *Gazetteer* records the mating arrangements for Sir Edward's cows, in the summer of 1814 – 'Number 14 My fine Heffer, Bull 1 June. Number 13, Bull the 4 June. Number 2, Bull the 20 May.' There is the fragment of an affidavit, sworn by a disgruntled tenant, who threatened to 'fight Sir Edwd with his own Sword,' for reasons that remain obscure.[451] Best of all is the *House Book* for the years 1808–12, a sturdy folio volume that somehow escaped the destruction of all the rest.[452] Here, day by day except Sundays, which he kept free from material concerns, Sir Edward recorded the details of household expenditure, of small debts and their subsequent payment, prices and purchases, of when and how things were done. He copied out recipes supplied by friends or magazines and noted down snippets of local news. His maths was unreliable – computing pounds of twenty shillings, each of twelve pence, was never easy – but the flavour of daily life at Mount Loftus is apparent on every page.

There is a touching contrast between the old-fashioned formality whereby Sir Edward notes the comings and goings of his eldest son 'the Colonel', the cost of a pair of stockings for 'Lady Loftus' or a hat for his unmarried daughter 'Miss Loftus' – and the simple, affectionate, day-to-day dealings with his numerous dependants. Payments for eggs or potatoes from the wives of his farm labourers or tenants, the purchase of a stout pair of boots or a coat for one of his servants, gifts or loans of money to pay for a funeral, to go on a journey or buy a cow – everything suggests a community that was close-knit, economically interdependent, socially informal, except on the rare occasions when Sir Edward exercised his authority to pursue a thief or distrain the goods of tenants who failed to pay their rents. A zest for country life is apparent on every page, as he records the price of some 'very fine lemons' and 'a monstrous large turbot', the arrangements for the management of his orchard, the arrival of 'two small fat cows' from Richfield, a present of partridges or a posy of flowers. There is also, unmistakeably, the goodness of the man himself – in his care for the wellbeing of all around him, his collection of recipes for dosing humans and animals, his numerous small kindnesses and occasional tetchiness, his curiosity, courtesy and quiet forbearance.

These accounts are primarily concerned with the day-to-day life of Sir Edward's family and immediate household, in the 'great house' and its gardens – which I explore in the next chapter – but numerous entries touch on the wider community that began just to the east of the house, in a cluster of buildings that formed the hub of the estate, like a small village. 'The Range' housed a granary and store as well as accommodation for the steward, the clerk and the herd. Next to it stood the dairies, the laundry, the blacksmith's shop and some cart sheds. Not far distant were the schoolhouse and dispensary that Sir Edward provided for his dependants. The stable yard was unusually large and well-appointed for an estate of this size, because Sir Edward's eldest son was mad about horses, which he bred, and there was more stabling in the fields above the yard – a series of small, stone-walled, slate-roofed byres, which dotted the meadows that covered the crest of the hill. It is said that Mount Loftus could stable eighty horses and ninety cows. There were two sets of kennels, one in the park for the harriers, the other in the haggard for the setters, and a racecourse for 'the Colonel' to exercise his horses and challenge his friends.

'About sixty men were constantly employed' at Richfield and Mount Loftus, according to my great-uncle Jack, quoting records from the 1780s, now lost. There were carpenters and smiths, gardeners and handymen, a coachman, grooms, kennel-men and a horde of less determinate labourers. 'A little stable boy, one Edward Byrne, was paid £4 a year, out of which the boy had to buy his own boots and brushes. A postilion was paid £8 a year & also had to find himself the same articles. Another was hired at £7 a year.'[453] By the early years of the nineteenth century Sir Edward paid for his servants' boots, seems to have dispensed with postilions, seldom used his carriage and kept very few riding horses; but otherwise little had changed. The Colonel's racing stud was more than sufficient to fill the stables and the yards swarmed with retainers.

Their number included Martin Dooley and 'old Grady', who did nothing much but had been around for ever; 'Brennan, my Boy' and Pat Neal, who worked in and around the house; the diffident clerk, Mr Sillitoe (who also acted as curate); and the indispensable Tom Kenna, the steward. Most trusted of all was James Maher, a long-standing tenant of the estate and Kenna's predecessor as steward, 'whose Fidelity and good conduct while living entitled him to the regard and the good wishes of all his Neighbours,' according to the beautifully engraved memorial at Powerstown church, 'Erected by his Landlord Sir Edward Loftus Bart, as a mark of respect,' following his death on 13 December 1815, at the age of fifty-six.[454]

The house and its demesne were encircled by a stone wall, built by Sir Edward in 1789–90, beyond which lay the villages of Powerstown and Ullard with their churches and graveyards, the tenanted land and the quarries – some 2,000 acres in all. Thirty miles south, in County Wexford, lay the Richfield estate: the ancient manor of Ballymagir. The old, moated house, approached by a drawbridge, was left unoccupied for most of this period but it was surrounded by nearly 5,000 acres of rich marshes, ideal for fattening livestock. These acreages are recorded in 'plantation measure' – but the combined total of the lands at Mount Loftus and Richfield, nearly 7,000 Irish acres, was the equivalent of more than 11,000 acres in modern terms. Drovers such as John Crowe were employed to herd black Kerry cattle between the two estates, taking two or three days for the journey, and Richfield was the Colonel's favourite place to graze his horses. It was also a great place to go wild-fowling and the steward, Robert Power, held a license as Sir Edward's gamekeeper.

Sir Edward cultivated rare strains of wheat and different types of potatoes, and was prepared to experiment with a wide variety of crops – '17 August 1809. Planted the Saffron [and] got a present from Mr Prim of 300 of Penton Cabbage Plants' – but numerous entries in the *House Books* recall the days when wealth was measured by sheep, cattle and horses. Most of the demesne lands at Mount Loftus and Richfield were given over to pasture and there is a strong sense of Sir Edward's personal engagement in the way that everything to do with livestock was recorded; the purchase of a 'Milch Cow & Calf' at Borris Fair –

'engaged to give 7 quarts of Milk, morning and Evening' – or a 'score of Mountain Sheep' from Boyan Flood; the sale of his Kerry cows at Goresbridge; the day when 'Nancy Cullerton's pet cow Calfed a Beautiful Heffer Calf fit to be reared'. These were things to celebrate, day by day.

Lists of supposed cures for various animal ailments punctuate the account books. In 1809 there was an outbreak of 'Disorder among Horses', and Sir Edward copied out a recipe from the *Correspondent*. 'Take 50 heads of Garlick Chop & Boile them in one Gallon of Sweet Milk for an hour then mix one pint of Linseed Oil, give the Horse about a pint thrice in the day.'[455] Sheep, by contrast, alternated between the indignities of 'Mr Proctor's Receipt for the Cure of Red Water in Sheep' – a hideous concoction of dung and soot, in which the suffering animals were supposed to wallow overnight before being dosed with 'three spoonfuls for three mornings between the 15 August and the 8 of September' – and the intoxication of 'Dr Thomas's Prescription for curing Magots in Sheep', which required a quart of best whiskey. All of which sounds like alchemy, or the medical incantations of 'country doctors and old women' quoted by William Tighe.

Enlightenment clearly had its limits, and one of those, for the Irish gentleman farmer, was any notion of self-sufficiency. The dining table at Mount Loftus may have been well supplied with tender young lamb and delicious beef, as it was with a variety of fruit from Sir Edward's garden, but this home-grown produce had to be supplemented with regular purchases of basic necessities – potatoes, flour, chickens and eggs. All of which was paid for out of the real income of the estate: the rent roll.

The scale of that income is something we can only guess at, since the relevant accounts have disappeared.[456] What the *House Books* provide instead are the details of numerous small transactions, glimpses of the relationship between a landlord and his tenants. Enlightened benevolence, as noted by Hall, is proved again and again by the evidence of loans, gifts and other kindnesses – but equally clear is Sir Edward's impatience when things went wrong. Both impulses are evident in an entry for 31 October 1808. 'Mr Michael Murphy has engaged to work the Quarry properly and that there shall be no Complaints by the Tenants of the want of Stone, as there has been, otherwise Sir Edward will take it from him & employ hands to make a proper opening in the Quarry & of course to work it as it should be.'

Real arguments were rare and there is no record of forced evictions at Richfield or Mount Loftus. Whenever Sir Edward became particularly grumpy about long arrears of unpaid rent he threatened the offenders with a writ or sent his steward to drive their cattle to the pound, as security for the unpaid debt, and life went on as normal. It was much the same with other disputes. When Edmund Furlong, one of the Richfield tenants, tried to enlarge his holding by altering 'the Bounds Ditch between the Glebe and Killogg,' Sir Edward sent Thomas Kenna 'to view the outrage' and 'ordered David Power if it was necessary to Lodge information' – but nothing more was heard of the case and Furlong continued as tenant for years thereafter. Likewise when the Mount Loftus tenants were repeatedly accused of felling trees in Sir Edward's park, dire threats were uttered and formal vows imposed on all the usual suspects never to offend again, but there is no evidence of real retribution.[457]

All the more surprising, then, that one small farm in Nighery – in Duncormick parish on the northern edge of the Richfield estate – became the scene of increasingly bitter confrontations, ending in violence. It began towards the end of 1809, when the tenant, Edmund White, was more than a year overdue with his rent.[458] White was habitually behindhand and Sir Edward's patience seems finally to have snapped, for he wrote to his Dublin lawyer, John Flood, to obtain a writ of enforcement and ensured that his steward, Thomas Kenna, was granted the powers of a Special Constable. Kenna set off in pursuit of White, first to Enniscorthy and then to Richfield, where he and John Biron 'took him on Tuesday morning just near his owne house,' and lodged him in Wexford Gaol. Then the negotiations began. White agreed to surrender his lease but claimed that he could not pay the arrears of rent, and applied to be released under the Insolvency Act. It took another fortnight before a settlement was reached and White was escorted by Kenna to Mount Loftus, where he signed a formal surrender of his lands and issued promissory notes for the outstanding amount, payable in instalments over the following two years – all of which was formally witnessed and stamped. The notes were never likely to be honoured but the legal fictions were preserved and the lands at Nighery were eventually relet, to Laurence Doyle.[459]

Up to this point the affair was a fine example of the Irish passion for litigation – White being as quick to cite the Insolvency Act in his defence as Sir Edward was meticulous in obtaining legal backing for his actions. I am reminded of Maria Edgeworth's contemporary comment, that 'almost every poor man in Ireland, be he farmer, weaver, shop-keeper, or steward, is, beside his other occupations, occasionally a lawyer. They all love law.'[460] But things took a turn for the worse, two years later, when Kenna was sent down to Richfield 'with orders to threaten to drive the Ballygow Tenants for the year's Rent in case they did not immediately pay the half year due' – and with a warning from Sir Edward 'to take due care that I am not defrauded by a certain person in Nighery.'[461] Sure enough, Doyle failed to pay, so Kenna returned on 28 October 1811 and 'drove McWhitty's farm' to seize his cattle as security for the debt. The reaction was sudden and dramatic. 'Mall Doyle and her family entered on the land forced ye Possession & carry'd away all goods, distressed & Burnd McWhitty's house pulled down a large Timber Sally [willow] tree and putting it down the Chimney placed on the top of it a large Cookes Bowle or Basket & named it the *Tree of Liberty*.'[462]

This was a violent challenge that dangerously evoked the revolu-tionary fervour of '98, as the furious Miss Doyle adopted the role of vengeful Hibernia, torching the house, tearing up a tree and turning her kitchen bowl into a symbolic Cap of Liberty. Sir Edward responded in kind, invoking the full sanctions of the law. Kenna was dispatched to lodge information with the local magistrate, Christian Wilson, and to serve an Official Notice of the Outrage 'on the Minister & Church Wardens of the Parish of Duncormack & High Constable,' while Michael Murphy and David Power were sent to seize the remaining crops at McWhitty's farm – 'to put my Hay on the Stables Loft, to dig out 24 Ridges of Potatoes on Nighery to get the Tenants to assist to take 'em out and to lock them up in Doyle's late House.' Letters were posted to the Wexford MP, Sir Frederick Flood, and a notice was drafted to insert in the official *Hue & Cry*, to set the chase in motion.[463] But once again, Sir Edward's bark was very much sharper than his bite. On 16 December he gave a pound to 'Dennis Bryan being in Rags, the

Man whose Life I saved, being concerned in Miss Doyle's Robbery & who I admitted [ie omitted] to prosecute.'

The damage to house and farm had a catastrophic impact on the rental value of what had formerly been a valuable tenancy. When James Harper from Bannow arrived at Mount Loftus on 3 December – 'to treat for White's late farm' – he came armed with 'a Recommendation from Luke FitzHenry of Ballygow' but was only prepared to offer six shillings an acre for a thirty-one year lease, and any hope of redress through the courts seemed a long way distant. It was not until the following March that Sir Edward was finally able to apply 'to the Grand Jury for Compensation for the Burning of Michael Whitty's house,' and at this point the *House Book* comes to an end, leaving the story unresolved – as I suspect it was, in reality.

Unresolved stories, fragments of daily life, are, in any case, all that we glimpse from most of the neat entries in Sir Edward's accounts, and behind these occasional dramas runs the more persistent reality of life on the estate: planting trees, mending roads and bridges, repairing the local church, maintaining the school and dispensary, and countless acts of personal benevolence. Trees were cheap ('two thousand of 5yr old Scotch Firs' cost £5) but roadworks were long and costly, involving dozens of men and horses, for weeks on end.[464] In the summer of 1809, for example, Sir Edward spent more than £40 on road-mending and a further £8 on repairs to Powerstown Bridge, which carried the road from Gowran to Graignemanagh. As for Powerstown Church, the work was never-ending. Repairs to the slate roof cost more than £15, in the autumn of 1809, and intermittent bills are scattered throughout the accounts for all manner of builder's supplies, for these and other tasks.[465]

That small church at Powerstown sheltered an even smaller congregation of Protestants but its ancient graveyard was the burial place for numerous Catholic families, as it had been for centuries past, and it seems that Sir Edward's main responsibility, as churchwarden, was to pay for the funeral expenses of his tenants and other dependants. Even the poorest cottagers felt obliged to spend a fortune on the wake, and few of them could afford it, so they 'borrowed' the money from their landlord. These 'loans' ranged in size from a modest thirty shillings for William Byrne Smith to bury his mother, to a substantial eleven guineas 'lent James Brandon to bury his wife.' Each was recorded in the *House Book* – but few were ever repaid.

Similar acts of kindness can be found throughout these accounts. Sir Edward 'lent' Anne Cullerton a few shillings to pay her Hearth Tax, and a few more to Mary Hunt to buy a pair of brogues, and he gave John O'Brien 'a present of £1' when he left to rejoin his regiment, 'to enable him to go on the Mail Coach to Corke,' so that he could arrive there before his pass expired. Other, more regular payments – from half a crown to a pound – were made to a small group of old retainers and others who claimed his sympathy. The monthly total was anywhere from seven to ten pounds.

In a more substantial way, Sir Edward provided for the education and physical wellbeing of his dependants. He employed Mr Curran the schoolmaster to teach their children to read and Mr Murphy at the dispensary to prescribe the latest medicines, from Messrs Boileau of Dublin. At the same time he continued to jot down almost any remedy that came his way, however improbable, and may well have pestered the long-suffering Mr Murphy to try a 'Cure for the Rheumatick Leg' (a decoction of oak leaves in beer, copied from the pages of the *Observer*) or the 'prescription powerfully recommended for the Hooping Cough & Small Pox' (an ointment made of the essential oils of 'Elder, Carraway & Rosemary with Rose Leaves and Camomile flowers, Rubbed to the Pit of the stomach') or the 'Receipt given by Mr O'Flahertie to make an Ague Plaister' (a mixture of turpentine, frankincense and Red Sanders, heated over a gentle fire, 'spread on White Leather, the size of a crown', and applied to the navel). But just in case that remedy for the aigue didn't work, Sir Edward also ordered a pound of 'Jesuits Bark' (quinine) from Boileau's.[466]

This instinctive tendency to combine the old with the new, not quite trusting either, was a habit he shared with his tenants. Living in a time and place where it still seemed possible to cure that most feared of scourges, smallpox, with an ointment of essential oils 'Rubbed to the Pit of the stomach', it must have been hard to adjust to the novelty of vaccination. As recently as 1796 Edward Jenner had proved that vaccinating with cowpox could immunise against smallpox, and that this was a safer method of protection than inoculating with smallpox itself, but terrified parents remained unconvinced. On 8 July 1811, Sir

Edward underlined the following entry in his *House Book*. 'Mr Murphy of the Dispensary was called on by me to view two Children in my Park that were Inoculated about a year ago by Doct' Stone with the Cow Pocks, the Parents not being Satisfied, had them Inoculated with the Common Pocks by one Doyle a Carpenter of Ballycabus. Mr Murphy has viewed the Children regularly to this date & pronounced the Children to be safe over the small Pox.'

I can hear a huge sigh of collective relief, but carpenter and doctor were probably still arguing, months later, as to which could claim the credit. And so it continued, in this small, self-absorbed community at Mount Loftus, while elsewhere, in another world, the slave trade was abolished, steam locomotion was hauling a new industrial economy into being and the Napoleonic Wars dragged on. Across the Irish Sea a new age had begun.

CHAPTER 37

Domestic Economy

Sir Edward's world contracted as he grew older, for he now stayed mostly at home, having disposed of his townhouse in Dublin after the Act of Union and locked up the old manor at Richfield, to save paying tax on a place that stood empty for most of the year. The household at Mount Loftus had also shrunk, from a swarm of children and servants to a family of three – Sir Edward, his wife Anne and their unmarried daughter Elizabeth – although the eldest son, Nicholas, was constantly in and out of the place, between barracks and racecourse, and the youngest, Francis, gradually returned to live there as his health proved unsuited to military life. The problematic widowed daughter, Mary Cary, tended to arrive with requests for money, but her children were welcome at Mount Loftus, particularly the youngest son, 'little Robert Cary', who was a favourite of Sir Edward.

To look after the family and guests there were now only three indoor servants, resident in the house itself – cook, kitchen maid and housemaid – but these were supplemented by a swarm of others who lived on the estate. Their terms of employment were formally recorded in the 'Servants Book', now lost, but their comings and goings occasionally surface in the household accounts, together with large supplies of food, 'for the Servants Quarters'. In February 1809 'Corporal Eustace was married to Margaret Henery my Kitchen Maid' and nine months later, in November, their baby was born – Sir Edward gave £1 to 'Corporal Eustace's wife for her Christening'. Bridget Murphy 'on leaving my service owed me 18s 10d', which left a balance due on her wages of little more than £1. In October 1810 Sir Edward found himself without a cook and wrote to one of his gardeners 'about his Sister who is a Cook to know if she be disengaged,' but it was not until 12 December that he was able to record, with evident relief, that Michael Murphy had gone to Enniscorthy 'to bring home Mrs Sheridan the Cook.' 1818 opened with a series of domestic upheavals. Margaret Worthington was discharged 'for frequently absenting herself contrary to repeated orders', but Sir Edward was prepared to give her a decent reference – 'Certified her being honest and sober during her service for five months.' She was replaced as kitchen maid by Elizabeth Kelly. A long-serving treasure of the household, Anne Cullerton, died at the end of January and was buried in Powerstown churchyard, but it took all her outstanding wages to pay for the funeral. Her successor, Jane Scott, 'commenced a House Maid' in February, at five shillings a week.

That sense of a small but rather too-frequently changing cast of female household servants contrasts with the seeming permanence of two favoured odd-job men, Brennan and Neal, who lived somewhere in the warren of buildings near the house and probably helped with everything from carrying in the turf – fuel for the fires – to waiting at table when there were guests.

'Brennan, my Boy' was one of those useful fixtures to be found in every Anglo-Irish household. Sir Edward records buying him a pair of 'very strong shoes' in 1809, and paying James May three shillings 'for making Brennan's Blue Jacket & mending his cloathes.' In June 1811 he gave Brennan another three shillings 'to buy a Pair of Stockings' and four pence for himself – not the wisest move, as it transpired, for Brennan 'got Immensely Drunk'. Keeping his servants away from the bottle was a problem that occasionally came to a crisis. In April 1818 'Pat Neille was Sworn not to drink spirits out of Sir Edward Loftus's house, not to drink any but what was aloud him by Sir Edwd or Col Loftus, the Oath administered by Col Loftus otherwise Sir Edward Loftus would discharge him, and but one Quart of ale in the 24 hours.' But Neal, like Brennan, had been around too long for summary dismissal and both were specially favoured – more than a decade earlier Sir Edward had arranged for them to learn to read and write. 'Desired Curran Schoolmaster to allow for an hour 3 times in the week to teach Neal and Brennan.'[467]

Life for this community of family and servants was centred on the comfortable, light-filled house, with its thirty-six windows and ten hearths, which Sir Edward had built about forty years earlier, after John Eaton finally surrendered his lease on the park and its lands. Somewhat perversely, to my eyes, the main rooms faced resolutely north, towards the picturesque ruins of Drumroe Castle – which Sir Edward had converted into a pigeon house – rather than taking advantage of one of the finest views in Ireland, down the back avenue to Mount Leinster, across the lovely valley of the Barrow.[468] It seemed a tall, ungainly-looking place as you approached up the front drive, but classically balanced as you swung round behind to enter through a pedimented porch (carved from the local granite), which focused the symmetrical Georgian façade of two main storeys and an attic. This apparent discrepancy between front and back was because Mount Loftus was built on a slope – its northern face was a full storey taller than the south and was dominated by a great demi-octagon bay, rising from a stone-flagged kitchen in the basement, to the attics, high above.[469]

It is there, in the basement, that I want to begin my exploration of the house. Cool cellars and storerooms were dug into the side of the hill behind the big north-facing kitchen, with its three tall windows onto the sloping lawn. There may once have been a brewhouse in one of the outbuildings – there are recipes for brewing in the account book – but as he grew older Sir Edward found it more convenient to stock his cellars with barrels of beer from Mr Flaherty of Graigue or Ephraim Burrows (who also supplied bread) and hogsheads of cyder from his closest genteel neighbour, Colonel Gore – to whom he paid £11-7-6 'for a pew in Grange Sylvia Church'. Pipes of port and casks of 'Sweet Mountain' or Bucellas were shipped on Mr Hayden's boat from Dublin, down the recently completed Barrow Navigation, and were bottled by Sir Edward – with enthusiastic help from Neal and Brennan, I imagine – and he noted his comments on particularly good consignments with an appreciation undimmed by his advancing age.

That relish was even more marked in his descriptions of the produce supplied by his tenants and their wives, or brought by carriers from the coast, or sent as presents by relatives and neighbours.

The Colonel's man returned from Richfield and brought from David Power one Widgeon, one couple of Plover with two couple of stone Plover or Sea Larks.[470]

Young Power came up and brought two pairs and half of my own Rabbits, two couple of Ducks, one couple of Widgeon [and] one hundred of oysters.

From Richfield 2 couple of Crested Fowl & two Turkeys, 3 Mullet
& one Trout. One couple & half of Beautifull Pidgeons from Taylor.
Mrs Cary sent a Brace of Partridge & a Brace of Snipe.
Mrs Cary sent a present of two Kidds.

Every few days Sir Edward bought several 'couple of Chickens' and
Mrs O'Brien supplied him with veal, but it is clear that what he really
loved was fish, and the accounts are full of mouth-watering descriptions.

2 pair of wonderfully fine soals 8s., a monstrous large turbot 15s., a
large John Dory & fine pair of Soal 5s., a very large turbot 12s. 6d. &
two large cod 7s. 7d., six dozen of Herrings 1s. 1d., 3 lobster and two
crabs 5s., three Haddocks 5s. 11d., a salmon from Elizabeth Canning
17 lbs at 8d. [per lb].

The fish were enormous – two salmon weighing a total of 17lbs were
described as 'small' – and oysters were bought by the hundred, for a
couple of shillings.

That sense of abundance continues with the lists of fruit – 'Four
dozen of very fine lemons, 10 doz of Oranges, two quarts of Bogberries,'
baskets of gooseberries from Mary Devereux, and vast supplies of apples
from Patrick Flin, who leased Sir Edward's orchards in 1809 'for Twelve
guineas and two thousand apples' per annum. That arrangement lasted
for less than a year, before Susy Watkins – who rented 'the Gooseberries
& Currants of Walled Garden & Orchard' at Richfeld for £6-10s. –
sent her son to Mount Loftus 'to take charge of the Orchard,' ensuring
regular supplies for the house. '31 October 1810, Mrs Watkins gave
this day one hundred apples for the Servants Quarters.'

Mary Hunt supplied Sir Edward with tobacco, at 2s 10d per lb, and
'many eggs' for 4s. 10d. – but eggs were also bought from 'May's
daughter' and 'Flin's wife' at three for a penny. In September 1809 Sir
Edward took delivery of a hundredweight of the finest flour from Mr
Buller's Mill, but returned it two days later, 'being fusty'. Potatoes from
Laurence Healy cost a shilling a stone, except for 'Darling Reds' which
were much more highly prized, at 1s. 8d. Sir Edward seems to have
enjoyed his greens – in April 1809 he 'Sent Miss Robinson a present of
Spinage Seeds'. For about a month every year, from early August, the
family ate mushrooms each day, supplied fresh from the fields at a

penny a plate. Tea was a luxury, at eight shillings per pound, and cakes were extravagantly brought from Carlow by the 'Carrie girl', at a cost of five shillings. 'A Bottle of the Essence of Mustard' was acquired in Kilkenny for 3s. 9d., where Sir Edward also bought 'a Bright Chopper for cutting meat in the kitchen, a Store for boxes of Candles [and] a Butchers knife in place of one lost by John Cullerton.'[471] But kitchens and larders were liable to vermin – '22 Dec 1808, Paid for Arsenic for poisoning Rats, 2s. 2d.'

Above stairs, over cool subterranean larders, a wide corridor-hall ran along the entrance front, from the east end of which rose the main staircase. At the other end, closest to the dining room, there was I think a service stair, leading down to the kitchen. The hall was filled with light from its two south-facing windows, and with the gentle ticking of a grandfather clock, one of two that were 'cleaned by Kelly' on 13 May 1811, for five shillings and five pence. Kelly was also employed to put 'Lady L's watch & Miss Loftus's in order' and Sir Edward was particular in noting the details of such valuable timepieces, in case they were stolen – 'My Watch James Gordon Dublin No 1103, Lady Loftus' Ferdinand Vigne London No 607.'[472]

Leading off the hall were the main reception rooms – 'the Large Parlour' in the central bay, with the dining room on the left, as you faced across the hall from the front door, and 'my own room' – Sir Edward's study – on the right, closest to the stairs. The parlour with its green-painted walls and three tall windows was the heart of the house, as I know from the accounts, because Sir Edward was meticulous in recording the details when he called in the chimney sweep, once or twice a year, and this was the most frequently swept flue. In February 1811, for example, he 'paid Quin for sweeping the Mt Loftus chimneys [six of them, including the Parlour] 4s. 4d.,' and he 'gave the Boy 5d.'. The little, soot-covered sweeper's boy, who clambered up the narrow stacks, must have been delighted to get a tip for his terrifying day's work – elsewhere he may have got nothing. The accounts also confirm that vast supplies of fuel were needed to keep the household warm – endless 'kishes of turf (cart-loads of slow-burning, sweet-smelling peat) at half a crown apiece, barrels of 'Sea Coal' at 6d. and heavy loads of 'Stone Coal' from the Kilkenny colliery at a shilling a hundredweight, plus substantial transport costs for horses and wagons.[473]

The fire in the parlour warmed Sir Edward's bones when age caught up with him and forced him to rest indoors – '4 March 1810. Went out to take the air after six weeks confinement' – but confinement did not mean that he stayed in bed. Throughout those six weeks he continued to administer the estate and keep his accounts, with the energy of a much younger man; and as soon as he was better he 'wrote to Mr Richard Radcliffe for a few of the Asparagus Potatoes.' His appetite had evidently returned.[474]

The *House Book* records the purchase of a 'Toast stand' from Mrs Meighan for £1, and a 'Breakfast Table Cloth' for £1 13*s.*, which suggests that breakfast was served on a small table in Sir Edward's study or the upstairs drawing room – but most meals were eaten in the dining room, albeit with less ceremony than of old. In 1809 Sir Edward had asked his Dublin man of business, John Flood, 'to buy me one of the Dumb Waiters' then in vogue, which enabled the family to help themselves rather than expecting everything to be served. When Colonel Gore or Sir Frederick Flood came to dine, one of the maids would have waited at table, helped by Brennan or Neal, on their best behaviour. They may have lacked the polish of well-trained footmen, but everyone in Ireland was used to that.

Business was conducted in 'my own room', where Sir Edward wrote his accounts, read the newspapers and smoked his long clay pipe. The management of his lands at Richfield and Mount Loftus occupied much of his time and there were letters to answer from neighbours soliciting his support, for one cause or another. Sir Edward gave short shrift to a 'Humbugging Letter from Mr McLaughlin' and 'an Electioneering Letter from Mr Shapland Carew' but was happy to sign a 'strong Memorial, to be transmitted to the Postmaster General, against Changing the Route of the Mail Coach [from] Thomastown to Waterford,' which had been drawn up by Colonel Gore. He also 'Gave Col Gore for Relief of Confined Debtors for Small sums, £2 5*s.* 6*d.*'[475] A much more difficult matter was the choice of his preferred journal. In May 1810 he sent £5 2*s.* 4*d.* to his Dublin man of business, John Flood, for six months' subscription to the *Dublin Evening Post* and *The Correspondent*, but changed his mind three months later, cancelled in a huff and then complained when the papers kept arriving – having previously made a fuss when they were late.[476] He decided to take 'a single weekly paper, called The Messenger', and later that year 'paid Mr Reynolds for five Months Subscription for the Harp newspaper, £1 2s. 9d.'[477]

On the first floor was Lady Loftus's drawing room, flanked by bedchambers for Sir Edward and his wife, and a couple of dressing rooms, one of which was furnished with the 'new Mahogany Tallboy' that Sir Edward bought at Websters Auction in 1810, for £3 18s. Up above was the airy attic floor, with at least three more bedrooms, including a large room with a wonderful view – which may have been where the unmarried daughter, Elizabeth, lived. There were no upstairs bathrooms or lavatories – so chamber pots were a regular purchase. The best cost three shillings each, but others were bought from Miss Stephenson for 1s. 4d. and a 'small one' for ten pence, for visiting children. Washing was presumably done in bedchambers or dressing rooms, with jugs of hot water carried all the way upstairs, and occasionally a tin bath would have been set before the fire. Purchases of soap were infrequent enough to catch my eye as I scanned the accounts – '9 April 1810. 2 Pieces of Windsor Soap, 1s.'

The house was filled with portraits. The florid, hawk-nosed features of Lord Loftus, Sir Edward's father, gazed down haughtily at his descendants in the hall, but there were other, more delicate things – exquisite chalk drawings of the young Sir Edward and his bride by Thomas Hickey, pastels of Elizabeth Loftus and Anna Maria Phillips by Hugh Douglas Hamilton, a cluster of silhouettes by Mr Thomason and three fine portraits of Sir Edward's children by Gilbert Stuart – all of which added up to some sort of image of social identity. More revealing, perhaps, are the omissions. A dull painting of the Extinguisher's first wife was dutifully displayed but there was nothing to recall his housekeeper and mistress, Sir Edward's mother, Mary Hernon; nor Mary Carroll, the shopkeeper's daughter from Goresbridge whose marriage to Sir Edward's namesake son caused such dismay; nor her daughter, Sir Edward's only grandchild, who had to wait until she was old, and the invention of photography, before her formidable profile could be recorded for posterity. But there were portraits of the Colonel's horses, views of the Mount Loftus estate and a treasured engraving of Sir Edward's hero, Lord Nelson.[478]

The library is equally informative, despite the haphazard nature of what survives.[479] Sir Edward and his wife enjoyed a diet of romantic fiction, scarcely different – except in its clothing of language and social mannerisms – from the escapist fantasies of airport paperbacks. She had once been an addict of the theatre but now read the eighteenth-century precursors of Mills & Boon – *The Happy Orphan*, *Evelina*, *Rash Vows* – and was one of the first to devour *Castle Rackrent*, that only too credible satire on Irish country life.[480] Edward preferred romances with an overtly sexual flavour (*Modern Couples*, *A Nunnery for Coquettes* and *Favourite Tales, translated from the French*) as light relief from weightier works – politics, travel and natural history, texts on economics and agriculture, English editions of the classics and Goldsmith's *History of England*. And he, too, tried to keep up with the latest bestsellers. In February 1812 he sent his long-suffering clerk, Mr Sillitoe, to Dublin to buy a pound of 'Jesuits Bark' [quinine] from Mr Boileau, druggist of Bride Street, and two pounds of 'Mr Foot's freshest snuff', together with '2 Vols of *I Think of the Times*, a new Novel', and a copy of *Coxes Magazine*. Sir Edward was most specific about the snuff (it had to be 'out of the day canisters in the Shop, half fine & half Course but not the Stalky Snuff.') but he had muddled the title of the novel. Mr Sillitoe managed to decipher what he meant and returned, a fortnight later, with *Thinks I to Myself*, a satire on fashionable life that ran through eight editions in the first year of its publication.[481]

The Loftus children, it seems, seldom read at all, except to consult the essential reference manuals of the landed gentry – almanacs, guide-books and the genealogies of horses and humans – but there were occasional exceptions. Francis, the baby of the family, owned a prettily bound edition of Fenelon's *Telemachus* – in which Odysseus' son becomes the hero of a political tract, arguing that kings are subject to social obligations, that war is an unnecessary evil and that man should live in the peace of universal brotherhood – while his sister's favourite, *A Sentimental Journey*, was described by Swift as his 'work of redemption'. More telling than any of these is the bookmark that Sir Edward left between the entries for Veyros ('a small Town and Castle in Portugal') and Vezelay ('a city of France') in *The Gazetteer, or Newsman's Interpreter*. This 'Geographical Index to all the considerable Cities, Patriarchships, Bishopricks, Universities, Dukedoms, Earldoms and such like' had been published in 1716 and was inherited by Sir Edward in 1759, when he inscribed his name inside the cover. Perhaps he had been thinking of travelling abroad with his newly wedded wife. Forty-five years later, at the age of eighty, he picked up the book again and began to browse, and then marked the page with a slip of paper on which he had noted, in his wonderfully legible hand, details of the mating arrangements for his cows, in the summer of 1814. And there the bookmark remained for the next hundred and eighty years until I, too, was browsing – and there it still remains, where I replaced it.

In his old age Sir Edward stayed mostly at home, with brief excursions to Goresbridge to settle a dispute with the local bakers, to Kilkenny for the assizes and to do some shopping, or to Borris Fair to buy a cow. He went to church on Sundays, and for the funerals of friends and servants, but for most of the week he was busy with the running of his estate and the keeping of his accounts. And he seems to have enjoyed the small pleasures of daily life, purchasing fruit trees for his garden, trinkets from the local pedlars for his wife and daughter, lottery tickets to share with his eldest son and constant supplies for the kitchen and cellar.

There was seldom need to go shopping in Kilkenny because pedlars came to the house, selling everything from pretty knick-knacks to lengths of cloth, and often had other skills, essential to such a household. 'Young Kelly my little Pedlar', for example, supplied '2 small Pocket Books for Lady L, a pair of Curling Irons for Miss Loftus, and a seal, a Nail Brush, an Ivory Marrow Spoon [and] a Bodkin' at a total cost of just under nine shillings, but he also maintained the clocks and watches at Mount Loftus and could evidently turn his hand to tailoring. In March 1809 he charged 11s. 4d. 'for making Miss Loftus's [riding] Habit' and the following year Mrs Kelly, the pedlar's wife, was paid a pound for making a 'Scarlet Net Cloake' for Lady Loftus. From 'Mr Gunning' Sir Edward bought '5 yards of fine Muslin at 5s. per Yard, 8 pocket Handkerchiefs at 4s [each], 2 yards and half of Nankeen Red at 2s. 2d. and a pair of Silk Stockings 8s. 1d.' and from 'Fitzgerald a Pedlar' he purchased 'a Handkerchief for Lady Loftus 3s., ditto for Miss Loftus 2s. 2d.' In October 1811 'young Kelly' persuaded him to take 'two Razors of his tipped with Silver on Tryal' – but Sir Edward returned them a month later, unsatisfied.[482] More successful was Mr Handy, who 'brought me one pound of the very best Spun Twine I have seen' and charged four shillings for this exceedingly superior string, in January 1812.

Luxuries were modest. Elizabeth's brother Francis, a captain in the militia, came back from Kilkenny with a new hat for her, which cost 16s. 3d., and a pair of gloves, for 2s. 8d. Silk stockings were necessary for formal occasions, but for everyday wear Sir Edward bought 'Black Worsted Stockings' from Brian McManus, gaiters from James May and shoes from Mr Flannery – who supplied sturdy, unsophisticated garments of much the same quality, at much the same price, for his servants. Miss Loftus, it seems, was more particular; her shoes and 'half boots' were made by Laurence Colfer of Wexford, for between seven and nine shillings a pair.[483] Elizabeth was famously fond of the garden which had been made for her above the house, but there is little evidence of any extravagance – a 'Garden Seat for Miss Loftus' cost two shillings and a couple of 'Bee Hives from Wm Garner' were ten pence each.

Her brothers' tastes were much more expensive. In November 1808 Francis was given an increase in his allowance, 'an extra £150 pa', while Nicholas drew a substantial income from the Richfield estate. Despite this, Sir Edward regularly paid their bills, including £2 8s. to renew the 'Sporting License for Captain Loftus' and £5 13s. 9d. for the Colonel's Race Subscription. Horses and hounds were an abiding passion, shared by most of the gentry, but Mount Loftus was exceptional even by the standards of a hunting county. Nicholas had the beginnings of what became a famous stud – complete with its own training course – and was always off to the Curragh with his racing friends, while his father was left to negotiate on his behalf for promising young horses. In December 1810 he 'sent Walsh the Colonel's Groom to Mr Proctor in Kilkenny to buy his Horse [and] gave him £40', but 'Proctor wanted forty Guineas' – a considerably greater price than the 7½ guineas that Sir Edward had recently spent on a horse for himself, from Pierce Hanrahan, or the 11½ guineas that he paid for a mule.[484] The old man may have indulged his son but was modest in his own affairs, and seems never to have been flush with cash. There was a good income from the tenants at Mount Loftus and Richfield, but the estate was still encumbered with the payment of a widow's jointure to old Lady Ely. As so often in Ireland, the economic reality was less splendid than it sometimes seemed.

Sir Edward's greatest worry was the increasingly precarious financial situation of his daughter Mary, who was the widow of a clergyman of sneering temper and apparently modest means. In the opening pages of the accounts all seems well. There are frequent references to Mrs Cary and her daughters, Luisa and Maria, coming to stay at Mount Loftus and of visits by her younger son 'little Robert Cary, on his way to the College in Kilkenny.' Sir Edward indulged them – '2 Boxes of Colours for the two Miss Carys' cost him a shilling in March 1809, and he gave Robert the princely sum of ten shillings in April – and Mary sent her father presents of partridge and quail, or of mushrooms, knowing how much he enjoyed good food. Luisa married a Captain Gibbs in September 1810. But the eldest boy was a captain in the army and the middle son, Bowen, seems to have been an expensive idler, despite being a clergyman like his father.

As early as 1809 there were occasional signs of trouble – 'lent Mrs Cary to send to her son, £50' – but Mary herself and various members of her children were in and out of the house quite regularly, and it was not until 1811 that matters took a serious turn for the worse. In April that year Mary Cary, her two elder sons and her son-in-law Captain Gibbs made frequent visits to Mount Loftus, clearly in trouble, and Sir Edward had to provide £164 10s. for Edward Cary's share of his mother's inheritance, which he was hard-pressed to find. The requests for money grew more urgent, until on 2 July 1811 he noted with some frustration, that 'Mrs Cary sent me a Volume of Accounts which I returned unexamined' and that he had received a letter from Captain Cary asking 'that I might let him have £25 for a short time, to which I have given an Answer that I was prevented by having advanced Large Sums to him and his family.' Sir Edward applied to his cousin Lord Ely 'for a Commision in his Regiment for Bowen Cary', apparently without success, and when Mary spent a few days at Mount Loftus at the beginning of September, he appears to have emphasised the need to economise. Shortly after her return home she wrote by Special Messenger to announce that her eldest son had let the family farm, Munfin, to 'Mr Mulrooney, Pilot Master of Wexford Harbour' – but the lease excluded the house and twenty acres of land, which Mary kept for herself. A month later Mrs Cary sent an urgent plea for help to her sister Elizabeth at Mount Loftus, on the same day that her carriage was sold to Maginnis of Kilkenny, for the knockdown price of

Nicholas Loftus, Viscount Loftus of Ely, 'the Extinguisher'. Portrait by unknown artist, 1758. Like his father, Nicholas wears an Irish linen scarf, and on the table beside him sits a book titled *Present State of Ireland*.

Sir Edward Loftus of Mount Loftus. Portrait by Thomas Hickey, 1759.

Anne Loftus (*née* Read). Portrait by Thomas Hickey, 1759.

Portrait by Angelica Kauffmann of Henry Loftus, Earl of Ely, his first wife France
Monroe, her nieces Dolly and Frances Monroe, and an Indian pageboy, 1771. Throu
the window is a glimpse of a classical temple in the grounds of Rathfarnham Castle

View of Rathfarnham Castle 1794, by George Holmes, showing the eighteenth-cent
alterations to the Elizabethan fortress, and its setting in an extensive park.

From the Mount Loftus archive. One of the Extinguisher's pair of pistols rests on a map of the Richfield estate, above Sir Edward's House Book, together with his book-plate of the family coat of arms and a bookmark recording the mating arrangements for his cattle. Under the House Book lies a photograph of Mount Loftus *c.*1895.

Portraits of the children of Sir Edward Loftus,
together with the 'Angelic Miss Phillips'.

(*top row*) Anna Maria Phillips and Elizabeth Loftus by Hugh Douglas Hamilton, 179
(*centre*) Miniature of Lieutenant Edward Loftus, 1791.
(*bottom row*) Captain Francis Loftus and Major Nicholas Loftus in the
uniform of the Kilkenny militia, *c.*1805.

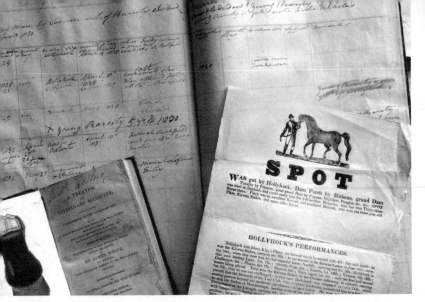

above) Memories of a sporting life. Sir Nicholas Loftus's Stud Book, together with a Treatise on Veterinary Medicine and handbill advertising 'Spot', one of the most successful offspring of the great 'Hollyhock'.

(*below*) Photographs of Mary Loftus and her husband Matthew Murphy *c.*1865.

(*above*) The last photograph of the Loftus siblings together, at Rackheath House in Norfolk, 1898. Jack, Nora, Frank, Pierse – with Belinda, their mother, seated on the sofa.

(*below*) Jack Loftus's family on Rosslare Strand, County Wexford, 1919. Pauline May (*née* Lichtenstadt) with her children Bettina, Patricia, Francis and Linda. Painting by Leo Whelan.

£17. Things were getting desperate, and a few weeks later Sir Edward had to send his daughter another £20 to meet her bills.[485]

The New Year started with a further loan of £30 to Bowen Cary and in March a letter arrived 'from Captain Cary – Consulting me on most material Business'. It was the first of a spate of messages as matters got worse. The crisis came suddenly and the account book records the story, with cryptic dismay. On the evening of 25 March 1812, 'Miss Maria Cary came to Mt Loftus' with the news that 'a most Extraordinary Occurrence happened, a Lady was arrested and carried to the Marchalsea [debtors prison] at Wexford on a Marked Writ for the sum of £126.' Sir Edward immediately got his eldest son to write out a draft for that amount payable on his Wexford bankers, Messrs Gleadowe & Company, 'for her enlargement, & I wrote to the Sheriff I would pay him the amount of an Execution laid on a Certain house.' Even in his private ledger he could hardly bear to acknowledge that the imprisoned 'Lady' was his daughter (Miss Maria's mother) and 'a Certain house' was her home at Munfin, now under threat of sequestration to settle her debts. The matter was urgent, both to relieve his daughter's distress and to put things right before any hint of this family shame could spread through the county. So Sir Edward 'sent off Tom Nowlan & James Maher at Eleven o'clock on the night – the former to take care of the Goods, the latter with the money to Wexford.' He also gave Maher a £1 note 'to pay for a Carriage from Wexford to Munfin,' to take his daughter home, and 'sent the Lady three, three-guinea Notes' for her immediate needs. On the next line of his accounts, seemingly without pause for thought, Sir Edward noted that he 'paid John Flin for 29 stone and half of Potatoes at 5d. [per stone].'

On 15 April Sir Edward 'went to Ross, saw Mrs Cary who satisfied me that what happened was through Error.' Whatever the truth of the matter, she seems to have managed to live within her means thenceforward, for no further crises are recorded in her father's accounts. Life at Mount Loftus resumed its tranquil pace, as far as the family was concerned.

In the wider world, however, this privileged life was the exception to a pattern of habitual lawlessness, interrupted by sudden dramas. Forgery, for example, was frequent – the accounts are full of references to dud or suspect banknotes – and postal theft was equally prevalent, to counter which Sir Edward sent banknotes cut in two, with the corresponding halves by a later post. Numerous petty offences related to the various regiments that were stationed in the locality, and their horde of camp followers. On 2 October 1809, for example, 'the Police Officers apprehended Peter Ennis, a Deserter from the Wexford Regiment' and sent him to Kilkenny, but Ennis claimed that he actually belonged to the 63rd Regiment, so Sir Edward 'wrote this date to Lt Col Pigott' to try to sort the matter out. On 5 Jan 1810, having discovered that he had authorised payments to support non-existent regimental children, Sir Edward wrote in haste to the local collector 'not to pay (having my signature) any of the Certificates of certain Soldiers wives of the Kilkenny Regiment being imposed on by them, they not having children.'

A few days later there was news of a 'most daring outrage . . . committed as supposed by the Graigue Boatmen'. A report in the *Dublin Journal* described how 'armed villains' went at night to the houses of three of Sir Edward's tenants. 'After breaking open the stable doors of William Henesey and P. Flynn, they brought out their horses and shot them dead. A shot was also fired at James Henesey's horse, which wounded it in the neck.' Various local grandees called on Sir Edward to discuss the case, including his neighbour Colonel Gore – who came twice in two days – General Wymard, Colonel Buller, Colonel Pack and the Dean of Ossary. The Barrow Navigation Company offered a reward of £100 and Sir Edward himself offered £50, 'for the discovery of such person or persons as were concerned in the Outrage'. But 'the cause this brutal and wanton act has not been ascertained' and nothing, it seems, came to light.

Another echo of old troubles – abduction clubs and the like – was heard when a local priest provided a certificate of marriage for Pierce Ryan and Mary Duggan, so that Sir Edward could issue an order 'to Liberate Pierce Ryan who stood committed for an assault' on poor Mary.[486] The account book records the bare bones of a story that must have been fraught with emotional drama – an abduction or rape, followed by a marriage that legitimised the assault.

In the background, never entirely forgotten, were the memories of '98. Habitual suspicion of strangers could, in such a context, prompt wild fears of sectarian plotting, on the slightest evidence. On 31 August

1811, for example, Sir Edward noted the seemingly ominous news that he heard 'from James Saunders of Killedmond permanent Sergeant' who told how 'Robert Lecky a Private in the Corps' went into Edward Byrne's shop in the nearby village of Borris, where he saw 'two strange Men, the one reported to have come from Dublin the other from some other part of Connaught'. Lecky heard 'one of the Strangers accost the other & said is it not time to go to Business.' He evidently suspected that mischief was afoot – the more so when he learnt that the 'strangers put up their Horses at Father Walshes who is Priest of Borris' – but there the story ends, unresolved.

And then there was the shooting of 'Young Muldowney of Mounteen More' in January 1812, when four nervous police officers went to execute a search warrant, 'which being Resisted was the cause of what happened.' Another victim of fear and stupidity.

Things continued in much the same way, as Sir Edward grew older. He still kept track of household expenditure and domestic news – there are records in his hand until a month before his death – but the management of the estate had been handed over to his eldest son, Nicholas, whose entries in the 'New Account Book' are much scruffier than his father's.

On 8 May 1818 Nicholas noted payments of £30 for a Gold Watch for his niece, Mary Loftus, and £11 4s. 6d. for a sudden profusion of mourning clothes. '21 pair of Stockens for Sr Edwd, 5 pair of Silk Stockens, 24 yards of Black Ribbon, one pair of Stays for Miss Loftus'; various articles for Lady Loftus, including three pairs of expensive silk stockings, three yards of lace, two of 'Black French Lace', ten yards of swan's-down and a black silk handkerchief, plus another '36 yards of Ribbon and 8 of Broad ditto'. Stockings for Sir Edward – but these were for others to wear, at his funeral; new stockings for the servants, silk stockings for the gentry, black ribbons to tie around arms or hats, black lace and a black silk handkerchief for Lady Loftus. The old man was close to death.

Those entries are almost the last, but the reckoning concludes with the payment of three brief bills – 'Eggs, 4d.; pd Miss Stephens, all clear 1s. 3d.; Eggs, 4d.'. Nothing more. Sir Edward Loftus died at the age of eighty-five on 18 May 1818. His wife survived him by three months, then she too was gone.[487]

CHAPTER 38

A Sporting Life

One of my childhood pleasures when visiting Mount Loftus was bellowing nonsense through a brass loudhailer that had once belonged to Colonel Nicholas, eldest son of Sir Edward. He used it to shout instructions to Joe Byrne and the stable lads as they exercised his horses, testing their pace as they raced around the park.

Nicholas loved racing, as he loved the chase in all its forms. He went shooting for wildfowl on the marshlands at Richfield, hunted his own pack of hounds across the hills of Kilkenny and followed the lures of passion through all the surrounding counties, and in Dublin, and on regimental postings in England. His only surviving bill of a personal kind is one for 1792 from Anne Smyth, Woollen-Draper of Dublin, which includes all manner of fashionable stuffs – *white galloon, orange & pink Striped Satin* – but the main expense was for the *black dutch Velvet, Sup^r double mill'd blue cloth, Sup^r buff cassimere* [cashmere] and *Bishops Court Hunt buttons* that denoted his membership of the smartest sporting set in Ireland, which met to hunt the fox at the seat of his cousins, the Ponsonby family in County Kildare, a few miles from the Curragh racecourse.

Two years later Nicholas was appointed captain in the newly formed Kilkenny Militia and made Deputy Governor of County Kilkenny – a position that demanded little in the way of formal obligations but was a mark of social standing. His military duties kept him busy for the next few years, but after the Act of Union at the turn of the century and his promotion to major in 1801, Nicholas had plenty of time for other pursuits. He served as Sheriff of County Kilkenny in 1801 and of County Wexford in 1805, but these were largely ceremonial roles and he was often to be found at Mount Loftus, or dining with friends at his club in Kilkenny, or off to the Curragh for the races. And it was around this time, probably in 1808, that Nicholas decided to train his own horses – so he laid out a racetrack in the park.

Early the following year, on 24 January, James Crealy 'took the length of the ground' while J Maher 'held the chains'. With the help of 'Walsh the groom' they concluded that one circuit came to 187 perch, which meant that three times round the track was just over a mile and three quarters. I love those ancient measures. A perch, pole or rod was the width of one of the furrow-long (furlong) strips of land in the open fields of medieval agriculture. Four perches to a cricket pitch, which is the length of 'Gunter's Chain', named after the mathematician Edmund Gunter, who published his description of it in 1624: 'We may measure the length and breadth by chains, each chain being four perches in length, and divided into 100 links.' For nearly three hundred years this was the essential instrument of English surveyors, lugged by bearers over deserts and mountain ranges, as they tramped their way across countries and continents, mapping the Empire at eighty chains to the mile. And how many chains to a furlong, I hear you ask? Ten, because even Mr Gunter was tempted by decimals.

Furlongs were the measure of the racetrack, as guineas were its currency. Its bible was the *General Stud Book*, recording equine genealogies stretching back to the 'foundation sires' of the late seventeenth century, and its social diary was the *Racing Calendar*, published annually, which traced the evolution of the sport from the early days of two-horse challenges to regular races, with cups and prizes and professional jockeys clad in their owners' colours. There could be no mistaking when Colonel Loftus had a horse in the running because he laid claim to the stark simplicity of white jacket and black cap, the colours of his coat of arms. These were the colours that flashed past the winning post again and again, as a horse called Hollyhock took Ireland by storm.

The story of this famous racehorse begins when Nicholas returned from a day's hunting and was accosted at the front gate of Mount Loftus by a hawker of holly sticks which he was selling for whip handles, who wanted 'his honour' to buy one. Nick bought a stick but was more interested in the bay horse pulling the man's cart, which the hawker agreed to sell to him for £5. For a year or two Nicholas rode 'Hollyhawk' as his regimental charger, and occasionally out hunting, but soon became convinced that he was capable of greater triumphs and put him in training as a racehorse. He won every race in the Irish calendar and a famous ballad, 'The Memory of the Splendid Hollyhawk', was composed when he died.

But memory is a tricky thing – for a name that seems to confirm the legend of a fine young horse bought from the shafts of a hawker's cart was spelt rather differently when it appeared in print, as 'Hollyhock'. And the horse acquired an impressive lineage, which was published in the *General Stud Book*: 'foaled in 1804, got by Master Bagot, his dam by North Star', with forebears that included Dorimant, Trunnion and Ripton's Sharper, all famous horses. So I checked the registry of thoroughbreds and discovered a comprehensive pedigree, stretching back to that renowned stallion, the Godolphin Arab.[488]

Such breeding matches the elegant, silver-mounted hoof, which is all that survives of this fabled steed. It is small, wonderfully neat, shod in a fine racing shoe – everything about it suggests a high-strung, elegant thoroughbred, dancing across the turf. But there were unexplained gaps in his pedigree and for the first few years of his life, Hollyhock was hidden from view – his earliest appearance on the racetrack was as an unknown four-year-old, winning sixty guineas in a sweepstakes on the Great Heath in Queen's County, in October 1808. He came from nowhere. So perhaps the legend was true – that a strong but unruly colt was given by his breeder to a hawker, from whom Nicholas Loftus acquired him, trained him and made him famous.

That fame can be traced in successive editions of the *Racing Calendar* and in a clipping from the *Kilkenny Moderator*, which I found tucked inside Hollyhock's silver-mounted hoof.[489] It is a record of his performances, 'during a very active and triumphant career' – winning fifteen King's Plates, 'for three of which he carried 12 stone 4lb, four mile heats'; the Kirwan Stakes, handicapped with two stone more than his nearest rival; two plates at Tullow, the Stakes at Maryborough, numerous sweepstakes; the Lemonfield Stakes, 'and a Plate there also'; the Challenge of the Kirwan Stakes, three times; and various two-horse challenge matches. The report also mentions that Nicholas Loftus withdrew Hollyhock from running in another Kirwan Stakes because he was handicapped to carry three and a half stone more than the eventual winner – 'which proved that the Stewards of the Turf Club considered him as a horse possessing powers beyond any moderate calculation.' And indeed they were right, for Hollyhock combined speed with astonishing stamina, which left his rivals gasping. On one remarkable afternoon, for example, he began by winning the Great

Ulster Stakes before beating Young Swindler in a challenge match for three hundred guineas – and then 'an hour after Hollyhock came out and won the Richmond Hundred – 20 to 1 against him.'

Thus it continued, for race after race. In 1810 Nicholas Loftus was promoted to lieutenant colonel when his regiment moved to Dublin – conveniently close to the Curragh. This was the year that Hollyhock first won more than a thouand guineas in prize money, plus whatever bets the Colonel laid on his prodigy. That wonderful form continued the following season, but persistent heavy handicapping eventually began to tell, as younger horses such as Pope and Waxy tested his supremacy. Hollyhock's winnings fell to around four hundred guineas in 1812, although he walked over the course in June to take the Marquis of Sligo's Gold Whip, without a challenger.

For most of that year he was described in the *Racing Calendar* as 'Mr Bruen's Hollyhock', for Nicholas Loftus appears to have sold him to a friend and neighbour, John Bruen of County Carlow. But this may have been some form of hidden partnership, rather than a true sale; for the horse was described in the *Racing Calendar* as 'Col Loftus's Hollyhock' on at least one occasion during the time he was owned by Bruen. A similar arrangement had occurred two years earlier – when 'Mr Wakefield's Hollyhock' won the Kirwan Stakes, but reappeared under Loftus colours two days later, to win the Challenge for the Kirwan. Such manoeuvres – apparently typical of other racing stables at this time – had more to do with the niceties of betting arrangements and Jockey Club rules than real transactions.

In 1813 Colonel Loftus was posted to England with his regiment, supposedly as a punishment on his fellow officers for engaging in too many liaisons with the ladies of the Viceregal Court. Any hopes that banishment might curb their riotous behaviour were soon abandoned, as the regiment cut a zigzag swathe of havoc from Manchester to Harwich to Portsmouth, and paused at Brentford to entertain their Honorary Colonel, Lord Ormonde, who was staying nearby.

They drank all the port and broke all the glasses and finished up by drinking all the claret in the town out of soup plates with spoons. Next day they had to cross a river. The revels were kept up till 4 am. They marched at 5. When they came to the river the officers marched through it and their men went over the bridge. The officers said it cooled their blood.[490]

Despite such excesses, the colonel's time in England was not entirely wasted, for Hollyhock went too, with the hope of repeating his Irish triumphs on English turf. Mr Bruen was so optimistic of his prospects that he arranged a challenge match for two thousand guineas against Mr Payne's 'Crispin', at the second spring meeting at Newmarket. It was a bold move, so 'Colonel Bruen, being anxious to ascertain what his chances of winning that race might be, hired Rival as a trial horse'. Hollyhock 'very cleverly' beat Rival in two successive trials, 'giving great odds of weight', which encouraged Bruen's friends, led by Colonel Nicholas, to place substantial wagers on the forthcoming match. Then, just as everything seemed to be going to plan, Hollyhock went lame, 'which ended his running'. It also meant that Bruen's friends were facing an expensive disaster, for the bets were 'pay or play' – their stakes were forfeit if Hollyhock failed to show. Desperate for a solution, Bruen remembered an obscure Jockey Club rule. 'All bets depending between any two horses either in Match or Sweepstakes, are null and void if those horses become the property of one and the same person, or his avowed confederate, subsequent to the bets being made.' He purchased Crispin and called off the match.[491]

Hollyhock's career as a racehorse was at an end, and he returned to Mount Loftus. His future, it seemed clear, was as a stallion, so Nicholas developed his growing expertise as a trainer into a serious study of thoroughbred breeding. His copy of the *General Stud Book* is inscribed 'Lieut. Colonel Loftus, Gosport 1814'.

While stationed at Gosport, the Kilkenny Militia took part in a Review of the Fleet by the allied sovereigns of Britain, Russia and Prussia, to celebrate the Treaty of Paris, which briefly brought an end to the Napoleonic Wars. Their band so pleased the Duke of York that he gave them a prominent role in the celebrations, while General Picton tried to persuade them to become a regular battalion and sail across the Channel to help keep the peace in Europe. The Militia decided not to risk their lives for England's glory – 400 were needed, but only 380 volunteered – and instead returned to Ireland. After postings in Cork and County Clare, Colonel Loftus marched the regiment home to

Kilkenny in 1816, to be disbanded. He and Colonel Wemyss were carried shoulder-high in chairs around the old city, as their men made mayhem for one last time.

A few silver forks, stamped with the regimental badge, found their way into Colonel Loftus's baggage as he returned from Kilkenny to Mount Loftus. But Nicholas came home with a more substantial prize: a mistress. The pursuit of pleasure – *two or three handfuls of light hearted flowers in their full bloom and a great Deal of the balsam of who cares* – had shaped his life for so long that it seems inevitable that his last great passion began as a reckless whim, a flash of desire. The wonder is that it lasted, changed, and somehow became a mercurial form of love.

'He was walking in the Barrack at Kilkenny when he saw one of his sergeants, Sergeant Meany by name, beating and abusing his wife.' Thus the story begins, in the words of my great-uncle Jack. I was brought up on endless versions of it, repeating a litany of memories from the distant past. The woman was beautiful – of course – and Nicholas reacted in a way that now seems shocking but appears to have satisfied all concerned. He made the sergeant an offer and purchased his wife on the spot.

Mrs Meany was installed in lodgings in Kilkenny, and then – after Nicholas inherited Mount Loftus following the death of his aged parents – she moved into Whalebone Hall, which he built for her accommodation a couple of hundred yards from the main house, with a stable for a favourite racehorse. It was said that Nicholas 'was never so happy as lying in the arms of his mistress above, hearing the neighing of the horse below.'

I clambered through the dilapidated granite shell of Whalebone Hall and gazed from the bedroom window across vast distances of the rich Kilkenny countryside, but I was never quite convinced by the stories of Mrs Meany. Then I came across a bill from the local handyman James Carroll to Sir Nicholas Loftus, dated 10 Jan 1822. It was an account for work done over the previous couple of years – repairs to the house and stables, painting, decorating and the like. On 16 March 1820 Carrol had replaced '2 Sqr of Glass in the parlour of Mrs Meany,' and charged two shillings and four pence for his work. On 22 August there was another pane of glass to replace, and again on 3 October, and then again in the following January. For the next ten months there was peace, before another pane was broken on Midwinter's Day, 21 December 1821.[492]

The bill suggests that Mrs Meany was a high-spirited woman, given to hurling things at her protector; how else to account for so much broken glass? But it also implies a more complex story and I began to suspect that the oral tradition might have been true in other respects, and that 'lying in the arms of his mistress above, hearing the neighing of the horse below,' Nicholas was indeed happy, and so was she – for a broken window may be a token of passion, not the sign of a broken heart.

It was the last straw for his sister Elizabeth, who decamped with their niece Mary and took a house on the Parade in Kilkenny, leaving Nicholas and Francis to a life of ceremonious carousing. Each evening, when they sat down to dinner together after a hard day's hunting or racing, Francis would raise his glass to Sir Nicholas; 'Brother, I wish to drink a glass of wine with you.' To which Nicholas would reply, with equal formality, before they opened another bottle.

Nicholas built up one of the best racing stables in Ireland while Francis bred a famous strain of red and white Irish setters.[493] They both loved hunting – hurtling over the green hills with a madcap assortment of like-minded friends. Some of these would stay the night, to save a long ride in the morning before the hunt began, and there was a regular routine for such visitors. An enormous breakfast, one of those classic Irish breakfasts, was followed by a visit to 'the Captain's setters' in the Haggard, then to the stables – filled with lovely horses – then a walk to inspect the harriers in their kennels in the park before returning to the house for a second 'hunt breakfast', washed down with brandy and liqueurs. Eventually the hounds were brought out and there was a fast, hard run, leaping over stone walls with a courage that was borne aloft on fumes of alcohol.

Sometimes they came to grief. A story is told of how Sir Nicholas was thrown and broke his arm when negotiating 'an ugly stone gap'. It was his own fault – he was riding with 'too severe a bridle' and had checked his horse as it rose to take the jump – but his friends assumed otherwise. They helped to get him mounted, in order to reach a surgeon, but advised him never again to ride this horse. 'At which Sir Nicholas coolly turned into the field by another gap, one-armed as he was and of course suffering much pain – and calmly remarking that he could not allow his awkwardness to bring blame upon an animal he so loved, and saying "Now, sir, do it your own way," the horse sailed most beautifully and safely over the very spot that had caused the accident.' [494]

Such a helter-skelter life was not conducive to careful record keeping and Sir Nicholas, in any case, cared little for such things. But his ambition to become a successful breeder as well as a trainer of race-horses required close study of equine genealogy; memory alone was not enough. So Richard Tattersall, head of the eponymous bloodstock auctioneers, presented him with a handsomely bound volume of neatly ruled blank pages, labelled *Sir Nicholas Loftus, Stud Book*.[495] It was an optimistic gift. Nicholas filled it in with some diligence at first but soon more scrappily, preferring – it seems – to keep most things in his head. He was certainly not prepared to confide to the written page the prices achieved for the progeny of his breeding – that column remained blank, much to my frustration. But he advertised his 'Sires to Stand at Mount Loftus this Season' with unmistakeable pride. Hollyhock's son Spot – whose 'beauty and gigantic powers are too well known to require any description' – and Prince, who was based at Richfield, commanded stud fees of five guineas each but Hollyhock himself still led the field: 'All Mares – Ten Sovereigns.' A locally printed poster for Spot included a summary of 'Hollyhock's Performances' to emphasise the stamina that was bred into his progeny, together with a genealogy of Spot's maternal lineage. This may have reassured those hoping to breed from him but reads to me like a crazy litany out of James Joyce – 'Dam Patch by Rubens, grand Dam Timidity by Potatoes, great grand Dam by Pegasus, Highflyer, Panglos.' [496]

More valuable than their stud fees were the colts and filly foals that sprang from such stallions, including the wonderfully successful Hesperus – winner of thirty-three races in England – and the neatly named Mount Loftus, a regular winner in Ireland and a racing advertisement for Sir Nicholas's stud.[497] These were the 'beautiful cattle' celebrated in Hollyhock's ballad, according to which the 'Lord Lieutenant and Many Great Nobles' came 'in Great Stile' to Mount Loftus and smiled with pleasure as they paid a fortune for the great horse's offspring. 'Should it cost us some thousands of Guineas, Here we'll buy a Young Hollyhawk.' [498]

All of those thousands of guineas were swallowed by Nick's extravagance. He lived in the style of an eighteenth-century patriarch, hospitable, generous, careless of the future. His neighbours despaired of the 'vast sums' that he spent on his horses, of which 'he seldom had fewer than one hundred in his stables,' and vowed that he never made money out of racing, 'probably because he was a truly honourable man'. But you are left with a sense of admiring wonder. 'When he hunted he had generally half a dozen or more mounted grooms in attendance, and made a very sporting appearance on *field* days among the members of the Kilkenny hunt. He had usually a good number of cows, but his grooms, his stable boys, and stable cats lapped up all the milk, without even allowing time for its *butyraceaus* qualities to develop themselves; in plain words, he had often occasion, we believe, to purchase butter for his own toast.'[500]

That mythical sense of a figure from the past pervades all such accounts from those final years. Here, for example, is the recollection of a stranger who found himself at Mount Loftus for one of those famous hunt breakfasts, and was persuaded to view the his host's horses, before the chase began.

> To such a man, and for such a breakfast, courtesy was due, and accordingly when we mounted, we dwelt a little, to see some young ones Sir Nicholas had in training so lightly tread the turf.
>
> 'Byrne,' said Sir Nicholas, 'I wish you would throw your leg across that little animal, and take him over some of those fences, it would gratify me very much indeed.' And now Jo Byrne to gratify him, did do the thing as few could do it – vaulting like a bit of gossamer upon the little racing saddle, he seemed to grow a part of the quadruped, he floated on as it were, all round about us, and sailed over sundry fences without a stirrup, to Sir Nicholas's great delight, and to all our admiration.[501]

That was in the early spring of 1829, a year of wonders and omens.

April saw the end of the Penal Laws, as Daniel O'Connell's great campaign for Catholic Emancipation achieved its long-sought goal. The Act was a compromise: Catholics could serve as MPs and hold public offices, but the property qualification for voters was raised from forty shillings to ten pounds, which drastically reduced the Catholic voting roll. For the time being, at least, Protestants felt secure in their Ascendancy. But this was the breath of change.

June was notable for a freak of nature, which reads like a fable of the times. 'A voluntary colony of silkworms' suddenly appeared at Mount Loftus, and settled on several spindle-trees. 'One tree was literally weighed down with them. And it is supposed there were not less than half a million worms actively spinning upon it.' The silkworms appeared to be in vigorous health and some reports claimed that excellent silk was produced, despite the absence of mulberry leaves. But it was feared they would soon expire, as probably they did.[502]

Then, at the end of November, Hollyhock died. He was buried close to the house, in a circle of five beech trees, and Sir Nicholas held a three-day wake in his honour – to which people came from miles around. Heroic quantities of booze were consumed by all and sundry, as toast after toast was drunk. Obituaries were published in the press and a ballad composed in his memory.[503] Its verses incorporate the essential elements of Irish myth – suffering Hibernia, a 'valiant hero' (Sir Nicholas), a legendary stallion ('The Splendid Hollyhawk') and woe to the English.

> When Guineas without intermission
> From out of their purses should walk
> They would turn home timorous to England
> Cursing Ireland and brave Hollyhawk
> But he disregarded their curses
> They were laughed by a man of great fame
> Who in Ireland always spends his fortune
> Sir Nicholas Loftus by name.

That legendary mourning was also, it seems to me, a wake for Georgian Ireland. The last, most wilful of the Georges died a few months later and was succeeded by his brother William, whose famously modest coronation seemed to catch a new mood, as demand for reform came to dominate every aspect of political life. Men like Sir Nicholas had shared with the old King a capacity to live their lives as if the eighteenth century would never end. Now, somewhat abruptly, they found them-selves facing a more challenging reality in which they seemed like fossils from another age. Confronted by the future, they lost their bearings. Some shut their eyes and clung to the prejudices of their class – but Nicholas had no time to turn away. Events came to meet him.

The issue was tithes. O'Connell's triumph in achieving Catholic emancipation made even more manifest this other injustice, whereby farmers of all persuasions, including Catholics and Dissenters, had to pay a levy to support the (Protestant) established church. Tithes could be socially divisive – they bore most heavily on smaller farmers and were levied in different ways from place to place – but a general sense of grievance, uniting landlord and tenant, had been rumbling away for years. Now the grumbles turned to war.

The Mount Loftus estate fell within the Catholic parish of Graiguena-managh, to which a new priest had been appointed in 1827. Martin Doyle was clever and strong-willed, and soon acquired a reputation for sharp practice in avoiding paying the tithe, despite being the tenant of some of the largest farms in the neighbourhood. Confronting him was the Protestant Rector, George Alcock, an old man, much respected, who now needed some assistance. Hence the arrival in 1829 of Rev. Luke MacDonnell, a 'hot headed and violent' zealot. The new curate soon complained that his salary went unpaid, because tithes went uncollected. There was good reason – the potato crop had failed that year, leaving many small farmers short of cash – but MacDonnell was unmoved by such excuses and decided to act as his own tithe agent, despite being legally debarred from doing so as a clergyman and magistrate. One of his first targets, inevitably, was the Catholic priest. This was the start of the 'Tithe War', which spread from Kilkenny to Carlow, and then to Wexford, Limerick and Tipperary, provoking the fiercest civil unrest since 1798.

As the dispute between the two men grew more polemical, Sir Nicholas tried to act as peacemaker. He invited Doyle to dine at Mount Loftus, on New Year's Day 1831, and offered to mediate between the rector and the parishioners. His proposal was accepted at a large anti-tithe meeting called by Doyle the following day, and for a while there was hope of a peaceful settlement.[504] But negotiations broke down, and the local magistrates – Sir Nicholas included – became increasingly alarmed as mass meetings across the county grew ever more violent. At the end of February they panicked and requisitioned a large force of constables, drawn from several counties, to enforce the law. A few days later, 120 armed police seized possession of cattle belonging to Martin Doyle, in lieu of the tithes that he still refused to pay.

Battle lines were drawn, and it was not long before the first deaths occurred, when police fired on a crowd resisting a similar seizure of cattle across the border in County Wexford. The year ended with the ambush of forty constables in Carrickshock, South Kilkenny. Thirteen of them were killed, including their captain.[505] And so it continued, as the tithe wars encouraged the violent expression of other, long-standing grievances. On 26 March 1832 it was reported that 'a messenger of Sir Nicholas Loftus was robbed, beaten, and left lying on the road by two men, on Tuesday, in the daylight.' The assault was blamed on the 'Whitefeet' – a secretive movement whose behaviour echoed the White-boys of fifty years earlier. [506]

It was at this sombre time, with a sense of his own mortality, that Sir Nicholas Loftus decided to set his tangled affairs in order. His original will has long disappeared and it was only by chance, in the London Library, that I came across a summary of it. And then I gasped – because I realised that the story of Mrs Meany had a sequel, erased from the family memory. Most of Nick's legacies were predictable enough – the bulk of the estate went to his surviving brother Francis – but there were other relatives for whom he wished to provide, and he made a few bequests from his own fortune. The recipients were John, Harriet, Charlotte and Susan, who had taken the name of Loftus 'at my desire,' being the children of Charlotte Meany, widow of Stephen Meany, late lieutenant in the 87th Foot.[507] The wording is careful – it identifies Mrs Meany as their mother but implies that her deceased husband was not the father. There can be little doubt of their true parentage.

Sir Nicholas died 'of a fever' on 16 August 1832, aged sixty-nine. Almost immediately the tidying up began. On 13 November his entire 'high bred and well-known Stud' was sold without reserve by Messrs Tattersall. All those lovely horses were dispersed and their stables stood empty. Even the record of that sale has disappeared, for the only surviving copy of the auction catalogue is nowhere to be found.[508] As for those children who sprang so unexpectedly to life in the book stacks of the London Library, they too vanished, after that tiny glimpse. And despite years of searching, I have found no further trace of them.

CHAPTER 39

Catholic Ascendancy

> I have heard old men talk about Sir Francis being wheeled out in
> his chair to sit in the sun on the gravel by the front door, & the old
> man calling to and feeding his peacocks.[509]

Life at Mount Loftus in the 1830s and '40s reminds me of a play by
Chekhov. Within the walled demesne, they lived out their roles against
the background of old family quarrels and a rapidly changing world.
Some were the agents of change, some the victims, but all of them had
personal preoccupations that eclipsed the wider social issues – and
running through each of their stories is the thread of endurance, a
quality that Chekhov loved.

Endurance woven with oddity. Sir Francis – a 'confirmed invalid' –
spent his days in bed, playing the violin. His spinster sister Elizabeth
planted silver coins in the garden, dreaming of the past. Their niece,
Mary, the Catholic daughter of an illegal marriage, was heiress to all
the family wealth. Her husband, Matthew Murphy, was the 'coming
man', whose ancestry was said by some to hide a scandal – but he liked
to plant trees, not chop them down. And we are conscious, as the
audience, that the Great Famine formed the next act.

After his brother's death, Sir Francis was determined to bring an
end to the years of racing extravagance. He continued to subscribe to
the Irish edition of the *Racing Calendar* but all the horses were sold and
even the landscape was changed.[510] 'He was not so selfish as to remove
and destroy the numerous walls that formed the paddocks his late
brother delighted in; but in order to make them harmonise with the
scenery, he planted them most successfully with ivy, both top and
bottom.'[511] But extravagance takes many forms and Sir Francis was not
immune to the old enticement – acquiring land. So when his neighbour
Lord Clifden offered to sell 'the lands of Barrowmount, Brook Hill
and Killeen with the Mansion House buildings and offices thereon,'
the temptation proved irresistible, even though it meant burdening the

estate with another big mortgage. Barrowmount adjoined Mount Loftus on its northern boundary – it rounded out the property very neatly – and rising agricultural prosperity made it look like a good investment.[512] And so, for a while, it was.

Sir Francis, in any case, was more concerned for the well being of his numerous dependents than extracting the maximum return from his estates. He gave 'daily employment to between eighty and a hundred individuals' and celebrated the completion of the hay harvest in the style of an eighteenth century patriarch. In July 1837, for example, more than a hundred and fifty of the poorer tenants and employees – men and women, mostly young – gathered for this 'annual entertainment' at long tables under a row of trees near the house, where refreshments were served. They were 'uniformly dressed at Sir Francis's expense – the men in new smock frocks, &c, and the women, with much taste and neatness, in green petticoats, short pink-striped wrappers, silk neckerchiefs and straw bonnets, and green ribbons.' Sir Francis rose from his sick bed to give a short speech of welcome, and then there was dancing. It reads like the memory of a dream.[513]

But the sharp realities of Irish politics were never far away, and Sir Francis's natural benevolence even stirred him to engage in local politics – as a somewhat unlikely radical. Prompted, I suspect, by his Catholic niece, he decided to take a lead on the issue of tithes, provoking raised eyebrows among his more conservative neighbours. In July 1838 *The Times* printed a report from its Dublin correspondent who referred with evident disdain to the 'multitudinous open-air meetings, called "great" by the Radical journals here', that were held throughout southern Ireland to protest against tithes. 'There is to be another "great" meeting on Sunday next, on the Hill of Coppena, in the parish of Graig, county of Kilkenny. Sir Francis Loftus, Bart., heads the requisition for this meeting.' You can sense the editor's disapproval.[513] Local opinion was very different. In autumn that year the strongly nationalist *Freeman's Journal* referred to 'that good man, and pattern for Irish resident gentry and landlords, Sir Francis Hamilton Loftus' – and announced a few months later that he had 'exonerated his tenants from paying the tithe charge.'[514]

But then, as if exhausted by too many big decisions, Sir Francis invited his sister and niece to keep house for him and increasingly retired to bed, where he spent long hours playing the fiddle, or reading. From time to time he would emerge to feed his peacocks, or to visit his Gothick privy in the garden, or to be driven round the estate as he gave orders for the planting of trees. 'But on some few occasions, when feeling stronger in health than usual, he broke from his self imposed seclusion.' And then, very occasionally, he might attend the meetings of the Gowran Farming Society – for his great interest, apart from music and the arts, was agricultural improvement. It seems like a deliberate turning away from all that he found confusing, as the last of a line of eighteenth-century rakes, marooned in the age of reform. But he lived for ever, like so many 'confirmed invalids', and he could talk for hours, to any who cared to listen – 'his mind stored with an intelligent study of the classics, and his memory teeming with reminiscences of eminent men and important events whose recollections now belong to history.'[515]

Memory, for his sister, was something to avoid – too much pain, long in the past. Elizabeth was in her seventies and had the determined dottiness of elderly spinster gardeners. She loved to be out-of-doors, in the 'new garden' that had been made for her above the house, in the time of Sir Edward – a large, gently sloping rectangle, sheltered by high stone walls, with rows of heated glasshouses where the tenderest plants could be grown. Elizabeth had to resort to various stratagems to encourage her gardener, Dennis Hickey, who seems to have preferred looking after his bees or pruning fruit trees to tending useless flowers. So she wrapped half crowns in twists of paper and buried them for him to find in flowerbeds that she considered well planted. And she taught gardening to her beloved niece, Mary, who laid out the 'Italian Garden' of formal parterre beds, hedged with box, complete with classical urns and statuary.

I remember as a child peering through an old iron gate into this half-wild paradise, overgrown but beautiful, a ghost of its former self. Marigolds and poppies sprang in tangled splendour within sprawling curlicues of box, and a few sweet grapes could sometimes be gleaned from the twisted branches of an ancient vine, in the ruins of a hothouse. There was a sweet, still, drowsy air – a sense that someone had gone for a nap long ago, and forgotten to return.

Mary had been nurtured in the company of good women – her mother Mary Carroll, her grandmother Margaret and her aunt Elizabeth – all of whom loved and cherished her. But her father had died when she was an infant, and Mary grew up uncertain of her place in the world – was she the illegitimate daughter of a Catholic girl from the village or the recognised heir to an old Ascendancy family? That uncertainty was compounded by attempts to make her conform to her Protestant heritage. Her great-uncle, Colonel Nicholas, had no heirs – so offered to settle £10,000 on Mary and have her educated abroad, but her mother would not hear of it unless she was brought up as a Catholic. Another attempt was made about the time that Mary came of age, when she was taken by her grandmother to live at Mount Loftus, in the hope that she would be assimilated into Protestant ways. But their relationship was never easy – Lady Loftus had always refused to recognise her son's marriage – and things grew much more difficult when Mary decided to marry Matthew Murphy.

Matthew was a tall, good-looking, serious and capable man, extremely well educated – one of his grandsons remembered that his letters were written in a beautiful, regular script and phrased in fine eighteenth-century style. His family lived at Pollagh House, half a mile from the back avenue to Mount Loftus, and was solidly prosperous. Theirs was the largest farmhouse on the estate – grand enough to have its own ballroom – and the Murphys were the most favoured tenants, as they had been for at least three generations. There is even a suggestion that they were illegitimately descended from old Lord Loftus; they shared that prominent nose. But none of this counted in Matthew's favour, for of course he was Catholic Irish. Despite the fact that both her husband and her granddaughter were the children of Catholic mothers, Sir Edward's wife was implacably opposed to what she considered a socially inferior match. In the face of such bad feeling Mary had to wait, and was only married after Lady Loftus was dead.

The wedding was finally celebrated in 1819, when Mary was twenty-eight and Matthew a couple of years older. By then much had changed. Unlike his mother, Sir Nicholas Loftus seems to have had few social prejudices, and unlike his father had no aptitude for estate manage-ment – so Matthew Murphy was employed as agent for both estates (Mount Loftus and Richfield) as well as looking after his own tenanted farm. This arrangement continued when Sir Francis succeeded his brother, except that by this time Mary Murphy was acknowledged as heiress to the family fortune, and she moved into Mount Loftus, together with her husband and their young family – three boys and two girls, the eldest being ten.

This oddly assorted household was strangely harmonious. Only one issue troubled relations between uncle and niece – that Mary refused to take the name of Loftus. She got out of it by saying that her eldest son could do so when he married, though she knew full well that the continuity of the family name had been linked to the inheritance of the family lands for generations past. It was written into the will of old Lord Loftus – for whom it far outweighed traditional considerations of legitimacy or posterity in the male line – and was something of a fixation for Sir Francis. He seems hardly to have cared that his heir was a woman and a Catholic, but he longed for Mary to call herself Loftus.

In every other respect, life at Mount Loftus continued much as it had in the previous century; the army of retainers, the hunters and the hounds. There may have been a new sobriety – I have a sense of everything being coated in brown varnish and plushly upholstered – but the young Murphy boys chased across the surrounding hills as their Protestant forebears had done, or went shooting on the marshes at Richfield, or fished in the River Barrow, while the house echoed to the sound of the violin, for hours at a stretch. He must sometimes have driven the rest of them mad, but Sir Francis was also a man of old-fashioned courtesy and benevolence who enjoyed spending time with the children, particularly the eldest son, John Murphy, whom he encouraged to read every book in the library and talked to for hours, on all manner of subjects. Occasionally Sir Francis would feel well enough to be driven around the estate with Matthew Murphy, discussing their shared passion for planting trees. Matthew was an upright man – he made sure that the rents were paid, but did so with decency – and his wife was a good and determined woman, whose care for the tenants reflected her own upbringing. She was loved and respected in the locality. All in all it seems to have been a peaceful life.

But outside the gates of Mount Loftus, Ireland was in turmoil. Daniel O'Connell with his 'voice of thunder' called a series of 'monster meetings' to demonstrate for repeal of the Union, and the radical nationalists of 'Young Ireland' (more revolutionary if less sectarian in their appeal) recalled the hopes and fears of '98. Arguments over the provision of university education and the use of physical force to obtain political ends reached across the social classes. Change felt inevitable. But all this arguing and shouting and plotting gradually petered away, and came to seem irrelevant, swamped by calamity. The summer of 1845 saw the arrival of the potato blight.

This new, more virulent form of blight rotted both stored potatoes and those in the ground, particularly the Irish 'Lumper', which formed the mainstay of people's diet in many regions. Kilkenny was less badly affected than the poor and crowded western counties – partly because there was greater agricultural diversity, including a wider variety of potatoes, and partly because it was simply more prosperous – but even here the effects were severe.

In 1846 the blight returned and the death toll sharply increased. The following summer brought a brief reprieve – a small crop but little blight – but in 1848 the pathogen once again devastated the crop and its effects continued well into the following year and to a lesser extent thereafter. These were the years of the Great Famine. Tens of thousands were forced into the Poor Law Unions (the dreaded workhouses) or were dependent for survival on some form of 'outdoor relief', including soup kitchens provided by public-spirited landlords. Up to fifteen thousand died of hunger and its related diseases. About a fifth of the population emigrated. Those were just the figures for County Kilkenny – in Ireland as a whole the death toll has been calculated at over a million.

The horrors of the Great Famine have been so well documented, so much argued about, that I shall not attempt to add any more to the story – and indeed, none of the family papers survive from this dreadful epoch. All that remains is the persistent memory of Mary Murphy's goodness and a vast iron 'famine pot', in which a thick soup was brewed up every day and dispensed to those in need. Mary's grandson, my great-uncle, wrote that she 'won the love and admiration of the whole countryside for her practical help and benevolence. Many a family in the district owes its survival to her generosity.' I think it was literally true, and his claim was echoed in her obituary, twenty years after the Famine had eased. 'Her whole life was spent in doing good; and her loss will be long and deeply felt by the poor of the neighbourhood, to whom she was an unsparing benefactress.' [516]

The aftermath of the Famine was a time of shock, in a land that was emptier and sadder year by year. In general, the larger landowners were worse off, as rents stagnated and rates rose. Many went bankrupt, while their more successful tenants grew prosperous as they consolidated their landholdings and switched from tillage to grazing. Those at the bottom of the scale, the smallest farmers and landless labourers, were the victims. Unable to feed themselves or evicted from their tiny land-holdings after failing to pay the rent, they fled for what they hoped was a better life, on the coffin ships to America. In 1837 there were 1718 inhabitants of Powerstown. By 1871 the church was roofless and many of the cabins unoccupied. Now, when you ask directions to the place, even from locals, most will shake their heads in perplexity.

The last decades of Sir Francis Loftus's life were years of disillusion-ment, political exhaustion, falling land values. O'Connell was dead, the 'Cabbage Patch Revolution' of 1848 had come to nothing. Ireland seemed peripheral, embittered, irrelevant. But particular, individual, local experience could often be very different, and the way these things were remembered suggests a more varied picture.

I have been looking at the old 'cartes de visite' for Sir Francis Loftus and his niece Mary, which were taken in the earliest years of commercial portrait photography. There is a sense of jumping from a timeless past into the modern age, even though these faded images, pasted onto small cards, have the stilted formality of Victorian prayer books. The likeness of Sir Francis may have been taken to mark his eightieth birthday, in 1857. It shows an old-fashioned man with long grey hair, frail and thin, wrapped in a thick coat and sitting in an upholstered leather chair. He has an elongated nose, steeply angled eyebrows, and a wide, mobile mouth that seems interrupted in the midst of an anecdote, uttered in the strangely accented language of former times, marked by the Irish brogue. The earliest picture of Mary was probably taken at about the same time, sitting in the same chair, when she was in her sixties. She stares steadily out at us, square-jawed and dark-haired (it may have been dyed), with a clear, capable look that has seen much. She knows her own mind. Other, later images show an older woman, fast becoming an archetype, like Queen Victoria. But most of all I am reminded that Mary Murphy was the spitting image of her grandfather, the Extinguisher – his beaked nose, strong chin and determined mouth. Replace her lace bonnet with an eighteenth-century wig and the likeness is almost shocking.

Sir Francis died at the age of eighty-seven, on 12 March 1864 – and his passing was marked with the style and drama of the previous century.[517] The funeral itself conformed to the classic pattern – all the servants and tenants wearing linen scarves of mourning, all the local gentry sending their carriages (and some of them present in person), fulsome epitaphs in the newspapers, interment in the family vault, and a disgruntled relative who pulled off his crepe band, threw it in the field and raced off home when he learnt that he was not the heir. This was the Reverend Cary (great-grandson of Sir Edward Loftus), whose Protestant fury at being disinherited by a woman named Murphy caused him to launch a chancery suit to set aside Sir Francis's will, on the grounds that Mary was illegitimate – since her mother was a Catholic, whose clandestine marriage to a Protestant was illegal under the old Penal Code.

But this eighteenth-century melodrama was resolved in the very different context of Victorian Ireland, and the outcome of the court case had none of the old, colonial, sectarian, sexist inevitability. On the contrary, after long arguments on either side it was determined in Mary's favour. She returned by train from Dublin – another sign of the times – and arrived at Goresbridge station, where her carriage was waiting to take her to Mount Loftus. But a great crowd of people was there to greet her, and they took her horses from the carriage and dragged it all the way home, two and a half miles, as she sat inside, weeping from emotion. And at night, it is said, all the surrounding hills were ablaze with fires to celebrate her victory.

That celebration, it seems to me, was a strange combination of the old, subservient, estate traditions and a new, radical sense that power had passed, that a woman, a Catholic, a shopkeeper's daughter, one of their own, had slain the dragon of Protestant Ascendancy. Hibernia had triumphed. But sometimes I feel that Mary's alarming likeness to her autocratic ancestors was more than skin deep; that the privileged Ascendancy ways were bred in the bone, inescapable – and the great divide, between the few who owned land and the mass that did not, was unbridgeable.

This, in any case, was the increasingly bitter theme of Irish politics in the second half of the nineteenth century. More and more it became a battleground, as traditional Anglo-Irish notions of the sacred nature of landed property were coloured by the grim reality of the Famine and its aftermath, the failure of an agricultural country to feed its people, the use of evictions to clear the land of the weakest, the hated middlemen, the absentee landlords.

Mrs Murphy – despite her name, her faith and her sex – was a member of the landed gentry, the Ascendancy, with the habits and the instincts of her class and some of its alarming fecklessness. She followed her uncle's example in deciding to buy more land and borrowed £10,000 to do so, but her choice was poor and it proved a bad investment.[518] Then she burdened the estate with charges to provide an income for her unmarried children – three great bearded men with nothing much to do, and their spinster sister – and she borrowed another £4,000 to enable her husband to buy a large house outside Dublin. By the time of her death, the annual interest on all those charges came to £3,500, accounting for more than half the total rent roll from all the lands in Kilkenny and Wexford. And Mary could be equally spendthrift of local goodwill. At the urging of one of her neighbours, the Hon Algernon Morton – a name Wodehouse might have relished – she went to court to defend her exclusive right to salmon fishing in the River Barrow, against those who claimed that it was a 'King's river', open to all. She won her case, but forfeited much sympathy.[519]

That strong-willed character, combined with the look of her fore-bears, made Mrs Murphy somewhat daunting as she grew older – but when she died in 1869, in her seventy-eighth year, they forgot her sternness, remembered her charity and came from miles to mourn her. As with her uncle's funeral, it was a classic Irish occasion. Employees and tenants 'wearing scarves and hat bands' staggered under the weight of her 'suite of coffins', as they bore her to the family vault in Powers-town churchyard. Her grand Protestant neighbours walked in the cortège, with their carriages following behind, alongside her bank manager, doctors, parsons and priests and assorted relatives, and many more who had come out of respect, affection or the hope of a party. Among them – walking to attend High Mass in a Catholic church, to mourn the woman who had disinherited him – was Mary's Protestant cousin, the Rev. Cary, reconciled at last to a world that had changed.[520]

CHAPTER 40

The Last Yellow Landau

In 1868, the year before his mother's death, John Murphy finally decided to marry, and chose as his bride a beautiful and spirited girl half his age. Or perhaps he was chosen, for Belinda Creagh was one of the 'crazy Creaghs of County Clare', whom nothing seemed to daunt. He was forty-six, she was twenty-three. He may have longed for this moment, after years of inertia and respectability – dominated by an old invalid and a stern matriarch – but I doubt he was prepared for the sudden change of pace.[521]

Belinda was a dashing and lively woman – no more than five feet high, but brought up with a rigorous routine of backboards and walking around with heavy books balanced on her head so that she had a beautiful deportment that made her seem taller, and always graceful. My grandfather remembered her 'faint delicious brogue' and her 'zest for life and energy and kindliness and charm'. Even in old age she had a sense of style, and one of my favourite images of her is provoked by the brief but wonderfully evocative summary in her last passport, issued when she was seventy, in 1921. The photograph shows a woman who seems much younger than her years, and the description is enchanting – *Forehead* High, *Mouth* Small, *Nose* Retroussé, *Complexion* Fair, *Face* Oval. The only sign of decrepitude is the note under *Any special peculiarities*, where she admitted to being 'somewhat deaf'. Her letters were written as she spoke – impulsive, stylish, irresistible – and her account books (scrawled in violet ink) convey that sense of vivid immediacy, even when recording the payment of £25 to Hove Town Council 'for my grave in Hove Cemetery'.

Belinda's married life with John Murphy began with a long honeymoon abroad. I think she must have dragged him there, for this was the first and as far as I can tell the last time that he ever crossed the Irish Sea. They stayed for a few nights in London, where they dined with her father and uncle, and Belinda was 'charmed with Westminster Abbey & its thousand relics of past centuries.' She bathed twice in the sea at

Ostend, loved Bruges, Ghent and Antwerp – 'the people are all so clean and neat looking' – but had mixed feelings about Brussels, where she disliked the fellow guests at her hotel – 'a number of English, none of very good class' – and dined badly. An excursion to the field of Waterloo provoked her to melancholy – 'a sad, sad place' – but she was comforted on her return to the city when she 'Saw the Queen quite close, walking by herself' and 'bought a bonnet at Madame Bertraud'. Cologne provoked dismay – 'a large dirty old town where they seem to possess no shoes' – and she was generally disappointed with the Rhine: 'nothing pretty or remarkable except the great volume of water.' When they arrived at Coblenz they had to make do with a second-rate hotel – 'the King and Queen of Prussia are here, so the place is crowded' – but Frankfurt struck her as a 'very nice town, good shops'. At this point her diary breaks off, but my grandfather recalls her telling him that she was paid great attention by a German general, who showed them the fortifications along the Rhine as he foretold the coming war with France. Slipped between the pages of her journal I found a couple of menus from the Grand Hotel in Paris, where they dined in a style that she wished to remember.[522]

When the newly wed couple returned to Ireland they moved into Pollagh House and then, about a year later, inherited Mount Loftus. It was a painful legacy, because old Mary Murphy left all her moveable belongings to her younger children, which they interpreted to mean everything that could be carted or driven away – all the family portraits, the silver, the furniture, even the gates from the fields, the cattle – everything removable. They took all that they wanted to Diswellstown House, near Dublin, and put the rest up for auction, leaving John and his young wife to bid for a few bits and pieces to furnish the empty house.[523] It caused a great deal of family bitterness, which took a long time to heal.

The estate, nonetheless, was still solvent, despite all the mortgages of previous generations and the charges laid on it by old Mrs Murphy to support her husband and their unmarried children.[524] Indeed, it seems to have been a time of surprising prosperity – or perhaps of reckless optimism – sufficient to sustain a much more lively social life than at any time for the previous forty years. And the new Mrs Murphy, Belinda Creagh, was determined to live to the full.

As the mistress of Mount Loftus, she was the one who set the pace. Her husband had spent so much time in the company of Sir Francis that he had absorbed an astonishing clutter of erudition – he was known as a 'Walking Encyclopaedia' – but was also infected with some of the old man's lethargy. He played his part in county life, as magistrate, deputy lieutenant and high sheriff, but lacked the drive to manage his estate or control his wife's extravagance. In fact he may have encouraged a show of style beyond what they could truly afford, because of his own desire for social recognition.[525] So the stables were full of horses, the kennels full of hounds, and Belinda became famous for her yellow carriages drawn by matched greys.

For the first decade of their life together, Mrs Murphy entertained lavishly and the house swarmed with guests, with constant house parties. Their social life was centred on hunting, shooting and racing – for which Kilkenny was famous – but there were also visits to be made throughout the neighbourhood, since most of the great eighteenth-century houses were still occupied by their owners. The Marquis of Ormonde – a Butler, hence related to Mrs Murphy – presided over local society from Kilkenny Castle, while closer to hand were Lady Clifden at Gowran Castle, Lady Tighe at Woodstock, the Desarts and the Bellews, and nearest of all, just across the River Barrow at Borris, the famous Mr Kavanagh.

This astonishing man was born without arms or legs – mere stumps instead of proper limbs – but somehow contrived to become an expert horseman, good shot, keen sailor, intrepid explorer, profuse letter-writer, Member of Parliament, enlightened landlord and devoted father of a large family. Belinda Murphy had her own vivid memory, to add to the tales of his exploits. She was being driven in a light Victoria to visit Mrs Kavanagh. They had crossed the bridge over the Barrow and were climbing uphill beside the high and winding wall of the Borris demesne when down around the bend came a coach and four, driven at speed by Mr Kavanagh. Belinda shrieked, since a crash seemed inevitable, but Kavanagh pulled up his horses with the reins fastened to the stumps of his arms, through the immense strength of his shoulders.

Guests at Mount Loftus ranged from hordes of relatives to the Lord Lieutenant, who enjoyed a long day's hunting with the Mount Loftus harriers, unaware that Belinda's cousin, General Creagh, had got up before dawn to lay a drag across the finest stretch of countryside. Lord Hartington – then serving as Chief Secretary – delighted his hosts by proclaiming the view down the back avenue to be the finest in the British Isles. The young Lord Cochrane came to stay, went shooting at Richfield and got marooned on the marshes – but agreed to stand as godfather to the Murphys' first-born son, Francis Cochrane Loftus, whose birth on 3 July 1873 was the excuse for celebrations on a feudal scale. 'The tenantry and labourers of the estate and neighbourhood collected, and by nine in the evening had piled an enormous bonfire, and by ten o'clock the hill blazed with tar barrels and bonfires. Dancing was kept up till morning. Many toasts were proposed, and ringing cheers given from the assembled hundreds for the health and prosperity of Mr and Mrs Murphy and their infant heir.'[526]

That strange sense of social deference had survived the long history of rural agitation, the horrors of the Famine, evictions and emigration – and constantly surprises me. The Irish newspapers around this time were filled with reports of a society that seemed immune to change, even as 'The Irish Question' became one of the dominant issues in British politics. There was a viceregal dinner at Dublin Castle which Mrs Murphy attended wearing 'a train and corsage of rich violet Lyons velvet, lined with white satin and trimmed with fine old point lace,' bedecked with pearls and amethysts and a diamond tiara. And then there were Lady Clifden's amateur theatricals, each December, when 'a large party of their friends and also the tenantry of the estate' filled the ballroom at Gowran Castle for a performance of *Cinderella*, in which Lord Clifden played one of the Ugly Sisters and Belinda Murphy's young daughters were cast as the Fairy Godmother ('in a tiny costume of white and silver, silver wings and wand') and the Duchess of Rattle-trap – a role unknown in the classic fable but one that proved strangely prophetic for the seven-year-old Nora. What on earth, I wonder, did the 'tenantry of the estate' make of it all? Perhaps they were simply content when the show was over and Lady Clifden gave them 'a splendid supper, after which dancing was begun and kept up until an advanced hour of the morning.'[527]

John and Belinda Murphy produced a rapidly growing family, for their two daughters were followed by three sons. The tall house at

Mount Loftus filled with children – all of whom were brought up to call themselves Loftus, for Belinda was determined to reclaim the ancestry that her husband had almost let slip. But the celebrations for the birth of the youngest – my grandfather Pierse, in 1877 – marked the last carefree moment before disaster.

From 1878 Irish agriculture was devastated by an immense increase in the importation of cheap grain from the prairie lands of America, opened up by the new railways. Cereal prices collapsed, which meant that tenants could no longer afford to pay their rents and most of the Irish estates – mortgaged to the hilt – were unsustainable. Davitt founded the Land League which, with the support of Parnell – successor to O'Connell, as Ireland's nationalist hero – instituted a nationwide campaign to negotiate lower rents and to resist eviction when landlords refused to compromise. Even the better landowners such as Kavanagh experienced the full force of accumulated bitterness, as the Parnellites swept the country in the 1881 elections. Kavanagh's defeat as a parliamentary candidate was celebrated by his own tenants lighting bonfires on the nearby hills, and by someone sending him by post a dead frog, with all four legs cut off.

The Land Wars affected everyone, good and bad, and the situation was so grave that the English government was forced to intervene. The Encumbered Estates Act provided a mechanism for the courts to take control of estates that were no longer able to meet their obligations. They were effectively nationalised, and then sold in parcels to the highest bidders. Within the space of a few years, vast swathes of the old Ascendancy landholdings passed into the hands of speculators or canny native farmers, and the pattern of colonial conquest was finally broken.

Mount Loftus was all too vulnerable to this sharp change in fortune. The extravagance of the previous decade suddenly seemed like madness, the reckless mortgages of past generations an insupportable burden. A sense of foreboding was compounded by immediate tragedy, which struck at the most evocative symbol of the old, careless enjoyment, the Mount Loftus Harriers. For it seems that the kennel-man, infected by the general gloom, took increasingly to drink. One Friday night he went down to Goresbridge and embarked on a bout that lasted until the following Monday or Tuesday, leaving the hounds unfed – and no one heard their howling because the kennels were far from the house.

Eventually he staggered home, failed to negotiate the steps up to his little room and fell into a yard full of ravenous hounds, which savaged and devoured him. The old stories, with hideous glee, insist that nothing was left but the soles of his hobnailed boots.

When news of this catastrophe reached the house, John Murphy took his gun and went down to the kennels with some men from the stables. He ordered the door to be opened so as to allow one hound to exit at a time, and as each one appeared he shot it, and killed the whole pack.

And then he fell ill with dropsy and retired to bed, incapable of action, leaving his wife to cope with an increasingly desperate situation. He buried himself in books and turned his face from the world. When his wife tried to talk to him about the future, and his sons, and their plans, his only suggestion was that they should all become farmers. In 1881 he died, leaving a bankrupt estate, a young widow and five children – the oldest of whom was ten, the youngest four. The first image to print itself on the mind of that four-year-old child, my grandfather, was his father's death.

> [I remember] being taken into a large bedroom at Mount Loftus and seeing a still, bearded figure on a bed, the corpse of my father. That is the only recollection I have of him, the only remembrance I have of seeing him. Next comes a clearer sharper memory of standing at the great bow window of the nursery and watching a long procession of carriages moving slowly down the front avenue; my father's funeral.

For a moment it seemed like the end. The estates of Mount Loftus and Richfield were taken over by the Encumbered Estates Court and most of the outlying land was let or sold. But this thoroughly Victorian melodrama of extravagance and retribution could not be complete without its moral – the purifying effects of disaster, repentance and hard work, leading eventually to glorious redemption.

Belinda Murphy was determined to hang on to what she could, and managed to lease back from the court the walled Mount Loftus demesne and the fields of Powerstown, together with Richfield and its famous pasture. She became a farmer, up most days before dawn to keep her accounts, feed her chickens and give the day's orders. There was, as before, a small army to supervise – her housekeeper, Mary Francis, and the girls in the dairy, and her gardener, her grooms, old Cullerton the coachman and all her other dependants – whose number seemed little less than it might have been a century earlier, though perhaps they worked a little harder. She raised cattle, fattened at Richfield, and pigs and horses and springer spaniels and poultry of all kinds – keeping what she needed and selling the rest at Kilkenny Fair or the other local markets. The springers were the most valuable, judging by Belinda's *Cattle Book* in which she recorded the prices realised for all manner of livestock. They sold for £12 apiece, twice the price of a bullock. Nothing escaped her attention.[528]

Through courage, stamina and constant hard work, Belinda Murphy managed to make the estate pay its way. There was sufficient to settle the rent and maintain her swarm of dependants, and somehow enough to send her children to Catholic schools in England and to keep up her own social life, if not at its previous hectic pace. Two friends in particular – Lady Ormonde and Lady Clifden – made a point of entertaining her, never allowing her misfortunes to cloud their affection, and all her neighbours held her in high regard. When all was well, and the weather was fine, she would set out in her yellow landau to pay them visits, and she was determined to be seen at all the great events of the social calendar. My grandfather remembered accompanying her in the landau to the Kilkenny Horse Show, and being greeted by 'a tall man with a great red beard and dressed in a long black coat and silk hat,' surrounded by men in dark uniforms. 'Seeing my mother shake hands and talk to the red bearded man, I also, dressed in my black velvet suit and with long golden curls, I also stepped forward and put out my hand and I remember well his bending down and gravely shaking it, but I could not understand why the men around him smiled or laughed. He was the Lord Lieutenant, "The Red Earl", Lord Spencer.'

What my grandfather may not have realised was that several of those 'men in dark uniforms' were the Red Earl's bodyguards, because the day after he arrived in Ireland for his second stint of office as Lord Lieutenant, in May 1882, his Chief Secretary and Permanent Under-secretary were murdered in Phoenix Park, on their way to the Vice-regal Lodge.[529] Even though he himself was sympathetic to many of the aspirations of the Irish Nationalists – he eventually became a convert to

Home Rule – Lord Spencer was a target for Fenian extremists. But their long, unforgiving struggle for Irish independence hardly seems to have touched the life at Mount Loftus. As so often in these family stories, the politics and the fierceness of Ireland's history have faded into the background – what they remembered was the colour of that yellow landau and the price of a pig at Gowran market.

Thus it continued for seven years, until another catastrophe almost broke Belinda Murphy's will. Her eldest child Linda, the favourite of all the family, had been sent to finish her education at a convent school in Paris. There she contracted typhoid. As soon as Belinda heard the news she rushed to be with her beloved daughter but arrived just in time to hold her in her arms before she died. This was in 1887, when Linda was seventeen. 'She is buried in Père Lachaise cemetery, in the family tomb of some French Marquis whose daughter was her great friend.' [530]

The shock of Linda's death, combined with the exhaustion of coping with all those long years of work and worry, prompted Belinda Murphy to consult a London doctor for the first time in her life. He ordered complete rest and a change of air, and recommended Bath. There she met Maurice Lindsay Coates – an Ulsterman, a Mason, a staunch Unionist and an active member of the Church of Ireland. He was in almost every way Belinda's exact opposite. But Mr Coates was wealthy, civilised and kind. She was thirty-eight, he was twenty years older. Within a few months he accompanied her on a visit to my grandfather's school, where he presented the small boy with a golden sovereign – untold wealth that his mother advised him to spend on a sow to keep at Mount Loftus, 'and thereby increase the sum greatly' – and within a year Maurice Coates and Belinda Murphy were married. It was as sudden a turn of fortune as any novelist could have wished for.

The source of Mr Coates's wealth was partly inherited (a family engineering works in Ulster) and partly a matter of luck. He owned a cotton mill and estate outside Belfast, which became enormously valuable as building land, to provide housing for the expanding city, and he speculated on railways and suchlike in Chicago, where he lost almost as much as he made. His wealth enabled Mr Coates to give up work when a relatively young man and to spend a few enjoyable years in Paris before devoting most of his life to his passion for shooting and fishing – which was probably the reason that he took a large country house in Norfolk, Rackheath Park, where he installed his new wife and her children.[531] He also acquired a love of good wine, and used to go regularly to Bordeaux to select the hogsheads of claret that would be shipped back to Norwich, to be bottled by his wine merchant. My grandfather recalled that 'Everyone had claret. When my brother and I went to boat on the broads or a long train journey back to school we always had a bottle of claret.'[532]

Life at Rackheath was extremely comfortable. The vast house was sumptuously over-furnished in late-Victorian style and came complete with a large conservatory, a covered stable yard, a lake and an extensive park – not to mention numerous servants, horses, carriages and other luxuries. It must have seemed the perfect happy ending. But this prosperous, easy, comfortable cocoon meant the abandonment of the delights and problems and ramshackle anomalies of Ascendancy life in Ireland; the sense of being rooted in a place and its people, for better and worse.

They tried to compromise – Belinda's brother, Symon Creagh, went to live at Mount Loftus, and kept things going as best he could, but it was never quite the same and when he died, in 1898, most of the furniture was sold and the place left derelict.[533] And so the neglect continued, as the old house fell into disrepair, the surrounding farms were sold by the Court, and Richfield too was sold.

And the yellow landau? It may have served for a while as a chicken roost, before, like so much else, it mouldered away – but it gleams in my memory of these tales, as bright as a buttercup.

Ned Cullerton (coachman) and 'Houlahan', Mount Loftus 1891.

INTERLUDE

CHAPTER 41

I remember. Mount Loftus in the 1880s

Jottings from the autobiographical notes of my grandfather, Pierse Loftus.[534]

I recall an old shawled woman leaning upon a stick walking slowly across the gravel towards the kitchen door. I had just been given a present, a cheap little pistol costing I suppose sixpence or threepence which fired little pink paper circles which made a very small noise. I ran towards the woman calling out 'I'll shoot you; and fired my little toy. The old thing at once collapsed on the ground crying out 'I'm kilt, I'm kilt entirely.' I screamed and they came up from the kitchen and gave the old woman whiskey.

Another memory is of the great stone floored kitchen at night with plenty of lights and many men and women. I remember dipping my head towards a tub containing apples floating in water and with fear watching people snatching raisins from a flaming dish, and melted lead being poured through a very large key into a bucket of water and the shapes formed being examined with laughter and interest. I suppose this must have been Halloween and my mother had brought in all the outdoor staff for the celebrations. I remember a fiddler sitting in the corner and everyone dancing jigs, and my mother seeing to everything and that everyone participated in the fun.

I remember a violent thunderstorm and being brought down to the cellar. The only person who ventured upstairs to report was dear old 'Faddy' – Mary Francis. She had been my mother's nurse in the old days in Clare and came to Mount Loftus as housekeeper and general help. Her old husband lived in the range of buildings near the house. That storm must have been a record event as three of my mother's horses were killed by lightning and several trees shattered.

I remember events about the farm – the killing of pigs, the making of sausages, the poultry yard, the various stone-walled paddocks with cattle and horses, the rick yard with its harvested stacks on small stone pillars, the cool dairy with great yellow-lined earthenware bowls for skimming the cream and the girls at the churns making butter. I remember how delicious was the taste of the cool buttermilk on a hot summer day and how often I went to drink it. Then there was the stable with the horses, and old Cullerton the coachman polishing the harness in his warm centre room. He was a most devoted servant though at times inclined to drink and on these occasions we small boys hurriedly retired before his swearing and grumbling and threats.

Then comes the memory of a meet of hounds at Mount Loftus when as a very small boy I was in charge of some man from the farm or stable and we stood near a big wood by the river and watched the hounds going through it. Suddenly from some bushes and bracken near us a fox stole out. I saw it and ran in front waving my cap and I fancy the fox turned back.

Then I recall how my brother Jack and I used to go out to collect mushrooms and bring them to a room in the range which had a fire and there fill them with small pats of butter and cook them on the hob. How good they tasted and how good too were the wild strawberries we gathered in the wood by the back avenue behind the cow house.

I remember the old house so well and how attractive it was – the long dining room with its brass-bound mahogany buckets and the two circular mirrors on the wall and the drawing room with its great bow window and the china and glass and the cosy library with one window facing the lawns (what we children called the Pleasure Grounds) and the other looking towards the long range of outbuildings and stables beyond. Then in the outer hall there was a long old sideboard and on it a glass case containing a stuffed badger and on that table we threw our caps as we entered the house.

We went to the chapel at Skeogh a couple of miles away and there we had a pew and I recall the penny I was given to put in the box. On one occasion my mother marched out with her family during the sermon, because the young curate was making violent political propaganda.

Another memory – a tall man standing by the library fire talking to my mother. I myself playing on the floor with a jointed wooden snake which Mr Adair, a leading estate agent, had just given me. Evidently my mother and he were talking politics for I remember suddenly asking – 'Which is the most wicked, Mr Gladstone or Mr Parnell?'. Alas I cannot remember the answer.

FAREWELL

CHAPTER 42

A Typical Victorian Family

There is a photograph of them with their mother – three young men in morning suits and their elder sister Nora in a pale floor-length gown, with a nosegay at her waist. Frank and Jack stare boldly at the camera, while my grandfather Pierse looks at us sideways, more reserved. As for Nora, she is glancing at someone else, out of frame, with an air of detachment. Belinda seems absorbed, content, momentarily still. She is tiny, but looks wonderful in her rustling silk dress, with her tall children perched around her. It is Christmas 1897 – the last time they would all be together – at their adopted home in Norfolk.

'What a typical Victorian family we were.' My grandfather's comment is layered with ambiguity, between what he remembered when he was old, what he wrote for posterity and what he actually experienced. That family photo, for example, was taken in the year of Victoria's Diamond Jubilee – 'the apotheosis not only of the great Queen but of England and our Empire' – and the formal clothes, ornate furniture and stilted poses depict the outward forms of solid respectability, the Victorian ideal. Reality was more uncertain, for none of Belinda's children had any prospect of inheritance. Their ancestral lands in Ireland were administered by the Encumbered Estates Court and their stepfather's wealth was destined for a nephew – they needed to live off their wits. But their appetite for adventure seemed to Pierse typically Victorian; the world was theirs to explore.[535]

'Nearly all the young fellows whom I knew or met and talked with had the ambition to leave England and carve out careers for themselves overseas, preferably in the British Empire. We believed in the Empire with a sincere faith, holding that it was the divinely appointed destiny of our people to spread abroad throughout the world, developing new lands and bringing justice and security and progress to savage peoples.' Those words may reek of their time, but they echo the arrogance of English adventurers, centuries earlier, as they set off to subdue the savage Irish.

The eldest brother, Frank, came closest to matching the imperial ideal. The family scrapbooks are filled with photos of him as cricketing hero, Sandhurst cadet, officer in the Inniskilling Fusiliers. His gaze is more open, less inward than his brothers, and his letters match his name: they are frank, simple and filled with a longing for action – 'bored with soldiering at home' – which came to seem an addiction, danger being the drug. A few months after he sat with his family for the Christmas photograph, he managed to get himself 'seconded to West Africa where he helped raise and train the first West African negro regiment,' in Sierra Leone.

The English had established a settlement for freed slaves on the coast of Sierra Leone in the eighteenth century. This might have seemed a nobler enterprise had they not also shipped out there sixty white prostitutes, which made only too plain that this was a place for the transportation of undesirables. Freetown's precarious history as a beacon of black liberation was undermined still further, a century later, when it became the base for a British advance on the hinterland, as part of the competitive 'scramble for Africa' by the European colonial powers. Britain claimed a Protectorate over these traditional tribal areas, and imposed a Hut Tax on every dwelling to help pay for the imperial infrastructure of roads, railways and administration, as they had done throughout their other colonies in Africa. Needless to say, this was much resented by the tribal leaders, and war broke out in 1898.

Frank's troops were engaged in suppressing this rising, and an evocative, sepia-tinted photo shows him with two fellow officers, their legs wrapped in puttees and their heads shaded by pith helmets, sitting outside a cluster of round mud huts with conical thatched roofs – imperial strangers in a 'primitive' land. One of them sprawls on a deckchair, seemingly asleep, while the others stare at the camera. Frank is unshaven and somewhat gaunt, but still preserves an air of eagerness and curiosity. A few weeks later, in January 1899, he was commanding the rear of a column of native troops as they filed down a twisting track, under constant attack from Kissi tribesmen who flitted in and out of the bush where the British could not follow. 'They gave us as lively a time as one could possibly desire,' and some of Frank's 'friendlies' deserted to the enemy. Eventually, after going to rescue one of his men who was wounded, Frank himself was 'hit in the tummy, low on the right side [and] bowled clean over.' It all seems eerily reminiscent of events in Ireland, exactly four hundred years earlier, when Archbishop Loftus's son was ambushed in the Wicklow hills by Irish tribesmen, who skipped across the bog and through the trees, 'knowing we cannot or indeed dare not follow them.' But Frank survived, after several days lying close to death, and was able to respond to his mother's frantic telegram – 'where wounded, how doing' – with the equally laconic response, 'Groin, doing splendidly'.

He was invalided home to recover and persuaded to join his mother and stepfather on a Mediterranean cruise. Mr Coates disliked the sea, hated 'being shut up' with a hundred fellow passengers, and 'could not bring his mind down' to enjoy 'the chief amusement on board, throwing a piece of rope into a slop bucket.' His grumpiness was compounded when he caught flu, which left him so weak that he could only go ashore for a few hours at Constantinople, 'when I had to lunch with the Sultan.' But he admitted that the lunch was good, and 'the Sultan looked exactly like the picture of him in Punch,' which partially consoled him – and he was pleased at the recovery of his wounded stepson, who rapidly gained weight and health, and seemed to enjoy himself. 'The ship was crammed with heiresses and there was a great deal of flirting.' But Frank was later teased by his youngest brother for failing to fix up a profitable marriage – 'I hear there were several beautiful gold-fish on board but you would not fish!'

Brother Jack, meanwhile, was prospecting for oil and coal in Mexico, having travelled there with his aunt Henrietta and her second husband, General Sir Richard Sankey, who had agreed to invest in a company set up by his nephew. The General was seventy years old, the walrus-moustached hero of numerous campaigns in Afghanistan and India, and Jack was a young man of twenty-two. Both of them seem to have been gripped by speculative fever and they had the backing of city friends, eager to seize control of Mexico's natural assets before the Americans got to them. There was no pretence of imperial destiny but the entire enterprise had a distinctly colonial air, for it depended on the benevolence of an autocratic dictator – adept at playing the Americans off against the English – and an unscrupulous assortment of European adventurers who flocked to Mexico as to a new gold rush.

The General believed in checking things out for himself, and wherever he went expected to deal with the man in charge. So they stopped en route in Washington to meet President McKinley at the White House and shortly after their arrival in Mexico City, in January 1899, they called on the 'great and strong President Diaz.' Diaz admitted that English investors were scarce because 'so many swindles had been propagated in the name of Mexico,' but seemed eager to help. He offered to place a gunboat at their disposal, to ease their journey to the oil fields of Papantia, and promised that if they found coal worth exploiting at Puebla he would arrange for the railway line to be extended direct to the mines – on condition that none of the coal was exported to the USA.

All seemed well, and Mexico City was full of diversions. Almost every night they went to the opera and social engagements of various sorts filled their diaries – giving Jack the chance to fall in love with a succession of young ladies. They also enjoyed a couple of narrow escapes, of the kind that make travellers' tales. Shortly after they arrived, while entering the cathedral, the General collared a thief who tried to steal his tie pin, and handed him over to the police. A few weeks later, while visiting the British Legation, they experienced an earthquake.

> The immense chandeliers swung so violently round and round that they almost touched the roof. The walls cracked and we went hard for the street where we all rolled about as if we were drunk. All the natives were praying on their knees with all their might & the street seemed to move up and down in waves while the tall electric lamp posts swayed about like trees in a breeze. The palace was cracked from top to bottom in three places and they say it was a sight to see the Cathedral towers swaying about. [536]

They came to no harm, but journeying by horseback across the roughest of tracks, up and down mountains and along river gorges, camping in villages with no inns and scant provisions, killing scorpions before they could close their eyes for the night, trying to evaluate the potential of mineral deposits with no experience to guide them – all of this proved too much for the General. The 'awful Mexican Saddles' caused him agonies of discomfort and a dose of dysentery forced him to cut short his stay, leaving Jack to carry on alone.

Jack discovered a seam of coal, nine feet thick, and 'an island off the coast containing a salt pan' – sufficient to convince him that he had found what he was looking for. But the Pacific Salt Company and Mexican coal proved frustrating investments. Neither Jack nor the General made any money out of them, 'and both had endless worries in subsequent years from their attempts to develop industries in Mexico.' All that now survives from their adventures is a lump of Mexican silver – a grandiose medal commemorating the opening of the Canal Porfirio Diaz in 1898. It serves as a paperweight.

And then there was Pierse, the youngest brother. While he was still at school, aged seventeen, his parents urged him to decide on a choice of career. His mother had vetoed the army because one brother was enough. His stepfather looked unfavourably on the suggestion of Oxford or Cambridge, followed by the Bar – too many years before he could earn his living. A family friend suggested dentistry; 'I shuddered at the idea.' Pierse himself was averse to any sort of office job, 'chained to a desk all day, working at books.' So he went for a walk with his best friend, striding around the school playground to discuss his future. The friend mentioned that his brother was a brewer and enjoyed his work – 'constantly on the move about the brewery inspecting vats & coppers & barrels.' Pierse immediately sat down and wrote a letter home, announcing his decision – 'and so my job in life was settled.'

To begin with that meant the traditional 'pupilage', trailing after the head brewer at Morgan's Brewery in Norwich for the best part of two years, learning not very much. – but this was followed by 'a year in Victorian London, at that time still an English city living in traditional ways and without a single motor vehicle of any kind.' Pierse studied chemistry by day with Mr Heron in Fenchurch Street and at night enjoyed the gaudy pleasures of the 'naughty nineties', for this was the heyday of the music halls, including the Empire and the Alhambra, with their 'promenades' thronged with prostitutes, the Palace and the Aquarium presenting 'living pictures' of classical scenes posed by naked girls – 'there was one girl in them an absolute Venus' – and midnight strolls down Piccadilly, 'in the course of which I was addressed by every conceivable term of endearment.' But alongside such temptations there was a constant round of lunches, dinners and dances, almost every night of the season. The extravagance was astonishing. A ball at one of the great aristocratic houses might cater for a thousand, with refreshments until five or six in the morning, and self-publicists like Alfred Harmsworth – owner of the *Daily Mail* – competed for the latest stars to entertain their guests. Jack Loftus went with his brother Pierse to Harmsworth's ball in Berkeley Square – 'Paderewski and Melba performed. People say Harmsworth paid P. £1,000 for the night!'

But Pierse knew only too well that this was a borrowed interlude and soon he was off on his travels, to learn the latest brewing technology. He began in Copenhagen, where he studied yeasts and bacteria with a pupil of Pasteur alongside students from Japan, Russia, France, Belgium and Germany. Pierse bought a tin bath for ten shillings and a 'loaded cane', weighted with lead, to protect himself from the 'huge dogs' – possibly rabid – that roamed the streets of the city. In Sweden he learnt lager brewing – and enjoyed smorgasbord and schnapps – before heading for Germany, taking with him his Danish bath and the boxing gloves that he had brought from England. He spent a few weeks in Stetten and then set off for Berlin. Two nights in luxury – 'at a first class hotel, where the notorious and beautiful Cleo de Merode was staying' – were followed by a month in an austere working-man's flat, kept by an old widow. It was very cold, and the boxing gloves and bath proved essential for keeping warm – he soaked his frozen bones in hot water and gave boxing lessons to his fellow pupils, an ill-tempered Prussian and a melancholy Frenchman. The Prussian soon gave up – Pierse hit him on the nose – but the Frenchman and he became friends and dined together every day, having first checked the evening newspaper to ensure that France and England were not at war, for this was a time of great diplomatic tension. And then they would head off to the Winter Garden, 'where Cleo de Merode was performing nightly.' I think Pierse was smitten. Fifty years later he looked back on this period as an enchanted age, in the 'kindly old civilised nineteenth-century Europe, where one mixed in fellowship with men of all nationalities and passports were not used or required.'

But the Great Powers of the 'kindly old civilised Europe' were busy carving up Africa, and Pierse landed a job with South African Breweries, on a three-year contract. He sailed on the *Carisbrook Castle*, in January 1899 – just as Jack arrived with his uncle in Mexico City, and their wounded brother Frank was travelling back from Sierra Leone, to convalesce in England. 'What a typical Victorian family we were.'

That untroubled colonial confidence, oblivious to the echoes of Irish history, was shaken during the voyage to South Africa by long conversations with two of his fellow passengers. One was a man called Jones – 'tall, thin, brown-faced, aquiline featured, striking personality' – who was 'one of the earliest pioneers of Johannesburg' and fiercely opposed to the imperialist dreams of Cecil Rhodes. The other was a 'vivid, dark haired impetuous and fearless' girl, with whom he fell gently in love as they spent 'tropical evenings on the boat deck, talking of life and literature.' Elizabeth 'Coos' Butler was the elder daughter of General Sir William Butler – a fellow Irishman and distant cousin of Pierse, recently appointed commander of the British troops in South Africa – and she seems to have shared her father's radical views, for the General was a man of wonderfully independent mind. A Catholic and protagonist of Irish Home Rule, he scorned the arrogance of British colonialism, sympathised with the fierce autonomy of the Boer republics, vehemently disagreed with the war-mongering stance of the High Commissioner, Sir Alfred Milner, and resigned his post when the government refused to back him. Eventually his warnings were vindicated and he chaired a commission of enquiry into the conduct of the Boer War, which produced a highly critical report, referring to 'Pantaloons in puttees & Harlequinades in helmets.' Assaulted by Mr Jones's liberal convictions and Miss Butler's teasing, Pierse's 'jingoistic imperialism' was turned upside down – 'for the time being, at any rate.'

After landing in Cape Town, Pierse endured an 'awful journey' to Johannesburg – 'a corrugated iron city' of streets lined with bars, which had sprung into existence following the discovery of massive deposits of gold in 1886. It was a classic gold rush settlement, a city of *uitlanders* – foreigners, most of them British – in the Boer republic of the Transvaal.

Tensions inevitably mounted. The Boer farmers – descendants of the original Dutch settlers – disliked the rough, hard-drinking miners and sharp European speculators who were rapidly transforming their dusty land into the richest state in South Africa. The *uitlanders* – who soon outnumbered the Boers – resented being treated as second-class citizens by the government of President Kruger, unable to vote and therefore powerless to protest against the taxes and other controls to which the mining industry was subject. Their cause was supported by the British government, which coveted the gold and longed to absorb the Boer republics, as part of a grand colonial plan that saw Britain's imperial edict stretching across the whole of Southern Africa – and the High Commissioner in Cape Town, Sir Alfred Milner, was doing his best to provoke a war.

Pitched into this cauldron of anger, greed and booze – 'I reckon that ¾ of the annual earned income of Johannesburg is spent in drink' – Pierse found it best to keep quiet about his newly acquired liberalism. Arguments were easily provoked and often ended in fights. But those shipboard conversations with 'Coos' Butler came vividly to mind when he received a long and entrancing letter from Cape Town, dated 19 May 1899. She admitted that 'I can't help teasing you', talked about riding for hours over the veldt, going to the races and winning her bets, and gardening every morning. 'I have got a horse, a dog & a kitten of my own now, & if I can get a young elephant will be quite happy – but as I don't see a chance of getting one I'm not happy. Are you 'appy?'

For the most part he was. Employed at the Castle Brewery, which had recently been constructed to slake the savage thirst of the *uitlanders*, Pierse's days were long, 'but there is very little book work, which is a great relief', and he enjoyed his life. 'Rides out on the veldt with the smell & pale blue colour of the eucalyptus woods, the sparkling air, & the ever pervading dull roar of the mines, the political excitement, the Music Hall & the Race meetings. The world seemed fair & before one stretched an endless life of adventure & success in the new and attractive land where life was so free & unrestricted & opportunities stood waiting for all.'

On those evening rides Pierse would often stop at a country bar, where 'a couple of bearded, roughly dressed [Boer] farmers' might greet him without malice – 'They were always friendly.' But there was also mounting tension, expressed in furious meetings in Johannesburg at which the miners were armed with iron bars and 'I myself carried in my inner breast pocket a whalebone & lead Life Preserver, which I had found in an attic at Mount Loftus, many years before.' A 'War Dance' was held, 'at the fine, brick built house of Mr & Mrs Dale,' where they swirled round the room to the music of Norman's band, dancing waltzes and polkas and a 'Galop'. 'In such light-hearted fashion was the prospect of war regarded in those distant days.' Pierse himself was under no illusions, and wrote to his brother Frank that 'if war does come we shall have very severe reverses,' for the terrain was ideally suited to the guerrilla tactics of the Boer snipers. Frank's advice to Pierse was 'to steer clear of politics, not to join any society with secret blood-and-thunder oaths, to refrain from making a rapid fortune in mining shares and to steer as clear of debt and the girls as you possibly can.'[538] He also advised him to treat the 'black brother' well, and never to address one as a 'damned nigger'.

By the beginning of July war seemed imminent and there was a general exodus from Johannesburg: '7,000 white people have left during the last fortnight & numberless natives.' In August Pierse was ordered by his employers to depart for the Natal Brewery in Pietermaritzburg, 'to assist in brewing the increased quantity of beer now required there,' as British troops poured into the town. Before leaving he was given a secret missive to deliver when he arrived, listing the names of carefully vetted recruits from Johannesburg who wished to join a new regiment, the Imperial Light Horse, which was then being raised in Natal. He also wrote to his brother Jack, enclosing a jingoistic letter that he hoped might be published in the British press. As Pierse frankly admitted, this reflected a drastic change of heart – for the atmosphere and war propaganda of the last few months had undone all the good work of those long conversations on the voyage from England – and he was now convinced that a fundamental principle was at stake. 'An Englishman shall not be treated as the member of an inferior race by a Dutchman before the eyes of the kaffirs.' My grandfather's language betrays such a complex of racial prejudices that it still has the capacity to shock – but this touchy, mean-minded 'principle' was one of the main reasons that the British went to war. The other was greed for gold, and from that, too, Pierse was not immune – for he concluded his letter by offering Jack 'the best tip going. The Boers will smash every bit of headgear on the mines & amuse themselves by chucking Dynamite down the shafts. One will be able to get shares of dozens of good mines for next to nothing. Buy really <u>first class</u> mines, only first class. Buy them when the smash comes – for the gold is there.'

Such unguarded revelations were suppressed a few years later when Pierse became involved in Irish politics – for Irish Nationalists regarded the Boer War as a touchstone of British perfidy; imperialism at its most ruthless. But in South Africa, at the time, war fever was contagious – and a few months after arriving in Pietermaritzburg Pierse enlisted in the Rifle Association, a territorial defence force with which he drilled at evenings and weekends. The news pleased his brother Frank, who was 'under orders for India' but was 'working heaven and earth for a transfer' to his old regiment, in order to get out to South Africa – 'Hoping to see you soon.'

War broke out in October 1899 with an invasion of Natal by the Boers, who laid siege to Ladysmith, Mafeking and Kimberley. As the first wild optimism of the British was overtaken by a series of disasters, the Rifle Association was on nightly patrol, expecting to be 'wiped out before morning by the Boer attack. I remember those nights, lying there by the river with the loud croaking of innumerable bull frogs – wondering when the attack would come.' But in the afternoons Pierse would take tea with the sisters of the Louis Botha – one of the leading Boer commanders – who were staying in the town after fleeing Johannesburg. As he himself wrote, it seemed like a different age.

Frank arrived in Durban in the first week of December. He sent a telegram to Pierse, and they met briefly at Maritzburg Station as his regimental train paused on its way to the front. His last note was scrawled in pencil from camp at Colenso on the eve of battle, 14 December.

My dear old Chap

We are starting to attack the Boer position at dawn tomorrow, and I should imagine will have about Colenso one of the biggest fights of the campaign. Accidents will happen and it is possible I may get hit. In case I do I am just writing these few lines by candle light to wish you good bye. You have always been a good brother and a good fellow in every way, though I am afraid I cannot say the same of myself.

Three days later, Frank's mother was coming out of Farm Street Church in London, early on Sunday morning, when she 'met a news-boy shouting awful battle hundreds killed & wounded.' She bought a paper and the very first name that she saw, in the list of those killed, was her eldest son. She collapsed in the street and was taken home by a policeman.

'Poor old Frank was killed in the front rank of the Irish Brigade, leading and cheering on his men.' That account, in a letter from the Colonel of the Inniskillings, suggests a heroic charge, the sort of 'splendid death' that he imagined the family wished to hear. But the truth was dour. Thousands of British troops had been ordered by the incompetent General Buller into an untenable position, in the bend of a river. The Boers – commanded by Louis Botha – swept them with fire from the surrounding hills and casualties were enormous. Pierse learnt what happened from one of Frank's fellow officers, Lieutenant Meldon.

> He cannot speak too highly of the way Frank led and encouraged his men. Meldon says it cheered him on & gave him courage. He was in the front line the whole way under awful fire & finally as they were lying down Meldon was wounded & in great pain. Frank bandaged him up & then took a rifle & lay firing when suddenly his head fell forward without a sound. He was shot through the head and killed instantaneously.[539]

The manuscript of Pierse's memoirs ceases at this point, as if he closed his eyes to the war. Letters between the surviving brothers were filled with family gossip – rumours about Frank's past, involving 'Miss Ramsey' and possibly a child, which they came to doubt were true – and more immediate news of Jack's life as a stock jobber and his unsuccessful attempts to secure a bride. And then there was the problem of Nora, which had been a running theme in Jack's letters to Pierse for much of the previous year, and seemed more insoluble than ever.

Their sister had a history of constant rows with most of her family, for Nora's view of herself – glamorous, stylish, admired – seems to have collided, all too often, with the prosaic fact that she was the eldest, unmarried sibling, and had nothing to occupy her life except 'society'. The dying days of Victoria's reign, for a woman who longed for pleasure, were immensely frustrating. 'She has an idea that London is very gay – balls, dinners and all that – & that she should be in the vortex of gay society.' But the Boer War had blighted such frivolity – 'Not one single ball. People have too good sense to go in for gaiety while our poor chaps are being killed every day.' So she screamed at her relatives, causing them such anguish that Jack wrote a glum note in his diary: 'Nora very wrong – a family talk and ultimatum.' Eventually – after hysterical scenes in Italy and in France, tirades against the wickedness of her family, ransacking Jack's desk to steal some of his letters and being threatened with confinement in a mental home – Nora was paid an allowance of £250 per annum on condition that she stayed away from their family home at Rackheath and stopped worrying her mother. Peace, of a sort, was restored.

But in South Africa the war was increasingly savage, as Kitchener enforced a scorched earth policy – burning the crops and houses of the Boers, salting their fields, poisoning the wells – and established the notorious concentration camps, in which tens of thousands died, most of them children. Yet again I am reminded of Elizabethan Ireland, and the horrors described by Spenser: 'they came creeping forth upon their hands, for their legges could not beare them, they looked like anatomies of death.'

No trace of this terrible conclusion can be found in the surviving letters from family or friends, or in Pierse's photograph album, or his unfinished memoir, or any of the family stories. Memory is blank.

The Victorian age ended on 21 January 1901, with the death of the old Queen. For forty years she had worn black for her long-dead husband, but the new King limited the period of mourning for his mother to three months. And for each of the Loftus siblings, this was a turning point.

Pierse returned from South Africa in 1902 with an appetite for politics and a determination to achieve financial independence. He persuaded his stepfather to buy him a stake in a small Suffolk brewery – Adnams of Southwold – and set to work with an energy that shocked the rest of the board. There was much to do and he was urgent to make his fortune. Restless and enquiring, he was excited by the imminence of change, and wanted to be part of it.

His brother Jack, by contrast, was nostalgic for an era that may never have existed. He wanted to live as his ancestors had done, in the tall eighteenth-century house, in the midst of its park, with numerous dependants. In May 1903 this suddenly seemed possible, when Mount Loftus demesne and Powerstown were put up for sale under the Encumbered Estates Act. His mother bought Powerstown for £3,000 and his stepfather put up the money for Jack to bid for Mount Loftus. 'The judge declared me the purchaser at £4,000. I had the place but nothing more, not a chair, table, spade or implement of any kind.'

And then he struck gold in the marriage stakes. After chasing Protestant heiresses who rejected him because he was a Catholic, Jack fell for a beautiful Jewish girl, Pauline May Lichtenstadt, the daughter of a wealthy stockbroker. They were married in November 1903. Just over a year later he took his 'young and lovely wife to Ireland, on her first visit to the home of his forefathers.'

> The party was met at Goresbridge by their steward and a landau and pair and drove to the front entrance gate where they were met by a large and enthusiastic crowd of tenants and friends. The gate was tastefully and gaily decorated with an arch of evergreens and the word 'Welcome' printed on a green background – the work of Mr Foote, the energetic Steward of Mount Loftus. Here the horses were unyoked and amidst cheers the carriage with its happy occupants was dragged up the avenue to the old Mansion House. Capt Loftus, with considerable emotion, standing in the carriage addressed the people in the name of himself and his wife and thanked them for the cordial reception. He hoped that soon he would be able to leave the city and come and live in their midst and that they should always cherish that good feeling and happy unity of spirit which had been displayed that day. The company were afterwards liberally entertained to refreshments and altogether a most enjoyable and harmonious evening was spent. Captain and Mrs Loftus left for London on Thursday evening.[540]

But where Jack saw the past revived, his wife saw damp and decay – and before she left, after this briefest of visits, had already decided that the 'old Mansion House' would not suit her, and needed to be replaced by something more modern. I also think that she wished to delay, as long as possible, her banishment from London and the society of her friends. So, at her urging, Jack had the much-loved house pulled down.

The adjoining range of buildings was adapted as a 'shooting and fishing lodge' for occasional visits, and eventually, when Jack decided to live there, he employed a local builder, 'who kept patching onto and pulling down the old range and in the end built a very ugly and inconvenient house indeed, most of which was burnt down in the thirties.'[541] But Jack was back at Mount Loftus, and wealthy enough to play his role as head of the family, benevolent landlord, patron of his locality. It was, in a way, as if nothing had changed.[542]

As for Nora, this was a time of liberation from the constraints of family life. Somehow she embarked on a glamorous career at Court and there is a wonderful photograph of her, statuesque, in a sweeping gown designed to flatter her figure. But reality was slightly stouter than the ideal she had in mind so she altered the photographic record with a swift stroke of the pen, adjusting her silhouette to the perfect line of fashion, and signed with a flourish – *Nora*. Though never truly beautiful she managed to convince enough men otherwise (including, it is said, the new King Edward) that she was able to dress her part with consummate splendour and a certain stylish amusement. Elizabeth Bowen described the type to perfection. 'Tall and handsome – nothing so soft as pretty, but in those days it was a vocation to be a handsome girl; many of the best marriages had been made by such. They carried themselves imposingly, had good busts and shoulders, waists firm under the whalebone, straight backs.'[543] So successful was Nora at playing this role that eventually, at the age of thirty-six, she snared an enormously wealthy American.

Robert Gardiner owned 78,000 acres of Long Island and a smaller, private island – acquired by an ancestor in 1639 – together with a Bay Shore house inherited by his family in the eighteenth century and a lavish apartment in New York. He commissioned a bust of Nora by Rodin, and married her at St Margaret's Church, Westminster, on 22 February 1909.[544] The local Long Island newspaper announced that Mr Gardiner's new wife was 'of ancient lineage, a beautiful and accomplished lady, speaking fluently several languages, and besides is a talented artist and amateur botanist.'[545] It was the apotheosis of a woman of modest means, who never let reality blight her prospects.

And thus, with varying degrees of enthusiasm, the surviving members of that 'typical Victorian family' left the nineteenth century behind and discovered modernity.

CHAPTER 43

Stumbling to Independence

In 1907 Jack returned to Mount Loftus after a visit to the International Exhibition in Dublin. He had enjoyed a good lunch, admired the displays from all parts of the British Empire – particularly the 'Somali Village' – and was furious that the Exhibition had been boycotted by the Nationalists as part of their campaign for Irish Preference. So he sat in his study to fume, writing notes on the spare pages of his cellar book in defence of Irish landlords and capitalist enterprise, and dismissal of what he saw as political posturing. 'Let those who preach Sinn Fein & those who preach Nationalism put down their money, risk it and start their industries and cease talking so much.' And then, on the same sheets of paper, he jotted down the estimated profits for another speculation in Mexican coal.

A few months later, across the sea in England, my grandfather Pierse Loftus was asked at very short notice to deliver a paper to 'an audience composed chiefly of English conservatives, who have made Unionism an integral plank of their political platform.' He chose as his theme 'The Irish Revival & Nationalist Ideals' – a seemingly neutral title that disguised a radical polemic, which he later thought prudent to forget. The only copy of his speech remained hidden in a folder, unread and unremembered for more than a century, until I found it in a chest in the attic.

Pierse declared at the outset that 'as an individualist my own tendencies are towards conservatism,' but that he utterly rejected orthodox Unionism. Having shocked his listeners awake, he soothed them by talking about various worthy schemes of a 'more or less non political' nature – the Gaelic League's efforts to revive the Irish language, the successes of the co-operative agricultural movement led by Sir Horace Plunkett, the work of the Industrial Development Associations, and the literary and artistic renewal inspired by such well-known names as Yeats and Lady Gregory. In fact, as Pierse scarcely acknowledged, each strand of this 'Irish Revival' had revolutionary implications. The Irish language was a marker of difference, even of exclusion, since it came to be a test of suitability for public office. Agricultural co-operatives provided a grassroots response to the evils of colonial 'landlordism', and Industrial Development Associations were a mechanism for Irish Preference, in defiance of the aggressive free-trade policies of the English government. Yeats, for all his misty allure, was a much more serious nationalist than his English readers realised.

Suddenly my grandfather shifted gear. 'As an Irishman intensely interested in the new genuine light appearing in the sky of his country after the quick fading and often disastrous brilliance of so many false dawns,' Pierse proclaimed his enthusiasm for a new political movement, Sinn Féin – 'Ourselves Only' – which 'was only officially started 26 months ago.' Sinn Féin was 'bitterly opposed to the parliamentary party led by Mr Redmond' – whose arguments for Irish independence had been corrupted by sending '80 voting machines to Westminster' – and it combined a simple message, 'the free Kingdom of Ireland is within you,' with a simple principle: 'No compromise on the constitution.' The new party believed that the Act of Union was 'illegal and invalid', that the English Parliament and law courts had no authority in Ireland, and was 'completely opposed to the enlistment of Irishmen in the British Naval or Military or police service.' It was determined to bypass the present government of Ireland by a combination of passive resistance and the establishment of its own parallel administration, headed by a National Assembly.

Pierse admitted that Sinn Féin's programme was 'astonishingly comprehensive and undisguised' and that it was opposed by the *Daily Telegraph*, the Catholic hierarchy, the leaders of the Labour Party and Irish Parliamentary Party – but declared his own wholehearted support. He also, most revealingly, quoted from Sinn Féin's official *Instructions to Branches*, which suggests that he himself was already an active member. 'Sinn Féin seems to me the most remarkable political movement of today – you will hear more of it shortly.'

That prediction – delivered by a young Irishman who had managed, hitherto, to convince them that he was 'one of us' – must have filled his conservative audience with dismay.

*

Later that year my grandfather stumbled back to his rooms in London, fuelled with 'much Burgundy' and chanting Fenian slogans, after a boisterous dinner with the Irish poet Padraic Colum. They had been celebrating the publication of Colum's first book, *Wild Earth* – a collection of poems that had originally appeared in *The United Irishman*, a paper edited by Arthur Griffith, the founder of Sinn Féin. Neither of them seemed much surprised when they arrived at Pierse's lodgings and 'found the Sinn Feiner – O'Mara – lounging in my most comfortable chair smoking my Turkish cigarettes and reading Yeats.' James O'Mara had been the Irish Parliamentary Party's MP for South Kilkenny, but resigned in 1907 to join Sinn Féin and, according to Pierse, was 'really the last man who should read poetry – he has too logical a mind.' True to form, O'Mara 'attacked Yeats as a renegade, and an English government pensioner, only to be answered by the poet's yet more passionate defence' – for Colum was a member of the Gaelic League, one of the founders of the Abbey Theatre in Dublin and a friend of Yeats, whom he enormously admired. 'In the midst of this hubbub the door opened & the MP came in – his face dropped as he saw O'Mara – but it was too late to retreat – so he joined our circle.' Pierse does not name him, but this must have been one of Redmond's Nationalists, furious at O'Mara's desertion but easily persuaded to stay by a glass of Irish whiskey and a classic Irish argument. That gathering of friends, disputing about politics and poetry, seems to me a perfect miniature of Irish nationalism, before things turned violent.

In 1908 Jack Loftus was appointed High Sheriff of County Kilkenny and decided that he needed somewhere grand enough to live for his year of office, since the hideous mansion that he had commissioned to replace his forebears' much loved home was still incomplete – building work having been 'much hindered by the wet seasons'. So he rented Barrowmount, a small estate with a fine eighteenth-century house adjoining the Mount Loftus demesne, which old Sir Francis Loftus had acquired from Lord Clifden but was lost in the crash of the 1880s. A few months later the *Kilkenny Moderator* announced the birth of his son and heir, Francis Coates Creagh Loftus, under the wonderfully eighteenth-century heading, 'Fashionable Intelligence'. The baby was presented with a silver loving cup, gold and coral rattle, silver porringer and spoon and a gold safety pin (for his nappies?). Time, it seems, was slipping backwards.[547]

Sinn Féin, despite its initial fame, attracted little support outside a small band of enthusiasts. It faded from view in the years immediately prior to the First World War and survived almost by accident – thanks largely to the English government, which mistakenly blamed it for the Easter Rising. So rapid was Sinn Féin's demise that Pierse's own allegiance switched, within three years, to the party that he had derided as ineffectual and terminally compromised by the machinations of Westminster. This change of heart occurred in 1910, when the Irish Parliamentary Party quite unexpectedly achieved its long-promised leverage on English politics. Two General Elections had been held within a year, each of which ended in the Liberals having a tiny lead over their Conservative rivals, but well short of an overall majority. The Irish Nationalists held the balance of power and the price of their support was a new bill for Irish Home Rule, which could now at last be enacted, since the block of the Lords' veto was about to be curtailed. This was the moment of political opportunity that persuaded Pierse Loftus to present himself as a parliamentary candidate for the constituency of North Kilkenny. He had also fallen in love and was newly married. Dorothy Reynolds was a young artist whose portraits were conventional but way of life seemed uninhibited – she may have encouraged Pierse to prove his ideals in practice.

He realised, of course, that he faced a great deal of scepticism, as an Irishman living in England, as a representative of the landlord class and as a young man with no record of struggle in the Nationalist cause. So he began his speech to the North Kilkenny Convention by paying tribute to his rivals, Patrick McDermott and Michael Meagher – both of whom were 'veterans of the battle' – but he argued that new blood was needed, and that his hero Parnell had achieved astonishing success because he surrounded himself with 'young untried men, who altered the face of Ireland.' Pierse claimed that for the past eight years he had concentrated on his business in England with the sole aim of placing it 'in such a prosperous condition that I could devote my whole time and attention to working for my country without payment,' and that during this time he had 'studied the Irish question & accumulated a library of

Irish books which would not shame Mr Redmond himself.' And then, with breathtaking aplomb, he brushed aside his opponents' accusations 'that I am a Sinn Feiner, that I am a Tory, that I fought against the Boers. I do not think it necessary to answer these, as they are simply untrue.'

Miraculous transformation of reality. My grandfather's boldness was in the classic style of Irish politics – never let the truth get in the way of a good story. For this was a man who had recently resigned from Sinn Féin, was about to join the Tory party, and was only prevented from fighting in the Boer War by the efforts of his family and friends. Less easy to deny was the fact that he came of the landlord class and 'was not bred up a Nationalist', but Pierse claimed this as an advantage. 'I am in the same position as Parnell, O'Connell & Edward Fitzgerald & I will say this: that – while fully admitting the curse landlordism has been to Ireland – that yet your most vigorous determined leaders, the men who meant business, were situate as I am – reared and educated as I am – and once they became Nationalist they became thorough Nationalists and today I stand before you as one who believes heart and soul in Irish Nationality.'

Pierse was fighting a losing battle. Though the *Kilkenny Moderator* later claimed that 'the Irish Nationalist Party would have found in him one of the most brilliant of their followers,' the North Kilkenny electors preferred a local man, one of their own, choosing a descendant of James Maher, who had served as steward at Mount Loftus a hundred years earlier, rather than a descendant of his employer, Sir Edward Loftus.

Having failed to gain a foothold in Irish politics, Pierse turned to polemics. He fired off letters to the newspapers, spoke frequently at meetings in Suffolk and London, and wrote his first book – more properly an extended pamphlet – *The Conservative Party and the Future*. Published in 1912, this seemed on the face of it another startling turn on his political rollercoaster – for the man who a short time earlier had dismissed as 'simply untrue' the notion that he was a Tory now set out his *Programme for Tory Democracy* in unambiguous language. But it was not, as many were swift to point out, the language of traditional Conservatism. *The Kilkenny People*, for example, published a long and enthusiastic review on 28 September 1912, but noted that 'the warmest praise for this admirably written and illuminating pamphlet comes from the "Daily Herald", the organ of the Labour Party, and having read it ourselves the difficulty that presents itself to us is to discover in what his Toryism consists – accepting that term in the sense in which it is usually applied, as representing a party of political stagnation and reaction – while on the other hand the democratic spirit that infuses and informs it is manifest in every page, almost in every line.' Pierse's vision of democracy included fixed terms for Parliament, a reconstructed Upper House, frequent use of the referendum, 'Land and Houses for the people,' educational reform, Home Rule for Ireland – and for England, Scotland and Wales. The best summary was indeed that of the *Daily Herald*.

> Mr Loftus believes in democracy. He believes in a State which considers the good of all, and not the good of a few. He wants strong Trade Unions, and Woman's Suffrage, and all kinds of wise things. One only wishes the Tory Party was as sensible and will bring them to pass. It is much more likely that Mr Loftus will become a Socialist, surely.

Those comments were acute. Pierse demanded action to redress working-class grievances and wrote a fascinating article towards the end of 1913, celebrating the *Daily Herald* as the authentic voice of labour unrest. 'This paper is edited with remarkable ability and day by day preaches doctrines of rebellion and revolution, and the leading articles are written with more fire and literary skill and beauty than those of any daily newspaper in England.' Pierse praised the *Herald*'s support for the Dublin strikers – in defence of the right to unionise – but thought their leader James Larkin and most of those who spoke on his behalf at mass meetings in the Albert Hall were 'cursed with an incurable mental sloppiness' and 'unworthy of their audience'.

Much the same thought seems to have crossed the mind of my grandfather's aunt – Henrietta, Lady Sankey – in relation to her favourite nephew.

> I was delighted with the pamphlet until I got to the 7th Chapter [Pierse's admittedly crackpot proposals for reforming the Upper House], which to my mind should never have been printed. I wish

you had consulted an experienced person knowing politics practically before giving your maddest reflections to the Publisher. I wanted to send your tract to Balfour & Lord Londonderry & Lord Charles Beresford all of whom I know and also Princess Louise hoping to get it passed on to the King but I am not so keen about doing so now.[549]

The politicians to whom Pierse sent copies seemed equally baffled. A traditional Conservative grandee took one glance at the title page before replying with brusque ill humour, 'I am not a Tory Democrat.' The sternest of Unionists, Edward Carson, wrote one of his typically ambiguous notes – 'The situation is a difficult one and of course is a constant anxiety' – but had no difficulty in drafting the entirely unambiguous Ulster Covenant, pledging to resist Home Rule by all means possible, which was signed by 500,000 Unionists in September that year. John Redmond – leader of the Irish Parliamentary Party – politely ignored my grandfather's pamphlet, but a more encouraging response came from Joseph Devlin, boss of the United Irish League, who suggested a meeting in London, to which he wanted to bring a young fellow Nationalist, Harry Boland. Pierse had dinner with Boland a few months later and was much impressed. He also made contact with George Gavan Duffy, the lawyer who later defended Roger Casement and several of those who were to lead the Easter Rising. But the real enthusiasts for his book were two campaigners for women's suffrage, Lady Aberconway and her daughter Priscilla Norman, both of whom were Liberals. Laura Aberconway claimed that 'your sense that the happiness of all is necessary to the full happiness of everyone, is I think the ideal of the Liberal party in the future,' while Priscilla teased Pierse as a secret ally: 'it leads me to think there must be a mistake somewhere, and that really you are one of us, a Liberal, if only you could endure to admit it.'

The most interesting letter came from Erskine Childers, whose own political trajectory was one of the strangest of all. He began as a committed Unionist, was converted to Nationalism by his American wife and achieved fame as the author of what many consider the first spy novel: *The Riddle of the Sands*. Childers (like the suffragettes) claimed Pierse for his own – 'I wish that you were a Liberal! – you seem nearer that than the other school! I quite agree with you that Toryism on its present basis of anarchy & barren negations is worthless to the country.' But most of his letter was strangely at a tangent. He pointed out a minor geographical error before commenting on the Irish Famine, which Pierse had blamed on the free trade policies of the English government – encouraging exports of food from Ireland when thousands were starving – while Childers placed greater emphasis on the repressive social history that had made the mass of the people dependent on a single crop, the potato. All of this was written in a crabbed, professorial hand and courteous tone of voice, slightly apologetic, which reminds me of an old-fashioned schoolmaster and which I find strangely moving – for two years later this mild-mannered man became a gun-runner for the Irish Volunteer Force. The German rifles that he bought for them and shipped to Ireland in his own yacht, given to him as a wedding present by his wife's father, armed the Easter Rising in 1916.

Shortly after Pierse's book was published, a new Home Rule Bill began slowly making its way through Parliament, despite the opposition of senior officials in most of the counties of Ireland – including Jack Loftus – who signed a letter to the *Irish Times* expressing their dismay. They strongly supported independence and dismissed the sectarian fears of Ulster Protestants, but they knew the strength of those fears, which they felt might scupper the Bill when enacted. They dreaded Partition. They were also concerned that the proposed method of election to a new Irish Parliament was based on too narrow a franchise and the financial arrangements were inadequate.[550] For very different reasons the Lords continued to delay matters for as long as they could, but their powers were now limited and the Bill was finally ready for Royal Assent in May 1914. All seemed more or less well, but at the last minute, in a devious parliamentary manoeuvre to placate the Unionists, an Amending Bill was passed for the 'temporary exclusion' of Ulster from the provisions of the new Act. It was much as Pierse had predicted the previous September, when he prophesied that backstairs deals and shabby manoeuvres would bring about Partition, and tried to warn the public in a letter to *The Times*.[551] His warning went unpublished, probably because it was too outspoken, and even he preferred to leave unsaid his fear that civil war would inevitably follow. 'As to what will happen in Ireland, I must leave to others the task of prophesying. The forces there, both Nationalist and Unionist, are so incalculable that I dare not attempt it.'

What actually happened was that the paramilitary Ulster Volunteer Force, inspired by Sir Edward Carson, imported German rifles to defend the Union, and the Irish Volunteers did likewise, – with the help of Erskine Childers – to oppose Partition. But just as civil war seemed imminent everything was altered. On 4 August 1914 Germany invaded Belgium and Britain declared war. The implementation of Home Rule was suspended for the duration.

In October 1914 Pierse Loftus's wife Dorothy sent a postcard from Suffolk to their infant son – whom they had packed off to Ireland for safety – with instructions to keep it. 'You will like this card when you are older.' It showed a boatload of Belgian refugees, landing in South-wold after crossing the North Sea – the first of several hundred to arrive in the town, which was only eighty miles distant from the Allied front line. Troops came and went on their way to war, and casualties were shipped back from Flanders to recuperate in the grand country houses of the local aristocracy, now requisitioned as hospitals. Pierse enlisted in a territorial battalion of the Suffolk Regiment and as a special constable, for which his duties included keeping nightly watch from the top of the church tower – spotting for illegal lights and on the lookout for air raids or invasion. Those fears were real, and persisted until the end of the war, but the actual damage was limited to a few small bombs, dropped from a lone Zeppelin, and a brief bombardment from the sea.

In 1915 Pierse and his wife were able to enjoy a short period of leave at Mount Loftus, where Jack was still living in considerable style, despite being a territorial captain in the Royal Irish Regiment. There are some fascinating photographs of the brothers, taken at this time. Pierse is soberly attired, sometimes in uniform, sometimes in a tweed jacket and breeches, but Jack's notion of how to dress for a wartime picnic beside the River Barrow includes a stiff winged collar and bow tie, white waistcoat, jaunty white hat and immaculately tailored suit. Even their moustaches are expressive – Pierse's is neat, close trimmed, while Jack's has a rakish twirl.

Ireland at this time seemed a place apart, distant from the front and distant in some way from the bitter quarrels of its own immediate past. For most Nationalists, as for most Unionists, normal politics had ceased to matter – and even those who regarded the Home Rule Act as an endlessly post-dated cheque committed themselves to the war. Only at the fringes was there any serious opposition, at least at first. The remaining adherents of Sinn Féin held back from what they saw as a British conflict, while the secretive Irish Republican Brotherhood – with the backing of two paramilitary organisations, the Irish Volunteer Force and the Irish Citizen Army – continued to plot for armed insurrection, inspired by a cult of martyrdom and the notion, shared by many who supported the war, that 'bloodshed is a sanctifying and cleansing thing.'[552] Eventually, to the amazement and disapproval of most of their fellow countrymen, they launched the Easter Rising, in April 1916 – timed to evoke the Christian symbolism of blood sacrifice. The Rising was doomed to failure and was defeated in six days and yet, thanks partly to the crude over-reaction of the British Government, it inspired the mythology of a nation that led, within a few years, to independence and civil war.

None of this had much evident impact on Jack Loftus. In 1916 he joined the newly formed Machine Gun Corps, was promoted to major and sent to Grantham for training. But then, as a diversion from the tedium of life in camp, he daydreamed of social glory – and petitioned the King to revive the family baronetcy, which had so unfortunately fallen into abeyance. In the midst of a European war he arranged for copies of his petition to be forwarded to the Lord Lieutenant of Ireland, the English Home Secretary and the Prime Minister – all of whom had other things on their minds. Needless to say, nothing came of it.

The following year, home on leave, Jack decided to take an inventory of everything of value at Mount Loftus. It provides a useful snapshot of taste and style in the furnishing of the house at that time, and lists a great number of pictures and objects that were lost in the fire, in 1934. But beyond its archival value, I am intrigued that this was something he felt he needed to do, at such a time. And then, in what seems another distraction, Jack thought he might stand for Parliament in the Kilkenny by-election of 1917. He drafted an address to the electors, declaring himself entirely in favour of Irish self-government but denouncing the Republican policy of the Sinn Féin candidate, William Cosgrave, 'because it can only lead to endless enmity with England and division & intrigue in Ireland.' Having read through his speech he must have realised that it was somewhat thin, and added what he hoped was an inspiring postscript. 'I am opposed to any safeguards and preferential treatments. The safeguard of any Irishman is with the justice of the people.' But that, too, fell flat – and having read it again, he wisely decided not to stand. Cosgrave, despite being then in prison for his part in the Easter Rising, was elected unopposed.

Pierse, meanwhile, had been sent to join the British Expeditionary Force in Northern France. He spent most of his active service as an instructor at the Army Musketry Camp, but seems to have fought at the front in the last stages of the conflict and was mentioned in despatches, 'for gallant and distinguished services in the Field'. I found his service medal in a drawer, together with a German decoration – the Merit Cross for War Aid, *'Für Kriegs Hilfsdienst'* – sad souvenir of the trenches. In a packet of cherished wartime letters there was one from his wife, Dorrie, which must have been written early in 1917, just as Pierse arrived in France. 'There is nothing to do but hope one day we will be together again – if love can hope to guard you, you know there is none stronger than mine for you.' In the same packet I came across an unused postcard of the main street of Fruges – a small town close to his camp – that Pierse bought from the local tobacconist, the widow Greuez. It shows a steeply sloping hill lined with whitewashed houses – some of which may have been bars or shops – a hideous church near the crossroads, old ladies clad in black, an air of poverty and absence. I think it reminded my grandfather of Ireland – it might almost have been Borris, across the river from Mount Loftus.

And that is all, for Pierse never seems to have talked about this time, or written about it. But the few photographs taken of him over those years tell their own story. The neat, self-contained young man who is pictured in his first uniform, or taking a few weeks' leave with his family at Mount Loftus, suddenly ages, seems weary – even as he sits with his young sons in a meadow, on a seaside holiday in Devon, still in uniform, with a model aeroplane in his hands and a faint smile on his lips, in the last year of the war.

It was then, in 1918, that a vast German offensive swept through the Allied armies, provoking Lloyd George to extend conscription to

Ireland for the first time. The response was a huge anti-conscription campaign, uniting the grievances and frustrations of many years in a surge of fury that enabled a revived Sinn Féin, now led by de Valera, to become the dominant political force in Irish Nationalism – and the Irish Republican Brotherhood, under Michael Collins, to reconstitute the Irish Volunteers as the Irish Republican Army. In the General Election that immediately followed the end of the war, Sinn Féin won a landslide and the Irish Parliamentary Party was almost wiped out. Behind the scenes, the IRA prepared for a campaign of guerrilla warfare. As the British government continued to procrastinate on the subject of Irish independence, the Sinn Féin members refused to take up their Westminster seats and established the first Dáil at Dublin, on 21 January 1919. That same day two IRA members, acting independently, shot two Royal Irish Constabulary officers in County Tipperary. It was the beginning of a war of independence that lasted for more than two years. Both sides committed acts of great savagery, but there was a particular, vindictive bitterness to the reprisals of the 'Black & Tans' – the paramilitary force recruited by the British government from soldiers who had endured years in the trenches. Many had their own reasons for hating the Catholic Irish but there was also, it seems to me, an acrid taste in the mouth – the hangover of the Great War.

When my grandfather was eventually demobilised, in February 1919, it was into a world that demanded his immediate attention, a long way from Ireland. The brewery needed re-organisation and its seaside hotels had to be reopened, after being closed for four years. There were two small sons whom Pierse scarcely knew and a wife who had learnt to live without him. It was also a sad world. Pierse was forty-one, many of his friends were dead and the light-hearted days of arguing about Yeats seemed gone for ever – but his own sense of social injustice was still fiercely alive. 'In despair with the apparently permanent domination of the Tory party by Lloyd George, and deeply shocked by the proceedings of the Black and Tans in Ireland, I made overtures to stand as a Liberal candidate.' And was rejected.

    Jack celebrated the end of war by commissioning a large family portrait of his wife and children, on the shore at Rosslare Strand in County Wexford. May Loftus holds a parasol to protect her from the sun, eleven-year-old Frank sits astride a pony, his sisters are barefoot – and the entire family is clad in the stylish informality that became fashionable in the 1920s, from Biarritz to East Hampton. This wonderful period piece paid no heed whatsoever to the memories of recent slaughter or to the hard, embittered fight for Irish independence that was then beginning – but the artist was Leo Whelan, whose most famous portrait, painted two years later, was of Michael Collins, Commander in Chief of the IRA.

At about nine o'clock on a dark and bitterly cold night, in January 1920, a procession of cars and horse-drawn carriages was travelling north of Kilkenny, on the way to a ball. As the leading carriage rounded a sharp bend in the road the driver heard a shout to halt, and 'two or three masked men sprang out and covered him with revolvers.' They pulled the carriage sideways, in front of a rough barricade of stones, as the first motor car was heard approaching. When the car pulled up, the driver and the male passengers were searched, and then all of them were bundled over a stile and into a meadow, and held under armed guard – but the carriage and its occupants were allowed to proceed on their way. 'Having bumped over the barricade they completed their journey and were in plenty of time for the ball.'

Another car arrived, and was halted, and its passengers joined the rest in the field. And then another, but this time the driver tried to accelerate through the ambush, only to be stopped when several shots were fired, puncturing the windscreen and bodywork – and the same fate met the next car, when this, too, tried to escape. 'The number of victims in the field was now growing.'

Then came two more cars and a carriage, the first of which was a Humber belonging to my great-uncle, Jack Loftus, and the second a Lancia Italia owned by Sir Hercules Langrishe – the carriage was Mr O'Gorman's. All were halted. A man in Lady Langrishe's party drew a revolver, but was immediately 'covered by one of the masked men,' who forced him to throw it over the hedge, 'where it was found the next morning by the police.'

At this point 'a well known city man and his wife, who were out for their evening "constitutional", walked into the midst of the scene,' all unsuspecting. They too were herded into the damp field and joined the rest – now about thirty-five in number, most of them in evening dress. Several of the ladies were very frightened but others seemed quite excited by the adventure, and a combination of chocolates, cigarettes and 'other dainties' – I suspect a hip flask or two – provided some degree of comfort, until an alarming din shattered the dark, as the IRA men took sledge hammers to the car engines. Eventually there was silence, and the gang's leader loomed over the hedge. He threatened the hostages with death if they dared to move before ten minutes had passed – then he and his men vanished into the night.

When the party-goers straggled back to the road they realised that they were never going to get to the ball – all six cars were wrecked, two had been turned on their sides and some were riddled with bullet holes. A few of the ladies were driven back to Kilkenny in the horse carriage, to alert the police, while the rest had little other choice than to walk the mile and a half to the city. But one increasingly frantic man, who had hidden a large bundle of cash at his first glimpse of the masked attackers, declared that it was lost. Having been through all his pockets he enlisted the help of the others in searching the field, before suddenly, shame-facedly, remembering that he had stuffed the notes in his underpants. This brief moment of comedy restored their spirits, and they all went home in better humour than might have been expected.

That contemporary account in the *Kilkenny People* prompts many questions. Why was the first horse-drawn carriage allowed to proceed on its way and the masked men's anger directed at the cars, rather than more obvious targets such as my great-uncle Jack or those other society people – Langrishe, Butler and Guinness were the best-known names – so easily identified in their evening dress? And how was it possible for the victims of the hold-up to enjoy their chocolates and cigarettes with such apparent insouciance? Somehow it seemed that all concerned knew their parts.

The key to this drama was a motor strike that had been called six weeks earlier, in protest against an order which obliged the owners of cars or vans to apply for a special permit before taking out their vehicles, as the government attempted to clamp down on the transport of arms and insurgents. The IRA had decided that if they could not use their cars, no one could – so it was the motors, not the people who were the object of their attack. But the ambush hurt most those who were in some ways closest to the attackers. For Loftus or Langrishe the loss of a car was a minor inconvenience, but for Cody, Kavanagh, Tierney and Mulrooney – owners of the four cars hired that evening – the strike was a disaster, since taxis were their sole source of income. They were all local men, almost certainly known to their assailants, and might have hoped that this would give them immunity – but the most savage revenge was reserved for 'blacklegs' who collaborated in any way with the Ascendancy.

Almost unnoticed in the escalating violence, a bill had been making its way through the English Parliament, which effectively gave legal substance to the messy Home Rule compromise that had been suspended on the eve of the Great War. The Government of Ireland Act – which became law two days before Christmas 1920 – made provision for two devolved Parliaments, in Belfast and Dublin, and some vague notion of a Council of Ireland that might link these two bodies. Ulster was happy, and proceeded to the elections that established a Unionist government for Northern Ireland, headed by Sir James Craig. Southern Nationalists ignored the Act, while silently accepting the reality of Partition as they fought for full independence. But the English government was acutely aware of a clause in the legislation which specified that if the Dublin Parliament was not operational by 12 July 1921, Southern Ireland would become a crown colony governed by martial law – an outcome that would have demanded a vastly increased commitment of armed forces and could only have made a bad situation even worse. On 24 June Lloyd George gritted his teeth and wrote an open letter to de Valera, as 'the chosen leader of the great majority in Southern Ireland,' inviting him to come to a conference in London, together with Craig, 'to explore the utmost possibility of a settlement.' De Valera refused to countenance Partition by sitting down at the negotiating table with the Premier of Ulster, or to negotiate without a truce. So finally, after a terrible year of increasing violence and brutal retaliation, with the deadline for the implementation of martial law coming closer by the minute, the longed-for Truce was finally agreed. It came into effect on 11 July 1921 and de Valera arranged to meet Lloyd George in London the following Thursday.

He arrived at Euston Station in the midst of a heat wave and was greeted by a frenzied crowd, fighting to get near him – 'they howled and screamed in the extremity of their enthusiasm.' 'Dev' may have anticipated something of this sort and was, in any case, determined to bypass the others in one-to-one discussions with Lloyd George. He wanted to be hidden away, out of the public eye. While his delegation made its headquarters at the Grosvenor Hotel on Park Lane, de Valera himself had arranged to stay at No. 5 West Halkin Street, close to Belgrave Square; the house that Jack Loftus had recently inherited from his aunt, Henrietta Sankey. It was centrally located, spacious, richly furnished and currently unoccupied – an ideal base for the crucial days that followed – but I wonder what de Valera made of the delicate watercolours by the late General Sankey that decorated every room, depicting scenes of imperial life in India and British campaigns in Afghanistan. Jack Loftus must by then have recognised that any solution, however much it pained his own sense of loyalty to the English Crown, was better than the continuation of things as they were, and had made contact with De Valera through his cousin, Máire de Butléir, a committed nationalist who had suggested the name of Sinn Féin to Arthur Griffith and was a close friend of Dev's wife. Jack may also have hoped that a settlement negotiated with his assistance might in some way strengthen his own position in the new Ireland, whatever shape that took. De Valera wrote two or three letters to him over the following year, which may have touched on these issues, but their correspondence has vanished, like so much else.

It proved, in any case, a fruitless mission. Each side held out for more than the other could concede, and clung to symbols of wording and allegiance that meant much to their supporters but blocked the first steps to practical independence. What Roy Foster has termed 'the politics of exaltation' trumped, yet again, the messy compromises of political common sense.

De Valera and Lloyd George continued a lengthy correspondence after the breakdown of negotiations but it was not until September that the two sides agreed to meet again. By then much had changed. De Valera knew that there was no prospect of achieving a republic and that any foreseeable treaty would be resisted by the most passionate of his supporters. He decided not to take part in the negotiations himself but agreed to send Michael Collins – as part of a team led by Arthur Griffith that included the irreconcilable Erskine Childers, as Secretary. The presence of Collins and the absence of de Valera were crucial to the shape of the final treaty. De Valera could never have allowed himself to negotiate anything less than the republic that he had so often and so passionately proclaimed, while Collins – with his clear military mind – knew that the first step was the most important, and the rest would eventually follow. What each of them feared and what each of them expected has been the subject of endless debate. My own view is that both foresaw what actually happened. De Valera expected a treaty to be signed – and overwhelmingly endorsed by the Dáil – which he would feel bound to reject. Collins, for all his courage, feared for the future. He purchased a fast two-seater aircraft that was kept on constant standby at Croydon, ready to fly him back to Ireland in case of need. The usual explanation is that he expected a breakdown in negotiations leading to an immediate resumption of hostilities, and knew that the British government had placed a price of £10,000 on his head, prior to the truce. I think he feared the contrary – that a treaty would indeed be signed, and the result would be civil war.

Negotiations began in London on 11 October and lasted nearly two months. After a clumsy start, with the full teams from each side confronting one another over the table, Griffith and Collins increasingly took the lead for the Irish. As the weeks dragged by they gradually made small concessions on trade and naval defence, while moving towards some form of Dominion status that stopped well short of de Valera's plan for a republic in 'external association' with the Commonwealth. They were recalled briefly to Dublin, apparently to stiffen their resolve, but eventually – overcome by exhaustion and by the threat of an immediate resumption of war – they signed the treaty at two o'clock in the morning of 6 December. The Irish Free State was born, Éire would have to wait.

A few hours later Collins wrote to his friend John O'Kane.

When you have sweated, toiled, had mad dreams, hopeless nightmares, you find yourself in London's streets, cold and dank in the night air. Think – what have I got for Ireland? Something which she has wanted these past seven hundred years. Will anyone be satisfied at the bargain? Will anyone? I tell you this; early this morning I signed my death warrant. I thought at the time how odd, how ridiculous – a bullet may just as well have done the job five years ago.

In the brief civil war that followed, more were killed than in the previous two years of fighting against the English. Several of those whom Pierse Loftus had known and argued with, in the days when the future seemed exciting, now found themselves opposed to the nation that they had helped to bring into being. Harry Boland was shot in a skirmish with soldiers of the Irish Free State, at Skerries Grand Hotel in Dublin. Erskine Childers was arrested for carrying a pistol, while on his way to meet de Valera, and sentenced to death by a military tribunal. He was executed at the Beggar's Bush Barracks, having insisted on shaking hands with each man in the firing squad. George Gavan Duffy reluctantly signed the treaty that he helped to negotiate and was appointed Minister of Foreign Affairs in the new Irish government – but resigned his post in protest at the killing of Childers, his long-standing friend. De Valera himself, though refusing to fight, led the political opposition to the treaty – a decision that he admitted, decades later, was the biggest mistake of his life. And Collins met his end, as he had foretold, in an IRA ambush.

I am reminded of the bleak conclusion of the republican Ernie O'Malley, who fought against the treaty. 'At one time it had been easy to blame the British for our faults and easy to interpret them in terms of conditions forced on us by historical necessity; now some learned to analyse cause and effect, to blame themselves and to face the evil necessity of power.'[554]

CHAPTER 44

The Fire

The aftermath of the civil war was a time of uneasy forgetting. Memories of the recent troubles were re-ignited by sporadic violence, but conservatism, poverty and a sense of disappointment stifled the 'politics of exaltation'. Dublin was scarred by the battles of the previous few years and the countryside, too, was changed. Many of the old Ascendancy families had closed up their houses – or had them torched by the IRA – and most of those who remained were no longer rich enough to keep up the old way of life, for their estates had long ago been parcelled off by the Encumbered Estates Court. Land re-distribution spread ownership more widely, but the dominance of pasturage as the most profitable form of farming worked in the opposite direction, forcing thousands of smallholders off the soil. Even the graziers were suffering from the worldwide collapse in prices that followed the Great Crash of 1929.

But life at Mount Loftus continued as if little had changed, for Jack's wealth was derived from his wife's inheritance, not from the land. His family went hunting and fishing and dancing as their forebears had done, and they were attended by up to a dozen domestic servants living in the house and its immediate outbuildings – plus gardeners, stable lads and others. In some cases the relationship between master and retainer was complicated by ancient history. Young 'Denny' Carroll, for example, was one of a swarm of Carrolls living nearby, all claiming kinship with Jack's great-grandmother Mary – the shopkeeper's daughter from Goresbridge who had caused such a scandal by marrying Edward Loftus in 1789. When Denny became Jack's chauffeur (in the late 1920s) both knew that they were cousins, but never spoke of it.

There is a small stone building in the walled upper garden at Mount Loftus, which once was used as an apple store. Various family members and visitors scratched their names and the date – in most cases no later than 1936 – on the whitewashed wall that is visible as you enter. Only when the door is closed is it possible in the dim light to make out a few inscriptions on the opposite jamb, normally hidden from view –

including a couple of outlined hearts, framing Denny Carroll's name, and a brief, scornful message. 'Mounkeys wanted in the zoo, I'd apply if I were you – do.'

I believe, but cannot prove, that it was lovelorn Denny himself who signed his name within the hearts – provoking Jack Loftus's second and favourite daughter, Patricia, to scribble her riposte. And I am reminded of a story that she told me, years ago. 'I remember one day in my youth having words with Denny Carroll, then my father's chauffeur. In the heat of the moment he shouted at me, "Ain't I your cousin?" With my riding whip in hand and flinging my hunting boots at him, I roared. "Get out, or I'll kick you out." He went.' Patricia was still in her teens, small but spirited, and Denny was three years older. I guess he made a pass at her – she was certainly scared and angry at what she thought was pure impertinence, and confused at his retort, not having been told the full family background. But Denny did not forget it. Not long afterwards Patricia was alone in the house when a band of drunken youths came up to Mount Loftus and started throwing gravel at the windows and threatening to break in. Patricia was quite undaunted. She threw water down on the men and called out, 'If you don't go. I'll get a gun and I'll fire,' before descending through the dark house and seizing a shotgun. Then she went outside and let off both barrels, into the air as she thought, but there was a yelp from the darkness as they vanished. Some years later old Mr Carroll died and she went to his wake, where Denny, the eldest son, fell drunk on her shoulder. 'Miss Patricia, Miss Patricia I forgive you. Didn't you pepper me well that night.'

Patricia told those stories with zest, as entertainment, but I can't help hearing an echo from long ago – of Lady Loftus's refusal to recognise the legitimacy of Mary Carroll's marriage to her favourite son, and the lingering bitterness of social exclusion.

Zest, at any rate, soon gave way to sadness. Jack's wife May died suddenly at Mount Loftus in February 1929, and his only son Francis returned from Cambridge with meningitis in April 1930, and expired at the age of twenty-two. Distraught and in need of company, Jack went to stay with his neighbours the Flemings, at Barracore House. There he met Emily Maud Scroggie, and a few months later they were married, 'very quietly' at Ealing, in January 1931.

Jack was fifty-five but seemed older and may already have been suffering from Parkinson's disease, which eventually overcame him. But despite the crash of 1929 he was still very well off and could be good company. 'Scroggie', as she was cuttingly referred to by Jack's children, was a woman of modest means and modest expectations. Born in India, daughter of a minor official of the British Raj, she had led a peripatetic life before ending up in Ireland, still unmarried at the age of forty-seven. As with so many genteel spinsters of that era, she seems to have been condemned to a humiliating routine of inviting herself to stay for months at a time with a circuit of acquaintances, and spending the rest of her life in dreary seclusion at Buswells Hotel, in Dublin.

It was a marriage of lonely people and perhaps for that reason provoked a lot of ill feeling. Maud seemed insanely jealous of all who had known Jack before they were married, and there were endless rows with his daughters – particularly with Patricia, her father's darling. Then, as Parkinson's disease took hold, she found herself acting as Jack's nurse. Scroggie may not have been the monster that family legend portrays, but she was certainly a sad and embittered woman, who saw others enjoying life in a way that had escaped her.

On Sunday 7 October 1934 there was a family party in Dublin to celebrate the christening of Jack Loftus's first grandchild – son of his eldest daughter Bettina and her gangling husband, Hal Grattan Bellew. The following morning, very early, Bettina's sister Patricia set off back to Mount Loftus, to exercise the hounds, while Jack and his second wife left at a more leisurely pace on a motoring tour of southern Ireland.

It was a bright, blustery day and Patricia was out riding all morning. She went home briefly to tell the cook that she wouldn't have any lunch, before driving to Graiguenamanagh to see the joint master of the hunt. Returning from Graigue at about three in the afternoon, she stopped at the Lodge to see the gatekeeper, Mrs Stafford. 'I'm going down to Goresbridge to catch the second post – is there anything you want me to get for you?' Mrs Stafford – who was reckoned a little loopy – replied in her absent-minded way, 'No, there's nothing I want. O yes, there was something, let me think. The cook was down here a few minutes back, and she do say the house is burning.'

Wondering whether this was just another example of Mrs Stafford's oddness, Patricia drove up the avenue to be confronted by a scene of mayhem. 'Flames were coming out of the roof, the men were tolling the stable yard bell, maids screaming, the telephone constantly ringing because the lines were on fire and no one doing anything useful.' Patricia's first thought was to save her dogs, trapped in her first-floor bedroom, so she dashed up a ladder but was dragged off by Denny Carroll, who climbed up himself and just managed to get them out through the window. Then Patricia took charge of operations. She realised that the only hope was to fill the huge water tank in the attic until it overflowed. 'Get the pump engine working and don't let it stop, whatever happens.' More and more helpers arrived – local farm-workers, the Civic Guards from Goresbridge – and she organised a human chain to salvage as much as they could. 'We rescued a fair number of books, which we spread on the lawn for safety.'

By this time the fire was roaring out of control, fanned by a strong wind, and it seemed that all was lost. And then the rafters fell in, the tank collapsed and Patricia's plan was seen to work, as a sudden flood of water doused the flames – 'But we saved the wrong end of the house, the servants' quarters.' At which point the fire brigade arrived. Lieutenant Duffy and his crew had come from the Curragh, fifty miles away, and were determined to make themselves useful. So they unreeled their hoses and began spraying water with indiscriminate enthusiasm, drenching the stacks of books that Patricia had so carefully saved.

Then the recriminations began, as she discovered that the fire had been started by Scroggie's maid, who had hung some of her mistress's clothes to air above the Esse stove that heated the hall. The clothes were wrapped in tissue paper, which scorched and fell on the stove, sending up a sudden flare of fire. The next day, when Patricia discovered the maid hanging more clothes up to dry above a stove in the stables, she exploded with fury. 'Don't you think you've done enough by burning the house down – do you want to destroy the stables as well?'

Those, at least, are her memories of this dramatic day – but the facts are more elusive. To begin with, it seems that Patricia's account of confusion and helplessness when she first arrived on the scene reflects her own sense of panic – blind to the efforts of servants and farm labourers, who worked like heroes to rescue what they could, before she got there. Eighteenth-century views of Mount Loftus and paintings of the racehorses bred by Sir Nicholas and of his brother's red setters were burnt to ashes, but a surprising amount was saved, even from the hall where the fire first started and from the upstairs rooms which must have been most difficult to get to when the flames took hold. Most of the family portraits survived, as did other cherished heirlooms, documents and books.

It is equally clear that Patricia's anger at Scroggie's maid was coloured by her bitter resentment of the poor girl's mistress. When Patricia told these tales it was as though she still felt Scroggie's malice, and blamed her for the disaster.

After the fire Jack and Scroggie moved to Barracore House, which they borrowed for about a year while the surviving servants' wing at Mount Loftus was patched together and the rubble cleared away. Jack Loftus died shortly after they returned to live there, in July 1936. A month later, in August, Patricia insisted on holding a great hunt party, on the eve of her wedding to an English naval commander, Temple Bayliss. Most of the local farmers were invited, many got very drunk and some were sick. Scroggie was outraged, and locked Patricia out of the house. She had to sleep in the stables and crept in early the next morning to dress for her wedding. It was the last great explosion of their long and bitter feud.

The year of the fire also marked the final twist in the strange political journey of Jack's brother Pierse – from Sinn Féin radical to Tory MP in the English House of Commons. On 15 Feb 1934 he won a by-election for the Lowestoft constituency in Suffolk, which he continued to hold for the following decade. It was the end to his dream of returning to Ireland, to the land where his family had lived for nearly four hundred years.

The dream, in any case, was a mirage – for the patched-up house and estate at Mount Loftus slowly but inexorably decayed. Bettina Grattan Bellew inherited the place after her father's death and went to live there with her husband and two infant children. The children grew up and gradually slipped away, to make their lives elsewhere, and Hal died in 1967. What remained of the estate was parcelled off bit by bit, trees colonised the park and the old stables fell into disrepair. When Bettina died in 1995 the house and its contents were sold. The place is still there. The rest is memory.

CHAPTER 45

In Powerstown Graveyard

A long procession wound through the avenue towards the chapel: first our carriage, then numbers of local carriages of the gentry, then farmers' carts, the men wearing a long white scarf about their hats or shoulders. After these, dozens of men on horses or ponies, each with his white scarf. It was a great turnout.

Approaching the graveyard I heard a strange piercing melancholy wail. This came from half a dozen or more old women with black shawls over their heads who were kneeling by the chapel. It was the old immemorial Irish 'Keen'.

After the service my aunts and I descended to the vault into which the coffin had been lowered, and my aunts walked around inspecting the coffins ranged on the shelves and, quite cheerfully, recalled old friends and relatives. Then we adjourned to the house, where we were entertained to a long, cheery, excellent lunch.

This is my grandfather's description of attending the funeral of an elderly cousin in Galway, in 1902, but the form was identical to that of every Loftus burial, for centuries past – and it seemed appropriate to honour that tradition as best I could. So I set out from the front lodge at Mount Loftus in search of Powerstown graveyard, hoping to discover the family vault with the coffins of my forebears 'ranged on the shelves'. Eventually, with some difficulty, I found the place, a mile or two distant from the house: a small church, roofless, with nettles filling the nave and goats grazing among the tombstones, a couple of fine old trees and peaceful views across green fields.

Graveyards are wonderful places for the burial of old disputes. I scraped away the moss from one of those tottering stones to find it inscribed with the name of John Eaton, whose battles with my forebears are long forgotten. Nearby I discovered another stone, 'Erected by Mrs Murphy of Mount Loftus in memory of her mother Mary Carroll & her grandmother Margaret Carroll.' Mary's marriage to Lieutenant Edward Loftus caused such family rows that she never took her husband's name and was buried outside the family vault. And then I found that vault, crouched at the edge of the graveyard, with a huge, twisted trunk of ivy clasped around its massive stone roof. The entrance had long ago been walled up: there was no way of gaining access.

So I perched on the churchyard wall and thought about my ancestors, pondering the ambiguous meaning of our family motto, '*Loyal au Mort*'. As a child I had assumed it was one of those phrases of boastful emptiness, 'loyal unto death' – it was only later that I realised the correct translation was something less obvious, 'loyal to the dead'; not loyal to the dead in general but loyal to the dead man. Many questions followed. Was that a statement or an injunction, and who was this dead hero? And what might loyalty mean, in such a context? Or was it simply a mistake by the heralds, bad grammar, when they should have written '*loyal à la mort*'?

As I gazed at the half-buried vault in Powerstown graveyard, in the soft light of that spring day, and imagined those coffins ranged on its dusty shelves, I was reminded of another motto, used at certain points in the family history: '*Prends moi tel que je suis*' (Take me as I am). So it seemed that I should honour them all, the good and the bad together, and not make judgements. Take me as I am – loyalty means accepting our shared history, my heritage.

It also means telling and retelling those tales that I heard as a child – giving life to the shades of the dead, as at a wake. And sooner or later, as at a wake, there comes a time to open the whiskey and remember a past that is filled with leaping shadows. This is the time for ghost stories.

Each of the Ascendancy families had its own hoard of horrors – a mordant litany of names and places, people, property and the devil – and ours was no exception. The best versions were told by my elderly cousin Patricia. Tiny but tough, a famous horsewoman in her day, she loved the shock of the story and never grew bored by the family repertoire. There was the pale eighteenth-century girl who was some-times glimpsed at Rathfarnham Castle, and the ghost with cloven feet who terrorised Loftus Hall, but the tale of the Mount Loftus kennel-man, eaten by his hounds, was the one that she told with the greatest glee – for she herself had learnt it in the most dramatic fashion, on a misty morning in 1930. Five couple of hounds had arrived to form the nucleus of a new pack of Mount Loftus harriers and were put in the Bull Yard, near Hollyhock's old stable. Patricia asked her father if some of the boys on the estate could help her to exercise the new arrivals, so he told two young Carrolls to give her a hand. She took them to the yard – but as soon as they heard the hounds give tongue the terrified brothers scrambled up the nearest tree and refused to come down. 'Wasn't your grandfather's huntsman eaten by the hounds?' Then they told her, as vividly as if it had happened the previous week, the story of the kennel-man's three-day absence on a drunken spree, and how the starving hounds devoured him when eventually he stumbled home. Patricia, near tears, went to her father and asked whether this was true. ' "Yes," said my Papa, "and nothing was left but his boots!" ' The kennel-man haunts the place even now – too vivid to be forgotten.

Stories such as these have been a way of preserving history, reinventing memory. But they also provide a means of forgetting, of exorcising nightmares by telling them as penny dreadfuls – tales so highly coloured that the real horror is hidden behind grotesque masks. Thus it is with all my family narratives. As I struggle to catch their stories, in rooms crowded with noisy ghosts, I am often distracted by louder conversations. Their words, in so far as I can make them out, are full of contradictions, ambiguities, uncertainties – but this is the reason I trust them. 'Take me as I am.' And I trust the old legends, told to me as a child. They might have been exaggerated, in the interests of drama, but they were not dressed up as moral fables. History, in those versions, is something living, immediate; memory is of the moment. These partial, lopsided, fragments of Irish history may not be true – not the whole truth – but they are real.

As the afternoon sun warms the stone slabs that roof the family vault in Powerstown graveyard, I rest my hand on one of them, relishing its weathered feel but also, half unconsciously, tapping it like a drum, as if sending a message to those interred below. As with all our ancestral tombs, this one is unmarked by any memorial or inscription. I like that anonymity, the lack of ostentation. But in telling these stories again, for future generations, I am also addressing the dead. Salutations.

Notes

Abbreviations used in the Notes:

SL Archive = Author's family archive

CSP(I) = Calendar of State Papers (Ireland)

CSP(D) = Calendar of State Papers (Domestic)

DNB = *Dictionary of National Biography*

NLI = National Library of Ireland

TCD = Trinity College Dublin

Chapter 2 Dissolution

1 Manuscript 'Life of Archbishop Loftus' (SL Archive)

2 *Itinerary in or about the years 1535–1543*, by John Leland (edited by Lucy Tomlinson Smith, London 1910).

3 The declaration of monastic vice was included in the preamble to the Act of Suppression (1536: 27 Henry VIII, c. 28). The report on 'Coram alias Coverham' by the government inspectors, 'Doctorem Layton et Doctorem Legh', is quoted by John Wm Clay in his edition of 'Yorkshire Monasteries, Suppression Papers' (*Yorkshire Archaeological & Topographical Association*, Vol. 48, 1912). William L'Anson published a detailed account of Coverham Abbey in the *Yorkshire Archaeological Journal* (Vol. XXV, 1920). An unpublished research paper by Guy Halsall, 'Coverham Abbey: a preliminary study in its History and Archaeology c.1187–1536' (York University, 1986), was kindly lent me by Harriet Corner, of Coverham Abbey. See also R. Fieldhouse and B. Jennings, *A History of Richmond & Swaledale* (Phillimore, 1978).

4 'Yorkshire Monasteries, Suppression Papers' (*Yorkshire Archaeological & Topographical Association*, Vol. 48, 1912). 'Wills & Inventories from the registry of the Archdeaconry of Richmond' (*Surtees Society*, Vol. 29, 1853).

5 William l'Anson, op. cit. William Page (ed.), *Victoria History of Yorkshire, North Riding* (1907). 'Feet of Fines for the Tudor Period' (*Yorkshire Archaeological & Topographical Association*, Vol. 8, 1890). 'Yorkshire Fines for the Stuart Period' (*Yorkshire Archaeological & Topographical Association*, Vols 53 & 58, 1915).

Chapter 3 A Radical Education

6 Manuscript 'Life of Archbishop Loftus' (SL Archive)

7 'Wills & Inventories from the Registry of the Archdeaconry of Richmond' (*Surtees Society*, Vol. 29, 1853)

9 CSP(I), Vol. 165, No. 32, June 1592

10 Loftus to Sir Robert Cecil, 13 September 1600. CSP(I)

Chapter 4 Faith in the Word

11 Alexander Craik, Bishop of Kildare, to Lord Robert Dudley, 30 April 1561. Sussex complained to Cecil, 22 July 1562, that 'The people, without discipline, utterly void of religion, come to divine service as to a May game.' E. P. Shirley (ed.), *Original letters and papers in illustration of the history of the Church of Ireland during the reigns of Edward VI, Mary and Elizabeth* (1851).

12 Sussex was much struck by Loftus's abilities as a preacher and wrote to commend him to Queen Elizabeth (29 November 1561) and to Cecil (25 December 1561). Helga Robinson-Hammerstein, 'Adam Loftus and the Elizabethan Reformation in Ireland: Uniformity and Dissent', in *Search: A Church of Ireland Journal*, Vol. 28 No. 1, Spring 2005.

13 James Morris (ed.), *Calendar of Patent and Close Rolls of Chancery in Ireland*, Vol. I, p. 471 (Dublin, 1861)

14 In 1562 Terence Danyell wrote to Lord Deputy Sussex to inform him that 'the Chapter be so sparkeled and owte of order as he can by no means assemble them to proceed to the election of Mr. Adam Loftus.' Rev. C. Scantlebury S.J., 'Rathfarnham Castle', in *Dublin Historical Record* (1951). Sussex passed on this message to the Queen 2 September 1562. E. P. Shirley (ed.), op. cit.

15 'Annals Civil and Ecclesiastical relating to the History of Ireland', manuscript compiled by Archbishop Adam's great-grandson, Dudley Loftus. (Marsh's Library, Dublin. Z4.2.7)

16 Manuscript 'Life of Archbishop Loftus' (SL Archive)

18 Elizabeth to Sir Nicholas Arnold, Justice of Ireland (6 January 1565), quoted in manuscript 'Life of Archbishop Loftus' (SL Archive)

19 Manuscript 'Life of Archbishop Loftus' (SL Archive)

20 Loftus to Cecil 16 July 1565. E. P. Shirley (ed.), *Original letters and papers in illustration of the history of the Church of Ireland during the reigns of Edward VI, Mary and Elizabeth* (1851).

21 CSP(I), 20 November & 13 December 1565. See also Helga Robinson-

Hammerstein, op. cit., and Jane Dawson, *Politics of Religion in the Age of Mary, Queen of Scots* (Cambridge, 2002).

22 C. H. Cooper (ed.), *Athenae Cantabrigiensis*, Vol. 2, p. 403 (Cambridge, 1861)

23 5 October 1566 & 3 November 1566. E. P. Shirley (ed.), op. cit.

24 'He is in my opinion the fittest man to profit god's church of any that I know of English birth.' Loftus to Cecil 22 January 1567. E. P. Shirley (ed.), op. cit.

25 'Nunc venit hora ecclesiam reformandi.' Sidney to Loftus 11 March 1567. E. P. Shirley (ed.), op. cit.. The Queen had originally proposed Adam Loftus's promotion to be Archbishop of Dublin in a letter to Sussex, 15 October 1563. E. P. Shirley (ed.) op. cit.

26 Sidney to Cecil, 4 March 1567. E. P. Shirley (ed.), op. cit.

27 Adam urged Cartwright's cause in a letter to Cecil, 5 December 1567, CSP(I)

28 Loftus to Cecil, 26 October 1570, CSP(I)

29 Transcripts of the letters from Goodman to Fitton and Loftus dated 11 April 1575 from Chester were kindly supplied by Dr Jane Dawson, who discovered them in the Denbighshire Record Office, *DD/PP/839* pp. 128–30.

30 Quoted from Dudley Loftus's manuscript 'Annals' (Marsh's Library, Dublin)

31 David Edwards, 'Beyond Reform. Martial Law & the Tudor Reconquest of Ireland' in *History Ireland*, Summer 1997

32 See, for example, the complaints of Archbishop Loftus regarding the Commissioners for Ecclesiastical matters, Ackworth and Garvey, and their responses, in 1578–9 (W Maziere Brady, op. cit..) or Sir Henry Sydney's account of the Diocese of Meath in a letter to Queen Elizabeth dated 28 April 1576 – Constantia Maxwell, *Irish History from Contemporary Sources 1509–1610* (London, 1923).

33 'The Roman Catholics, in Dublin especially, frequently repaired to the Protestant churches at the same time that they adhered to the worship of the Mass'. Dudley Loftus, 'Annals' (Marsh's Library, Dublin, MS Z4.2.7)

Chapter 5 Death of an Archbishop

34 The letter from the Privy Council to Sir William Drury, 11 February 1578, is quoted in full in the manuscript 'Life of Archbishop Loftus' (SL Archive)

35 Loftus to Walsingham, 15 September 1580, CSP(I)

36 CSP(I), July 1580–July 1581, passim

37 CSP(I), May–September 1581

38 Even Spenser, the least merciful of men towards the Irish and an admirer of 'good Lord Grey', recorded in his *View of the State of Ireland* (1633), that 'complaint was made against him, that he was a bloodie man, and regarded not the life of her subjects more than dogges, but had wasted and consumed all, so as now she [Queen Elizabeth] had almost nothing left, but to raigne on their Ashes.'

39 See David Edwards, op. cit.. for the evidence of Grey's brutality and Loftus's opposition to it. CSP(I)

40 Lord Justice Loftus to Burghley, from his palace of St Sepulchre's, 5 November 1582. CSP(I). See also *View of the State of Ireland* (London, 1633, but circulated in manuscript at an earlier date)

41 Lords Justices to Privy Council, 12 September 1583, CSP(I)

42 Philip O'Sullivan Beare, *Historiae Catholicae Compendium* (Lisbon, 1621) – from the translation included in Constantia Maxwell, *Irish History from Contemporary Sources* (London, 1923)

44 I am quoting from Loftus's will, his only reference to past misdeeds

Chapter 6 A College for Learning

45 Loftus sent a letter from Dublin on 29 September 1596, marked 'Haste, post haste'. It reached the Palace of Nonsuch five days later, on 4 October – but this was exceptionally fast. Messages to England mostly took longer, often a matter of weeks, if the winds were contrary. CSP(I)

46 In November 1595, at the age of sixty-two, Adam Loftus accompanied the Deputy, Sir William Russell, into Connaught, to suppress the latest uprising, 'though the time of the year be unseasonable for my old and sickly body to undertake any long journey.' (*DNB*)

47 Graham Kew, *The Irish Sections of Fynes Moryson's Unpublished Itinerary* (Dublin Manuscripts Commission, 1998)

48 Sir Henry Wallop to Walsingham, 8 April 1585, CSP(I)

49 For Adam's original request for a grant of these lands, see Loftus to Burghley, 15 September 1582. CSP(I). For the Archbishop's tenure of Rathfarnham at 30 shillings rent, see F. E. Ball, *History of County Dublin*, Vol. 2, p. 119 (1903). Loftus 'was the builder of both Rathfarnham Castle and Knocklyon Castle. He was also the proprietor of vast estates in the Rathfarnham and Tallaght area, including Scholarstown, Oldcourt, Tymon, Woodtown, Killakee, Ballycragh, Ballycullen

and Mount Pelier Hill.' Pat Comerford, 'An Irishman's Diary', *The Irish Times*, 2 April 2005.

50 The earliest surviving letter sent from 'Rathfernan' is from Loftus to Walsingham, in favour of Mr Avery Randolph (a regular courier of the Archbishop's letters), dated 30 September 1585. CSP(I). When Loftus moved to Rathfarnham, he allowed his wife's relatives, the Purdons, to live in the old archiepiscopal castle at Tallaght. F. E. Ball, *History of County Dublin*, op. cit.

51 Kieran R. Hickey, 'A geographical perspective on the decline and extermination of the Irish wolf *canis lupus* – an initial assessment', in *Irish Geography*, 33 (2000). See also the 'Annals Civil and Ecclesiastical' of Dr Dudley Loftus (Marsh's Library, Dublin., MS Z4.2.7) for 1582.

52 Manuscript 'Life of Archbishop Loftus' (SL Archive) provides detailed evidence of Perrot's instructions and his intentions.

53 'The ungodly gain that this archbishop doth suck out of that church to pump up himself, his children and friends, is so sweet that he cannot endure any man to look towards it.' *The Letter Book of Lord Deputy Sir John Perrot. Analecta Hibernica 12* (Dublin, 1943)

54 Loftus to Burghley, 12 August 1585, CSP(I)

55 Manuscript 'Life of Archbishop Loftus' (SL Archive). This version quotes verbatim from numerous contemporary documents and is close to Adam's own detailed account in a letter to Hatton, Burghley and Walsingham. CSP(I) 12 July 1587. Other quotations are taken from various letters in CSP(I), except for that on Ambition, which specifically refers to Loftus in his quarrel with Perrot and is transcribed from the manuscript 'Life', cited above – which gives as its source *The Government of Ireland under Sir John Perrot from 1584 to 1588*, by E.C.S. (London, 1626). The British Library catalogue identifies 'E.C.S.' as Sir Edward Cecil

56 Perrot's insults on the Council were reported in a letter from Loftus to Burghley, 4 December 1586. CSP(I). Roger Turvey, *The Treason and Trial of Sir John Perrot* (Cardiff, 2005) is my source for two of Perrot's 'treasonable' remarks against the Queen – the third was from F. E. Ball, *History of County Dublin*, op. cit.

57 For much of this background information, see Steven G. Ellis, *Ireland in the Age of the Tudors* (1998). Sir Henry Wallop – Treasurer and former Lord Justice – endured a fierce row with Perrot within a fortnight of the Deputy's arrival, and had to apologise to Walsingham for his 'passionate disposition.' Wallop to Walsingham, 9 July 1584, CSP(I).

58 Loftus to Burghley, 22 September 1590, quoted in W. Maziere Brady, *State Papers concerning the Irish Church in the time of Queen Elizabeth* (1868)

59 The extract from the Archbishop's speech 'at ye General Assembly in ye Tholsel soon after ye Quarter Sessions of St John ye Baptist in 1591' is taken from the manuscript 'Life of Archbishop Loftus' (SL Archive).

60 'It was strongly influenced by Trinity College, Cambridge, the protestant stronghold from which it took its name and much of its academic arrangements.' T. W. Moody, F. X. Martin, F. J. Byrne, *A New History of Ireland*, Vol. III (1976). The Queen made plain in a letter to the Lord Deputy, Chancellor and Council of 29 December 1591 (transcribed in manuscript 'Life of Archbishop Loftus' (SL Archive) that the college should be modelled on those in Oxford and Cambridge, but left the details to Loftus and his brother-in-law the Bishop of Meath, who had experience of those universities.

61 The Queen's view of the new college's purpose is quoted from her letter of 29 December 1591 (see previous note). The contemporary Catholic view is taken from a *Petition to the Pope from Irish Catholics in Exile*, 1595–8, quoted in Constantia Maxwell, *Irish History from Contemporary Sources 1509–1610* (1923).

Chapter 7 Signior Gloriosus

62 Barnaby Riche, *The Adventures of Brusanus, Prince of Hungaria* (London, 1592)

64 See Andrew Trollop to Walsingham, 12 September 1581. CSP(I)

65 Christopher Goodman to Archbishop Loftus, 11 April 1575, DD/PP/839. p. 130

66 Adam gave Cecil a goshawk and a tercel – a male hawk, usually a peregrine. 16 July 1565, CSP(I).

67 Legge to Burghley, February 1590. *CSP(I)*. Riche acted as informer for Legge's inquiries and accusations, which leads me to suspect he may have written the more colourful phrases of his reports. Thomas Herron, *Studies in Philology*, No. 3 (University of North Carolina Press, Summer 2008).

68 CSP(I)

69 For full details of this fight, as described by Riche, see T. M. Cranfill & D. H. Bruce, *Barnaby Riche: A Short Biography* (University of Texas, 1953).

70 *The Adventures of Brusanus*, in which Loftus figures as Gloriosus, was registered in October 1592, and *Greenes Newes Both from Heaven and Hell* in February 1593. Thomas Herron, *Studies in Philology*, No. 3 (University of North Carolina Press, Summer 2008).

71 Loftus to Burghley, 17 September 1592, CSP(I)

72 *The answers of the Lord Chancellor to certain articles objected against him by Barnaby Ryche and Robert Legge*, Ratharnham, 17 September 1592, CSP(I)

73 Loftus to Cecil, 1 June 1600. Fenton to Cecil, 1 June 1600, CSP(I)

74 Loftus to Burghley, 14 September 1594, CSP(I)

75 Loftus to Cecil, 27 September 1597, from Rathfarnham, CSP(I)

76 Loftus to Cecil, 28 March 1600, CSP(I)

77 Loftus to Cecil, 20 January 1600, CSP(I)

78 Loftus to Cecil, 19 January & 28 March 1600, CSP(I)

79 Manuscript audited by Sir James Ware and countersigned by members of the Irish Privy Council, sold at auction by Bonhams on 23 March 2004. Present whereabouts unknown.

80 This charge against Loftus was published by Fitzsimmons in 1611, in a short book written after his release, based on notes made during his time in captivity. *Justification and Exposition of the Divine Sacrifice of the Masse* (facsimile reprint by Scolar, 1972). See also Loftus to Burghley, 7 April 1600 & 9 February 1601, CSP(I).

81 Sir Arthur Chichester to Viscount Cranborne, 25 February 1605, CSP(I)

Chapter 8 Band of Brothers

82 *Henry V* was written in 1599, and may have been the first play to be performed at the Globe Theatre, which opened that year.

83 Graham Kew, *The Irish Sections of Fynes Moryson's Unpublished Itinerary* (Dublin Manuscripts Commission, 1998)

84 Edmund Spenser, *View of the State of Ireland*, published by James Ware, p. 34 (Dublin, 1633)

85 Steven G. Ellis, *Ireland in the Age of the Tudors 1447–1603* (London & New York, 1998)

86 The charge that Archbishop Loftus had fostered his children with the O'Byrnes was made by Barnaby Riche and denied by Adam as 'shameless slander'. 17 September 1592, CSP(I). J. Venn & J. A. Venn, *The Book of Matriculations and Degrees in the University of Cambridge*

1544–1659 (Cambridge, 1913)

87 Sir Edward Waterhouse (Chancellor of the Irish Exchequer) to Walsingham, 28 August 1589, CSP(I)

88 Loftus to Walsingham, September 1589, CSP(I). Adam referred to his son as 'a young man, meet to be lyked'. Walsingham died the following year.

89 Lord Chancellor Loftus to Burghley, Rathfarnham, 17 September 1592, CSP(I)

90 Archbishop Loftus to Secretary Wilson, 15 August 1580, cited by P. H. Hore, *History of the Town & County of Wexford*, Vol. IV (1904). For slavery see the evidence collated by Prof. A. Gwyn in *Analecta Hibernia* No. 4, October 1932, and the more recent work by Robert Davis, *Christian Slaves, Muslim Masters: White Slavery in the Mediterranean, the Barbary Coast, and Italy 1500–1800* (2004).

91 Contemporary description of Bagenal cited by J. J. N. McGurk (*DNB*)

92 Bishops Loftus and Jones, to the Privy Council, 21 August 1591, CSP(I)

93 Camden's *Britannia, Newly Translated into English* [by] *Edmund Gibson* (London, 1695)

94 Graham Kew, op. cit.

95 Bagenal to Burghley, November 1593, CSP(I)

96 Tyrone to the Lord Deputy and Council, 11 October 1593, CSP(I)

97 Tyrone to Lord Chancellor Loftus, 11 October 1593, CSP(I)

98 Loftus to Burghley, 16 October 1593, CSP(I)

99 *ODNB*. Tyrone himself is said to have bribed Fitzwilliam with sacks full of gold.

100 Tyrone to the Privy Council, 5 November 1593, CSP(I)

101 Galloglasses were professional soldiers, of Scottish descent, who fought with a distinctive axe.

102 Loftus to Cecil, 16 July 1596, 28 March 1601, CSP(I)

103 P. H. Hore, *History of the Town and County of Wexford*, Vol. 1, p. 278 & Vol. IV, pp. 293–4 (London, 1904)

104 P. H. Hore, *History of the Town & County of Wexford*. Francis Elrington Ball, *A History of the County Dublin* (1902)

105 Loftus to Cecil, 17 July 1597, 28 March 1601, CSP(I)

106 Edward's command of a foot company in Bagenal's army, at the battle of Yellow Ford, is recorded in the notes of Jack Loftus (SL

Archive).

107 Letter from the Irish Council to Tyrone, signed by the Lords Justices (Loftus and Gardiner) 16 August 1598. Quoted in the notes of Jack Loftus (SL Archive)

108 Loftus to the Hon Lords of Her Majesty's Privy Council, Friday at 10 o'clock forenoon 18 August 1598. Quoted in the notes of Jack Loftus (SL Archive)

109 The Queen to the Lords Justices, Greenwich 12 September 1598. Quoted in the notes of Jack Loftus (SL Archive)

110 Graham Kew, op. cit.

111 Captain Linlye to Sir Robert Cecil, 12 July 1599. Quoted by Daniel MacCarthy, 'The Disaster of Wicklow', *Journal of the Kilkenny and South-East of Ireland Archaeological Society*, Vol. II, New Series (Dublin, 1859)

112 Henry Harrington to the Lord Chancellor [Archbishop Loftus] 29 May 1599, quoted in Daniel MacCarthy, op. cit.

113 For a near-contemporary account of warfare in Ireland, see T. Gainsford, *The Glory of England* (1618), quoted by Constantia Maxwell, *Irish History from Contemporary Sources* (London, 1923)

114 Reports by Sir Henry Harrington and Captain Linlye to Sir Robert Cecil, 12 July 1599, quoted in Daniel MacCarthy, op. cit. A contemporary map of the battle is preserved in Trinity College Dublin Library, MS 1209-005

115 'There is gone out of the Chancellor's house this last night eight of his servants to the enemy.' John Clifford to Sir Robert Cecil, 30 June 1599, CSP(I)

116 'Of the English, 140 men were slain, together with Clifford himself, and Sir Alexander Ratcliffe, of Odsal, and as many wounded; nay they had all been lost but for the valour of the horse.' Camden, quoted by Daniel MacCarthy, op. cit.

117 Sir Robert Cannon to Cecil, 12 June 1600. CSP(I)

118 Loftus to Cecil, March 28 1600. CSP(I)

119 Lodge, revised Archdall, *The Peerage of Ireland* (1789)

120 Edward Loftus married Anne, daughter & co-heir of Sir Henry Duke of Castle Jordan, County Meath. A French law dictionary, published in 1588 – inscribed with Edward's signature and with a later note that 'This book belonged to Sir Edward Loftus son of Primate Loftus d. 10 May 1601' – was acquired by Archbishop Narcissus Marsh with other books and manuscripts belonging to the Orientalist Dudley

Loftus (Marsh's Library, Dublin Z4.5–18)

121 Graham Kew, op. cit.

122 CSP(I)

123 *Pacata Hibernia* (compiled by George Carew, Earl of Totnes, and edited by Thomas Stafford) is the most vivid account of the last years of the Elizabethan pacification of Ireland, from the English point of view. It was written shortly after the events it describes but not published until 1633.

124 Edmund Spenser, *A View of the State of Ireland*, p. 72

125 For a detailed analysis of the colonial process see Nicholas Canny, *Making Ireland English 1580–1650* (Oxford, 2001)

Chapter 9 A Trew Discription

126 Francis Jobson's map is preserved in the library of Trinity College, Dublin (TCD, MS 1209/64)

Chapter 10 A Peaceable Kingdom

127 For details of chalice and paten see P. H. Hore, *History of the Town and County of Wexford*, Vol. 4, pp. 336–7 (London, 1900–11); and Sweeney, *Irish Stuart Silver* (Dublin, 1995)

128 'Gossipred' meant god-parenting, standing as sponsors at baptisms.

129 My copy of Temple's book was published in 1698 (at another critical moment for the Protestant Ascendancy) and was bound with a collection of violently sectarian tracts – 'The Jesuits Unmasked', 'The Devil turn'd Casuist or the Cheats of Rome' and several similar rants.

130 TCD 1641 Depositions, online transcript, depositions of Thomas le Strange and Thomas Scott, *MS 814, fol 231v & fol 141r*. This archive of contemporary depositions at Trinity College Dublin, now fully transcribed and published online, is the single most important resource for the events of 1641 and their immediate aftermath.

131 TCD 1641 Depositions, online transcript, examination of John Pue, MS 810, fol 211r. Edward Loftus served in Sir Charles Coote's regiment under his cousin, Sir Arthur.

132 CSP(I) 1641, p. 256; 1660, p. 389. See also *The Humble Answer of Nicholas Loftus Esq to the Petition of Christopher Simms* (London, 1646, Early English Books Online)

134 P. H. Hore, *History of the Town and County of Wexford*, Vol. 4, p. 331 (London, 1904). Lodge, *The Peerage of Ireland*, Vol. IV (Dublin,

1754)

135 In 1623 Nicholas Loftus married Margaret Chetham, heiress of
     'Thomas Chetham of Nuthurst in Lancashire, and of Hackettstown
     in the County of Dublin'. They had eight sons and six daughters, of
     whom four died young. Lodge, op. cit.

136 TCD 1641 Depositions, online transcripts, MS 819, fols 270r-270v,
     fols 272r-272v

137 TCD, 1641 Depositions, online transcript, deposition of Henry
     Palmer, MS 818, fol 88r-88v

139 TCD, 1641 Depositions, online transcript, deposition of Robert
     Browne, MS 818, fol 208r

140 Sir Adam Loftus to Sir Robert King in London, 14 February 1642.
     British Library, Thomason Collection, E134/29. Drogheda was
     relieved a fortnight later, as Edward Loftus announced to Sir Robert
     King, in 'Joyfull News from Ireland'

141 'The Particular Relation of the Present Estate and Condition of
     Ireland', British Library, Thomason Collection, E134/29

142 James Howell, *Mercutius Hibernicus: or A Discourse of the late
     Insurrection in Ireland* (Bristol, 1644)

143 Edmund Borlase, *The History of the Execrable Irish Rebellion* (London,
     1680)

Chapter 11 Joyful News from Ireland

144 *Joyfull Newes from Ireland*, London Library, P2913/18. This is the
     same edition as Thomason E137(22)

145 Thomason's collection of Civil War Tracts is now in the British
     Library.

146 The astrological war produced some of the most obscure pamphlets
     in Thomason's collection. Its flavour can be sampled in William
     Lilly's *A Prophesy of the White King and Dreadful Dead-man Explained*
     (1644) Thomason E.4(27); John Booker's *A Bloody Irish Almanack*
     (1646) Thomason E.328(14); and George Wharton's *Bellum
     Hybernicale: or Ireland's Warre Astrologically demonstrated* (1647)
     Thomason E.365(21).

147 *Grand Plutoes Remonstrance* was a savage fantasy that implicitly
     identified King Charles with 'his Hellish Maiestie [who] is pleased to
     declare 1. How far he differs from Roundhead, Rattle-head, or Prick-
     eare 2. His Copulation with a Holy Sister 3. His deere affection to
     Romish Catholikes, and hate to Protestants 4. His Oration to the

Rebells.' Thomason Tracts, E138(11). This pamphlet appears to have been written as a response to another by the Royalist John Taylor – *The devil turn'd round-head: or, Pluto become a Brownist. Being a just comparison, how the Devil is become a Round-Head? In what manner, and how zealously (like them) he is affected with the moving of the Spirit. With the holy Sifters desire of copulation (if he would seem holy, sincere, and pure) were it with the Devil himself.* (London, 1642)

148 *Joyfull Newes from Ireland* was printed in several editions, the first of which seems to have been published by John Frante between 27 February and 7 March 1642. Thomason Tracts, E137(13). Another edition was printed by H. S. & W. Ley together with *A copy of a letter sent from a Privy Councellor to Mr Fenton Parsons.* Thomason E137(22). My own copy of was published as the second half of *Two Letters of Note*, 'Printed in the Yeare 1642'. Thomason E138(10). I have somewhat abridged the original text.

Chapter 12 A Family at War

149 Sir Arthur Loftus was listed as Captain of a Foot Company prior to the rebellion, in charge of a 'Lieutenant, Ensign, Chirugion, Serjeant and Drum, and fourty four Soldiers' (according to a list of army officers in Sir James Temple's *Irish Rebellion*). His *True Relation of the late Expedition, etc.* was published in London, 1642. (London Library, P2913/14)

150 A bill survives for the Naas garrison's consumption of wine – 'Sir artur loftes' owed £5 15s. 0d. and 'leftenant loftes' £3. TCD 1641 Depositions, online transcript, Addition of John Match, MS 813, fol 337v.

151 See *A Full Relation, not only of our good successe in generall, etc.* (London, 1642) London Library, P2913/13

152 *Exceeding Good Newes from the Neweries, Victorious Newes from Waterford* and *True Newes from Cork.* British Library, Thomason Collection, E143/18, E144/1, E147/18

153 *A Letter Sent to His Majestie Concerning His Majesties Resolution to go into Ireland* was dated 23 April 1642 and published in London by Robert Barker (SL Archive).

154 An example of Loftus's commitment to his role as Deputy Treasurer of War is the Commision issued to him in June 1642 'to set forth One Ship to Sea at his own Charges, of about Forty-five Ton, for the Service of *Ireland.*' *House of Commons Journal Vol. 2*, 18 June 1642

155 Nicholas Loftus's statement of Royalist conviction is quoted by John

Presteigne, whose unpublished Loftus genealogy was compiled in the late eighteenth century. GL Archive. Loftus's Royalist allegiance is confirmed by the generally reliable Lodge, *The Peerage of Ireland* (Dublin, 1754).

156 Lodge, *The Peerage of Ireland*, Vol. IV, p. 338. Dudley Loftus was killed in 1627, during the Duke of Buckingham's disastrous expedition to the Isle de Ré, in support of the French Protestants besieged at La Rochelle.

157 Edward Loftus lost a great deal when the rebels occupied his lands in Wicklow, stole his cattle, horses and crops and ruined his house. TCD 1641 Depositions, online transcript, deposition of Hugh Madden ex parte Edward Loftus, MS 811, fol 75r

158 TCD 1641 Depositions, online transcript, examination of Robert Doughtie, MS 815, fol 402r–405r

159 TCD 1641 Depositions, online transcript, deposition of Thomas Molineux, MS 811, fols 154v–157v

160 Irish Council to Nicholas Loftus, 25 April 1642. Cambridge University Library, MS Ad 4246, f 51v. See also the *House of Commons Journal* for April–July 1642, passim

161 Edmund Borlase, *The History of the Execrable Irish Rebellion*, Appendix (London, 1680). The Council's proclamation was dated 10 June 1642; one of the signatories was Adam Loftus.

162 The Council to Nicholas Loftus, 11 August 1642 (Cambridge University Library, MS Ad 4246, f 75)

163 Letter to Lord Percival, 3 September 1642, cited in *House of Lords Journal*, Vol. 5, 5 September 1642

164 P. H. Hore, *History of the Town and County of Wexford*, Vol. 4 (London, 1900–11)

165 For letters from the Irish Council to England, see Cambridge University Library, MS Ad 4246, ff 112, 124v, 125, 125v.

166 Devereux fortified his family home of Ballymagir, in County Wexford, with 'a breastworke mote & drawe bridge'. TCD 1641 Depositions, online transcript, examinations of William Stafford and Nicholas Maylor, MS 819, fol 270r–272r

167 CSP(D), 22 September 1645

168 CSP(I), 13 January, 19 January 1646

169 CSP(D), 22 June 1646, CSP(I), 2 July 1646

170 CSP(I), Addenda, 3 July, 9 July, 11 August 1647

171 CSP(D), 24 December 1646

172 CSP(I), Addenda, 11 August 1647

173 20 January 1648 (Cambridge University Library, MS Add 89, f207)

174 CSP(I), 4 July 1648.

175 See John Gilbert, *History of the Irish Confederacy and the War in Ireland*, Vol. VII, pp. 325–8 (Dublin, 1891).

176 Sir Maurice Eustace to Ormond, 8 October 1647. John Gilbert, op. cit., Vol. VI, pp. 206–7 (Dublin, 1890)

177 CSP(I) Addenda, 30 November 1647, 25 January & 3 April 1648. Sir Adam Loftus was appointed to be the receiver of the cash.

178 The Committee at Derby House to Sir Adam Loftus. CSP(D), 1 May 1648

179 For Ormond's account of the taking of Rathfarnham see *The Irish Sword*, Vol. XXI, No. 86 (Winter 1999), pp. 372, 376. His letters to the King were written a fortnight after the event, when it was already clear that history needed careful explanation. Parliament's version is preserved in a partially illegible pamphlet, *Perfect Summary of Exact Passages in Parliament*, Issue 22 (London, Monday 6 August 1649) in the Burney Collection at the British Library (not to be confused with similarly named and numbered pamphlets in the Thomason Collection). Dudley Loftus's account is preserved in the Bodleian Library, MS Tanner 25, fols 67r–68v.

Chapter 13 The Wrath of God

180 Andrew Marvell, *Horatian Ode upon Cromwell's return from Ireland*. Cromwell described himself to Speaker Lenthal as 'an instrument of God'.

181 Cromwell's letter to Lenthall describing the sack of Drogheda (17 September 1649) was published in *Letters from Ireland, relating several great Successes it hath pleased God to give unto Parliaments Forces* (Edward Husband, London, 1649).

182 *Paradise Lost*, 2, 249. 'Hail horrors, hail Infernal world, and thou profoundest / Hell Receive thy new possessor: one who brings / A mind not to be changed by place or time.'

183 See James Scott Wheeler, *Cromwell in Ireland* (Dublin, 1999).

184 In April 1647 the Catholic Confederacy seized Nicholas Loftus's lands in Wexford to pay for their garrison at Duncannon. CSP(I), 6 April 1647

185 Hore, op. cit., Vol. 4 (citing Carte's *Life of Ormond*)

186 Hore, op. cit., Vol. 4

187 Hore, op. cit.

188 'Wogan was a native of Kildare who had been raised as a Protestant in Wales. He served Parliament in the English Civil War, but changed sides in 1648.' James Scott Wheeler, op. cit.

189 John Gilbert, op. cit., Vol. VII; Addenda, Bellings to Ormond, 16 October 1649. Hore, op. cit., transcribes the word 'patrons', as quoted above, but Gilbert reads it as 'passions'.

190 See Cromwell's letter to Lenthal (Speaker of the House of Commons) 19 December 1649, quoted by James Scott Wheeler, op. cit.

191 Dudley Loftus manuscripts (Marsh's Library, Dublin, V.3,2,19); quoted by John Prendergast, *The Cromwellian Settlement of Ireland* (London, 1970)

192 Borlase, op. cit.

Chapter 14 Taking Possession

193 Gabriel Beranger visited Loftus Hall in 1780 and described seeing 'Strongbow's Sword'. Hore, op. cit., Vol. IV, pp. 378–9. Family tradition has it that the sword was given to the National Museum of Ireland, but no record of it can now be found – and according to Dr Andy Halpin, a curator at the National Museum, the sketch reproduced by Hore represents a Scottish claymore, rather than 'the Anglo-Norman two-handed sword' which the caption indicates. Jack Loftus recorded that the sword was initialled AR – presumably Alexander Redmond..

194 Lodge, *Peerage of Ireland* (London, 1754)

195 D'Alton, *History of the County of Dublin* (Dublin, 1838)

196 Walter Harris, *The Whole Works of Sir James Ware*, (London, 1739/46)

197 J. T. Gilbert, *History of the City of Dublin*, Vol. I (Dublin, 1854)

198 All quotations from Boate's work are taken from the edition published in 1726 (with additional contributions from Thomas Molineux and others), which was reissued in 1760.

199 I am quoting from the notes of my great-uncle, Jack Loftus, whose description of the state of Ireland immediately after the civil wars is based on contemporary testimony.

200 Nicholas Whitty of Dungulph, James Lewis of Graig and Robert Redmond of the Hall (together with about thirty-five of their dependants) were listed for transplantation in 1653, and assigned land in Connaught. Hore, op. cit., Vol. VI, p. 503.

201 Survey of the Loftus Hall estate by Charles Frizell for Henry Loftus, 1771 (National Library of Ireland)

202 *An Act for assuring, confirming and settling of Lands and Estates in Ireland* (September 1656)

203 The Irish Census of 1659 showed the extent of the Loftus family's landholdings, just before the Restoration.

204 CSP(I), 1664

205 Hore, op. cit., Vol. VI, passim

206 John Cliffe lived with his wife at his father-in-law's castle of Dungulph, before it was occupied by Henry Loftus. Hore, op. cit., Vol. VI, p. 614

207 *Journal of the Old Wexford Society*, No. 3, 1970–1, pp. 43–6

208 National Library of Ireland, MS 33,030

209 *Analecta Hibernica*, Loftus Papers No. 89, as quoted by J. B. Loftus (SL Archive)

210 Lodge, *Peerage of Ireland*, Vol. IV (Dublin, 1754)

Chapter 15 The Gift of Tongues

212 Dudley Loftus, *An History of the Twofold Invention of the Cross* (Dublin, 1686) Cambridge University Library, 753.a.92

213 *Acts of the Apostles* 2:4–11 (Tyndale translation)

214 M. Mansoor, *The Story of Irish Orientalism*, pp. 21–5 (Dublin, 1944). See also George Thomas Stokes, *Some Worthies of the Irish Church* (London 1900).

215 Robert Gorge's four-page life of Dudley Loftus is now in the Bodleian Library – MS Tanner 25, fols. 67r–68v.

217 Stubbs, *History of the University of Dublin*, p. 84 (quoted in Stokes, op. cit.)

218 Marsh's Library, Dublin, Z4.2.11

219 TCD 1641 Depositions, online transcript, deposition of John Higginson, MS 810, fol 344r

220 F. E. Ball, op. cit.. John Gilbert, *History of the City of Dublin*, Vol. I, pp. 37–8, 41, Vol. II, pp. 67–8 (Dublin, 1854–5, reprinted 1972). Constantia Maxwell, *Dublin under the Georges*, pp. 185–6 (Dublin, 1946). *The New Grove Dictionary of Music and Musicians*, edited by Stanley Sadie (London, 1980). William Smith Clark, *The Early Irish Stage* (Oxford, 1955)

221 Katherine van Eerde, *John Ogilby and the Taste of His Times* (London, 1976)

222 Van Eerde, op. cit.

223 Dudley Loftus manuscripts (Marsh's Library Dublin, V.3.2.19)

224 P. H. Hore, *History of the Town and County of Wexford*, Vol. IV (London, 1904). See also E. M. Johnston-Liik, *History of the Irish Parliament 1692–1800* (6 vols, Ulster Historical Foundation, 2002).

225 Dudley Loftus, *The Proceedings Observed in the consecration of the twelve Bishops* (London, 1661) Cambridge University Library, 3406.c.14

226 Dudley Loftus, *Oratio funebris habita post exuvias nuperi Johannis Archiepiscopi Armachani in ecclesia cathedrali Dublini* (Dublin, 1663). Copies are in Marsh's Library, Dublin, and Cambridge University Library.

227 Harris, op. cit.

228 Lodge (revised Archdale), *Peerage of Ireland*, Vol. VII (1789)

229 The original contract between 'Signora Francesca Lucretia Plunketta' and 'Dudleio di Casa Alsata', signed Dud: Loftuseo and witnessed by Jo. Higgin, Mary Flood & Anne Renolds (5 July 1666) is now in the British Library (Add 21135, f. 35)

230 [Dudley Loftus], *The Vindication of an Injured Lady* (London, 1667). The only surviving copy appears to be that which originally belonged to Loftus and was eventually given with other of his papers to the Bodleian Library by Narcissus Marsh. Radcl.e.40(9)

231 CSP(D), 1668, p. 283

232 [Dudley Loftus], *Lettera Esatoria Di mettere opera a fare sincera Penitenza, etc* (1667). I am grateful to Andrew Palmer for providing me with a translation.

233 Dudley Loftus, *The Case of Ware & Shirley* (1669) Cambridge University Library, 1130.d.10

234 See William Smith Clark, *The Early Irish Stage* (Oxford, 1955) citing CSP(I) *1666–69*, pp. 566–7.

235 Dudley Loftus, *The first marriage of Katherine Fitzgerald (now Lady Decies) contracted in Facie Ecclesiae with John Power, now Lord Decies, Asserted by Dudley Loftus DLL and Judge of the Prerogative Court in Ireland* (London, 1677) Cambridge University Library, 518.h.3(2)

236 Harris, op. cit.. p. 255. See also A. P. W. Malcomson, *The Pursuit of the Heiress*, p. 26 (Ulster Historical Foundation, 1982).

237 Vatican Library, Rome, *Barberini Latin* MSS 8626

238 Richard Bagwell, *Ireland under the Stuarts* (London, 1916)

239 Walter Harris, *History of the City of Dublin*, p. 347ff. (London, 1766). CSP(D), 2 September 1673, 23 October 1673, 31 October 1673

240 Fifteen letters from Dr Dudley Loftus to Sancroft, dating from 2 August 1680 to 6 March 1686, are preserved in the Bodleian Library, Tanner Collection MSS.

241 Dr Twells, *Life of Dr Edward Pocock* (London, 1816)

242 *Papers of the Dublin Philosophical Society 1683–1708*, Vol. 1, edited by K.T. Hoppen (Irish Manuscripts Commission, Dublin, 2007)

243 Richard Simon, *Histoire Critique du Vieux Testament* (Paris, 1680). The first English edition appeared in 1682.

244 Marsh's *Essay on Sounds with Proposals for the Improvement of Acoustics* was presented to the Royal Society in 1683.

245 The Dublin Society's fascination with freaks of nature continued despite Dudley Loftus's scorn. *A Discourse on the Dissection of a Monstrous Double Catt* was 'read before the Dublin Society by Dr Mullen' and printed in Number 174 of the *Philosophical Transactions* (Oxford, 1685).

246 Harris, op. cit., p. 254

247 Rev. John Barrett, *An Essay on the Earlier Part of the Life of Swift* (London, 1808)

248 For the reference to angles and triangles see Loftus's judgement *In the Case of Ware and Shirley*, quoted above.

249 For corrections to my translation of the Latin sections of Swift's satire I am grateful to Dr Neil Hopkinson.

250 University of Glasgow Library, MS Hunter 73 (T.3.11)

251 Twells, op. cit.

252 E. M. Johnston-Liik (op. cit.) dates Dudley Loftus's second marriage to 11 May 1693.

253 Harris, op. cit.. Dudley's last publication appeared the year that he died: *Clear and learned explication of the history of Our Blessed Saviour Jesus Christ taken out of above thirty Greek Syriack and other Oriental authors by way of Catena by Dionysius Syrus and faithfully translated by Dudley Loftus* (Dublin, 1695). Marsh's Library has a copy.

254 Marsh's Library – Z4.2.7. Turn the book upside down and running the other way through the pages are brief entries in a much neater hand, which seem to be the beginnings of an earlier manuscript by Dudley, a dictionary of the English language.

Chapter 16 A Tangled Web

255 *Letters from Orinda to Poliarchus* [i.e. Cotterell] (London, 1705)

256 The copy of Katherine Philips's *Poems* owned by Frances Jones (and twice signed by her, on the end leaves at front and back) is essentially the 1669 edition, with the title page from 1667. It seems to have been issued thus by the publisher, rather than cobbled together at some subsequent date.

257 Richard Jones (later Lord Ranelagh) was twice married into one of England's great political families, the Cecils. His first wife, Elizabeth Willoughby, had a Cecil mother, and his second, Margaret, was the daughter of James Cecil, Earl of Salisbury, by his wife, Lady Margaret Manners, daughter of the 8th Earl of Rutland. She was therefore a double cousin of Thomas Coningsby's previous mistress – Lord Scudamore's wife, Frances Cecil – who also had a Manners for a mother.

Chapter 17 The Golden Ball

258 John P. Prendergast, *The Cromwellian Settlement of Ireland*, p. 343 (1870)

259 CSP(I), 25 April 1661

260 CSP(I), 25 February 1663

261 CSP(I), 25 March 1663

262 CSP(I), 28 March 1663, 25 April 1663

263 CSP(I), 'About January' 1666

264 CSP(I), 27 January 1666

265 CSP(I), 1660–70, p. 672

266 *The Rawdon Papers*, edited by Rev. E. Berwick (1819). On 16 June 1670, three years after 'Addy' Loftus's dog abandoned the fight at court, John Evelyn saw an Irish wolf-dog 'beat a cruel mastiff' at the Bear Garden. Edward MacLysaght, *Irish Life in the Seventeenth Century*, 3rd edition (Cork, 1969)

267 Historical Manuscripts Commission, 6th Report, Appendix Part I, p. 368

268 CSP(D), 30 August 1672.

269 CSP(D), 23 September 1674 & 9 December 1675. The warrant signed by Charles II is in the British Library (Stowe, 206 f. 79).

270 CSP(D), 15 July 1679

271 CSP(D), 19 July 1679

272 CSP(D), 27 August 1679, Ranelagh to Conway

273 CSP(D), 1 September 1679

274 The Board of the Green Cloth existed until recent times, as I discovered one day when strolling up St James's and found myself passing the door to its discreet but expensive offices. It supervised various aspects of the royal finances, as it had done for centuries past, but was abolished in 2004.

275 CSP(D), 20 January 1680, Loftus to Conway

276 CSP(D), 19 June 1680, James Sloane to Conway

277 CSP(D), 29 September 1680

278 *CSP(D)*, 9 November 1680

279 CSP(D), 22 February 1681

280 Undated [1689] letter from Adam Loftus Viscount Lisburn to William III, in British Library (Add. 32095 f. 329): 'If yr. Majsty have not already disposed of Mr Skelton's employ in France [Skelton was James II's envoy to Versailles] & shall think me worthy thereof, I shall . . . &c., &c.' The letter is in a secretary's hand but boldly signed 'Lisburn'.

281 Manuscript of the Earl of Fingal: XI; 63. This account was written in 1711, possibly by Plunkett.

282 John Dunton, *Teague Land: or A Merry Ramble to the Wild Irish (1698)*, edited by Andrew Carpenter (Dublin, 2003)

283 Manuscript of the Earl of Fingal, XI, 63

284 This story eerily echoes the death of Adam's uncle Walter at the Siege of Youghal, forty years earlier. As with Adam, the cannonball that killed him was suspended above his tomb.

Chapter 18 On the Hook

285 *A Chorographic Account of the Southern part of the County Wexford* by Robert Leigh, Esq., of Rosegarland, written in 1684, is described by P. H. Hore in *History of the Town and County of Wexford*, Vol. 4 (London, 1904) as a manuscript in the possession of 'Sir Thomas Phillipps, Bart., Middle Hall, Worcestershire'. Hore's father, H. F. Hore, published a transcript of Leigh's account in the *Journal of the Kilkenny and South-East of Ireland Archaeological Society*, Vol. II, 1858–9. A more recent transcript is included in Billy Colfer's masterpiece, *The Hook Peninsula* (Cork University Press, 2004).

286 Robert Leigh, *A Chorographic Account*, op. cit. See also P. H. Hore, op. cit., Vol. V, p. 36.

287 The original deed of trust, dated 30 August 1666 ('Analecta Hibernica', Loftus Papers, No. 89), is missing, but was transcribed by J. B. Loftus (SL Archive).

288 Robert Leigh, *A Chorographic Account*, op. cit.

289 'The network of stone walls was encouraged by Loftus, who allowed a rent reduction on land enclosed by walls built by tenants.' Billy Colfer, *The Hook Peninsula* (Cork University Press, 2004)

290 See H. V. Hart-Davis, unpublished 'History of the Mansell Family'.

291 See W. E. H. Lecky, *Ireland in the Eighteenth Century*, Vol. I, p. 116 (2nd edition, London, 1902), and L. M. Cullen, *The Emergence of Modern Ireland* (London, 1981).

292 P. H. Hore, op. cit., quoting a contemporary description of the charter ceremonies by J. M. Paruen.

293 Old Corporation Books of Ross, quoted by Hore. See also extracts from the Corporation Books printed by Col Philip Vigors in the *Journals of the Royal Society of Antiquaries of Ireland*, July 1892, October 1892, June 1894.

294 George Story, *An Impartial History of the Wars of Ireland* (London, 1693). My quotations from the treaty of Limerick are taken from Story's narrative.

295 Robert Leigh, *A Chorographic Account*, op. cit.

296 Bodleian Library, MS Clarendon 88, ff 260–5. The letter was dated 12 May 1693.

297 Loftus papers in National Library of Ireland. (NLI, Loftus 16)

299 Lecky, op. cit., notes that 'The Lord Chancellor Bowes and the Chief Justice Robinson both distinctly laid down from the bench "that the law does not suppose any such person to exist as an Irish Roman Catholic." '.

300 CSP(I), 1707, p. 314 (C2, 44, No. 6131)

301 On 27 October 1713, the Portrive of Bannow was listed as Robert Burnett, and the Burgesses were John Cliffe, Anderson Sanders, Nathaniel Boyse, Joshua Nunn, Nicholas Codd, Anthony Cliffe, Jacob Boyse, Chas Harrison, Nicholas Loftus, Samuel Boyse, Richard Curtis and William Milling. Those names were transcribed by Jack Loftus from *The Corporation Book of Bannow* for the years 1703–14 – before he presented it to the Royal Society of Antiquaries of Ireland, of which he was a member.

Chapter 19 Lilliburlero

302 Bishop Burnet, *History of His Own Time* (1724)

303 *Brewer's Dictionary of Phrase and Fable* (14th edition, 1989)

304 *A Short Character of His Ex[cellency] T[he] E[arl] of W[harton]* is said to have sold 2,000 copies on the day it was published, in December 1710

305 Lewis Melville, *The Life and Writings of Philip Duke of Wharton* (1913)

Chapter 20 The Extinguisher

306 Colonel Rudgeley's petition is quoted by P. H. Hore, *History of the Town and County of Wexford*, Vol. 4, p. 408 (London, 1904).

307 The Report of the Commisioners of Revenue on the state of the Irish lighthouses is recorded in a letter from the Duke of Ormond to the Lord High Treasurer of England, 1 August 1704. *Calendar of Treasury Papers*. See also Bill Long, *Bright Light, White Water* (Dublin, 1993).

308 P. H. Hore, op. cit., quoting a petition from Edward Elsmere, Collector of the Port of Ross, in 1728

309 *The Dublin Gazette*, August 24–7, 1728, quoted by P. H. Hore, op. cit.

310 P. H. Hore, op. cit.

310A *The Gentleman's and London Magazine*, September 1761; *London Evening Post*, 20 September 1761.

Chapter 21 The Present State of Ireland

311 The tripartite publication of Prior's *List of the Absentees*, the anonymous *Present State of Ireland* and Swift's *Modest Proposal* was titled *A View of the present state of affairs in the Kingdom of Ireland* (London, 1730).

312 Several editions of Prior's pamphlet exist, the first of which dates from 1729.

313 For further details on Prior see Desmond Clarke, *Thomas Prior 1681–1751* (Dublin, 1951), and for the Society's publications see the same author's *Bibliography of the Publications of the Royal Dublin Society from 1731 to 1951* (2nd edition, Dublin, 1953).

314 See *The Founders of the Dublin Society* (Dublin, 2005). I am grateful to Mary Kelleher, archivist of the Society, for additional information, including the fact that the William Loftus recorded in this publication as a member of the Society in 1731 is an editorial error of transcription for Nicholas Loftus.

315 The paper on hop cultivation was read by Prior on behalf of an English correspondent, Captain William Cobbe.

Chapter 22 Captain Freney's Blunderbuss

316 Freney's blunderbuss was loaned by Bettina Grattan Bellew of Mount
Loftus to Rothe House Museum, Kilkenny. Since her death, the
museum has claimed that it was given to them and refused to return
it or even to acknowledge its provenance. Alas and shame.

317 'By the Lords Justice and Council of Ireland, A Proclamation . . .
given at the Council-Chamber in Dublin, the 13th Day of January,
1748 – ' proclamation reproduced in an edition of Freney's *Life &
Adventures* edited by Frank McEvoy (Kilkenny, 1988). The original
*The Life & Adventures of James Freney, commonly called Captain Freney,
written by himself* was published in Dublin in 1754 – but his legend
was such that popular editions were still being published as chapbooks
more than a century later – and again in recent times.

318 *Recollections of John O'Keefe, written by himself* (London, 1826)

319 O'Keefe, op. cit.

320 See Michael Holden, *Freney the Robber* (Cork, 2009).

321 In quoting Garret Drake's affidavit I have removed some of the legal
terminology inserted by his Lordship's attorney Thomas Stopford
('Said Plaintiff', 'This deponent', etc) and restored it to the first
person, to replicate the actual language used by Drake, but otherwise
have preserved it unedited. It is dated 4 February 1763. (SL Archive)

322 Most of the deeds relating to the sale of the Mount Eaton estate, and
the lawsuit, are now in the National Library of Ireland, NL Loftus
70, 79, 103, 106, 108, 114, 119, 123, 125, 150, 167, 169, 170

323 SL Archive

Chapter 23 A Scandalous Settlement

324 'An Inventory of the Effects of the late Lord Loftus in his Trunks at
Sir Edward Loftus's at his death, Taken the 6th of January 1764 in
the presence of Henry Loftus, Charles Tottenham, Nicholas Gordon
& Charles Caldwell Esqrs on the part of Lord Loftus, and Sir Archd.
Acheson, Counrs McAuley & Hamilton, Richard Parson Esqr. on
the part of the Execors of Lord Loftus.' (SL Archive)

325 Details concerning Mary Hernon noted in the 'Acct. Between Sir
Edward Loftus and Captain Nicholas Loftus relative to the Effects of
the late Lord Loftus', 5 June 1769 (SL Archive). Mrs Hernon's house
may have been in New Ross, because the accounts include payment
of £4 for a year's rent 'for a House in Ross'.

326　Eyton Poutts to Lord Arran, 7 January 1764 (PRONI Ms T3200/1/12). Thanks to Dr Anthony Malcomson for this reference

327　Captain Nicholas Loftus is described in Lord Loftus's will as 'my reputed or natural son by Mary Hernon', whereas Edward is simply described as 'my reputed son' and his mother is never mentioned (NLI, MS Loftus 134A)

328　Lord Loftus's surviving will is dated 1758 (at about the time of the marriage of Edward Loftus) and three successive codicils were dated 1760, 1762 and 1763 (NLI, Loftus Archive)

329　Information from various documents in SL Archive

Chapter 24　Portraits of a Marriage

330　I can no longer look at the actual portraits, but photographs of them, for the originals were sold by a cousin at the Mount Loftus sale, in 1995, and are now in a private collection in Ireland. Alas!

331　J. T. Gilbert, *A History of the City of Dublin* (Dublin, 1861), quoted by Anne Crookshank and the Knight of Glin in *Ireland's Painters 1600–1940* (Yale, 2002)

332　Edward Loftus was in his early twenties when he was married, and Anne may have been a year or two older. 'The Hon Captain Loftus' married 'Anne, 1st dau. & co heir of Rev. Paul Read, Rector of Leckpatrick Co. Tyrone, by Elizabeth, dau. of the Rev. James Hamilton of Tullybrick & Castlehill, Co. Down' on 18 March 1758. (George Edward Cokayne, *Complete Baronage*, Vol. V, 1906).

333　Edward was educated at Wakefield before he and his brother Nicholas were recorded in the register of Kilkenny School on 14 June 1749, at about the age of fifteen, or possibly younger. T. U. Sadleir, *The Register of Kilkenny School*; Series 6, Vol. 14 of the *Journal of the Royal Society of Antiquaries of Ireland*, 1924

334　Edward Loftus's rental account book for *c.*1768 occupies a few pages of what later became his son Nicholas's account book (SL Archive)

335　Calculating the purchasing power of money over time is notoriously difficult, but an income of £4000 in 1783 was probably the equivalent of over £500,000 today.

336　See *Finn's Leinster Journal*, 29 July 1769, NLI and notes of Jack Loftus (SL Archive).

337　*The Gazetteer, or Newsman's Interpreter: a Geographical Index to all the considerable Cities, Patriarchships, Bishopricks, Universities, Dukedoms, Earldoms and such like* (London, 1716). The copy purchased by John

Ferguson (who later became the second husband of Edward Loftus's mother-in-law) was inherited by Edward in 1759, when he inscribed his name inside the cover.

338 The only surviving details of the dispute between Anne Loftus and her relatives are contained in a legal brief on behalf of Edward and Anne in an Exchequer suit brought against them by Isaac Read and Isabella Steward, Widow (née Read), dated 26 January 1761. NLI, Loftus 105.

339 NLI, Loftus 189

Chapter 25 The Ghost of Loftus Hall

340 The quotations about 'The Ghost of Loftus Hall' are drawn from various newspaper articles in the family archive. The earliest of these, 15 December 1934, is by John O'Brien, from *The [illegible] and Weekly Gazette*. Another version, by Leo Bowes, appears to have been published in the 1950s, but the cutting has been clipped to exclude all identification of the paper and date. The longest and most circumstantial version is that by Thomas P Walsh, *Munster Express Christmas Supplement*, *c.*1965. This article quotes various witnesses to the haunting, the most recent of them being the Rev. Charles Dale, tutor to the young Marquis of Ely, in 1867. Another version is told by Kevin Myers, 'An Irishman's Diary', *The Irish Times*, 18 May 1983. A wildly inaccurate video is now on sale in local tourist shops, if one may speak of accuracy in such a context.

341 Fr Broaders was parish priest on the Hook from 1725 to 1774. He lived at Knockaneduff as a tenant of the Loftus Hall estate, on a farm that was described in a 1771 survey by Richard and Charles Frizell (NLI, MS 4153) as 'cold ground, but may be improved'.

342 Kevin Myers, 'An Irishman's Diary', *The Irish Times*, 18 May 1983

Chapter 26 The Late Said Earl

343 Manuscript record of 'The Personal Examination of Lord Ely before the Commissioners and Jury the 24th day of January 1767' (SL Archive)

344 Richard Moore was one of a dynasty of furniture makers, and was in business in Capel Street from 1730 to 1769. He was grand enough to be made Freeman of the City of Dublin in 1728, Master of the Upholders' Guild 1733–4, Member of the Common Council 1732 and 1750. Knight of Glin & James Peill, *Irish Furniture*

Chapter 27 To Assert my Honour

345 Sir Jonah Barrington, *Personal Sketches of his own Times*, Vol. II (2nd edition, London 1830)

346 I have relied for much of my background information about the history of duelling on James Kelly, 'That Damn'd Thing Called Honour'. *Duelling in Ireland 1570–1860* (Cork, 1995)

347 Notes by J. E. B. Loftus (SL Archive)

348 The details of Edward Loftus's quarrel with his half-brother Henry are recorded in *The Case of Edward Loftus Esq; submitted to the Public* (Dublin, 1768). A copy of this pamphlet was in the National Library of Ireland, according to a letter from the librarian, Patrick Melvin, dated 25 June 1982 – but it had vanished by the time that I enquired there, in 1998. Another copy survives in the British Library.

349 The fact that Henry Loftus referred to his half-brother as 'Ned Hernon' is recorded in the testimony of Nicholas Loftus Hume, the 'Idiot Earl', in the long-running case of *Loftus* v. *Hume*. A transcript of that evidence is supplied in the printed record of the Appeal to the House of Lords, heard on 27 April 1775 (NLI, ILB 34 i 5)

Chapter 28 Count Loftonzo

350 Private collection. The Dublin Society motto refers to Virgil's *Aeneid* (Book 1, lines 460–1). Aeneas finds pictures of the Trojan war on a building at Carthage and turns weeping to Achates: 'What region on earth is not full of [the tales of] our labours? Behold Priam. Here too are the rewards of glory.'

351 Thanks to Frances Egan for a copy of the entry in the *Royal Dublin Society Proceedings*, Volume 9–10, for a 'General Stated Meeting' of the Dublin Society, 4 March 1773

352 William Temple, 'Topographical Description of Dalkey', *Exshaw's Magazine* (1770) – quoted in Francis Elrington Ball, *A History of the County Dublin*, Vol. I, p. 59 (London, 1902)

353 Rathfarnham with its demesne was bought for £17,500 from Thomas Connolly on behalf of Nicholas Loftus Hume, 2nd Earl of Ely, in April 1767, three months after his trial for idiocy. F. Elrington Ball, *History of the County Dublin*, Vol. II (1903)

354 Knight of Glin & James Peill, *Irish Furniture* (London, 2007) p. 170; Stephen Redmond, 'Behind the Wall; a Rathfarnham Mystery' in *Ecclesiastical Record* (n.d.) pp. 15–7; John, 5th Marquis of Ely, *A Famous Castle, Reminiscences of the lovely Dolly Munro* ('Printed for Private Circulation', c.1890)

355 British Library, Add MS 22228 f. 121

356 'If Sir George Macartney will be so kind as to grant this liberty to Mr Loftus, he will lay him under much more obligation than by making him a Privy Councillor.' Loftus to Macartney, 17 June 1769. Knight of Glin & James Peill, *Irish Furniture* (London, 2007) p. 170

357 For Stuart see Julius Bryant, ' "The Purest Taste" – James "Athenian" Stuart's work in Villas and Country Houses', in Susan Weber Soros (ed.) *James 'Athenian' Stuart (1713–1788): The Rediscovery of Antiquity* (New Haven & London, 2007), pp. 300–4, and Howard Colvin, *A Biographical Dictionary of British Architects, 1600–1840*, pp. 998–1003 (New Haven & London, 2008). For Chambers see John Harris & Michael Snodin (eds), *Sir William Chambers, Architect to George III* (New Haven & London, 1996).

358 The only surviving drawing connected to Henry's renovation of Rathfarnham was found among the papers of William Newton, an architect who competed unsuccessfully to design the Royal Exchange at Dublin in 1769 and was acquainted with James Stuart, for whom he worked as an assistant in the 1780s. RIBA, British Architectural Library, SC72/8

359 Lady Shelburne's Diary, 6 August 1770. Copy of this extract supplied by Alastair Lindsay.

360 The semicircular bay on the east of the castle is shown in Thomas Roberts' *View of Rathfarnham Castle* (1769) and may have been commissioned by the previous occupants.

361 Chambers to Loftus, 29 January 1771. For the evidence of the Dining Room wallpaper, I am grateful to Alastair Lindsay, former architect of Rathfarnham's restoration.

362 The description of the park in 1914 is from an undated clipping of *The Irish Catholic*. There is no mention of the gatehouse in Chambers' correspondence with Loftus and I believe it to be Stuart's work.

363 Alastair Lindsay, 'Rathfarnham Castle, A case study in Conservation', unpublished memo for the Office of Public Works, Dublin notes that 'The Apollo sunburst ceiling is similar to one in the Casino at Merino', designed by Chambers.

364 The description of Dollymount is taken from William Handcock, *History and Antiquities of Tallaght*, p. 90 (Dublin, 1877/1899, reprinted 1991). A sketch corresponding to this description can be found in Francis Elrington Ball, *History of the County of Dublin*, Vol. III, p. 41 (1905)

365 *Maps of the Lordships and Manors of Loftus Hall, Fethard, and Templetown in the County of Wexford*, drawn by Richard and Charles Frizell in 1771 (NLI, MS 4153)

366 The final decision in the case of Henry Loftus v. Rochfort was in the Irish House of Lords, on 24 March 1784, almost a year after Henry's death. The votes were even until the Lord Chancellor gave his casting vote in favour of Loftus

367 'The members considered under the influence of Mr Ponsonby, Ld Shannon, the Loftus's and Tottenhams, who are all related and connected together amount in the whole to 47.' David Large, 'The Irish House of Commons in 1769', *Irish Historical Studies*, Vol. 11, No. 41, p. 45 (March 1958). See also Thomas Bartlett, 'Opposition in Late Eighteenth-Century Ireland', *Irish Historical Studies*, Vol. 22, No. 88, p. 326n (September 1981).

368 This extract comes from the second of two letters, dated 23 February 1771 (signed 'Pascal' but generally believed to have been written by Langrishe), which were widely circulated before being subsequently republished in *Baratariana*, pp. 145–50 (Dublin, 1773).

369 According to a footnote in *Baratariana*, it 'was originally published in detached portions in the *Freeman's Journal* in April and May 1771.' A slim version was published in book form in 1772, followed by 'the second edition, corrected and enlarged', in 1773.

370 *Baratariana*, p. 180 (Dublin, 1773)

371 See Anne Cruikshank & the Knight of Glin, *Ireland's Painters, 1600–1940*, p. 163 (New Haven & London, 2002). For details of the music from Niccolo Piccinni's 1760 opera see Barra Boydell, *The Ely Family and Musical Life in 1770s Dublin* (Kauffman symposium at the National Gallery of Ireland, 2005).

372 *Georgian Society Records*, Vol. II, pp. 120–3 (Dublin, 1911)

373 Brian MacGiolla Phadraig, *Ely House, a detailed guide to its Classical and Georgian features* (Dublin, 1982). See also the Knight of Glin & James Peill, *Irish Furniture*, p.160 (New Haven & London, 2007).

374 Lady Ely's 'attic theatre' at Ely Place seated about sixty and the *Freeman's Journal* for 19 April 1785 records the performance of a tragedy (*The Distressed Mother*) and a comedy (*All the World's a Stage*) performed there by her friends. Brian MacGiolla Phadraig, *Ely House*, p. 18 (Dublin, 1982).

375 One of these silver tokens (now in a private collection) is illustrated in *Ireland's Painters* (New Haven & London 2002) by Anne Crookshank and the Knight of Glin, who date it between 1780 and 1790.

376 Onslow letters, compiled by Harriet Loftus: Surrey History Centre G173/26/10

377 The quotation is an altered version of Milton, *Paradise Lost*, 11, 26

Chapter 29 Receipt for a Person in Love

378 SL Archive

379 The verse was signed 'John Hayes', i.e., Sir John Macnamara Hayes, 1st Baronet (*c.*1750–1809) (*DNB*)

380 So widespread was the image of the Irish fortune hunter, on the lookout for a rich wife, that elaborate satires were published on this theme. See, for example, *The Irish Register, Or a List of the Duchess Dowagers, Countesses, Widow Ladies, Maiden Ladies, Widows, and Misses of large Fortunes in England, as register'd by the Dublin Society, For the Use of their Members. Together with the places of their several Abodes.* (Dublin Printed: London reprinted for T. Cooper, 1742).

381 The most comprehensive account of the abduction of the Misses Kennedy can be found in *Matters of Felony* by Margery Weiner, Heinemann (London, 1967). See also [Rt Hon. J. E. Walsh], *Sketches of Ireland Sixty Years Ago* (Dublin, 1849)

382 The best account of Peg Plunket's life is her own, republished as *The Memoirs of Mrs Leeson, Madam*, edited and introduced by Mary Lyons (Dublin, 1995).

383 *Drewy's Derby Mercury*, 15 December 1780, quoting a report from Dublin dated 8 December. 'Pomona Green' was an eighteenth-century term for apple green, derived from the Latin.

384 *Drewy's Derby Mercury*, ibid

Chapter 30 The Angelic Miss Phillips

385 *Portrait of Lady Loft* was sold by Christie's, 12 May 2006

386 See M. J. Young, *Memoirs of Mrs Crouch* (London, 1806).

387 Entry on Anna Maria Crouch, *DNB* (2004–11)

388 For a good contemporary account of eighteenth-century theatre, see Carl Philip Moritz, *Journeys of a German in England*, translated by Reginald Nettel (London, 1983).

389 M. J. Young, *Memoirs of Mrs Crouch* (London, 1806)

390 Harriet Horncastle Hook's *Double Disguise* (with music by her husband James Hook) was first performed at the Theatre Royal in Drury Lane, 8 March 1784.

391 Nicholas Loftus's bill from Ann Smyth, Woollen-Draper of No. 2, Parliament Street Dublin, for 1791–3, survives in my family papers.

Chapter 31 City of Rogues

392	Valentine Lawless, Baron Cloncurry, *Personal Recollections of the Life and Times* (Dublin, 1849)

393	*Buck Whaley's Memoirs* (written in 1797) edited by Sir Edward Sullivan (London, 1906). Unless otherwise attributed, quotations in this chapter are from this source.

394	See *The Hibernian Magazine*, October 1788.

395	To the dismay of some of his friends, who had bet against this outcome, the following notice warned them that the Buck was back and their wagers lost: – 'June 7th. We can now speak positively of Mr Whalley's return from his Jerusalem expedition, on the issue of which so considerable sums depended. He is at present in London, and will shortly proceed from thence to revisit his friends in this kingdom.' *The Hibernian Magazine*, June 1789

396	For further information on 'The Sham Squire' and Lord Clonmel (and on John Magee's revenge at 'Fiat Hill') see W. J. Fitzpatrick; *Curious Family History; or, Ireland before the Union* (Dublin, 1869)

397	Jonah Barrington, *Personal Sketches of his Own Times* (1827–32)

398	Valentine Lawless, *Personal Recollections of the Life and Times* (Dublin, 1849)

399	*The Memoirs of Mrs Leeson, Madam* [aka Peg Plunkett], edited by Mary Lyons (Dublin, 1995)

400	Chamberlain's bill for the china, dated 13 December 1814, came to £118 5s. 6d. SL Archive

401	Lady Jane's will is dated 10 November 1830, and is in her own hand. (SL Archive)

402	These details were reported as 'An extraordinary case of insanity' in the *Annual Register* (April 1838) and reprinted by Desmond O'Flanagan in the *Dublin Historical Record*, Vol. 47, No. 2, Autumn 1994.

Chapter 32 The Volunteer Banners

403	The 'Grattan Banners' were sold at the Mount Loftus auction on 11 July 1995 and acquired by the National Museum of Ireland

404	A transcript of the report in *Finns Leinster Journal* is preserved in the notes of J. E. B. Loftus (SL Archive). I have been unable to trace a surviving copy of the relevant issue in any library. This famous mushroom is also referred to in *Matters of Felony* by Margaret Weiner (London, 1967).

405 *Book of Entries and Petitions*, October 1780, Irish Record Office, quoted by W. E. H. Lecky, *A History of Ireland in the Eighteenth Century*, Vol. II, p. 40n (London, 1897)

406 Notes of J. E. B. Loftus, SL Archive

407 National Gallery of Ireland

408 Leeds City Art Gallery, Lotherton Hall

409 Contemporary manuscript copy of Brutus's 'Letter to Lord Carlisle Lord Lieutenant of Ireland who Landed the 24th of December 1780' – signed 'Brutus', and dated 27 December 1780 (SL Archive).

410 Fitzgibbon's remark is quoted in R. F. Foster, *Modern Ireland 1600–1972* (London, 1988).

411 R. F. Foster, op. cit.

412 A transcript of Sir Edward Loftus's letter to Napper Tandy is preserved in the notes of J. E. B. Loftus (SL Archive). The original was lost in the fire at Mount Loftus in 1934.

412A *Dublin Journal*, 14 September 1784.

413 A transcript of the proceedings of the Kilkenny Congress is preserved in the notes of J. E. B. Loftus (SL Archive). The original was lost in the fire at Mount Loftus in 1934.

414 Langrishe's remark is quoted by J. A. Froude, *The English in Ireland in the Eighteenth Century*, Vol. II (London, 1874).

415 Drennan's remark is quoted by James Kelly in 'Parliamentary Reform in Irish Politics', Chapter 6 of *The United Irishmen*, edited by David Dickson, David Keogh & Kevin Whelan (Dublin, 1993). The imagery was topical, for this was the height of the balloon craze.

Chapter 33 Five Miniatures

416 Six miniatures are recorded in a Mount Loftus inventory of 1917; five survive. The missing portrait was probably of the youngest brother, Francis.

417 Sue McKechnie, *British Silhouette Artists and their work, 1760–1860* (London, 1978). Thanks to Katie Coombs of the Victoria & Albert Museum for directing me to this work.

418 Stephen Wells, conservation framer, drew my attention to the evidence of the glass.

419 Cennino d'Andrea Cennini, *The Craftsman's Handbook*, translated by Daniel V. Thompson (Yale University Press 1933, reprinted by Dover Publications)

420 For a vivid contemporary account of multiple occupancy, above a shop, see Fanny Burney's *Evelina*, first published anonymously in London in 1778, and in Dublin a year later. Anne Loftus's copy (from an edition published in 1784) survives in my library.

Chapter 34 1798, A Family Divided

421 *A Review of the Conduct of Administration during the Seventh Session of Parliament* (Dublin, 1790) was Wolfe Tone's first pamphlet, which he published under the pen-name 'The Independent Irish Whig'.

422 The first Dublin edition of *Rights of Man* lacked any indication of printer or bookseller – for fear of prosecution – but the title page claimed that 'This edition has been printed under the direction of The Whigs of the Capitol'.

423 Edward was 'his father's favourite and the best looking of the family', according to the notes on our family history compiled by my great-uncle Jack Loftus (SL Archive).

424 Edward Loftus was commissioned as Cornet in the 1st Regiment of Horse Ireland 17 December 1783, and Lieutenant in the 4th (Royal Irish) Dragoons 31 January 1790. *Army List* 1784, 1791

425 *General Evening Post*, London, 7 April 1791

426 *Public Adventurer*, London, 6 April 1790. See also L. M. Cullen, 'The 1798 Rebellion in Wexford: United Irishman Organisation, Membership, Leadership' in *Wexford: History and Society*, edited by Kevin Whelan (Dublin, 1987); Kevin Whelan, 'Reinterpreting the 1798 Rebellion in County Wexford', p. 15, in Dàire Keegan & Nicholas Furlong (eds), *The Mighty Wave* (Dublin, 1996)

427 A contemporary report of this meeting – presumably a printed broadside – was lost in the Mount Loftus fire in 1934, but my great-uncle Jack Loftus transcribed a copy in his notes on the family history (SL Archive).

428 A copy of this *Address To the People of the County of Wexford* (sold at auction by Mealy's/Adams, 19 April 2011) was inscribed on the reverse 'Ld. Loftus' – suggesting that it was distributed to figures of political influence throughout the county, even those like his Lordship who seemed opposed to all reform.

429 Jonah Barrington, *Personal Sketches of His Own Times* (London, 1832)

430 William Farrell, *Carlow in '98* (Dublin, 1949) – the autobiographical account of a United Irishman who drew back from violence but was caught up in the Rising and whose life was saved by Mary Cary (née Loftus).

431 William Farrell, *Carlow in '98*

432 Rev. James Hall, *Tour through Ireland* (London, 1813)

433 Ibid.

434 'First-hand account of the Battle of Kilcumney by Sir Edward Loftus' quoted in an article in *The Kilkenny People*, date missing.

435 *DNB* (London, 1898)

Chapter 35 A Dishonourable Union

436 *The Party: A New Song* – a printed squib attacking those who deserted the Irish administration during the Regency crisis in early 1789 – was found amongst the Killadoon papers, at Killadoon, Celbridge, County Clare

437 George Edward Cokayne, *Complete Peerage*, Vol. V, pp. 66–7 (London, 1926)

438 Details of the acreage and rent roll of the Loftus estates quoted from Howard Evans, *Our Old Nobility* (London, 1909)

439 Jonah Barrington, *Personal Sketches of His Own Times* (London, 1832). See also P. H. Hore, *History of the Town and County of Wexford*. Vol. 5 (London, 1906).

440 Details of Pitt's letter are taken from J. G. Swift MacNeill, *Titled Corruption* (London, 1894).

441 Howard Evans, *Our Old Nobility* (London, 1909)

442 It required a private Act of Parliament in 1807 to break the will of Henry Loftus, Earl of Ely, and enable the house that he built in Ely Place to be sold.

Chapter 36 A Gentleman Farmer

443 Carl Philip Moritz, *Journeys of a German in England*, translated by Reginald Nettel (London, 1965)

444 *The Gentleman Farmer. Being an Attempt to Prove Agriculture, By subjecting it to the Test of Rational Principles* (Dublin, 1779) was one of a spate of books on farming that helped to elevate its social status. Its author was Henry Home, Lord Kames, a central figure of the Scottish Enlightenment.

445 Sir Edward Loftus's letter to the Dublin Society 'On the Culture of Potatoes' was dated 27 April 1806, and published in the Society's *Proceedings* the following year. Seed potato sales of Red Apple and Minion Cup are recorded in Sir Edwards' 'House Book' (SL Archive).

446 *Journal of a Tour in Ireland, performed in August 1804* (London, 1806)

447 William Tighe, *Statistical Observations relating to the County of Kilkenny, made in the years 1800 & 1801* (Dublin, 1802). The day that Tighe presented his work for publication by the Dublin Society (8 July 1802) Sir Edward Loftus presented a model of a new plough.

448 Tighe's footnote on *Verbena officinalis*, vervain, which he found growing wild in pastures and roadsides is worth quoting in full. 'This plant is regarded with a superstitious veneration, derived from ancient idolatry – and it is esteemed as a sovereign remedy in many cases. When the country doctors among the common people, or old women, pull herbs for medicinal purposes, they always add some superstitious invocation, and most plants are taken up "in the name of the Father, the Son, and the Holy Ghost"; but when vervain is pulled, this particular incantation is used,

> Vervain that growest upon holy ground,
> In Mount Calvary thou wert found,
> Thou cur'st all sores and all diseases,
> And in the name of the holy Jesus
> I pull you out of the ground.'

449 Sir Edward joined the Dublin Society in 1765 and remained a member until his death. *The Founders of the Royal Dublin Society* (*RDS*, 2005)

450 Rev. James Hall, *Tour through Ireland* (London, 1813). Though published in 1813, the tour seems to have been undertaken in 1808–9.

451 The affidavit is dated 2 November 1812, and indicates that the 'Deponent', William McDaniel, had been directed by Sir Edward Loftus to pay his rent to someone called John Murray, to which McDaniel replied that 'he took no land from Murray & would pay him no rent & that he would fight said Sir Edwd with his own Sword.' It seems that the surviving sheet is the final part of a longer deposition.

452 The 'House Book for 1808–12' is a vellum-bound volume of thick, creamy paper, and the entries are almost entirely in Sir Edward's hand. It is the closest we have to a diary. A second account book survives, for the first five months of 1818, but this is a much scrappier affair, written on a few blank pages that have been sewn into a crude quarto binding together with 'The Town and Country complete Family Account-Book for the year 1808'.

453 Quoted from the notes of Jack Loftus, based on records of the Mount Loftus and Richfield estates that were lost in the fire of 1934 (SL Archive)

454 The memorial to James Maher cost £2-5s-6d (bill rendered by Thomas Bergius 18 January 1818).

455 Sir Edward's eldest son, Nicholas, owned a copy of White's *Veterinary Medicine*, which was clearly well used, with several pages heavily dog-eared and notes scrawled in the margins, suggesting that his horses suffered from a variety of ailments, including inflammation of the eye, 'stomach staggers' and other alarming symptoms.

456 A note on page 262 of the *House Book* (9 November 1809) itemises the half-year rental payments for a dozen Richfield tenants, totalling just under £300 – i.e. £600 in a full year – plus almost £200 outstanding from the previous settlement. It is not clear what proportion of the Richfield rent roll was represented by this incomplete list.

457 The stealing of timber from the park was evidently a recurring problem. The '1808/1818 Family Account Book' has 'a Copy of Affidavit' bound in at the beginning, which includes what appears to be an almost complete list of the Mount Loftus tenants, thirty-three in total. Each of them was asked to swear an affidavit, not to plunder the park and to inform on any who did so.

458 Nighery was spelt Nicharee on a map of the Richfield estate at the time of its sale, towards the end of the nineteenth century.

459 The *House Book* details the sequence of events, from 12 December 1809 – when James Crowe was sent to obtain a 'Specialty' from the High Sheriff of Wexford for Thomas Kenna to enforce a 'marked writ' on Edmund White – to 13 April 1810, when Laurence Doyle finally took possession of White's farm.

460 Maria Edgeworth, *Castle Rackrent* (Dublin, 1800)

461 'Driver – a man who is employed to drive the tenants for rent; that is, to drive the cattle belonging to tenants to the pound.' Maria Edgeworth, *Castle Rackrent*.

462 See Kevin Whelan, *The Tree of Liberty*, (Cork, 1996).

463 *Hue & Cry* was the official police gazette – but 'the Police Magistrate refused inserting my Advertisement, on Acct of it not being attested on Oath'. It was not until a week or so later that the correctly sworn notice was accepted for publication.

464 The large purchase of Scotch Firs was made in December 1808, and they seem to have been planted alongside the drive. A month later, on

23 January 1809, Sir Edward 'Sent Js Maher to Kilfane to buy 2 Dozen of young Scotch Firs to [illegible] in the trees planted in the Avenue, Cost 1s. a Dozen'. Compare that with the extravagant price of £10 for seven Peach trees (2 Montaubaum, 2 Nobless & 3 Royal George), bought from Mr Robinson of Kilkenny on 24 November 1810.

465 For details of expenditure on the church and for purchases of other builder's materials, see the 'House Book', 31 December 1808.

466 Aigue meant malaria, which was endemic in Ireland – although increasingly rare – until late in the nineteenth century.

Chapter 37 Domestic Economy

467 30 August 1809

468 See Jack Loftus, *Tales of Old Mount Loftus* (manuscript, copy in SL Archive).

469 The layout of the ground floor and basement is taken from a description provided by my grandfather, P. C. Loftus, in his autobiographical notes (SL Archive). The layout of the upper floors conforms to the evidence of Sir Edward's *House Book* and to the pattern of similar houses described by Maurice Craig, *Classic Irish Houses of the Middle Size* (London, 1976).

470 27 November 1808. *Stone Plover or Sea Larks* – probably turnstone, a coastal bird similar to a small plover.

471 17 November 1809. These items were bought from Mrs Meighan, who later supplied him with a toast-rack.

472 James Gordon, Watchmaker, was listed at 41 South Great George's Street in Sir Edward's copy of the Dublin Directory for 1804.

473 A 'Kish' of turf weighed six-hundredweight, according to Philip Luckombe, *A Tour through Ireland* (2nd edition, London 1783).

474 4 November 1810, Sir Edward noted down the Rev. Thomas Davis's 'Recommendation of the following Effective Medecine for the Gout, which he tried & found of Infinite use to him Eau Medicinale de Huson, 29 Dame Street'. This may well have been some form of laudanum.

475 23 October 1809

476 15 August 1810

477 19 November 1810

478 The Mount Loftus inventory for 1917 lists three views of the estate – 'Mt Loftus', 'Mt Loftus from Co Carlow', 'Goresbridge & Mt Loftus' – painted in 1790, immediately after the demesne wall had

been completed. There were four portraits of racehorses – Hollyhock (1809), Whalebone (1814), Hesperus (1825) and Ambrosio – and a picture of the Colonel's hounds (1819). Two of the racehorse paintings hung at Mount Loftus in Sir Edward's lifetime, the others being painted after his death; all were lost in the fire of 1934. The 1917 inventory also lists '4 old Dublin engravings 1760 by Jas Moulton fine old frames' and a number of political cartoons and cockfighting prints.

479 '600 books, mostly old' were listed in the 1917 inventory, but many were burnt in the 1934 fire. Less than 200 survived that can be identified as having come from the original Mount Loftus library. Many of them have Sir Edward's bookplate pasted inside the front cover – engraved with the arms that were awarded to him in 1763.

480 *Castle Rackrent* was published anonymously in 1800 but was immediately recognised by her acquaintances as the work of Maria Edgeworth. Anne Loftus inscribed her name on the title page of the first Dublin edition and her husband added his own inscription, 'By Miss Edgeworth'.

481 *Thinks-I-to-Myself. A Serio-Ludicro, Tragico-Comico Tale* by Edward Nares was first published in 1811 and went through eight London editions and a comparable number of American editions before the end of 1812.

482 4 October/12 November 1811. *Young Kelly Pedlar* is identified in these entries as Michael Kelly.

483 The Colfer family still lives on the Hook, in County Wexford. Billy Colfer was a noted local historian, author of a wonderful book on the Hook.

484 16 October 1811

485 7 December 1811. 'Mrs Cary sent to me for £20, sent her £20.'

486 8 October 1811. Rev. Mr Wm Delatruntes Parish Priest of St Carrice's Certificate of the Marriage of Pierce Ryan & Mary Dugan the 8th of October 1811 Witness thereto Michael Ryan & Mary Kelly. Gave an Order to Governor Lee to Liberate Pierce Ryan who stood committed for an assault on Mary Duggan.

487 Sir Edward was eighty-five years old at the time of his death, according to notices in the *Edinburgh Advertiser* and *Baldwin's London Weekly*, May 1818. His illegitimate younger brother, Colonel Nicholas, died at Godalming in 1819 or 1820, when his life interest in the Wexford estates reverted to Sir Edward's eldest son.

Chapter 38　A Sporting Life

488　An entry in Sir Edward's House Book for 7 July 1810 – The Captain went to see Hollyhauke run at the Carlow Races – preserves the original pronounciation of the horse's name, as do the entries in his son's Stud Book. SL Archive. Hollyhock was born in 1804 and died on 30 November 1829, according to a note in Nicholas Loftus's handwriting, in his copy of the 'General Stud Book'.

489　*Kilkenny Moderator*, 2 June 1830. The report was about six months after Hollyhock's death, evidently based on information provided by Sir Nicholas Loftus.

490　Details of the regimental history are extracted from the notes of Jack Loftus (SL Archive).

491　See *Sporting Magazine*, 1831; *Bury and Norwich Post* (19 May 1813); the *Racing Calendar* for 1813, and *Kilkenny Moderator*, 2 June 1830.

492　SL Archive

493　Extracts from Francis Loftus's sporting diary, containing 'the oldest pedigree of any Irish setters that I have been able to find,' were published by Col J. K. Millner, *The Irish Red Setter* (London, 1924).

494　The story of Sir Nicholas's accident while hunting was told by 'a relative, who was present' to the anonymous author of *Ierne: or Anecdotes and Incidents During a Life Chiefly in Ireland* (London, 1861), written during the lifetime of Sir Nicholas's brother Sir Francis.

495　There is a note on the flyleaf of this 'Stud Book' in Nicholas Loftus's handwriting – 'The Gift of Richard Tattersall Esq.'. Another note, on the same page, records that *Hollyhock* 'died at Mount Loftus November 30 1829'. There are pencil notes on the first page, recording Tattersall's instructions to the binder – '3qr Dimis [?]/ ½ Bd Russia lettd on/ the Back/ Stud Book/ on Side/ Sir Nicholas Loftus.' The paper is watermarked Brocklesby & Morby 1823 (SL Archive).

496　Undated poster advertising Spot, printed by Abm Denroche, Printer, High-Street, Kilkenny (SL Archive)

497　A two-handled silver cup survives in the ownership of a cousin – 'Won at Salisbury, England / Anno 1826 / by Hesperus / son of Hollyhock / Dam Rally by Waxy.'

498　A handwritten copy of *The Memory of the Splendid Hollyhawk* – six verses, of eight lines each – survives amongst the family papers. It appears to be a contemporary copy, said to have been written by his groom shortly after Hollyhock's death in 1829 (SL Archive).

500 *The Quarterly Journal of Agriculture*, Vol. ix, p. 485 (William Blackwood, 1839)

501 *Ierne: or Anecdotes and Incidents During a Life Chiefly in Ireland* (London, 1861)

502 *Leinster Journal*, 20 June 1829. The story was picked up by *The Imperial Magazine* in London and *Nile's Weekly*, in Baltimore, and reprinted in *An Arrangement of British Plants* by William Wittering (London, 1830) and *The Book of Butterflies, Sphinges and Moths* by Thomas Brown (London, 1832)

503 *The Kilkenny Moderator* published a summary of Hollyhock's triumphs, while the *Sporting Magazine* noted his age (twenty-four) and stated that 'He was the best race horse of his day in Ireland.' The story of Hollyhock's wake and burial in the park was recorded by my grandfather, P. C. Loftus, who heard it when a boy at Mount Loftus. The horse's grave is still there, marked by a stone in the centre of the circle of trees.

504 See *Freeman's Journal*, 6 January 1831

505 Much of my account is summarised from that by Michael O'Hanrahan, 'The Tithe War in County Kilkenny 1830–1834', in *Kilkenny: History and Society* (Dublin, 1990).

506 *The Times*, 29 March 1832. A slightly fuller account in the *Morning Post*, 28 March 1832, noted that the messenger was robbed of a parcel that he was delivering to Sir Nicholas from Kilkenny.

507 Sir Nicholas Loftus's will was dated 1 May 1831. George Edward Cokayne, *Complete Baronage*, Vol. V. (London, 1906)

508 The sale 'By Messrs. Tattersall, on 13th and 14th Nov' of 'The entire high-bred and well-known Stud of the late Sir N. Loftus, Bart., consisting of upwards of 100 Lots, the greater part thoroughbred, viz. Stallions, Brood Mares, young Stock, and 14 Hunters, masters of great weight, and well bred enough for Leicestershire' was advertised in the *Morning Post* on 23, 29 and 31 October, 3 and 10 November 1832. Tattersalls annotated catalogue for the sale was included in a list of the family documents compiled at Mount Loftus in 1976, but disappeared some time in the next two decades.

Chapter 39 Catholic Ascendancy

509 Note by Pierse Loftus, *c.*1950 (SL Archive). See also Jack Loftus, *Tales of Old Mount Loftus* – manuscript notes (SL Archive).

510 Sir Francis subscribed to Robert Hunter's *Racing Calendar* until at least 1848 – which is the last edition surviving from the Mount Loftus library.

511 *Ierne: or Anecdotes and Incidents During a Life Chiefly in Ireland* (London, 1861)

512 Mary Loftus settlement 1866 (SL Archive)

513 *Freeman's Journal*, 27 July 1837

514 *The Times*, 2 July 1838, quoting a report from Dublin dated 29 June

515 *Freeman's Journal*, 25 October 1838, 25 January 1839

516 *Kilkenny Moderator*, 16 March 1864

517 *Kilkenny Moderator*, June 1869

518 Sir Francis's obituary, *Kilkenny Moderator*, 16 March 1864.

519 Mary spent £10,000 to buy poor townlands near Borris, according to the notes of her grandson, Jack Loftus (SL Archive).

520 Notes of Jack Loftus (SL Archive)

521 *Kilkenny Moderator*, July 1869, records the attendance of 'Rev. P. R. Cary', from County Wexford.

Chapter 40 The Last Yellow Landau

522 Information from the notes of Pierse Loftus (SL Archive)

523 Belinda Murphy's diary of her honeymoon begins when they arrived in London on 31 July 1868 and breaks off at Frankfurt on 3 September, when they 'parted with our courier Summerfield, he returned to London.' The menus from the Grand Hotel in Paris are dated 10 and 19 October 1868 (SL Archive).

524 The printed bill of sale for the auction 'by order of the executors of Mrs Murphy' survived in the Mount Loftus archives until at least 1976, but has since disappeared. Belinda Murphy's sister, Henrietta Creagh (later Lady Sankey) seems to have rescued some of the family heirlooms at the auction, to keep them in the family.

525 Belinda Murphy may have brought some money of her own to the marriage, and a draft deed survives dated 16 April 1969, setting out the terms whereby her relative Edmond Hogan – a physician and surgeon of County Clare – agreed to pay £2000 to John Murphy on condition that he allowed his wife an additional £100 per annum as 'pin money' and bequeathed her the un-entailed estates in Wexford when he died. SL Archive

526 SL Archive and NLI, Loftus Papers

527 'Rejoicings at Mount Loftus', *Irish Times*, Saturday 5 July 1873

528 *Kilkenny Moderator*, 23 December 1876, 8 December 1877

529 'Cattle Book' begun 1887 is the only surviving document from Belinda Murphy's years as a farmer. A small, fat volume, the pages interleaved with pink blotting paper, it records the purchases and sales of livestock, as well as the letting of various parcels of land to different smallholders. All the entries are in Belinda's bold, distinctive hand (SL Archive).

530 'One of my earliest recollections is of the gloom in my old home in Ireland when the news came of the murder of Lord Frederick Cavendish.' Pierse Loftus; notes for a family history. (SL Archive)

531 Pierse Loftus; manuscript notes for an autobiography (SL Archive)

532 Ibid.

533 Ibid.

534 Ibid.

Chapter 41 I remember Mount Loftus in the 1880s

535 Pierse Loftus, manuscript notes for an autobiography (SL Archive)

Chapter 42 A Typical Victorian Family

536 Pierse Loftus's memoirs, together with letters to Pierse from his family and friends, a few copies of letters sent by him at this time, and diaries and notebooks belonging to Pierse and his brother Jack, are the sources for most of the information in this chapter. (SL Archive)

537 Manuscript diary of J. B. Loftus (SL Archive)

538 Frank Loftus's warning against secret societies was quite specific, because Cecil Rhodes had set up just such a society, with the aim of establishing a federation of white Anglo nations – which was intended to dominate the entire world.

539 Pierse Loftus obtained leave to go up to the camp at Colenso, and arrived there the day before Christmas Eve, 1899. A few days later he wrote to Jack. 'I had always hoped and expected that we three, who have always been so united & such friends, would have stood together for years to come, back to back. It feels now as if a great part of ones life had gone out.' (SL Archive)

540 'Rejoicings at Mount Loftus', *The Kilkenny People*, Saturday 14 January 1905

541 See Jack Loftus; *Tales of Old Mount Loftus* transcript. (SL Archive).

542 On Tuesday 5 July 1910, in *The Dublin Gazette*, it was announced that 'The King has been graciously pleased to grant unto John Edward Blake Loftus in the county of Kilkenny, Captain 4th

Battalion Royal Irish Regiment, a Justice of the Peace for the said county and High Sheriff thereof in the year 1908, and his brother Pierse Creagh Loftus, His Majesty's Royal Licence and Authority, that they and their issue may continue to bear the Surname of Loftus only instead of that of Murphy, and also that they may bear the Arms of Loftus proper, to be borne therewith as his and their principal Arms quartered with those of Murphy.'

543 Elizabeth Bowen, *Hand in Glove* (1952). The story was set in Ireland, in 1904

544 The engagement of Robert Alexander Gardiner and Nora Loftus was announced in the *New York Times*, 8 February 1909, only two weeks before they were married – which seems unusual enough to provoke speculation.

545 *Sag Harbour Express*, Suffolk County New York, 18 March 1909

Chapter 43 Stumbling to Independence

547 *Kilkenny Moderator*, 19 February 1908, 27 May 1908

549 Arthur Balfour was leader of the Conservative party, and had served as Chief Secretary in Ireland under Lord Londonderry, when the latter was Lord Lieutenant in 1887. Londonderry subsequently served in various ministerial capacities, and when the Liberals came to power he became the most vocal Unionist in the Lords, adamantly opposed to Irish Home Rule. Lord Charles Beresford, Admiral and MP, came from a family with vast estates in Ireland, and deep-rooted conservative prejudices. Princess Louise was sister to the King, Edward VII.

550 Collective letter to the *Irish Times*, 21 October 1912, signed by the Lieutenants, Deputy Lieutenants and other senior officials, in counties north and south of what later became the border.

551 The draft of Pierse Loftus's letter is dated from Southwold, Suffolk, 23 September 1913, and is headed 'A Political Prophesy'.

552 The claim by Patrick Pearse, leader of the Easter Rising, that 'bloodshed is a sanctifying and cleansing thing', met its best riposte from James Connolly. 'We do not think that the old heart of the earth needs to be warmed with the red wine of millions of lives. We think anyone who does is a blithering idiot.' In one of the strangest conversions of this strange history, Connolly changed his view and joined Pearse in the Dublin GPO, on Easter Monday 1916. Both were executed.

554 Ernie O'Malley, quoted in Richard English, *Ernie O'Malley: IRA Intellectual* (Oxford, 1998)

Index